DATE DUE		

Disaffected Democracies

Disaffected Democracies

WHAT'S TROUBLING THE TRILATERAL COUNTRIES?

Edited by Susan J. Pharr and Robert D. Putnam

PRINCETON UNIVERSITY PRESS
PRINCETON, NEW JERSEY

Library of Congress Cataloging-in-Publication Data

Disaffected democracies : what's troubling the trilateral countries? /
edited by Susan J. Pharr and Robert D. Putnam.
p.   cm.
Includes bibliographical references and index.
ISBN 0-691-04923-8 (cl : alk. paper) — ISBN 0-691-04924-6 (pb : alk. paper)
1. Democracy.   2. Europe—Politics and government.   3. Japan—Politics and government.
4. United States—Politics and government.   I. Pharr, Susan J.   II. Putnam, Robert D.
JC421.D57   2000   320.9182'1—dc21   99-049292

This book has been composed in Galliard

The paper used in this publication meets the minimum requirements of ANSI/NISO
Z39.48-1992 (R 1997) (*Permanence of Paper*)

www.pup.princeton.edu

10 9 8 7 6 5 4 3 2 1

10 9 8 7 6 5 4 3 2 1
(Pbk.)

To

C.B.B. and S.A.

and to

R.W.P.

with deepest

appreciation

Contents

Tables

Figures

Preface

THIS BOOK SEEKS to unravel one of the central problems galvanizing the attention of policy-makers and scholars alike at the outset of the twenty-first century: why, in some of the world's oldest democracies, in an era in which democracy as a form of government has triumphed worldwide, is public confidence in leaders and the institutions of democratic governance at or near an all-time low? Capitalizing on research conducted in Europe, the United States, and Japan representing a full range of possible answers to this question, the book results from a research project that brought together a small group of leading scholars to compare ideas and findings on public trust—the conditions that undermine it and, alternately, that sustain and revitalize it—in relation to democratic governance. The book is a twenty-fifth anniversary successor volume to a provocative and highly influential 1975 work, *The Crisis of Democracy*, which was initiated by the Trilateral Commission on the health of democracy in the Trilateral countries (Crozier, Huntington, and Watanuki 1975).

The book arises out of two streams of intellectual activity in which the organizers have been centrally involved. The first is a project of the Trilateral Commission. Recognizing the profound changes that have occurred since the original *Crisis of Democracy* volume appeared (e.g., the end of the Cold War and the rise of transnational community-building efforts), the commission several years ago asked Robert Putnam to assemble a group of distinguished social scientists to take a fresh look at how the Trilateral democracies were faring. In September 1994, in collaboration with others, Putnam assembled 14 leading scholars from the United States, Europe, and Japan (several of whom contributed chapters to this book) at a workshop in Cambridge, Massachusetts, for a lively and free-wheeling discussion. On the basis of those exchanges, consultation with others, and short think-pieces prepared by participants, Putnam reported to the commission in Copenhagen in April 1995. It was generally agreed, by both workshop participants and commission members, that the many problems that have emerged in the Trilateral democracies since the original report was issued fully merited a major collaborative study of the kind offered here. This book, then, is a logical outgrowth of these earlier intellectual activities and focuses on a central theme that emerged from them: declining public trust as a pervasive problem in the Trilateral democracies.

Second, the book is the final major project of the "Democratic Governance" portion of a program of activities funded by multiyear grants from the Carnegie Corporation, Ford Foundation, and Rockefeller Foundation (Arts and Humanities division) through the American Academy of Arts and Sciences over the period 1994 to 1999 on the broad theme of "Social Capital, Democracy, and Public Affairs." This program, too, was directed by Putnam, and its activities have included a rich variety of research and public initiatives coordinated by a steering committee made up (in addition to this volume's authors) of Peter B. Evans (Department of Sociology, University of California at Berkeley) and Theda Skocpol (the Departments of Sociology and Government, Harvard University). Consonant with its broad public policy goals, some activities have featured outreach, such as workshops held around the United States with community leaders and activists to develop strategies to foster social bonds through voluntary groups. Others, led by Evans, have been academic in focus and have explored the relationship between social capital and economic growth in developing countries. Cumulatively, the project has been at the center of a burgeoning debate among scholars in universities and on the Internet on social capital—the forces that give rise to it, its impact on economic development and growth, and factors that erode it.

The current project is a major intellectual activity of the initiative, taking up questions about the health of democratic governance in a Trilateral context. Although the initiative has had an overall focus on social capital, the Trilateral democracies project has assumed from the outset that social capital is only one possible piece of the puzzle among many in any search for why confidence in government and in the institutions of representative democracy has eroded in the advanced industrial democracies. Indeed, our intent has been to spark as broad an inquiry as possible by bringing together some of the best theoretical and empirical work available.

DEMOCRACY AND CONFIDENCE IN GOVERNMENT: THE PROBLEM

Exploring the conditions for democracy and for successful democratic governance is a venerable enterprise extending back to Plato. In the second half of this century, as a large part of the world emerged from colonialism, the problem of how democracy might be made to flourish in unfamiliar soil preoccupied some of the best minds and took on great urgency in a Cold War context. In this quest the older democracies— then conceived as models—attracted much scholarly interest. As Europe, North America, and Japan deepened their cooperation, attention shifted from what the older democracies might have done right to their common problems. The Trilateral Commission report of 1975 argued that North America, Western Europe, and Japan were in the grip of a crisis of governability: social demands were rising, outstripping the capacity of states to respond in an era of slower economic growth, while authority was on the decline. The prognosis, echoed in a number of other works from the same era, was somber; the future of democracy itself appeared to be in question.

Although the authors agreed on this conclusion, each portrayed the problem in his region somewhat differently. Samuel P. Huntington, writing on the United States, saw American governmental institutions being overwhelmed by a "democratic surge" in the form of greater demands for equality and participation. For Europe, Michel Crozier stressed the collapse of traditional values and institutions and increased social mobilization. Japan, Jōji Watanuki held, was something of an outlier in relation to these problems; there, traditional values, coupled with strong economic performance, constrained citizen demands for greater participation. The implicit question was whether the problems identified in the older democracies would eventually emerge in Japan as well. In sum, the authors saw the future of democracy in the Trilateral countries as grim.

Looking at the course of developments over the past quarter century, the fit between reality and the report's prognostications is close in some areas, but less so in others. Its economic forecast appears to have been remarkably accurate. Although the details vary by country, the rising prosperity of the early postwar decades did, in fact, continue to give way to lower growth and higher inflation and unemployment. Interdependence, recognized as a significant force in the original report, has proceeded, though at a pace far more rapid than anyone might have envisioned in 1975, transforming the context in which national leaders and institutions operate, particularly in Europe.

But the social and political dimensions of what has evolved are far more complex than the report predicted. Democracy itself has triumphed as a result of the end of the Cold War, an occurrence that no one in 1975 could have predicted convincingly, leaving democracy as a set of institutions and values even stronger today than before. As Max Kaase and Kenneth Newton conclude in the final work of a five-volume series on the theme of *Beliefs in Government* that focuses on Europe, democracies have shown remarkable resilience and "can stand considerable internal and external pressure while at the same time adjusting to changing environments" (1995, 16). But problems of governance in the advanced industrial democracies persist. Concerns in earlier decades about market failure had shifted by the 1980s to fears of "government failure"—the belief that less government is better. Advanced by Reagan, Thatcher, Kohl, Nakasone, and many other leaders, "less government" and "deregulation" have become slogans that few political hopefuls, whatever their party, can fail to echo. At the same time, however, citizens' support for existing government programs that address their specific needs is largely undiminished, constraining the ability of public officials to reduce government's role and manage national budgets. In place of demands for greater participation, as envisioned in the original Trilateral report, there is a great deal of evidence to suggest that public cynicism targets not only national political leaders, but also a wide range of institutions. In Japan, for example, public distrust of national-level politicians, which has been endemic in the postwar era, has now spread to the country's once-vaunted national bureaucracy and local officials as well (Pharr 1997a).

Indeed, it is a remarkable irony that just at the moment when liberal democracy has defeated all its enemies on the battlefields of ideology and politics, many people in the established democracies believe that their own political institutions are faltering, not flourishing. The larger issue today, at the outset of the twenty-first century, is not whether democracy will survive or, indeed, whether it is in crisis, but how well leaders and institutions in democracies can meet the expectations and needs of their citizens.

Unraveling the reasons behind declining confidence in government and political leaders is a major focus of contemporary debate among scholars, journalists, public opinion specialists, and others. The *Beliefs in Government* series has provided a rich base of evidence for comparing developments in Europe with those in Japan and North America. A major research volume on American distrust of government (Nye, Zelikow, and King 1997) and another on trends in democracies worldwide (Norris 1999) lay the groundwork for the present study but also highlight the need for work that looks across a range of countries broad enough, but also sufficiently similar, for meaningful comparisons. New data sources largely unavailable to Crozier and his colleagues now make it possible to undertake such an exercise focused on the advanced industrial democracies, with considerably more empirical precision than was possible in the past. These include data from the World Values Surveys (which include Japan and the United States as well as European countries), Eurobarometer results, and new survey sources in Japan.

Meanwhile, a vast literature on political institutions and social change in the various Trilateral countries now makes developing generalizations across the region easier than was the case decades ago, when *The Crisis of Democracy* was written, and that literature explores numerous candidate causes of citizen disillusionment with politics. Robert Putnam's *Making Democracy Work: Civic Traditions in Modern Italy* (1993), which advances the proposition that rich social capital stores promote good government, has stimulated research on the relationship among civic disengagement, social capital, and democratic governance. A forthcoming work by Putnam looks at social capital in a number of industrial countries to explore further its explanatory power (Putnam forthcoming). In his recent research on civic disengagement in America (1995a and 2000), he has joined any number of other scholars in focusing on the effects of television on civic disengagement and disaffection (Patterson 1993; Fallows 1996; Pharr 1997a). New work takes up the problem of political ethics as it affects citizens' evaluations of their leaders (Pharr forthcoming; della Porta and Vannucci 1998). Other analysts link disaffection and popular malaise in the advanced industrial democracies to a general loss of national purpose that accompanied the end of the Cold War (Maier 1994).

A wealth of other explanations have attracted attention: the effects of regionalism, global economic and other transborder forces, and emerging supranational organizations on the ability of national leaders to address problems; the end of the postwar economic boom and a variety of economic ills, from unemployment in Europe to lags in real income in the United States (until the mid 1990s); the decline of political parties; race and ethnicity as sources of disaffection; and others. Indeed, so much work is proceeding on so many fronts that a central need today has been to make sense of it all by bringing together scholars at the forefront of research on different pieces of the puzzle to develop a framework of analysis that can make sense of what has been occurring to varying degrees and in different ways across Trilateral countries and across time.

The Causes Are Political

Within this stream of new literature, what sets this book apart is its focus on the world's oldest and most established democracies and the time span it covers, roughly from 1975 to century's end. With its focus sharpened in this way, it offers the most coherent framework to date for thinking about citizen disaffection with government and the institutions of representative democracy. The chapters, each based on original research employing different approaches and methodologies, offer varying interpretations of these trends. Measures of confidence include commitments to, confidence in, and evaluations of political parties, parliaments, political elites, and public authorities ("government" in the American sense). Among the indicators highlighted in the book are trends among the Trilateral countries more generally and within individual countries in attachment to and evaluation of political parties, approval of parliaments and other political institutions, assessments of the "political class" (politicians and political leaders), and assorted evaluations of what many have called "public trust."

Although our interpretations often diverge, the framework we adopt regards public satisfaction with representative institutions as a compound of the *information* available to citizens, citizens' *criteria of evaluation*, and the actual *performance* of these institutions. Performance might have

deteriorated because of declines in the *capacity* of political agents to en-
act citizens' interests and desires, or in the *fidelity* with which they reflect
those interests and desires. Such a framework, it should be added, is in
no way obvious in relation to previous research, which has traced declining confidence in government to a variety of nonpolitical sources. The
causes of decline in confidence, we find, lie not with problems in the
social fabric (although we do see an important *indirect* relation between
social trust and social capital, on the one hand, and political confidence,
on the other); nor are they the result of general economic conditions, the
end of the Cold War, the media (in any simple way, at least), or many
other factors, often studded with proper nouns (e.g., Nixon, Vietnam,
Lockheed) that previous observers have offered as explanations. The
problem, we hold, is with government and politics themselves, and we
show why.

This book project, it may be noted, has had certain advantages over
previous projects on similar general themes. The single most momentous
change of the past quarter century has undoubtedly been the end of the
Cold War, a development so recent that it is only beginning to be possible to take its measure. Meanwhile, the years 1993 and 1994 brought
major political turmoil and transformation to several leading democracies, including Japan and Italy. Developments in those countries
receive particular attention here for this reason, but it is only now, with
the political, economic, and institutional context stabilizing in these
countries, that changes of such magnitude can be probed for their possible effects on the bonds between citizens and government.

The authors of this volume have major debts on many fronts. We owe
particularly heavy ones to the Ford Foundation, whose funding made the
project possible, the American Academy of Arts and Sciences, which administered it, and the Rockefeller Foundation, which hosted us and our
fellow researchers at the spectacular Bellagio Study and Conference Center in Villa Serbelloni on Lake Como between June 29 and July 3, 1998.
Samuel P. Huntington, who provided an unofficial link to the earlier Trilateral project, served as a general discussant for the sessions in Bellagio,
as did Ralf Dahrendorf, whose vast experience as a scholar and policy-
maker in Europe made him a remarkable resource to us all. To both of
them we express heartfelt appreciation. The participants in the original
1994 discussions in Cambridge that gave shape to the project all deserve
our thanks. They include Alan Brinkley, Jean-Claude Casanova, Robert
Dahl, Peter Dobell, David Gergen, Charles B. Heck, Stanley Hoffmann,
Samuel P. Huntington, Junko Katō, Anthony King, Theodore Lowi,
Terry M. Moe, Paul Peterson, Giovanni Sartori, the late Seizaburō Satō,
Fritz Scharpf, William Schneider, and Theda Skocpol. The report emerging from those Cambridge sessions, entitled "Revitalizing Trilateral De-

mocracies," was drafted by Casanova, Putnam, and Satō. The Cambridge meetings and the Trilateral report were generously supported by the Rockefeller Brothers Fund.

The authors want to express special thanks to the many people who contributed to the volume in innumerable ways, including Jeffrey Boutwell of the Academy; Michael Lipsky, our program officer at the Ford Foundation; Colin Campbell and Russell Phillips, President and Executive Vice President, respectively, of the Rockefeller Brothers Fund; Charles B. Heck, North American Director of the Trilateral Commission; Susan Garfield at the Rockefeller Foundation and Gianna Celli, Acting Director, and Nadia Gilardoni, Conference Coordinator, at the Rockefeller Study Center in Bellagio; Louise Kennedy, Robert Putnam's assistant, who joined us in Bellagio and contributed to the success of the conference in many ways; Paul Talcott, Christian Brunelli, and Jessica Wolf, who provided research assistance and other help relating to the project; Maurits van der Veen, who served as rapporteur at the 1994 Cambridge session; and Theda Skocpol and Peter Evans. Frank J. Schwartz performed superbly both as rapporteur at the Bellagio conference and as editorial coordinator for this book, and Emily M. Morris served as the ever gracious and efficient project coordinator. Finally, we are grateful to Sylvia Coates for preparing the index to this volume and to Malcolm Litchfield, Chuck Myers, and Joanne Daniels for bringing the book to press so expeditiously. To all we owe thanks, though the conclusions and any errors of fact or omission are, of course, our own.

Cambridge, Massachusetts
Susan J. Pharr
Robert D. Putnam

Foreword

Samuel P. Huntington

THE REPORT ON "The Governability of Democracy" that Michel Crozier, Jōji Watanuki, and I prepared for the Trilateral Commission in 1975 was published as a book entitled *The Crisis of Democracy*. Looking back on it 25 years later, I think that perhaps the most important point to note is that whether or not democracy was in crisis in the Trilateral countries in the mid-1970s, many well-informed people thought it was. Declining economic growth, high inflation, escalating government deficits, uncertainties in international trade and finance, mounting political volatility and instability (including the forced resignation of President Nixon), unsettling incidents of radical terrorism, and resurgent Soviet assertiveness all led people to focus on the incapacities and limitations of existing political regimes in the industrialized world. This pessimism was dramatically reflected in Willy Brandt's widely reported belief that "Western Europe has only 20 or 30 years more of democracy left in it; after that it will slide, engineless and rudderless, under the surrounding sea of dictatorship, and whether the dictation comes from a politburo or a junta will not make much difference" (*The Economist*, March 23, 1974, p. 12).

These concerns prompted the Trilateral Commission's director, Zbigniew Brzezinski, to propose and the commission to authorize the study we undertook. Our book detailed at some length the problems confronting Japan, the United States, and Europe; it explored in depth the conditions in each country and analyzed the extent to which these conditions differed or resembled one another. The report identified three types of challenges facing democratic countries: *contextual challenges* arising from the external environment, such as the security threats posed by the Soviet Union and communism, the oil price increases, and imbalances in the international economy; *social trends*, including the increasing power of populist movements, intellectuals, the media, and other forces; and *intrinsic characteristics* of democracy that, as highlighted by Tocqueville, Lippmann, and Schumpeter, were likely to contribute to its weakening or undoing. These were, we said, "a key element in the current pessimism about the future of democracy:" (Crozier, Huntington, and Watanuki 1975, 8).

These challenges, we argued, were leading to the delegitimation of governmental authority, mounting political demands that pointed to the overloading of government, the fracturing and disaggregation of political parties and political purposes, and intensified parochialism and disagreements among democracies on international issues. Our volume concluded with a series of recommendations designed to deal with these problems, including measures for promoting sustained economic growth and the reduction of poverty, strengthening executive and legislative institutions, reinvigorating political parties, restoring a more balanced relationship between government and media, slowing the expansion of higher education, achieving more participation of workers in the organization and management of the workplace, and creating a permanent Trilateral institute, funded by private and public bodies, to study and provide recommendations for dealing with the common problems of the advanced industrial democracies.

Our report differed from other Trilateral Commission products in that it was not designed as a consensus document consisting of broad generalizations acceptable to most European, Japanese, and American elites. It was instead meant to be analytical, provocative, and political. It stirred up far more controversy than any other Trilateral Commission document before or since and made several leading commission members, David Rockefeller among them, rather unhappy. The report was heatedly debated at the commission's Kyoto plenary meeting in May 1975; several commissioners vigorously criticized it, particularly the section on the United States, which I drafted. The report and the book attracted widespread attention and were excerpted, quoted, and discussed in virtually all the major media organs in the United States and, to a considerable extent, in other Trilateral countries. Debate on the "governability of democracy" continued for almost two years in commission publications and elsewhere. A few, but only a few, of our specific recommendations materialized in Trilateral countries in the years that followed.

Our study has been criticized by some, including at least one contributor to the present volume, for portraying a "crisis of democracy" when there really was not one. Crises and catastrophes, however, can be prevented only when people take seriously the possibility that they may occur. Prophecies of disasters are more likely to be self-nonfulfilling than self-fulfilling. I would like to think that our volume may have played some minor role in the broad intellectual and political movement that developed in the 1970s to point to the limitations of government and that led to the economic and social policies associated with Ronald Reagan, Margaret Thatcher, and their counterparts in other advanced industrialized democracies. That process, indeed, began in the United States with the deregulation movement initiated by the Carter administration, almost all of whose top leaders, from the president and vice president on down, were Trilateral Commission members.

The Crisis of Democracy differs significantly from the current volume edited by Susan J. Pharr and Robert D. Putnam. Writing at a time of pessimism about the future of democracy, we were concerned with the impact of a variety of economic, social, demographic, and international challenges to the stability, legitimacy, and effectiveness of democracy in the Trilateral countries. In social science jargon, these challenges were our "independent variable," and democratic government was our "dependent variable." We began our study by setting forth the former and then attempted to explore their implications for the latter.

Pharr and Putnam pose the title question, "What's Troubling the Trilateral Countries?" Compared to the situation that existed in the 1970s, one is tempted to answer, "Not much." In contrast to the 1970s, the 1990s have been a time of widespread and understandable optimism, at times euphoria, about democracy and its future as the political system destined to take hold everywhere in the world. The advanced industrial democracies not only triumphed in the Cold War but have also created an integrated global economy, achieved unmatched material prosperity for most of their people, and virtually eliminated the possibility of fighting wars with each other. Significant ideological or institutional alternatives to democracy are nonexistent among industrialized societies. As Pharr and Putnam point out, there is "no evidence of declining commitment to the principles of democratic government . . . on the contrary, if anything, public commitment to democracy per se has risen in the last half century" (introduction, this volume).

Although serious challenges to democracy are currently lacking, this does not mean that none will appear in the future. The challenges that arose in the 1970s were in considerable measure a product of the demographic explosion ("Baby Boom") that produced extraordinarily large numbers of people then in their late teens and twenties. The current combination of generally effective democratic institutions and widespread lack of confidence in those institutions may well reflect the middle-aging of the Boomers. Different problems for democracy are likely to arise as this huge generation becomes elderly. All democratic governments are already concerned with their ability to provide the pensions and other retirement benefits that have come to be expected. That problem, however, may be exacerbated by another development. In Europe and North America, the Boomers are overwhelmingly native-born, white Christians. In varying degrees, the work force is becoming non-native and nonwhite in America and non-native and non-Christian in Europe. Ethnic, racial, and cultural divisions could thus coincide with a generational division and reinforce the differences between generations over their responsibilities to each other. This could be a central challenge confronting Western democracies on the *fiftieth* anniversary of our report on their governability.

In the contemporary sea of democratic achievement and well-being, however, Pharr and Putnam find one perplexing island of failure. In our 1975 volume we noted that the challenges to democratic government then observed had produced, at least in the United States, a dramatic decline in public confidence in government. Now, 25 years later, while the challenges we enumerated have disappeared, the low confidence in government in America and other Trilateral countries has not only continued but deepened. How can this be explained? Why, given the widely hailed "triumph of democracy," have people in most advanced industrial democracies become more disillusioned with their political leaders and institutions? Pharr and Putnam's thinking and this book begin with their dependent variable, the decline in confidence, and then work backward to attempt to identify the independent variables responsible for this anomalous development. This volume explores a tremendously fascinating and important question and provides a variety of complex, perceptive, and imaginative answers to it.

Disaffected Democracies

ONE

Introduction: What's Troubling the Trilateral Democracies?

Robert D. Putnam, Susan J. Pharr, and Russell J. Dalton

A QUARTER CENTURY AGO Michel J. Crozier, Samuel P. Huntington, and Jōji Watanuki argued that the nations of Europe, North America, and Japan confronted a "crisis of democracy." Their starting point was a vision, widespread during the 1960s and 1970s, of "a bleak future for democratic government," an image of "the disintegration of civil order, the breakdown of social discipline, the debility of leaders, and the alienation of citizens" (Crozier, Huntington, and Watanuki 1975, 2).

The central thesis of the subtle, nuanced, and wide-ranging analysis by Crozier and his colleagues was that the Trilateral democracies were increasingly overloaded by more and more insistent demands from an ever-expanding array of participants, raising fundamental issues of governability. Within that common framework the three authors offered somewhat distinctive diagnoses of the problems facing their respective regions. In Europe Crozier emphasized the upwelling of social mobilization, the collapse of traditional institutions and values, the resulting loss of social control, and governments' limited room for maneuver. Huntington asserted that America was swamped by a "democratic surge" that had produced demands for more equality and participation, political polarization, and less effective political parties and government. His provocative therapy was to "restore the balance" between democracy and governability. By contrast, Watanuki argued that Japan did not (yet?) face problems of "excessive" democracy, thanks in part to rapid economic growth and in part to its larger reservoir of traditional values. Whatever the regional and national nuances, however, the authors sketched a grim outlook for democracy in the Trilateral countries: delegitimated leadership, expanded demands, overloaded government, political competition that was both intensified and fragmented, and public pressures leading to nationalistic parochialism.

In historical perspective the sense of crisis that permeated *The Crisis of Democracy* may have reflected the confluence of two factors: first, the surge of radical political activism that swept the advanced industrial democracies in the 1960s, which began with campus protests in the United

States over civil rights and the Vietnam War and was then echoed in the events of May 1968 in France, Italy's "Hot Autumn" later that year, and student upheavals in Japan; and second, economic upheavals triggered by the oil crisis of 1973–74 that were to result in more than a decade of higher inflation, slower growth, and, in many countries, worsening unemployment. The Trilateral governments were thus trapped between rising demands from citizens and declining resources to meet those demands. Moreover, governments' legitimacy was suspect in the eyes of a generation whose motto was "question authority." Crozier, Huntington, and Watanuki warned that these ominous developments posed a threat to democracy itself.

A quarter century is an opportune interval after which to revisit the issue of the performance of our democratic institutions. The intervening years have witnessed many important developments in our domestic societies, economies, and polities, as well as in the international setting.

Most dramatic of all, of course, was the end of the Cold War, symbolized by the fall of the Berlin Wall in 1989. If it did not signal the end of history, the removal of the communist threat surely did mark the end of a historical epoch. It transformed the fundamental underpinnings of security alliances and eliminated the principal philosophical and geopolitical challenge to liberal democracy and the market economy. In some of the Trilateral countries it also coincided with, and to some extent triggered, an intellectual and ideological revolution. In each country it transformed domestic political calculations and alignments in ways that are still being played out.

Economically, the decades that have followed the appearance of the Crozier-Huntington-Watanuki volume were distinctively less happy than those that preceded it. The oil shocks of 1973–74 and 1979–80 drew down the curtain on that fortunate, early postwar combination of high growth, low inflation, and low unemployment. Although economists differ on the origins of the pervasive slowdown, virtually all econometric analyses confirm the view of the man and woman in the street: Western economies took a turn for the worse around 1973–74, and recovery was a slow and uncertain process. The immediate inflationary effects of the oil crises were overcome by means of stringent monetary policies, but economic malaise continued. In subsequent years Europe had unprecedentedly high structural unemployment, the United States endured sharply reduced rates of real wage growth, and after 1992 Japan experienced the longest recession in the country's postwar history.

"Interdependence" was already widely discussed in the early 1970s, and integration of the world economy has continued at a rapid pace in the years since. International trade has grown faster than gross domestic products, and foreign investment more rapidly than either of them. Western economies are even more porous internationally now than when Crozier and his colleagues wrote, and our economic fates even more intertwined. Nowhere is this more true, of course, than in Europe: the European Union has taken shape and extended its reach to an increasing number of policy domains with stunning speed. Moreover, the rise of newly industrializing economies challenges the competitiveness of all the Trilateral countries. Finally, immigration from the less to the more developed nations of the world has accelerated, creating new difficulties and social tensions.

Socially and culturally, these decades have witnessed significant change in all our countries. Increased mobility and growing individuation have eroded traditional family and community ties. Some observers believe that the trend toward declining respect for authority that Crozier, Huntington, and Watanuki underscored has continued apace in all sectors of society, and others see evidence of increased tolerance of diversity. The role of women in economic life (and to some extent in public life more generally) has expanded. The expansion of higher education during the 1950s and 1960s continues to boost the university-educated share of the electorate. The electronic media have transformed how we spend our leisure time as well as how we follow public affairs. In many of our cities problems of drugs, crime, homelessness, and blight are even more visible now than a quarter century ago. Finally, older people occupy a growing share of the populations in all Trilateral countries, which is certain to have major consequences for both social and economic policy in the decades to come.

Political change over the past quarter century is a pervasive theme of the present chapter and this entire book. Nevertheless, one factor in particular deserves special emphasis at the outset. When *The Crisis of Democracy* appeared, citizens in the Trilateral world were still primarily concerned about market failure in sectors as diverse as social services, culture, and the environment, and demands for government intervention to redress those failures were ascendant. This ideological climate fed the preoccupation of Crozier, Huntington, and Watanuki with governability. As symbolized by the advent of Thatcher, Reagan, Nakasone, Kohl, and similar figures elsewhere, however, public concern had shifted by the early 1980s from *market* failure to *government* failure. Responding to, and in part encouraging, this sea change in public opinion, conservative leaders proposed a reduced role for government, and this ideological shift to the right was accelerated everywhere by the discrediting of state socialism after 1989. Facing an altered electoral marketplace, political leaders everywhere now call for less government—less bureaucracy, less regulation, less public spending—although policy has yet to catch up with rhetoric (as demonstrated by Alesina and Wacziarg, this volume). Even a relatively liberal Democratic president in the United States has proclaimed that "the era of big government is over." In one sense, the problem of "overload" identified by Crozier and his colleagues appears to have solved itself: many people seem to have concluded that government action is not the answer to all their problems.[1] Yet citizens still hold government responsible for their social and economic well-being, and cutting "entitlement" programs remains difficult everywhere.

Against this backdrop of geopolitical, economic, social, and ideological change, how should we assess the current status of the advanced industrial democracies of North America, Western Europe, and Japan? Because we seek a response to this question that should be as widely applicable as possible, we stress features common to the Trilateral democracies rather than the equally interesting unique features of each national case.

At the outset we want to emphasize a distinction that Crozier and his colleagues felt less need to stress: the distinction between the effectiveness of specific democratic governments and the durability of democratic institutions per se. On the one hand, we see no evidence in any of these countries that democracy itself is at risk in the sense of being supplanted by an alternative, undemocratic political regime or by social or political anarchy. On the other hand, we do see substantial evidence—much greater than that available to Crozier and his colleagues 25 years ago—of mounting public unhappiness with government and the institutions of representative democracy throughout the Trilateral world.

Earlier alarm about the stability of democracy itself, which Crozier, Huntington, and Watanuki were in part responding to and in part amplifying, now seems exaggerated. The happy contrast between political developments in the advanced industrial democracies after World Wars I and II is indeed dramatic. Within two decades after the end of World War I, fledgling democracies had collapsed in Italy, Germany, Spain, and Japan, and more established democracies elsewhere were under siege. Now, more than half a century after the end of World War II, democratic regimes are deeply rooted throughout the Trilateral world and have multiplied in other parts of the world as well (Huntington 1991). Bearing in mind the tragic failures of democracy in the interwar period, it was entirely natural in the first decades after World War II for observers of Western politics to ask whether it could happen again. Political science has a poor record of prognostication, especially with respect to radical change, and we should not be too presumptuous in writing about such funda-

---

[1] Polls do not, in fact, generally confirm the thesis that ordinary citizens' views about the proper role of government have shifted nearly as much as has the climate of elite opinion. Equally important, however, there is little survey evidence that citizens have become more insistent on government action in recent decades.

mental issues, but with half a century of democratic stability under our collective belts, the answer is almost certainly no.

The case for this optimism does not rest on the simple passage of time. Decades of surveys in North America, Western Europe, and Japan yield little evidence of diminished support for liberal democracy among either mass publics or elites. If anything, the opposite is true: commitment to democratic values is higher than ever (Norris 1999; Klingemann and Fuchs 1995; Kaase and Newton 1995). In sharp contrast to the period after World War I, no serious intellectual or ideological challenge to democracy has emerged. Whether tracked over the more than five decades since the end of World War II or the decade since the fall of the Berlin Wall, opponents of democracy have lost support. Even where public discontent with the performance of particular democratic governments has become so acute as to overturn the party system (as in Japan and Italy in 1993–95), these changes have not included any serious threat to fundamental democratic principles and institutions. In this sense we see no significant evidence of a crisis of democracy.

Nevertheless, to say that democracy per se is not at risk is far from saying that all is well with the Trilateral democracies. The premise of this book is that public confidence in the performance of representative institutions in Western Europe, North America, and Japan has declined since the original Trilateral Commission report was issued, and in that sense most of these democracies are troubled. In the remainder of this chapter we first trace this decline in confidence, examining each region in turn and then the Trilateral world as a whole. Second, while recognizing that the causes of public disaffection with government and representative institutions are complex and many-faceted, we offer a framework or model for understanding them. Individual contributors to the volume work within this framework to offer varying interpretations for observable trends.

SYMPTOMS OF DISTRESS:
PUBLIC EVALUATIONS OF POLITICS AND GOVERNMENT

Public attitudes toward democracy can be assessed at various levels of abstraction. We find no evidence of declining commitment to the principles of democratic government or to the democratic regimes in our countries. On the contrary, if anything, public commitment to democracy per se has risen in the last half century. At the other extreme, our study is not concerned with day-to-day evaluations of specific leaders, policies, and governments (in the European sense of the word); we assume that evaluations of this kind of governmental performance will rise and fall in any well-functioning democracy. Thus, this book is about neither a "crisis of democracy" as such nor the ebbs and flows in the popularity of particular incumbents. Rather, our concern is with popular confidence in the performance of representative institutions. Among the specific indicators we focus on are trends in

- attachment to and judgments of political parties,
- approval of parliaments and other political institutions,
- assessment of the "political class" (politicians and political leaders), and
- assorted evaluations of political trust such as agreement or disagreement with survey statements like "the government [or "most elected officials"] don't care much what people like me think," "parties are only interested in people's votes, not in their opinions," and so on.

Whatever the "normal," background level of public cynicism and censure of politics, citizens in most of the Trilateral democracies are less satisfied—often much less satisfied—with the performance of their representative political institutions than they were a quarter century ago. At a minimum it is a shared premise of the contributors to this volume that the evidence in support of this generalization deserves to be taken seriously.

North America

The onset and depth of this disillusionment vary from country to country, but the downtrend is longest and clearest in the United States, where polling has produced the most abundant and systematic evidence.[2] When Americans were asked in the late 1950s and early 1960s, "How much of the time can you trust the government in Washington to do what is right?" three-quarters of them said "most of the time" or "just about always." Such a response would sound unbelievably quaint to most people today. This decline in confidence followed a decade or more of exceptionally turbulent political conflict—the civil rights movement, Vietnam, Watergate and its successor scandals—that transformed American politics. Third-party challengers for the presidency, divided government, a term limits movement, and other political developments signaled the public's increasing disenchantment with the political status quo (Wattenberg 1996; Nye, Zelikow, and King 1997). Public confidence in the ability and benevolence of government has fallen steadily over this period. The decline was briefly interrupted by the "It's Morning in America" prosperity of the Reagan administration, and even more briefly by victory in the Gulf War, but confidence in government ended up lower after 12

[2] The most comprehensive assessment of the evidence for declining confidence in government in the United States, as well as initial evaluations of alternative explanations, is Nye, Zelikow, and King (1997).

years of Republican rule. Indeed, of the total decline, roughly half has occurred under Republican administrations and half under Democratic ones. The economic prosperity of the late 1990s has seen an uptick in confidence in government, but the figures still remain well below those of the 1970s, much less the halcyon days of the late 1950s and early 1960s.

Public opinion data tell the story of this decline. For example, whereas two-thirds of the American public once trusted the government to do what is right, only 39 percent felt this way in 1998. In 1964 only 29 percent of the American electorate agreed that "the government is pretty much run by a few big interests looking out for themselves." By 1984 that figure had risen to 55 percent, and by 1998 fully 63 percent of voters concurred. In the 1960s two-thirds of Americans rejected the statement "most elected officials don't care what people like me think"; in 1998 nearly two-thirds of Americans agreed. This negative assessment applies to virtually all parts of the apparatus of government. Those people expressing "a great deal" of confidence in the executive branch fell from 42 percent in 1966 to only 12 percent in 1997, and equivalent trust in Congress fell from 42 percent in 1966 to 11 percent in 1997 (Lipset 1994; Lipset and Schneider 1983).

Almost every year since 1966 the Harris Poll has presented a set of five statements to national samples of Americans to measure their political alienation:

- The people running the country don't really care what happens to you.
- Most people with power try to take advantage of people like yourself.
- You're left out of things going on around you.
- The rich get richer and the poor get poorer.
- What you think doesn't count very much anymore.

Every item on this list has won increasing assent from Americans since the opinion series began. In the late 1960s—at the very height of the Vietnam protests—an average of barely one-third of Americans endorsed these cynical views; by the early 1990s fully two-thirds of all Americans concurred. By almost any measure, political alienation has soared over the last three decades (Harris Poll, February 1994).[3] A single comparison captures the transformation: in April 1966, with the Vietnam War raging and race riots in Cleveland, Chicago, and Atlanta, 66 percent of Americans *rejected* the view that "the people running the country don't really care what happens to you." In December 1997, in the midst of the long-

---

[3] Although systematic data on political alienation in America before the advent of regular national surveys in the 1950s is sketchy, some evidence suggests that alienation had declined from the mid-1930s to the mid-1960s. See Lane (1965).

est period of peace and prosperity in more than two generations, 57 percent of Americans *endorsed* that same view (Harris Poll).

If less abundant and dramatic, the evidence from Canada conforms to this general picture. In addition to the normal fluctuations of the political cycle, ratings of specific political parties and individual leaders and confidence in the major institutions of Canadian politics and government have fallen over the last two decades. The dramatic collapse of the Conservative Party in 1993 illustrated the growing tensions within Canadian politics. Reflecting these political trends, the segment of Canadian voters who agree that "the government doesn't care much what people like me think" swelled from 45 percent in 1968 to 67 percent in 1993, the proportion who feel a "great deal" of confidence in political parties slipped from 30 percent in 1979 to 11 percent in 1999, and confidence in the House of Commons fell from 49 percent in 1974 to 21 percent in 1996 (Dobell and Berry 1992, 5–9; LeDuc 1995; Clarke et al. 1995). By 1992 only 34 percent of Canadians said they were satisfied with their system of government, down from 51 percent as recently as 1986 (Adams and Lennon 1992). Although Canadians express their views in a more muted tone than their American neighbors, they are also increasingly discontented with the performance of their political system.

Europe

Comparable trends in public opinion in Europe are more variegated, but there, too, the basic picture is one of spreading disillusionment with established political leaders and institutions. (Although other chapters will explore important intra-European differences in the levels and trends of discontent, this chapter intentionally focuses on commonalties among the Trilateral democracies.) Trust in politicians and major political institutions has fallen over the last quarter century in countries as diverse as Britain, Italy, France, and Sweden.

Britons' traditional deference to elites has been replaced by growing skepticism. In 1987, for example, fewer than half of Britons believed that either civil servants, the national government, or local councils could be trusted to serve the public interest (Jowell and Topf 1988).[4] And while 48 percent of the British public expressed quite a lot of confidence in the House of Commons in 1985, that figure had been halved by 1995. Public protests over government decisions had become a common feature of

---

[4] A longer time series asking about the honesty and ethics of members of Parliament is available from British Gallup. In 1982 only 26 percent of the British public gave MPs a low or very low score on this scale, but this increased to 43 percent in 1993. A similar question asked by Canadian Gallup shows an increase in negative sentiments from 39 percent in 1982 to 49 percent in 1992 (Hastings and Hastings 1994, 312).

politics in a nation once known for popular deference to political elites. As a symbol of this spreading skepticism, a series of high-profile Parliamentary committees in the 1990s studied issues of government corruption, ethical standards in politics, and campaign finance abuses. Sweden, which invented the consummate welfare state and was once widely considered to have found a happy "middle way" between the free-for-all of market capitalism and the oppression of state socialism, is emblematic of Europe's troubled mood. The proportion of Swedes who rejected the statement that "parties are only interested in people's votes, not in their opinions" decreased from 51 percent in 1968 to 28 percent in 1994 (Listhaug 1995). Even after the onset of the trend of decreasing political trust, a majority (51 percent) of Swedes still expressed confidence in the Riksdag in 1986; by 1996, however, only 19 percent did.

Especially striking are the patterns for the postwar democracies of Germany and Italy. Although political support grew in these nations during the postwar decades, the trends reversed at some point, and support has now eroded significantly from postwar highs. For instance, the percentage of Germans who said they trusted their Bundestag deputy to represent their interests rose from 25 percent in 1951 to 55 percent in 1978; it had declined to 34 percent by 1992 (Noelle-Neumann and Koecher 1993, 657). Other survey questions point to a general erosion of Germans' trust in government since the early 1980s. Similarly, student unrest and extremist violence in the 1970s first strained Italians' postwar democratic agreement, and then public skepticism broadened and deepened with the political scandals of the past decade, signaled most dramatically by the radical restructuring of the party system in the mid-1990s. Thus, the percentage of Italians who say that politicians "don't care what people like me think" increased from 68 percent in 1968 to 84 percent in 1997.

At least until recently, such trends have been less visible in some of the smaller European democracies. Still, patterns of growing political cynicism have become more common in Austria, Norway, Finland, and other small states during the past decade. Almost everywhere, it seems, people are less deferential to political leaders and more skeptical of their motives.

Across Europe the pattern of declining political support has apparently accelerated in the past decade. The authors of a purportedly exhaustive account of European public attitudes toward politics and the state up to the beginning of the 1990s did detect "a more skeptical attitude on the part of citizens toward the reality of democracy," but they strongly discounted talk of a "democratic crisis" (Klingemann and Fuchs 1995, 440–41). A more recent and authoritative evaluation of all the relevant long-term evidence, however, found "clear evidence of a general erosion in support for politicians in most advanced industrial countries" (Dalton 1999, 63). Moreover, the second survey found that by extending the time-span and the cross-national breadth of the data, the empirical evidence now presents a clear and striking picture of the erosion of partisan attachments among contemporary publics. . . . If party attachments reflect citizen support for the system of party-based representative government, then the simultaneous decline in party attachments in nearly all advanced industrial democracies offers a first sign of the public's affective disengagement from politics. . . . Rather than a transient phenomenon or merely linked to distrust of incumbents, public skepticism has at least partially generalized to political institutions and may thus be a continuing feature of democratic politics (Dalton 1999, 65–66, 68)

Japan

Public evaluations of politics and government in Japan reveal similarly disturbing trends. While *The Crisis of Democracy* portrayed Japan as an outlier, buffered from travails the authors saw looming elsewhere by a deferential political culture in which state authority was accepted (Crozier, Huntington, and Watanuki 1975, 3–9, 161–70), Japanese citizens' disillusionment with government and political institutions has if anything proved to be more persistent than elsewhere in the Trilateral world. To the extent that they can be known from the limited data available, Japan began the postwar era with confidence levels at a low point. With a generation of leaders discredited by wartime defeat and with the new democratic institutions imposed by the Occupation as yet untested, it is little wonder that political uncertainty prevailed, as attested to by extremely high proportions of Japanese responding "don't know" to survey questions. By the 1960s confidence in democracy per se was well established, and people's evaluations of government and politics had improved somewhat from these abysmal beginnings, but they nevertheless remained low relative to those in most other advanced industrial democracies (Flanagan et al. 1991; Richardson 1974). Although the mid-1980s witnessed a brief upturn, confidence levels declined noticeably in the politically turbulent and economically distressed 1990s. The long-term trends toward less deference to political leaders, diminished loyalty to established political parties (including the long-dominant Liberal Democratic Party, or LDP), and increased political dissatisfaction all predate the scandals that finally brought down the LDP in 1993 after 38 years of uninterrupted rule.

The proportion of Japanese voters who agree with the deferential view that "in order to make Japan better, it is best to rely on talented politicians, rather than to let the citizens argue among themselves" has fallen steadily for 40 years. Although this is probably a good indicator of the *strengthening* of the cultural and sociological foundations of Japanese democracy, the proportion of voters who feel that they exert at least "some influence" on national politics through elections, demonstrations, or expressions of public opinion fell steadily between 1973 and 1993. In other words, Japanese voters have become less and less satisfied over the last 20 years with their limited role in politics, and less content to leave public affairs in the hands of political leaders. This is the backdrop against which a series of political corruption scandals broke prior to 1993, discrediting the LDP and causing public esteem for political leadership to decline still further. In yet another sign of a downturn in confidence, trust in the country's once-esteemed elite civil servants has also plummeted over the past decade.

TRILATERAL TRENDS IN POLITICAL CONFIDENCE OVER THREE DECADES

When we step back from surveying the Trilateral landscape region by region, the picture that emerges is disturbing. Long series of national election studies or reputable commercial public opinion surveys provide extensive evidence of how public sentiments have changed over time. Evidence of the declines in political support has been more apparent in three areas that we examine in this section: disillusionment with politicians, with political parties, and with political institutions.

Politicians

If public doubts about the polity surfaced only in evaluations of politicians or the government in power at any particular point in time, there would be little cause to worry. After all, citizens' dissatisfaction with an incumbent government routinely spurs voters to seek a change in administration at the next election and then extend support to the new incumbents. In that case disaffection is a healthy part of the democratic process. Because citizens have the power to "throw the rascals out," democracy has a potential for renewal and responsiveness that is its ultimate strength. But if dissatisfaction is generalized to the point that citizens lose faith in the entire political class, then the chances for democratic renewal are seriously diminished.

The patterns we have described separately, region by region, appear to be common to most Trilateral democracies. Table 1.1 reports the time trends for a commonly asked battery of political trust questions developed by the American National Election Study.[5] The questions deal with

---

[5] The per annum change coefficient is the simple regression trend line of the opinion over time. For example, the −.385 coefficient for Austrians' belief that parties are interested only in their votes means that this opinion decreases by .385 percent a year, or 3.85 percent

politicians as a political group, or tap general feelings of trust in government or government officials. Just as American skepticism about government and the politicians who run the government deepened over the past 30 years, these same downward trends appear in the nearly dozen nations for which long-term opinion series are available. Sweden and Canada also have relatively long series of political trust measures, and both nations have experienced a steady erosion in confidence in politicians from the late 1960s that rival the rates of change found in the American opinion series (Clarke 1992; Holmberg 1998).

Until the 1970s gauging trends in the rest of Europe and Japan was hampered by a lack of systematic surveys asking comparable questions, but as research centers in other Trilateral democracies took shape, comparing trends among the advanced industrial democracies became more practicable. By the mid-1990s there was evidence of long-term declines in confidence in politicians and government in Austria, Finland, and Iceland (e.g., Ulram 1994; Borg and Sänkiaho 1995). Shorter time series for Britain and Japan also point to growing public disenchantment with politicians (Curtice and Jowell 1997). Even in Trilateral nations that only recently began to gather data on the basis of standard survey questions, there are indirect indications from other data sources that trust in political leaders was higher before these data series began.[6] In general terms, the evidence of declining trust is more convincing in nations where the data series are more extensive and cover longer periods of time.

When data for recent decades are assembled today, the picture that emerges is stark. Overall, *there is evidence of some decline in confidence in politicians in 12 out of 13 countries for which systematic data are available.* The convergence of results across Trilateral democracies is striking, because each has experienced its own unique political events over the past quarter century. Although the decline is not universal,[7] there is a

---

a decade. When cumulated over several decades, as in the United States, these small per annum effects can generate significant changes.

[6] For example, if the American time series had begun in 1976, as do many other national series, the marked drop in trust would be much less evident. The respective 1976–96 coefficients would be trust (.057), leaders are crooked (.114), and don't care (−.721).

[7] The sharpest deviation from the pattern of declining trust is the Netherlands: the two longest Dutch opinion series show statistically significant improvements between 1971 and 1994. These are the only two statistically significant positive coefficients in the table. We suspect that the Dutch time series begins too late to capture the stable period of Dutch politics before the end of pillarization and the realignment of the party system in the late 1960s (which would be equivalent to U.S. opinion levels before the drop in trust in the late 1960s). For example, in his study of Dutch electoral behavior, Rudy Andeweg (1982, 183) maintains that the Provo violence of 1965–66 damaged the legitimacy of not just government authorities, but of authority more generally, and that these patterns continued into the 1970s.

TABLE 1.1

Confidence in Politicians in 13 Trilateral Countries (per annum)

Nation	Change	Period	N of timepoints
Austria			
Only interested in votes	− .385	1974–96	4
MPs lose touch	− .577*	1974–96	4
Politicians don't care	− .297	1974–96	4
Britain			
Only interested in votes	− .339	1974–96	6
MPs lose touch	− .292	1974–96	6
Canada			
Government doesn't care	− .541*	1965–93	7
MPs lose touch	− .524*	1965–93	7
Denmark			
Politicians don't care	− .185	1971–94	9
Finland			
Only interested in votes	− .389	1978–91	11
MPs lose touch	− .495*	1974–94	11
Germany			
Officials don't care (a)	− 1.270*	1969–94	5
Officials don't care (b)	− .661	1974–94	4
MPs lose touch	− .525	1974–91	3
Iceland			
Politicians trustworthy	− .850	1983–95	4
Italy			
Officials don't care	− .451*	1968–97	5
MPs lose touch	− 1.353	1968–91	3
Trust government	− 1.165	1968–91	3
Japan			
Many dishonest politicians	− 1.943	1976–92	3
Netherlands			
Only interested in votes	.785*	1971–94	8
MPs don't care	.903*	1971–94	8
Norway			
Only interested in votes	.115	1969–93	4
MPs don't care	− .286	1969–89	3
Sweden			
Only interested in votes	− 1.326*	1968–94	9
MPs don't care	− .815*	1968–94	9

TABLE 1.1 (*continued*)

Nation	Change	Period	N of timepoints
United States			
Trust government	−1.226*	1958–96	10
Politicians don't care	−.817*	1952–96	12
Leaders crooked	−.426*	1958–94	10

Notes: Table entries are unstandardized regression coefficients of time on each variable. The original variables are coded so that negative regression coefficients indicate a decrease in trust over time. *p < .05.

Sources: The respective National Election Study series in each nation.

general pattern of spreading public distrust of politicians and government among the citizens of Trilateral democracies. The political process undoubtedly faces strains when an increasing number of people distrust those individuals who are running the institutions of democratic governance.

Political Parties

For more than a century political parties have played a central role in the theory and practice of democratic government. To be sure, classical philosophers conceived of democracy as a kind of unmediated popular sovereignty in which "the people" ruled directly, but they had in mind the context of a small city-state and never imagined that democratic government could function in societies as large and complex as today's Trilateral nations. If the greatest modern political innovation—representative democracy—overcame this hurdle of scale, it required intermediary institutions to link citizens to their government, aggregate the increasingly diverse universe of conflicting social and economic interests into coherent public policies, and ensure the accountability of rulers to the ruled. With the advent of universal suffrage, these functions came to be performed by political parties throughout the democratic world.

Although parties have long been the target of vociferous criticism, without them, the eminent scholar E. E. Schattschneider (1960) once asserted, democracy would be unthinkable. One need not be blind to the deficiencies of partisanship nor romanticize the democracy internal to party organizations to recognize the importance of parties to representative government. Joseph Schumpeter (1952, 269) once defined democracy as "that institutional arrangement for arriving at political decisions in which individuals acquire the power to decide by means of a competitive struggle for the people's votes." Although Schumpeter did not specifically emphasize the role of parties in this competition, his theory did clarify how parties contribute to democracy. Just as firms in a free market are led to innovate and to satisfy consumers by a combination of self-interest and the rules of open competition, so too, this theory explained, does party competition provide the linchpin between voters and public policy and the mechanism for turning disparate "special interests" into some version of "the public interest." Just as brand names allow consumers to choose on the basis of past experience and to penalize shoddy performance, so too do party labels ensure that voters can reward the successful stewardship of public affairs and punish incompetence or dishonesty. Partisan "brand loyalty" gives political leaders the right incentives: they are free to innovate and make difficult decisions that may be painful in the short run, while they remain accountable to their constituents in the long run. Parties, in short, make the political marketplace orderly. Parties offer other advantages. They can rise above the public's feelings about individual politicians; party supporters can be dissatisfied with a set of candidates, yet remain committed to the party's goals and the principle of representative democracy that parties signify.

Because of their centrality to democracy, people's feelings of attachment to or identification with political parties are one of the most widely studied of political attitudes, with fine-tuned efforts to measure both affinities toward specific parties and acceptance of the general system of party-based democracy (Weisberg 1981).

Signs of the public's waning attachments to political parties first emerged in several Trilateral democracies during the 1970s (Dalton, Flanagan, and Beck 1984). The collapse in citizen engagement with political parties over the decades since is as close to a universal generalization as one can find in political science (Dalton 1999). Card-carrying membership has always been less important for American than for European parties, but the proportion of Americans who reported that they engaged in party work at least once during the previous year fell by 56 percent between 1973 and 1993, and the proportion who reported attending a campaign rally or speech fell by 36 percent over the same period. Comparably massive declines in party membership have been registered in most Trilateral countries over the last 25 years (Putnam 1995a; Scarrow 1997). As attachments to political parties have eroded, electorates have become more volatile and skeptical. A comprehensive look at this pattern of weakening party ties, or "dealignment," reveals that popular identification with political parties has fallen in almost all the advanced industrial democracies. *The percent of the public expressing a partisan attachment has declined in 17 out of 19 of the Trilateral nations for which time series data are available.* The strength of party attachments was separately measured in 18 nations: all show a downward trend (Dalton 1999).

Seldom does such a diverse group of nations reveal so consistent a trend. The only major variation is in the timing of the decline. Dealignment in the United States, Great Britain, and Sweden has been a long-term and relatively steady process that moved partisanship to a lower baseline level. For example, 65 percent of the Swedish public claimed party ties in 1968 compared to only 48 percent in 1994. In other countries the change has been more recent. French and Irish partisanship has eroded over the past two decades. German partisanship, which had grown during the early postwar decades, began to weaken in the late 1980s and dropped off markedly in the 1990s. The collapse of the Progressive Conservative and New Democratic Parties in the 1993 elections accentuated a similar trend toward dealignment in Canadian politics. A detachment from parties accelerated in the 1990s in Japan and Austria, too, in response to a breakdown of political consensus in both nations (for Japan, see Ōtake, this volume). Specific variations aside, the overall pattern is consistent and striking. If party attachments represent the most fundamental type of citizen support for representative democracy, as many scholars assert, then their decline in nearly all advanced industrial democracies offers strong and disturbing evidence of the public's disengagement from political life.

Beyond reflecting dissatisfaction with politicians and current party leaders, weakening partisan ties also signal a growing disenchantment with partisan politics in general. For example, responses to several questions from the American National Election Study indicate a trend of declining faith that parties and elections are responsive to the public's interests (Dalton 1996, 271). A variety of other evidence points to Americans' growing disillusionment with political parties as agents of democratic representation (Wattenberg 1996). Along with other factors, disenchantment with political parties fueled public demands for major electoral reforms in Japan, Italy, and New Zealand. Across most Trilateral democracies, more citizens are now maintaining their independence from political parties and the institutions of representative democracy that they represent.

Political Institutions

In the Trilateral democracies, citizens' skepticism about politicians and political parties extends to the formal institutions of democratic government. It is one thing for citizens to be skeptical of the president or the prime minister (or even the group of politicians in parliament); it is quite different if this cynicism broadens to the institutions of the presidency and the legislature.

Because of its abundance of long-running, high-quality public opinion surveys, the best evidence once again comes from the United States. One question gauges confidence in the officials running the three branches of

American government (Blendon et al. 1997). In the mid-1960s a large proportion of Americans expressed a great deal of confidence in the Supreme Court, the executive branch, and Congress, but that confidence dropped dramatically by the early 1970s, and slid even further for the executive and Congress over the following two decades. Significantly, it is the Supreme Court, the least partisan and political institution, that has best retained the public's confidence. By the mid-1990s barely a tenth of the American public had a great deal of confidence in the people running the executive branch or Congress—dramatic evidence of Americans' dissatisfaction with government.

Table 1.2 presents data on trends in confidence in parliament for 14 Trilateral democracies.[8] Parliament is the prime institution of representative democracy, the link between citizens and elites. Thus, we focus on public images of parliament as a key institution in the structure of democratic politics.

The time coverage and the extensiveness of the evidence varies considerably across nations, but the overall pattern is quite apparent. *In 11 out of 14 countries confidence in parliament has declined.* Although the evidence does not rise to the level of statistical significance in a number of cases (largely because of the limited number of time points), the overall pattern is quite striking. And in those five countries (Britain, Canada, Germany, Sweden, and the United States) for which the most extensive data are available, the drop in confidence in the national legislature is both pronounced and statistically significant. Additional data on the erosion of confidence in parliament appears in Kenneth Newton and Pippa Norris's chapter in this volume.

Citizens' declining confidence in the institutions of democratic government extends beyond parliament. Using the 1981 and 1990 World Values Surveys, a separate analysis evaluated confidence in the armed services, judiciary, police, and civil service as well as parliament. Although some institutions have scored gains in public trust over time, the general downward trajectory is clear. On average, confidence in these five institutions decreased by 6 percent over this single decade (Dalton 1999; Inglehart 1999). In fact, only Denmark and Iceland displayed absolute increases in institutional confidence during the 1980s, and those increases were small.

The trends described here are not homogeneous across all the Trilateral countries. The degree and timing of growing distrust of political leaders, dissatisfaction with government performance, and estrangement

---

[8] Where possible, we use separate national survey series because these tend to have a longer time span and more frequent measurements. When such data are not available, we track confidence in parliament on the basis of the 1981 and 1990 World Values Surveys.

TABLE 1.2
Confidence in Parliament in 14 Trilateral Countries (per annum)

Nation	Change	Period	Source (N)
Belgium			
Parliament	.444	1981–90	WVS (2)
Britain			
Parliament	−2.399*	1981–96	Gallup (8)
Parliament	.666	1981–90	WVS (2)
Canada			
Parliament	−1.152*	1979–96	CIPO (8)
Parliament	−.385	1981–96	WVS (3)
Finland			
Parliament	−2.266	1981–96	WVS (2)
France			
Parliament	−.888	1981–90	WVS (2)
Germany			
Parliament	−.992*	1984–95	IPOS (11)
Parliament	−1.533	1981–96	WVS (3)
Iceland			
Parliament	−.500	1984–90	WVS (2)
Ireland			
Parliament	−.333	1981–90	WVS (2)
Italy			
Parliament	.222	1981–90	WVS (2)
Japan			
Parliament	−.133	1981–96	WVS (3)
Netherlands			
Parliament	1.000	1981–90	WVS (2)
Norway			
Parliament	−.533	1982–96	WVS (3)
Sweden			
Parliament	−2.242*	1986–96	SOM (10)
Parliament	−.133	1981–96	WVS (2)
United States			
Congress	−.565*	1966–96	Harris/GSS (21)
Congress	−.917*	1973–97	Gallup(19)
Congress	−1.066	1981–96	WVS (3)

Notes: Table entries are the per annum change in the percentage expressing a great deal or quite a lot of confidence in each institution. *p < .05.

Sources: World Value Surveys (WVS) data are from the 1981–83, 1990–94, and 1995–98 surveys; other data are from individual national survey series.

from established parties vary greatly, depending on national traditions, specific political events, the effectiveness of individual leaders, and so on. Generally speaking, the trends are clearer in the larger countries—and clearest of all in the largest of all—and less visible—or, in a few cases, almost wholly absent—in some of the smallest countries (on the latter phenomenon, see Katzenstein, this volume).

Quite apart from any temporary disenchantment with the present government or dissatisfaction with particular leaders, most citizens in the Trilateral world have become more distrustful of politicians, more skeptical about political parties, and significantly less confident in their parliament and other political institutions. Compared to the state of public opinion at the time that Crozier, Huntington, and Watanuki wrote, the political mood in most of our countries today is not just grumpy, but much grumpier.

WHY WORRY?

Although public concern over these trends is widespread, it is nevertheless reasonable to step back and ask whether we, as citizens of the Trilateral democracies, should be worried about the many signs of erosion in popular confidence in government and the institutions of representative democracy. Some observers would offer a resounding "no," offering three main arguments, all of which are represented in this book. The first holds that a critical citizenry signals not illness in the body politic, but rather the health of democracy, and that the real challenge is to explain not the long-term decline in confidence, but why it was as high as it was in the 1950s and early 1960s, especially in the United States. A variation on that same view sees value change, driven by prosperity, technology, and other factors, creating a more critical citizenry that while debunking the political status quo is also forcing new issues such as environmentalism and women's rights onto the political agenda, thus reforming and revitalizing democracy (see Dalton, this volume).

A second objection holds that while established forms of political participation like parties have suffered a loss of support, new forms such as referenda and "town-hall"-style fora and an upsurge in certain types of grassroots activism including social movements that are more broad-based than in the past have supplanted previous forms of political engagement (see Tarrow, this volume). A third objection proceeds from a particular perspective on the appropriate relation between government and citizens. The task of government, this view holds, is to give citizens not necessarily what they want, but what they need, and thus sound and appropriate policies are the best measure of governmental performance. Confidence levels are immaterial as long as the public supports the government enough to comply with its laws, pay taxes, and accept conscription.

Although each of these arguments has merit, most, if not all, of the contributors to this volume see reason to worry that voters' "report cards" on their representative institutions in the Trilateral democracies have generally become more critical—and often much more critical—in recent decades. We do not believe that this sour mood is a precursor of the collapse of Western democracy. But, for the most part, we do hold that a decent respect for our fellow citizens' views compels us to consider why they are increasingly distrustful of, and discontented with, their political institutions. If the decline in public confidence is justified (because of growing corruption, for example), then we might applaud citizens' ire but not its cause, just as we would be glad to have discovered a child's fever without being glad that her temperature was high.

The point of view adopted in this book is that if citizens are less satisfied with their representative institutions, this is a politically relevant and important fact. However, none of us argue that popularity is the sole measure of democratic performance, and all of us recognize that governments often must (or should) take actions that might reduce their popularity in the short run. That said, we are not in full agreement about whether public satisfaction per se is a relevant measure of democratic performance. Some of us believe that democracy is not (just) about making citizens happy, and that it is also supposed to facilitate "good government," whether or not citizens are pleased with government actions. Others of us endorse the more populist view that what is distinctive about democracy is that the ultimate criterion of performance is citizens' collective judgment, so if public confidence declines over the long run, that is prima facie (though not irrefutable) evidence that the performance of representative institutions has declined.

For disaffection in particular countries, explanations have been offered that are studded with proper nouns: Vietnam, Nixon, Craxi, Mulroney, Thatcher, Recruit, and so on. Such interpretations offer important insights into the national catalysts for democratic distress, but it seems surprising that so many independent democracies just happened to encounter rough water or careless captains simultaneously. Although we do not discount the importance of specific national factors, we seek more generalizable explanations.

TOWARD A MODEL FOR EXPLAINING DECLINING PUBLIC TRUST

Unraveling the question of why confidence in government has declined to varying degrees across the Trilateral world is a complex task. While the contributors to this volume do not always agree on which factors matter

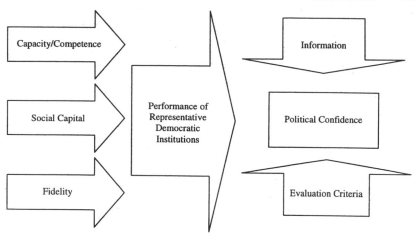

Figure 1.1. Explaining Confidence in Government and Political Institutions: A Model

most, we do agree on a general framework of interpretation for the causes of the decline. Public satisfaction with representative institutions is a function of the information to which citizens are exposed, the criteria by which the public evaluates government and politics, and the actual performance of those institutions (see Figure 1.1). Thus, a decline in satisfaction might be due to a change in any of these variables.

First, the accuracy and comprehensiveness of publicly available *information* about democratic performance might have changed. Logically, this might be due to either deterioration (worse information about good performance) or improvement (better information about bad performance), but the most common interpretation is that voters have over time become better informed about their governments' performance, particularly about the leaders' conduct in office (e.g., corruption), even though malfeasance per se might not have worsened. Some studies of the media and public confidence (see Norris, this volume) are relevant to this interpretation of our central dependent variable.

Second, the public's *criteria for evaluation* of politics and government might have changed in ways that make it objectively more difficult for representative institutions to meet those standards. This in turn might be due to either or both rising and diverging expectations. If public demands on government spiral insatiably upward, satisfaction could fall even if performance remains unchanged. In part, this was the interpretation offered by Crozier, Huntington, and Watanuki. If the heterogeneity of public desires increases, either by polarization along a single dimension or by divergence across multiple dimensions, then it becomes more difficult for government to identify any feasible set of policies that would satisfy its constituents. Some chapters in this book, particularly those by Alberto Alesina and Romain Wacziarg and by Russell Dalton, adopt this interpretation. Alesina and Wacziarg suggest (inter alia) that growing heterogeneity of voters' views about issues on the evolving public agenda has necessarily increased the distance between government policy and the preferences of the average voter. Dalton argues that many voters' criteria for judging government (especially the process of government) have evolved in a "postmaterialist" direction, thus increasing the discrepancy between their aspirations and government performance.

Third, the *performance of representative institutions* might have deteriorated. Measuring performance objectively is a challenging task, of course. Because it is reasonably well established in most of the Trilateral countries that cyclical fluctuations in citizens' evaluations of incumbents correlate with macro-economic indicators, one obvious approach is to measure macro-economic outcomes (inflation, unemployment, growth, and the like), and several of our authors investigate this relationship in their chapters (see Alesina and Wacziarg and also Pharr, this volume). Their findings contribute to a growing body of work that generally discounts this as the primary explanation for the decline in public confidence in political institutions (Nye, Zelikow, and King 1997; Norris 1999). As Nye and his colleagues (1997, 10–11) note with regard to the United States, for example, the largest decline in confidence occurred over the high-growth decade between 1964 and 1974, and confidence actually increased during the recession of the early 1980s.

Once these economic measures are set aside, there is little agreement over which dimensions of performance are relevant across countries, time, and individual citizens. One obvious measure might be gains or losses in social welfare, and, indeed, Peter Katzenstein argues here that levels of confidence have remained high in countries in which social welfare guarantees are secure (e.g., some of the small democracies of Northern Europe) while they have dropped elsewhere as a result of rollbacks of the welfare state. Testing such a hypothesis runs into the problem of how to measure governmental performance on social welfare, however. If we use government outlays, we run up against the fact that despite the rhetoric hailing "small government," government transfers (which are heavily skewed toward social programs) as a percentage of GNP have increased strikingly in the Trilateral countries precisely over those decades in which confidence has decreased (see Alesina and Wacziarg, this volume). Alternatively, to measure results like increased longevity and improved health would fail to take into account the many factors other than government policies (e.g., diet, economic prosperity) that produce them. Another problem is choosing a point in time at which policy success or failure can be judged. For example, some people believe that the American war in Vietnam or the process of German reunification constituted massive policy failures that contributed powerfully to declining political confidence; other observers might argue that, in the long run, these policy "failures" represent historic successes.

POSSIBLE EXPLANATIONS FOR DETERIORATION IN THE PERFORMANCE OF
  DEMOCRATIC INSTITUTIONS

Thus, objective measures of policy performance have obvious limits. When searching for why citizens feel the way they do about their government, their subjective appraisal of governmental performance is what ultimately matters. The fact that public confidence has declined can be taken to mean that governmental performance is less satisfactory than it once was. Most contributors to this volume consider citizens' falling confidence in government to be focused specifically on political institutions and to have principally political roots, a position strongly supported by the evidence presented by Newton and Norris. We concentrate, then, on identifying broad explanations for the deterioration of governmental performance. These can be collected under two rubrics.

The first of these is declines in the *capacity* of political agents to act on citizens' interests and desires (see Figure 1.1). Thus, we seek to identify forces that may have undermined the ability of national governments to implement their chosen policies and respond to citizen demands in a satisfactory way. The principal such force is internationalization, which creates a growing incongruence between the scope of territorial units and the issues raised by interdependence, reducing the output effectiveness of democratic nation-states. Fritz Scharpf advances scholarship in this area by specifying precisely why internationalization creates complex problems for democratic representation. Pointing out that confidence levels have remained high in some of the smaller Trilateral democracies—precisely those countries that are most dependent on the global economy and thus most affected by internationalization—Katzenstein, on the other hand, contests that argument.

The second broad explanation concerns declines in the *fidelity* with which political agents act on citizens' interests and desires. Within this category fall arguments about failures of political leadership, failures of political judgment on the part of voters, and deterioration of the civic infrastructure (or social capital) by means of which interests are articulated and aggregated. Susan Pharr distinguishes between policy performance and conduct in office to demonstrate that misconduct in office is a far more powerful predictor of Japanese confidence levels over the past two decades than a number of other possible causes. Looking at Italy,

France, and Germany, Donatella della Porta shows how political misconduct in the form of corruption can create "blessed" versus "unlucky" communities. While agreeing with Pharr on the importance of corruption in prejudicing citizens' views of government in Japan, Hideo Ōtake makes the case that partisan dealignment there is due primarily to the failure of Japanese voters to reward political entrepreneurs who have sought to realign party competition along more productive and relevant policy dimensions. Sidney Tarrow argues that the political reforms induced by social movements might actually improve performance and thus confidence in government in the long run, even though those social movements were initially motivated by popular distrust of political authorities.

One final problem relating to the issue of fidelity arises from the complex relationship among three sets of variables: confidence in government; governmental performance; and civic engagement, social capital,[9] and social trust. A key issue is precisely how an erosion of social capital and social trust may affect citizens' confidence in government. Several authors explore this relationship using individual-level data (see Newton and Norris and also Pharr, this volume). Confirming the findings of other recent work, they establish that a person's degree of social trust or level of civic engagement have little or no *direct* effect on his or her confidence in government (Newton 1999; Hall 1997). What Newton and Norris go on to show, however, is that by adversely affecting governmental performance, social trust in particular does *indirectly* affect political confidence levels, as Figure 1.1 suggests. Low levels overall of social capital and social trust in any given society contribute to poor governmental performance, which in turn adversely affects all citizens to varying degrees; as a consequence, they will give the government low marks. Metaphorically speaking, no citizen (no matter how high his or her *own* social trust or civic engagement) can escape the rain produced by poor governmental performance, which is perhaps produced in part by the social disaffection or civic disengagement of his or her neighbors. Looking at aggregate- rather than individual-level data for a number of Trilateral nations, Newton and Norris find strong support for this indirect "rainmaker" effect of declining social trust on citizenries' confidence in government. Their work thus supports the earlier claims of Robert Putnam

[9] By analogy to physical and human capital, some scholars have introduced the term "social capital" to refer to the norms and networks of civil society that enable citizens and their institutions to perform more productively. Without adequate supplies of social capital—that is, without civic engagement, healthy community institutions, norms of mutual reciprocity, and trust—democracies and market economies may begin to falter.

(1993; see also Putnam 2000 and Putnam forthcoming) about these relationships.

This chapter has reviewed a large body of evidence to demonstrate that over the quarter century since Crozier and his colleagues issued their report, citizens' confidence in governments, political parties, and political leaders has declined significantly in most of the Trilateral democracies even though the depth and timing of this decline have varied considerably from country to country. Some commentators may tell their fellow citizens that the problem is "just in your head"—a function of unrealistic expectations rather than deteriorating performance—but we are inclined to think that our political systems are not, in fact, performing well, although perhaps for reasons beyond their immediate control. These criticisms of governments and leaders do not necessarily translate into a "crisis of democracy" that threatens constitutional and representative government. Nevertheless, the fact that representative democracy per se is not at risk does not imply that all is well with our political systems. Indeed, most of our fellow citizens believe that all is *not* well. Due regard for their views, as well as a prudent concern for the future, suggests that we should explore the sources of this democratic discontent.

PART I

Declining Performance
of Democratic Institutions

The Public Trust

Russell Hardin

WHAT ARE WE to make of the apparent decline in confidence in government across the Trilateral democracies? Why does it happen? Does it matter? I propose answers to these questions and speculate on their implications for democracy. Although there are probably many causal factors in any change this grand and widespread, I will focus on a related pair of changes in the nature of the policies faced by governments in the advanced industrial democracies. Their historical focus on economic issues—whether to use central planning or to rely on the market—has largely been settled in favor of the latter in a remarkable shift in global conditions over the past two decades or so. At the same time the range of policy issues at stake has grown more diverse and technically more complex, and therefore evidently harder to handle successfully.

Before turning to explanations and implications, I wish to address three conceptual issues of the uses and abuses of the terminology of trust. First, is trust in government analogous to trust in another person, or is it a very different notion? It clearly is *not* analogous to personal trust most of the time (Hardin 1998a). A personal relationship involving trust is far richer and more directly reciprocal than a citizen's relationship to government. Hence, we should speak not of trust in government, but of confidence in government. It should be clear that this notion is a partial analogue of trust, as spelled out below. That is what licenses the loose vernacular use of the term trust even in the context of a citizen's relation to government. But it is only a partial analogue, and much of the force of claims of trust does not apply to claims of confidence. For many writers, declining trust suggests a normative problem. Declining confidence does not so readily provoke normative concerns.

The second issue is that we should be concerned with trustworthiness rather than with trust (Hardin 1996), because if we wish to induce changes somewhere, it is most likely in the former. We do not commonly want to increase trust without first enhancing trustworthiness. If there have been changes in citizens' propensity to trust government, the first supposition we should make is that those changes are rooted in changes in the trustworthiness of government and not in changes in our trustfulness, credulity, or basic psychological makeup (see Newton and Norris, this volume).

Finally, we should recognize that trust involves an expectation that the trusted has both the right motivations and the competence to fulfill the trust. Unless there is good evidence to suppose politicians have become less honorable in recent decades, we should probably focus our attention on problems of *competence* rather than motivation.[1]

There is one other conceptual issue to be addressed: the nature of social capital, which is thought by some observers to be declining in the United States. If they are right, its decline might contribute to the loss of confidence in government in the United States, but not likely in most other Trilateral democracies.

Once these conceptual issues are out of the way, we can turn to explaining the apparent decline in confidence in government that shows up in surveys in many of the Trilateral nations. I will assume that responses to survey questions on trust are not evidence of mere credulity. Rather, they are evidence of belief that governmental performance is failing in some way relative to past performance. I will focus on one explanation of declining confidence in government in the section "Competence and Motivation." Its consequences for politics and government will then be discussed under "Democratic Theory." Government today may be no more nor less competent than it was two generations ago, but its agenda may have changed in ways that make it *seem* less competent relative to the problems it faces. In particular, the relatively simple conflict over whether to engage in central planning or let markets operate has largely been settled in favor of markets. The issues that now dominate political agendas in the advanced industrial democracies are much less systematically related to one another than these economic issues were, and they are often technically complex and beyond popular understanding. But because a failure to deal with them is often not beyond popular understanding, governments increasingly seem to be maladroit.

TRUST IN GOVERNMENT

Discussions of trust have become commonplace in the analysis of governmental responsiveness and citizen attitudes toward government (Bianco 1994), in efforts to understand differential economic success across societies (Fukuyama 1995), and in discussions of the relations between cli-

---

[1] I am inclined to assume with David Hume that many government officials are no more public-spirited than most citizens and that by far most of the success government has in achieving public purposes turns on incentives that guide individual officials in their actions (Hardin 1998b). Hence, it is unlikely that the public spiritedness of officials has declined markedly.

ents and various professionals, such as doctors (Barber 1983). It is common in these discussions to suppose that trust is essentially good because it has good consequences and, hence, to suppose that generally higher levels of trust would be good. Many recent, well-received works make strong claims for the value of trust and thus at least implicitly for the value of enhancing trust (Luhmann 1980; Putnam 1995a; Putnam 1995b; Fukuyama 1995). If we wish to understand the role of trust in society, however, we must get beyond the flaccid—and often wrong—assumption that trust is simply good. This supposition must be heavily qualified, because trusting the malevolent or the incompetent is foolish and even harmful.

Even if trust is important in society, it does not follow that trust in government is important or even meaningful. Much of the shock value of the countless polls that supposedly testify to declining trust in government and other institutions depends on the presumption that trusting government is roughly analogous to trusting a person. For the most part, this is an incoherent assumption. To say that I trust you suggests several things. First, I expect you to do certain things. Second and third, I think you have the motivation and the capacity to do those things. And finally, if my trust is specific to you, I think you are motivated to do those things because they benefit me, not merely because you might have wanted to do them anyway or were being paid to do them independently of the fact that they are in my interest.

In French there is no neat equivalent of the English verb *to trust*. The nearest counterpart is *avoir confiance*, to have confidence. The French term is apt for what most English speakers presumably mean when they say, "I trust that the sun will rise tomorrow, as always." Here the use of "trust" is otiose. It adds nothing beyond saying that I expect the sun to rise or that I understand the physics of the sun's rising daily. Of course, the vernacular allows for the use of "trust" in such trivializing ways, but there is not much of interest in such uses of "trust." It is similarly trivializing to say of most people that they trust government or government officials whom they do not know personally or have a relationship with rather than to say that they expect the government and its officials to do certain things.[2] Some of the standard survey questions on trust in government, in fact, do not even use the terminology of trust. That the respondents mean trust is imputed to them by researchers.

---

[2] Niklas Luhmann (1980) speaks loosely of "system" trust, which is merely the confidence one has in the larger system of legal enforcement, monetary policy, and so forth. It is not trust in any useful sense of the word any more than my expectation that drivers will stay to the right in North America is a matter of trusting them to have my specific interests at heart.

Can typical citizens meaningfully trust government in the way that they do trust their friends and other associates? In general, no. For me to trust you, I have to know a fair amount about you. My knowledge might be wrong, and I might therefore mistakenly trust or distrust you. But in general, for me to trust you I must believe your motivations toward me are to serve my interests, broadly conceived, with respect to the issues at stake. I could believe this if I believed any of the following things. First, because you value our relationship enough to want to maintain it, you will want to fulfill the trust I place in you.[3] Second, you value me enough to include my interests in your own, as a parent, lover, or close friend might do. Or third, you have such strong moral commitments to, say, fidelity that you will want to fulfill my trust.[4] Although some officials might want us to believe that the second holds for them, only the first of these attitudes can plausibly be attributed to most government officials. But even that asks too much in the sense that few of us can know many government officials and their commitments well enough to judge whether they actually value their relationships with us. It is conceptually possible that someone might trust government or, rather, a government agency in this sense, but that would be very demanding epistemologically because it would require vast knowledge (Hardin 1998a and Hardin 1999a).

At present, to my knowledge, no elected government official knows me at all. Although some have met me, I suspect that they have long since forgotten me. (Some have long since forgotten their mothers.) It is implausible that any of them is motivated by concern for my interests. True, many of them want my vote and the votes of people like me. But in this they may be merely self-serving and opportunistic, and they may just as soon not serve my interests when *that* will help them get elected. If I trust them in the trivializing, vernacular sense discussed above, that is what I trust them to do: act opportunistically. It would be silly for me to say I trust those officials the way I trust many of my associates.

Because there is no evidence that people actually trust government in the ways they do trust some persons, and because it is very difficult to see how they sensibly could, it makes sense analytically to speak of declining confidence in government rather than declining trust. We should therefore interpret all the survey data on the subject to be about confidence, not trust, in government. Being confident in an agency might be epis-

---

[3] We may refer to this reason for trusting as encapsulated interest; that is, my trust in you is encapsulated in your interest to fulfill my trust (Hardin 1991, 1992).

[4] One cannot sensibly be thought to have a moral commitment to fulfill trusts *tout court*. If I did, and you happened to trust me to do something I would and should never do, then the fact that you trusted me to do so would morally bind me to some extent. Nevertheless, some writers actually suppose one is morally obligated to fulfill trusts.

temologically easy as a mere generalization from its past behavior without any genuine knowledge about anyone in the agency.

Finally, there is a widely held view that government *needs* the trust of citizens if it is to work well. This view is perhaps a variant of the claim of Émile Durkheim and Talcott Parsons that social order rests on shared normative commitments (Parsons 1968, 89–94). This is not the place to quarrel with that extraordinary and virtually unresearchable claim. But the more recent view of the role of trust can make sense only if by trust is meant essentially confidence and, perhaps, some element of cooperativeness. Government might need this much if it is to gain citizen compliance with sometimes hard laws, such as those concerning taxes and conscription (Levi 1997). If government needs trust in the strong sense in which our personal relationships need trust and trustworthiness to prosper, then it has been failing us throughout the history of modern democracy and virtually must fail because most citizens simply cannot trust government that way.

TRUSTWORTHINESS

The point of wanting more trust in personal relations is that trust facilitates cooperation, but it is hard to see why more trust per se is wanted. We want As to trust Bs to do Xs (Hardin 1991). When we think of the problem in this unpacked form, we immediately focus on specific devices to get the Bs to do Xs; that is, we focus on the *trustworthiness* of the Bs. For example, the massive system of contract enforcement in any flourishing market society serves agents who do not genuinely trust each other with respect to anything in particular—who, indeed, need not even know each other well enough to be trusting without backing from the law. Nevertheless, the system enables them to enter into very complex cooperative relations that are mutually beneficial. The very specific confidence in compliance with a legal contract is grounded in the system of contract enforcement. Or, as is true in many ongoing business relations, it is iterated or repeated interaction that gives the parties an incentive to behave well now because they want the relationship to continue in the future. For example, if I regularly supply your firm with some input and you object that the quality of one of my shipments is poor, it will be in my interest, if possible, to make the shipment right regardless of the terms of our contract because I will want to keep your business. I could insist on the letter of the contract, but then you might find an alternative supplier for your future needs.

Although contemporary writings commonly posit trust as the relevant variable in explaining differential success in cooperation, the crucial variable is typically the trustworthiness of those who are to be trusted or relied upon. If popular assessments of government—as measured by responses to such vague questions as "How much do you trust government to do what is right?"—suggest declining confidence, we should similarly suppose that the problem to be explained is declining performance or responsiveness on the part of government. If we think there are problems inherent in declining trust, we might attempt to address them by encouraging more trust or, alternatively, attaining greater trustworthiness. Clearly, if a person, such as your child, were distrustful, you would want to encourage that person to be more trusting only if trust were justified, that is, if the people to be trusted were trustworthy. If we can tell at all accurately from our experience with them whether particular people are apt to be trustworthy in certain circumstances, we will then trust them as much as their trustworthiness merits.

How should we interpret responses to standard questions on trust in government? It is not plausible to treat them as articulately responsive to any reflective sense of trust, of what trust is and how it works. But they presumably do reflect people's real experiences. Hence, they are implicit assertions about the trustworthiness or reliability of relevant others. Again, if there are changes over time or differences across contexts in the level of trust that people express in responding to survey questions, we should look to changes or differences in the behavior of those who are supposedly trusted for an explanation. Hence, if confidence in government is declining, we should address that problem by enhancing government competence.

COMPETENCE AND MOTIVATION

In conceptual work on the subject, it is commonly assumed that trust has two quite distinct dimensions: competence to perform what one is trusted to do and motivation to perform. For example, I could distrust you to baby-sit for my child because I think you are incompetent or because I think you would be malevolent toward the child. Unfortunately, these two dimensions are often not separated. For example, the main survey questions on trust in government in the United States (in the National Election Studies series) do not separate them. Other data suggest that citizens think that neither the integrity nor the competence of officials is in decline, and there are also data that point in opposite directions on both these issues. The data on declining confidence in government seemingly entail that citizens think that at least one of these factors is in decline. Or perhaps, as discussed below, there is another background factor that leads to declining confidence in government despite the continuing integrity and competence of officials.

Because the dimensions of competence and motivation are independent, we must assess these two considerations separately if we are to understand the decline in confidence in government. Judging the motivations or commitments of government agents can often be difficult. But if we suppose that there is little reason to think that such agents are more venal or untrustworthy today than they were a generation or two ago, then declining confidence in government would essentially reflect governmental failure.

Why might governmental performance be in decline? The tasks that government takes on may have grown more complex and difficult, yet the capabilities of government may not have kept pace with the increased burden. World War II required massive mobilization and imposed great demands on government. For the United States, the war in Vietnam required less massive mobilization, but, in some ways, it imposed even greater demands on the military because it was radically more complex than the war in Europe and the Pacific. While the apparent competence of the military in World War II may have produced fairly high levels of confidence in government, the apparent incompetence of the military in Vietnam may have produced low levels of confidence. Recall the quip, after the war in Iraq was over but the war in Bosnia raged on, that the American military does deserts but not mountains and jungles; this makes precisely the point that judgments of competence depend to some extent on the ease of the task. Of course, we might adjust our evaluations to match the differing difficulty of various tasks. But we might be poor at doing that and the citizens of any nation might be inclined to judge their government competent or incompetent on the basis of how well it masters the tasks it actually faces rather than how well it could master some hypothetical task.

Some of the changing attitudes to government and its agents may therefore be structural in origin. For the United States, the war on poverty, the war in Vietnam, and the war on drugs all sounded simple enough for a nation with a long history of winning wars. But all these efforts failed fairly conspicuously, and many citizens may have concluded that a government that once was relatively competent had turned into one that was relatively incompetent. Failures of aspects of massive welfare systems in other Trilateral nations similarly suggest government incompetence. Indeed, government's share in the economies of many nations may be distressing to many of their citizens. Similarly, the banking disasters of the United States and Japan suggest remarkable incompetence in an arena in which government was ostensibly engaged in careful oversight.

In other areas government may actually perform better today than it did in the past, and it may face less difficult problems. John Mueller (1999) argues that economic theory has advanced to the point that it might now generally be helpful to economic policy-makers. He compares economics today to medicine about a century ago. The Flexner Report, whose impetus came from the medical educational group of the American Medical Association, concluded that sometime around the beginning of the twentieth century, going to an American doctor was finally more likely to benefit patients than to harm them (Flexner 1910). Similarly, Mueller supposes, following the advice of economists today is, at last, more likely to benefit than harm economic performance. Much of that advice in many nations is now to leave the economy alone to a substantial degree and to let the market work. It is, of course, a corollary of letting the market run its course without massive intervention that government escapes the burden of being judged for the success or failure of its economic planning. Economic policy was once the major cleavage between parties in many democratic societies, whether the Republican and Democratic Parties in the United States or the Conservative and Labour Parties in Britain. Today it is increasingly economic policy on which they concur.

SOCIAL CAPITAL

Although the changes in agenda that might undercut confidence in government are a problem for all advanced industrial democracies, a decline in social capital is perhaps unique to the United States. It does not merit extended treatment here, but it might be useful to see how it could matter (for a critical discussion and survey of views of social capital, see Hardin forthcoming b). Social capital is defined as "features of social organization, such as trust, norms, and networks, that can improve the efficiency of society by facilitating coordinated action" (Putnam 1993, 167). If a decline in confidence in government in the United States partly results from a decline in social capital, the central element of the notion at issue is participation in various public-spirited and social-group organizations. Such participation seems to be declining in the United States (Putnam 1995a), but not in the other Trilateral democracies.

   To keep this discussion tightly focused, I will refer to "organizational" and "network" capital rather than to the more inclusive and amorphous "social" capital. Although there is a tendency to speak of social capital as though it were a particular kind of thing that has generalized value, as money very nearly does, it must vary in the sense that what is functional in one context may not be in another. Consider an example. Teenagers network in two quite different ways (Heimer 1990). In many communities they come together by coordinating on one spot—the local square where there might be cafés or other points of teenage interest, the local park, or the outdoor basketball court of a local school. In other communities, especially well-off and suburban ones, they come together by making deliberate arrangements over the telephone. Perhaps both groups create and use a kind of social or network capital, but the two kinds are quite different. Moreover, the skills involved in one kind might be more widely useful. In particular, deliberate organization via telephone calls might be good practice for the kind of organizing adults must do in typical bureaucratic settings, in neighborhood politics, in managing the lives of their children in a school system, and so forth. Although coordinating on a spot for meeting is quite generalizable in principle, in actual practice it is likely to be of relatively little use. Incidental investment in developing the one kind of network capital may have much larger payoffs in the long run than does investment in the other kind.

Investment in network capital through participation in socially directed organizations—that is, organizations with relatively collective purposes, such as some of those that Putnam (1995a, 1995b) discusses—may be displaced by more deliberate investment in networking for personal advantage. Indeed, people with political aspirations might participate in socially directed organizations *in order to* benefit personally from the network ties and reputational advantages they gain from such activity. In the end, there might therefore be no overall decline in network capital, but specific forms of capital might well decline. Because this may follow simply because people's goals have shifted, it would be wrong to conclude prima facie that a decline of network capital in socially directed organizations *leads* to changes in goals.

Note that organizational and network capital provide two quite different values. First, the organizations and networks can be directly enabling; they themselves can be the vehicles we use to accomplish various purposes. For example, I may use my network to prompt my son's school to be more responsive to him. Second, they can be an arena in which we develop particular forms of human capital; they can teach us how to do things that might be more generally valuable outside the context in which we learn them. For example, after I learn how to run a meeting or organize a group of people to participate in a Parent-Teacher Association (PTA), I might use those skills in other contexts. It makes sense to reserve the terms *social, organizational,* and *network capital* for the first of these, for organizations and networks as vehicles for accomplishing our purposes. In a sense the organizations and networks are instances of social capital. The second value, the development of individual capacities, is clearly important, but it is more a matter of human capital as traditionally discussed by Gary Becker (1975) and others.

How do network and organizational capital benefit us? Do they benefit us by what they can do, that is, by what the network or organization can do? Or do they benefit us by what they enable us to do by means of the human capital we develop in networks or organizations? If there is a decline in the social capital represented by such groups as the PTA or bowling leagues, that might reduce both the human capital for managing other people in spontaneous contexts and the availability of actual organizations and networks to help us accomplish various things.

Francis Fukuyama argues that participation in such networks and organizations prepares us psychologically for the demands of working in modern firms. As a consequence he supposes that social groups are good for the economy indirectly through the human capital they produce (Fukuyama 1995). Let us try to unpack this idea. The argument is that spontaneous sociability leads us to join various social organizations; participation in these organizations prepares us psychologically for working in large firms. This argument might seem to apply to a developing nation or to a subpopulation, such as immigrant groups or ghetto poor, that has not been incorporated into the economy. But how are these groups different from the new labor forces that staffed the Industrial Revolution? The nascent industries of Europe and North America evidently created their own human capital. It seems unlikely that much of the necessary human capital was created in voluntary social organizations. Once underway, the developing economies of our time should also generate the human capital they require.

Perhaps the kinds of human capital needed today are different and are likely to be produced in social organizations such as local political groups and sports clubs. Or, more plausibly, some variant of Fukuyama's argument might apply to the special kind of human capital or psychology peculiar to the entrepreneurs who are needed in the drive to develop a market economy. If this is the essence of his idea, it does not seem important to most of the Trilateral nations, in which capitalist enterprises are alive and well and in which the generation of relevant human capital is handled by universities and business schools, experience on the job, and entrepreneurial families, whose offspring tend to be much more enterprising than the average person. The entrepreneurs who have made the biggest difference to the exploding computer and information industries have included youngsters such as Steve Jobs and Bill Gates.

So what is to be said of the somewhat anomalous case of North America, where the social capital embedded in voluntary social group organization seems to have declined sharply over three decades? If this decline is problematic, it could be because we will have fewer such organizations to use for political and other ends, or because such organizations will produce less of the human capital that might be needed in the polity and economy. These effects may not both be important. Indeed, one of the plausible explanations for the decline of voluntary groups is that dual-career marriages reduce the time available for participation in such groups. But dual careers might at the same time give both partners many opportunities to learn how to manage people, even how to organize them for action. Hence, the decline in opportunities for developing such human capital through participation in voluntary social groups might be offset—or surpassed—by opportunities to learn these skills in professional life. If so, then the main loss attributable to declining organizational capital is the loss of available social organizations that can be used for wider purposes, whether political or otherwise.[5]

In sum, we want to know two quite different things about the apparent decline in organizational capital in North America. Does it disable us politically by reducing access to voluntary and social organizations that are useful for furthering our political goals? And are we individually disabled by our declining participation in such organizations? For the first question, there are two quite different issues at stake in the two quite different kinds of organizations in which participation is apparently declining. Voluntary *political* organizations, such as neighborhood action groups, would seem to be much more useful in helping us achieve political goals than are *social* organizations such as choral groups and bowling leagues. Yet the data on declines in these two broad classes of groups are quite similar (Putnam 1995a). Their decline evidently has much less to do with their purposes than with the characteristics of participation in them, as is suggested by many of the explanations proposed for their decline. We are not dropping out of specifically political organizations, but out of voluntary organizations in general.

DEMOCRATIC THEORY

Communitarians assert that people have become more skeptical of government because the social organization of our lives has changed (Etzioni and Diprete 1979). There may be an element of truth in this claim (but see Newton and Norris, this volume). Other observers contend that politicians' styles have changed, as in the shift from traditional campaigning to the marketing of candidates, especially via television. As noted earlier, I wish to concentrate on a different causal nexus to argue that *the underlying political issues have changed* in ways that reduce confidence in government.

There have been two mutually exacerbating changes. The first is a big system shock: the essential end, at least for the near term, of the focus on economic distribution and of the management of the economy for pro-

[5] The supposition that the production of relevant forms of human capital—forms that might be especially important in our political lives—is increasingly handled through our professional experiences in organizations may be false. Perhaps we *are* increasingly in deficit, relative to earlier generations, in developing such politically relevant human capital. It will not be easy to resolve this question empirically.

duction and distribution. The second is the slow and steady rise during the postwar era of often complex issues that are unrelated to one another. Together these two changes now preclude the organization of politics along a single left-right economic dimension. Those citizens coming of political age over the past generation in the Trilateral democracies might not recognize the political organization that prevailed for generations—and even centuries—in many of these countries. Their concerns are a hotchpotch of unrelated issues that are not the obvious domain of any traditional political party. The era of a simple, widely acknowledged, main political issue has passed.

Perhaps the fundamental problem we face is therefore an ongoing re-definition of democratic politics and participation. When democracy shifted from small to larger societies and therefore had to become representative, when it shifted from the selection of representatives by lot, as in Venice, to selection procedures that turned politicians into a professional class, and when it shifted from more or less free-for-all elections to party-dominated contests, there were reasons to rue the changes as somehow bad or tending toward less democracy. But at some level it would be hard to say any of these moves was a mistake because they were virtually necessitated by social circumstances.

We may have entered another transitional era, with democracy shifting from coherent, party-dominated contests to free-for-all elections of a new kind in which citizens' competence to judge candidates and issues may be in decline (even, perhaps, in their own view) because the complexity and diversity of issues makes them extremely difficult to understand and package. Citizens' reduced confidence might not be worrisome, however. To some extent, *we are losing confidence in government precisely because we no longer think we need it in the important realm of the economy.* We evidently had more confidence in government when it was trying to manage the economy, but arguably without much success.

The Focus of Politics

For virtually the entire history of modern democracy, politics has been organized around economic issues. Indeed, the central worry of many of the authors of the U.S. Constitution, the first system of broad democracy, was the threat that genuine democracy posed to property and its privileges. Previously, the economic conflict took a fairly specific substantive form in support for particular interests against others, such as landed estates or plantations versus manufacturing and urban interests. It eventually became a more abstract conflict between the state and the market (especially in Europe) or between business in general and other groups (especially in the United States). Postwar Japan has been an anomaly with its near consensus on mercantilist management of the economy for the benefit of industry and agriculture and its lack of an anti-statist party. Its peculiarly deep and lasting economic difficulties in the 1990s may derive primarily from its past mercantilist policies and the incapacity of its virtually hegemonic statist party to jettison those policies and reduce the role of the state in the economy.

The economic conflict had both a domestic and an international form: greater equality versus untrammeled liberty, communism versus the free market. The institutional form of the domestic issue was central planning versus laissez faire. The issue was never quite that simple, of course. The typical corporation wanted regulatory, subsidy, and tariff policies that would specifically benefit it against a fully free-wheeling market; industrial workers wanted job and wage protection; professional groups wanted restrictive licensing and regulation; farmers wanted subventions, some variant of price supports, and protection against imports of food; and all of these groups wanted more competition among the other groups. Extant corporations may now have to endure more laissez faire than they ever wanted because upstart corporations often thrive in competition with older ones. The general movement toward laissez faire has not been equally quick in all of the Trilateral nations, but, in part because of the globalization of corporations and the loosening of trade restrictions, the trend is similar everywhere except perhaps Japan.

Now, however, we seem to be in an era in which the economic division is no longer crucial because we have reached near-consensus on how to handle the main economic problems: we generally handle them by letting them handle themselves. With the passing of the division over economics, there is no similarly cogent, simple dimension on which to organize political contests. We may have to deal with economic crises in the future, and we may disagree over how to do that, but we seem to have accepted (to a greater or lesser extent, depending on the country) a basic reliance on the market and have increasingly given up on central planning to organize our economies.

The former left-right antagonism has been reduced to a very short spread from those who prefer more generous welfare programs to those who prefer somewhat less generous programs, and the difference between the two positions represents a very small fraction of national income. Radical reorganization of the economy to achieve some degree of equality or fairness is now virtually off the agenda. Perhaps because the causal relations are not well understood, the split over welfare policy often seems to be as much a matter of tone as of content. For many people it is a difference that is easily outweighed by formerly minor concerns such as items on the social agenda and regional preferences. The odd result is that politics may be noisier and seemingly more intense and even bitter, but it is less important. The rise in volume may be a temporary, transitional phenomenon. We will not know for sure until we have lived with the politics of marginal issues for a longer period of time. Just possibly, people now have the social capital as well as the leisure time to organize intensively over marginal issues.

The European story is more sharply drawn than the North American because it hangs very much on the fact that socialist and even communist parties enjoyed wide support in Europe. These parties were somewhat tarnished by the economic failure of communism in the East. That failure was itself a consequence of government incapacity to plan and run an increasingly complex high-tech economy, in which entrepreneurial creativity seems to be crucially important. That part of an economy evidently cannot be run from the top down—how can one command young people to go out and create a new industry the way Steve Jobs, Bill Gates, and others did?—but must be allowed to run on its own if it is to prosper. With their former central agendas essentially dead, European parties of the left may follow the lead of the American Democratic and Republican Parties to become politically vague and opportunistic. Such leaders as Tony Blair and Gerhard Schröder may follow Clinton's path of unsystematic policy despite rankling older socialists.

Citizens

Citizens may be justified in lacking confidence in government's ability to handle many of today's important issues. Yet citizens who supposed that they could do better than their governors have voted in U.S. referenda to adopt policies with unexpected, grim consequences. In many cases of policy-making by referendum, citizens are arguably misled—or they mislead themselves—to believe the issues are far simpler than they are, and they vote simplistically. Consider two examples, one very briefly because it is funny and another at greater length because it is depressingly grotesque. The two examples are peculiarly American; indeed, they fit the view of many people in other nations that American politics is uniquely bizarre.

California's Proposition 3 in 1998 was intended to correct a blunder that would prevent the state's delegates from being seated at national party conventions. An earlier law had opened the state's primaries, but the national parties sensibly do not permit delegates chosen in open (that is, nonparty) primaries to vote in their conventions. Unfortunately, the proposition to correct this blunder was too intricate for voters, who killed it, although it seems implausible that a majority of voters meant to deprive themselves of a voice in the national conventions that select presidential candidates. State officials now hope to thwart the supposedly popular will by distorting the process in ways that will let California delegates be seated in the conventions of the year 2000 (*New York Times*, November 15, 1998). At some level, this was not even a difficult choice, but it was complicated by a blunder in the writing of the proposition.

Let us now turn to a deplorable and very important example. According to Susan Estrich (1998), the California referendum that introduced the clumsy and destructive "three strikes and you're out" policy for dealing with repeat felons was grossly misconceived, yet it was enormously popular. That law requires mandatory longer prison sentences for felons with at least one prior conviction for a serious or violent felony. "The result of mandatory laws and punishment by slogan," Estrich observes, "is that we spend more and more money locking up less and less violent people." In an early case to which the new law was applied, a pizza thief was sentenced to a term of 25 years to life for his petty theft, with no possibility of parole before serving at least 20 years (*New York Times*, March 5, 1995).

The California law was a response to the kidnapping and murder of a young girl, Polly Klaas, by Richard Alan Davis, a recently released kidnapper. The public outcry over that murder led to a referendum requiring longer sentences for felons with at least one prior conviction for a serious or violent felony. Although Polly's father initially pushed that referendum, the text of the law that was put to voters was so stupid that Klaas withdrew his support. In particular, the law does not require that the new crime be violent, and it bars judges from assessing the dangerousness of the person committing the crime. The law lumps minor felons and kidnap-murderers together as people who should live out much of their lives in jail in order to protect society.

Ironically, Davis was originally serving a mandatory, maximum 16-year sentence for a prior kidnapping. He was released after only eight years under a California law that halved the sentences of all those convicts already in jail in order to make more room for newly convicted offenders, the largest number of whom were probably petty drug offenders. The law did not distinguish among convicts on the basis of the violence of their crimes (Massing 1998). Of course, the three-strikes law that was adopted by referendum increased the problem of prison overcrowding that prompted the release of Davis, which led to Polly's murder.

Governor George Pataki of New York has dealt with similar problems by sensibly releasing minor drug offenders to make more room for violent offenders. He has done this quietly, perhaps because punishment by slogan would trump him if he were too assertive about the policy. For a lover of democracy, it is distressing to defend actions on the part of a public official that counter the popular will. But the nature of the popular will on such complex issues is also distressing, as it would likely be even to an individual voter who had the opportunity to discuss the issues quietly rather than through sloganeering groups.

Although these two referendum issues were relatively simple, they were too complicated for voters to grasp. This is not surprising if we suppose, as rational choice theorists since Anthony Downs (1957) have done, that voters have little incentive to vote and therefore even less incentive to figure out how to vote their interests (Hardin forthcoming). As policies become more complex and the electorate grows, these considerations weigh more heavily, and they militate against citizens' voting intelligently. Moreover, as issues become more diverse, there is little hope of parties' aligning as coherently as in the formerly neat division between economically conservative and economically liberal, and the accountability of elected officials becomes increasingly murky. Governmental failures—as in many Great Society programs or the Vietnam War in the United States, elaborate welfare programs in Europe, and complicated supports for farmers almost everywhere—however, are relatively clear even to ill-informed voters. Hence, even if voters may not know enough to vote well, they may often have compelling reasons to think that government is incompetent.

If an individual behaved as incoherently as the electorate and legislature of California in the three-strikes example, we would probably deride that individual as hopelessly irrational. Here is a brutally brief summary: because a kidnapper was released after only eight years under one cavalierly ill-conceived law, a pizza thief was incarcerated for at least 20 years under an even more cavalierly ill-conceived law.

The problems of cyclic preferences analyzed by Kenneth Arrow (1963) and C. L. Dodgson may become increasingly common in an era when political issues are as diverse as they seem to be now. Such issues as the environment, safety, and the social agenda of the religious right do not fit easily into the agendas of traditional political parties. The association of environmental policy with the left, at least in the United States, happened for the accidental reason that the initial targets of environmental regulation were such corporations as electric utilities and steelmakers. But environmental protection is not inherently contrary to the interests of individuals at any point on the economic spectrum, and it is therefore natural that it should be championed by a separate party under Germany's system of proportional representation rather than by the traditional parties of the left or right.

A similar story can be told of automotive safety equipment. While American auto makers long opposed the introduction of airbags, other, especially German and Swedish, manufacturers have made the same systems part of their sales appeal. It is very hard to see safety as a left-right issue. If anything, one might suppose that the less affluent, who are traditionally associated with the left, might be less inclined to favor such innovations than the more affluent. Indeed, as is also true of the less developed nations, the poor typically view environmental and safety regulations that raise costs to be less in their interests than do the well-off (Hardin 1999d).

Finally, the Republican Party's embrace of the social agenda of the religious right in the United States might seem natural today, but it would have seemed unlikely to an earlier generation who regarded the Democratic Party as populist and the Republican Party as more libertarian. William Jennings Bryan, one of the most grotesque of the populist backers of an early part of the social agenda, was a Democrat who, admittedly, had long since outlived his intelligence when he argued the case against teaching evolution in Tennessee schools in the notorious Scopes Trial. Teddy Roosevelt, who was not quite a free-thinker and maybe not sophisticated enough to know whether he was a libertarian but who was still an individualist, was a Republican. The Republican Party may have mortgaged its soul to the religious right in order to win votes in the South after Lyndon Johnson, a southern Democrat, fought for civil rights.

In the face of such issues we will not be able to hold public officials accountable except for oddly assembled packages of positions on seemingly unrelated issues. As a result we may conclude that our officials are incompetent and therefore untrustworthy because they cannot handle such complexity. Admittedly, the politics of issue X are more perverse in the United States than in most nations, but the current agendas of all the Trilateral democracies are messy and no longer fit the left-right economic dimension of the past.

The success of today's economic policy, if it holds, may mean that citizens have less reason to believe that parties capture their interests in a summary way. Hence, they have one less clue for deciding how to vote intelligently. It would be a saving grace if government policy mattered less now. If the economy can perform well without government tinkering, and if we do not face other major crises, perhaps government will seem less important than it once did. But even then its tasks may be so diverse and complex that it must often fail in dealing with them, so that citizens will continue to find it incompetent and will lack confidence in it. In the most sanguine scenario, the government of the next decade or so might enjoy the credit, falsely, for economic performance for which it has little responsibility. Once the reasons for economic prosperity are more fully understood, however, national leaders may no longer be able to win credit for that prosperity, as Bill Clinton and some leaders of Japan's Liberal Democratic Party in the 1980s have done. Leaders will then be judged by their supposed successes or failings on other issues.

What we face now is a transition to a way of aggregating the ill-articulated preferences of citizens who cannot take the time to understand the issues being decided in their names well enough even to know their own preferences. We want representatives to represent us in the sense of serving our interests (Hardin forthcoming), but we want them to do that for us even in the face of the sad fact that we ourselves do not know what would serve our interests, and we might judge them harshly even for happening to serve us well merely because we do not realize that they are doing so.

Politicians

The two most popularly successful politicians of our time have been Helmut Kohl and Ronald Reagan. Reagan escaped much of the burden of complexity because he predated the events of 1989 and took partial credit for them. In keeping with traditional political divisions, Reagan stood with Margaret Thatcher for a smaller government role in the economy. In dealing with the more complex issues of his time, he was the Great Simplifier. If we could get rid of some of those polluting trees, we could reduce smog in Los Angeles; if we could get the welfare queens with their Cadillacs off the welfare rolls, we could balance the budget; and if we could end the threat of nuclear devastation with Star Wars, life would be lovely. Such ideas ranged from the silly to the fatuous, but they were wonderfully simple, and they helped give Ronald Reagan a virtually free ride as president.

Kohl was the one major leader who handled the events of 1989 well enough even to profit from them, while the response of George Bush, for example, bordered on stolid stupidity. Kohl's ideas were as simple as Reagan's, but they happened to be politically important and even profound rather than silly. They were to unify Germany and to unify Europe, two of the most constructive international political moves of the second half of the twentieth century and rivaled only by Mikhail Gorbachev's ending of the Cold War and demolition of the Soviet empire. The details involved in carrying out Kohl's ideas may be complicated and difficult, but what George Bush in his dreadful abuse of English called "the vision thing" was clear and simple in each of these ideas. The striking thing about Kohl's success, which must be envied by leaders in other democratic nations, is that it was grounded in genuinely simple, focused ideas that deeply mattered. In this respect he was historically lucky. Few leaders face such simplicity and clarity of purpose. Those few have mostly been in times of war and massive economic failure. Kohl had the extraordinary luck to face two creative and positive goals, and he had the political sense to grasp them.

Barring such luck, politicians can no longer focus their campaigns on issues as simple as the economic division that served through the time of Reagan and Thatcher. Declining confidence in the capacity of elected officials to handle policies on diverse, complex issues coupled with the fact that these issues cannot be defined systematically as party issues, pro or con, may push candidates for public office in opposite directions.

Many political aspirants may attempt to enhance their appeal by adhering more rigidly to policy commitments on well-defined issues, such as environmental protection or, in the United States, the social agenda of religious values. Other candidates may follow the lead of Bill Clinton, Tony Blair, and Gerhard Schröder and avoid association with very much at all. They can rise not merely above party; they can rise above issues. They can campaign on almost nothing beyond personal appeal and the promise that they will serve us well no matter what issues may arise.

In the United States Bill Clinton would have been the next most successful politician after Reagan if he had been able to control his adolescent libido. His brilliant political move was to relegate party definitions of positions to the past, blurring the old distinctions. Or maybe it was not a brilliant move, but the product of his character. Even here Reagan had led the way by running the largest peacetime deficits in American history, contrary to his supposedly deeply held Republican convictions. If it had not been for the related rise of the social agenda and its happenstance attachment to the Republican Party, Clinton might have sailed through his presidency with the ease displayed by Reagan. Despite his partial disgrace, however, the seemingly deliberate lack of much systematic content in his views may still provide the model for future politicians.

Candidates will not necessarily choose one of these strategies—a single-issue focus or generalized vagueness—but those who do are likely to enjoy greater success. It is clearly easier to get elected with a single-issue focus in the amorphous, decentralized U.S. system than in political systems in which national parties have more control over the agenda and candidates. Outside the United States, then, generalized vagueness may be the choice of national parties and successful candidates.

CONCLUDING REMARKS

Much of the apparent decline in confidence in government may simply express intolerance of ambiguity. The clarities of an earlier era are gone. People who do not like ambiguity may think they see politics clearly by focusing on a single, unambiguous issue and neglecting all the rest. Forget the impossible ghetto or immigrant community—save the whales or stop abortions. These citizens might still lose confidence in government if they believe that it does not share their justifiable concern with issue X. People who can handle ambiguity might be more comfortable with ill-defined candidates and parties that may do little more than look good.

Although the significance of current domestic issues in the Trilateral nations may be less than it once was, conflict over these issues may be more fractious—not necessarily more heated or deeper, but merely more fractious. Earlier problems may have been fundamentally more difficult, but at least it was relatively clear what the issues were.

In 1840 John Stuart Mill (1977, 175) wrote that America had few outstanding public leaders for the enviable reason that "America needs very little government." He wrote before the Civil War, two world wars, the Great Depression, and the Cold War, when a bit of government might have been useful. Now, though, a century and a half later, his quip may begin to apply not only to America, but also to other advanced industrial democracies. We may begin to think of memorable public leaders as people who could maintain themselves in office with great success rather than as people who accomplished anything for us. And we may praise them, as Clinton is praised today, not for their policy accomplishments, but for their talent in mastering their roles. We will lack confidence in government, but if we are lucky, it will not matter that government is incompetent to handle our marginal issues very well.

The U.S. Constitution, as designed principally by James Madison, was intended to obstruct government, not to enable it. The government it was especially designed to block was state government, because the often petty state governments frequently stood in the way of economic life and development at the end of the eighteenth century (see Hardin 1999c, especially ch. 3). What Madison ideally wanted, however, has in some respects come to pass only recently with the slow scaling back of the statist regime that was put in place in the 1930s, largely to deal with the overreaching power of business. If the social agenda crowd, the mercantilist-statist right, or the socialist-statist left were to control government, a Madisonian would consider it a disaster. In Madison's view people need government to maintain order, but they do not need it to run their lives, as any of these groups would want it to do.

We may finally have entered an era when government can be incompetent to manage many of its problems, and *it does not matter* very much. It will not matter as long as there are no massive crises to manage and the government does not revive Hamiltonian desires for mercantilist management of industry or socialist desires for central planning. What we have done to a large extent is back down from 1930s statism in the United States, Bismarckian and socialist statism in Europe, and mercantilist statism in Japan.[6] The shift may be slower outside the United States, and, indeed, Japan continues to be remarkably mercantilist despite the fact

[6] Outside the Trilateral democracies, many other nations have also backed away from socialist statism, both in the former communist bloc and in the Third World (except for the Islamic world, which almost everywhere remains mired in statist control of economic and social policy, typically at the hands of men utterly ignorant of any social or economic theory, or even devoid of ideas entirely). The development of the Third World now appears, retrospectively, to have been massively hampered by its rough adherence to socialist statism, which must rank among the great historical disasters for the harms it has brought. For example, Nehru's autarkic statism doomed two generations of Indians to at best halting progress in overcoming massive poverty and illiteracy.

that Japanese firms have been extraordinarily successful in world competition and probably do not need the protections their state still provides.

The remarkable intellectual feature of all of this is that the statist vision that once seemed to be good and even necessary now seems wrongheaded. Maybe we were not wrong before, but the preconditions of our earlier view no longer apply. The economy is finally close to free-standing. Although pockets of it always have been, these pockets were usually in minor industries, local areas, or innovative sectors. Now the economy is free-standing even in standard core activities. Perhaps even more important, business no longer seems to want to control government, which, in many nations, it has learned it does not need for its own management. Hence, the weakening of government does not matter as much as it once would have because we do not need strong government to resist the tendency of business to push for mercantilist advantage. The rise of statism was in part an antidote to politically ruthless business, but we may no longer need it. The dread of corporate power that was once commonplace (Dewey 1935) is virtually gone in the advanced economies.

The nearest equivalent to Madisonian theory in the twentieth century has been Austrian economics as represented by F. A. Hayek among others. Although theirs is ostensibly an economic theory, its most cogent insights are of broad social theory. An especially odd aspect of the current hegemony of Austrian and Madisonian views—even without those labels attached—is that they were almost purely theoretical: in the past there was no way to test them on the ground. But now they have been and are being tested, and they seem to be acquitting themselves very well. Madison himself was not willing to practice his theory once he was in office, and perhaps Hayek et al. would not have been either. But the monitory example of the Soviet world, admittedly a bad version of socialist statism, and the severely trammeled markets of the more prosperous West gave us a chance to see a crude, perhaps second-best test of the Austrian-Madisonian views.

This assessment, made in medias res, might turn out to be grossly optimistic, a mere extrapolation from the most positive aspects of current changes. But for the moment the Austrian and Madisonian schools seem to have the right vision. That is a stunning turn, perhaps even more stunning to those on the traditional left than to Millian libertarians. Its most impressive consequence is the reversal of the long historical trend toward increasing state hegemony over the economy and, potentially, all else when the state fell into bad hands, such as Stalin's or Hitler's. But for that very reason contemporary worries about declining state capacity may be grounded in understandings of the past that are irrelevant to the present and near future.

THREE

Confidence in Public Institutions:
Faith, Culture, or Performance?

Kenneth Newton and Pippa Norris

SOME 25 YEARS AGO a report of the Trilateral Commission on *The Crisis of Democracy* (Crozier, Huntington, and Watanuki 1975, 158–59) concluded that "Dissatisfaction with, and lack of confidence in, the functioning of the institutions of democratic government have thus now become widespread in Trilateral countries." Since then there have been periodic expressions of concern when other commentators have echoed this theme, using survey data to show that citizens are dissatisfied and disillusioned with the central institutions of representative democracy in the advanced industrial democracies (e.g., Miller 1974; Niemi, Mueller, and Smith 1989; Dogan 1994; Dalton 1996, 268–69, Dalton 1999; Nye 1997a, 1; Nye and Zelikow 1997; Norris 1999). A recent study of the United States presents extensive evidence drawn from different surveys showing that confidence in Congress, the federal government, the executive, and the presidency have all fallen since the 1960s and 1970s. In terms of public confidence, Congress, the White House, and the executive branch now rank very low on lists of 14 or more public and private institutions (Ladd and Bowman 1998, 120–21, 142–45).

Like the authors of the Trilateral report before them, some analysts are most concerned about loss of confidence in the main institutions of democratic government: parliament, the executive branch, parties, the courts, police, the civil service, and the military (e.g., Orren 1997; Dalton 1999). Others are also worried about the erosion of public esteem for various private institutions, including major companies, the mass media, trade unions, and the church (Lipset and Schneider 1983), and suggest that the decline of public confidence in a wide range of central institutions indicates a problem extending beyond political life (Dogan 1994; Dalton 1996; see, however, Listhaug 1995). Another group of analysts focus on a loss of social trust among citizens as a significant indicator of social and political malaise (Putnam 1995a, 1995b; Dalton 1996).

An erosion of confidence in the major institutions of society, especially those of representative democracy, is a far more serious threat to democracy than a loss of trust in other citizens or politicians. Political leaders come and go with swings of the electoral pendulum, and trust in them may rise and fall with citizens' evaluation of their performance in office. A wealth of evidence suggests that trust in leaders or particular administrations is subject to greater short-term fluctuation than confidence in institutions. However, institutions are large, impersonal, and broadly based, and the public's estimation of them is less immediately affected by particular news items or specific events. Thus, loss of confidence in institutions may well be a better indicator of public disaffection with the modern world because they are the basic pillars of society. If they begin to crumble, then there is, indeed, cause for concern. Furthermore, many observers argue that in our large-scale and impersonal modern world, social and political stability and integration increasingly depend on confidence in institutions rather than trust in individuals, so vibrant institutions matter more to contemporary democracies than does the quality of interpersonal relations among citizens (Luhmann 1988; Dunn 1984; Giddens 1990; Seligman 1997). For all these reasons, this chapter regards confidence in institutions as the central indicator of the underlying feeling of the general public about its polity.

Previous studies have debated whether or not there has been a significant or long-term erosion of public confidence in modern institutions across different societies (see Listhaug and Wiberg 1995, 298–322; Nye and Zelikow 1997, 263–64; Dalton 1999; Newton 1999). Some assert that the figures show a mixed pattern, with no clear trends for any given set of institutions, nations, or periods of time. In some instances the confidence figures fall, but in others they rise, and in others still they are more or less constant. After examining public confidence in ten sets of public and private institutions in 14 Western European nations between 1981 and 1990, Listhaug and Wiberg (1995, 320) concluded: "The data from the two European Values Surveys do not demonstrate that there has been a widespread decline in the public's confidence in institutions during the 1980s." Although they observed a decline of confidence in "order" institutions, they noted that "confidence in other political institutions is either stable, as in the case of the civil service and parliament, or, as with the education system, has become stronger."

Listhaug and Wiberg based their conclusions on data up to 1990. Newer evidence from a wider range of nations suggests that the world may have changed since then (Norris 1999). Klingemann (1999) demonstrates how support for parliaments suffered a marked erosion during the 1990s, while Inglehart (1999) has documented a decline in confidence in hierarchical and traditional institutions like the military and the church. Shifts of this type in public attitudes in the Western world since 1990 may have resulted from the collapse of the Soviet Union, which made it easier for established democracies to be openly critical of themselves in-

stead of closing ranks in self-defense, as they did during the chilly decades of the Cold War. The world also became more complex in the late
1980s and 1990s, not least for Trilateral democracies, which faced increasing difficulties due to international competition and the pressures of
globalization. Perhaps things have changed enough since the long boom
of the 1960s and 1970s and the end of the sharp division between East
and West to make 1990 or thereabouts the start of a new political era.

The first task of this chapter is to use the most complete comparative
data currently available to establish long-term trends of confidence in
institutions in the Trilateral democracies. On the basis of that data we
then investigate the underlying causes of the patterns revealed and develop an explanation for them.

CONFIDENCE IN INSTITUTIONS DURING THE 1980s

Most studies of confidence in institutions have been confined to Western
Europe or North America, but we can compare public opinion in a wider
range of advanced industrialized democracies included in both waves of
the World Values Survey (WVS) conducted in the early 1980s (1981–84)
and the early 1990s (1990–93).[1] These include almost 47,000 respondents in 17 Trilateral democracies (listed in Table 3.2). This group of
nations comprises most of the established democracies in the world, and
it is broadly representative because it includes both major economic
powers like the United States, West Germany, and Japan and smaller
social-democratic states like Belgium and Norway. These nations also
possess a wide array of political systems and institutional structures, such
as presidential versus parliamentary executives, federal versus unitary
states, and consensual versus majoritarian systems, which is important if
we are to be able to generalize about systematic variations in support.

Institutional confidence was measured in the World Values Survey with
a four-point scale using the following question: "Please look at this card
and tell me, for each item, how much confidence you have in them. Is it
a great deal (4), quite a lot (3), not very much (2) or none at all (1)?"
The survey compared public support for ten institutions, which can be
divided into public-sector institutions, understood as those most closely
associated with the core functions of the state (including parliament, the
civil service, the legal system, the police, and the army), and other institu-

---

[1] To produce a consistent universe for comparison over time, we dropped countries like
Australia and Switzerland that were included in only the first or second wave. For consis-
tency we also excluded East Germany from the comparison and dropped all countries in the
World Values Survey outside the Trilateral region.

TABLE 3.1

Confidence in Public and Nonprofit/Private Institutions in the Trilateral Democracies

	Early 1980s	Early 1990s	Change	Coefficient of Association (sig.)
Public Institutions				
Police	74%	70%	−4%	.10**
Legal system	61	55	−6	.13**
Armed forces	61	46	−15	.28**
Parliament	48	43	−5	.10**
Civil service	46	43	−3	.06**
Nonprofit/Private Institutions				
Education system	63	64	+1	N/s
The church	54	50	−4	.09**
Major companies	44	48	+4	.08**
The press	38	40	+2	.04**
Trade unions	39	38	−1	.03**

Note: The proportion of respondents in 17 advanced industrial democracies who replied that they had "a great deal" or "quite a lot" of confidence in these institutions. The coefficient of association and significance is measured by gamma. *p < .05 **p < .01 N/s = Not significant.

Sources: World Values Survey 1980–84, 1990–93.

tions in the private and nonprofit sectors (the education system, the church, major companies, trade unions, and the press).[2]

Table 3.1 shows the pattern of public trust when the data are pooled across all 17 nations under comparison. The most important finding is that during this decade, *all the public institutions examined suffered a significant (if varying) decline in confidence.* The sharpest fall (−15) points) occurs in confidence in the armed forces, which may reflect the military's reduced standing in the post-Cold War era or cultural shifts undermining support for hierarchical and authoritarian institutions (Inglehart 1999). During the 1980s there was also a modest but significant erosion of confidence in the legal system and police as well as in the civil service and parliament. It is striking that confidence in legislatures, the

[2] As previous studies have suggested (Lipset and Schneider 1988), it should be noted that the precise dividing line between state and nonstate institutions is not clear-cut. The education system is often largely but not exclusively within the public sector, for example. In the same way, established churches can be seen as part of the state. This study nevertheless distinguishes between those institutions that can be regarded as most closely associated with the functions of the state and those in the nonprofit and public sectors.

Table 3.2
Confidence in Parliament in the Trilateral Democracies

Nation	Early 1980s	Early 1990s	Mid-1990s	Change: Early 1980s to Early 1990s
Finland	65%	34%	33%	−31%
Norway	77	59	69	−18
Spain	48	38	37	−10
France	55	48		−7
United States	52	45	30	−7
Canada	43	37		−6
Ireland	52	50		−2
W. Germany	51	50	29	−1
Italy	30	30		0
Sweden	47	47	45	0
N. Ireland	45	46		+1
Japan	28	29	27	+1
Britain	40	44		+4
Belgium	38	42		+4
Denmark	36	42		+6
Iceland	48	54		+6
Netherlands	45	53		+8

Note: The percentage of respondents in 17 advanced industrial democracies who replied that they had "a great deal" or "quite a lot" of confidence in parliament. The coefficient of association and significance is measured by gamma.

Sources: World Values Survey 1980–84, 1990–93, 1995–97. Data for the mid-1990s are drawn from Klingemann (1999).

main representative institution linking citizens and the state, is consistently ranked almost 30 points lower than confidence in the police.

The trends across institutions in the nonprofit and private sectors are mixed and inconsistent: While confidence in the church declined, for example, trust in the education system remained stable, and public support actually increased slightly for major companies and the press. Thus, problems of confidence have been more pervasive in the public than in the private sector.

Given their importance as the key institution of representative democracy, concern has focused on low support for legislatures. We can examine how confidence in parliament changed from the early 1980s to the early 1990s, with trends in some countries updated to the mid-1990s on the basis of Klingemann's data (1999). Table 3.2 displays an even more mixed pattern than we have observed so far, with a far steeper fall of confidence in parliament in countries like Finland (−31 points) and Spain (−10 points) than in others like the United States and Canada. More important, there are significant cross-national variations during the

TABLE 3.3
Confidence in Public and Private Institutions in the Trilateral Democracies

Nation	Public Institutions Confidence Scale			Private Institutions Confidence Scale		
	Early 1990s	Change 1981–90	Significance	Early 1990s	Change 1981–90	Significance
Finland	12.69	−1.61	**	11.96	−0.74	**
Norway	13.69	−0.90	**	12.91	+0.03	
Spain	11.80	−0.90	**	12.35	+0.40	**
United States	13.36	−0.69	**	13.16	−0.38	**
Ireland	13.58	−0.50	**	13.23	−0.12	
Sweden	12.78	−0.50	**	12.07	+0.14	
Belgium	11.67	−0.42	**	12.36	+0.06	
Canada	13.03	−0.41	**	12.85	−0.09	
Britain	13.57	−0.41	**	11.55	−0.43	**
Italy	11.33	−0.40	**	12.24	+0.82	**
Denmark	13.54	−0.36	**	12.34	+0.20	*
Japan	11.96	−0.34	**	11.16	−0.16	
W. Germany	12.61	−0.25	**	11.66	+0.15	*
Netherlands	12.49	−0.23	*	11.92	+0.10	
N. Ireland	14.01	−0.20		12.59	−0.36	
France	12.41	−0.07		11.99	+0.27	*
Iceland	12.69	+0.73	**	12.62	N/a	
All of the Above	12.57	−0.62	**	12.31	−0.01	

Note: Mean confidence in five public and five private institutions in 17 advanced industrial democracies. The significance of the difference in group means is measured by Anova. *p < .05. **p < .01. N/s = Not significant.
Sources: World Values Survey 1980–84, 1990–93.

1980s: support for parliament actually *rose* in seven of the 17 nations under comparison, most notably Denmark, Iceland, and the Netherlands. The overall erosion of support for public institutions across the Trilateral region that we have observed therefore disguises some important differences among nations.

To explore the pattern further, we created two confidence scales, one for public and one for private institutions.[3] Cross-national comparison on the basis of these scales (see Table 3.3) confirms a striking and important

---

[3] The measures of confidence in the ten institutions were summed to form two consistent 20-point scales measuring confidence in public institutions and confidence in private institutions. These scales proved suitable for analysis because the separate items were highly intercorrelated, producing scales with a normal and nonskewed distribution with high reliability (Cronbach's Alpha = .77 for the confidence in public institutions scale and .66 for the confidence in private institutions scale).

pattern: during the 1980s *confidence in public institutions declined consistently, if in varying degrees, in all but one society* (Iceland). In contrast, the pattern of confidence in private institutions proved more mixed: it fell significantly in Finland, the United States, and Britain, but increased significantly in Spain, Italy, Denmark, West Germany, and France. Based on this evidence, we conclude that there are important cross-national variations in confidence in particular public and private institutions, as we would expect, in terms of both the level of confidence and the direction of trends over time. Although this shows clearly that there is no general loss of support for all social institutions in the Trilateral region, the evidence does indicate declining confidence in *public* institutions in virtually all the Trilateral nations during the 1980s. The political and governmental problems that have been so widely discussed in the United States are not sui generis, but are evident to a greater or lesser extent elsewhere.

THEORIES OF TRUST AND CONFIDENCE

What can explain this loss of public confidence in the central institutions of representative democracy? It is important that there has been a consistent loss of confidence in public institutions but not all private institutions. So too is the fact that the problem does not seem to spill over more generally into distrust of other citizens (Newton 1999). This makes the search for causes both easier and more difficult. It suggests that the problem is not a general malaise affecting all, or even many, aspects of modern life, but a specifically political and governmental one. Blame cannot easily be laid at the door of intensified global economic competition or the unemployment and slow economic growth these have produced in the Trilateral democracies. If economic hardship were the cause, then one might expect confidence in major companies to tumble, but it has not. On the contrary, the collapse of communism seems to have heightened faith in capitalism and business corporations. The limitation of the problem to specifically political and governmental institutions suggests that broad and general theories of social and economic crisis are inappropriate.

Nor does the much discussed tendency of the contemporary mass media to report scandal, corruption, and disaster provide an adequate explanation. Although the amount of time people spend watching television is associated with some indicators of political apathy and disaffection, viewing television news and reading newspapers is associated with civic mobilization and support for the political system (see Norris, this volume). Indeed, general theories suggesting that contemporary society has become increasingly individualist, competitive, materialistic, fragmented, globalized, or impersonal do not get us very far because they should apply equally to social trust and to confidence in a wide range of private institutions, but they do not. Thus, we have to look elsewhere for plausible explanations. There are at least three schools of thought on how to explain the erosion of citizen confidence in public institutions: those that focus on the social-psychological features of individuals; those that look to the cultural environment of individuals, groups, and communities; and those that concentrate on governmental performance.

Social-Psychological Explanations

One school treats trust and institutional confidence (or distrust and lack of confidence) as basic aspects of personality types. According to Erikson (1950), feelings of inner goodness, trust in others and oneself, and optimism form a "basic trust" personality trait that is formed in the first stages of psychological development as a result of the mother-baby feeding experience. Basic personality traits, it is argued, are enduring and general, influencing many aspects of behavior (see Allport 1961; Cattell 1965). Early and seminal work of the social psychologist Morris Rosenberg (1956, 1957) also argues that alienation, trust in people, and beliefs that people are fundamentally cooperative and inclined to help others combine to form a single "trust in people" scale. Because of their psychological history and makeup, some individuals have an optimistic view of life and are willing to help others, cooperate, and trust. Because of their own early life experiences, others are more pessimistic and misanthropic. They are thus inclined to be guarded or alienated, more distrustful and cautious of others, and pessimistic about social and political affairs and about people and politicians in general. In this regard trust is an affective orientation that forms part of our basic personality and is largely independent of our experience of the external political world.

In a discussion of political trust, Gabriel (1995) highlights the assumptions of the social-psychology approach (without subscribing to them himself) when he observes that it contrasts "trusting people" and "cynics." According to Easton (1965, 447), "the presence of trust would mean that members would feel that their own interests would be attended to even if the authorities were exposed to little supervision or scrutiny." Similarly, Gamson (1968, 54) suggests that trusting people expect the political system to work as they wish "even if left untended." In other words, there are trusters and there are cynics who carry their political perceptions around with them without much reference to the performance of the political system or its leaders.

The social-psychological approach has the obvious limitation that it is hard-pressed to explain changes in trust among large segments of a country's population, but it must be taken seriously because of its importance in shaping the literature on trust. The current approach to trust and confidence is based less on the specific tenets of the social-psychological school than on an assumption growing out of it about how to interpret standard survey questions on the topic. Responses to such questions, many people assert, tell us something about the individuals who express the attitudes rather than about the world in which they live. Hence, studies of trust and confidence tend to concentrate heavily on the individual characteristics of trusters and cynics, and rarely on the social and political circumstances that are associated with levels or trends in trust.

If the social-psychology view is right about trust as a character trait, then one would expect a fairly close association at the individual level between social trust and confidence in public institutions. Any suggestion that there are different types of trust and confidence, that they can vary independently of one another, or that the same person can express one type but not another challenges the theory.

The Social and Cultural Model

Posing an alternative the to the social-psychological model, some social theorists hold that the ability to trust others and sustain cooperative relations is the product of social experiences and socialization, especially those found in the sorts of voluntary associations of modern society that bring different social types together to achieve a common goal. The theory goes back to Alexis de Tocqueville and John Stuart Mill, both of whom emphasized the importance of voluntary associations and social engagement as training grounds for democracy. Many contemporary writers pursue the same theme, discussing society's ability to inculcate "habits of the heart" such as trust, reciprocity, and co-operation (Bellah et al. 1985), emphasizing the importance of civil society in generating cooperative social relations (Coleman 1990; Inglehart and Abramson 1994; Sztompka 1996), or focusing on trust or civic culture as a basis for stable and peaceful democracy (Almond and Verba 1963; Inglehart 1990, 1997c; Ostrom 1990; Rose 1994; Mischler and Rose 1997; Newton 1997c; Rose, Mischeler, and Haerpfer 1998).

The social and cultural model essentially argues that individual life situations and experiences—especially higher education (Doring 1992), participation in a community with a cooperative culture, and involvement in voluntary activities (Geertz 1962; Ardener 1964; Williams 1988)—create social trust and cooperation, civic-mindedness, and reciprocity between individuals. This in turn helps create strong, effective, and successful social organizations and institutions, including political groups and governmental institutions in which people can invest their confidence. Such organizations and institutions in turn help build trust, cooperation, and reciprocity, as well as confidence in other institutions. In short, there is a direct and mutually reinforcing relationship between the types of people who express trust and confidence on the one hand and strong and effective social organizations and institutions on the other. If this is true, we would expect to find that people who express attitudes of trust toward others are likely to express confidence in public institutions and to be well integrated into voluntary associations and other forms of cooperative social activity. This association should also be tested at the individual level.

The Institutional Performance Model

The third model, presented in the introduction to this book, focuses on the actual performance of government as the key to understanding citizens' confidence in government. Trust and confidence are regarded neither as personality traits nor as the direct products of social conditions that are associated with a democratic culture or well-developed social capital. Instead, because all citizens are exposed to government actions, confidence in political institutions is likely to be randomly distributed among various personality types and different cultural and social types. Government institutions that perform well are likely to elicit the confidence of citizens; those that perform badly or ineffectively generate feelings of distrust and low confidence. The general public, the model assumes, recognizes whether government or political institutions are performing well or poorly and reacts accordingly.

This theory has three implications. First, given accurate sampling techniques, reliable research procedures, and sensible survey questions, responses to questionnaire items about institutional confidence are likely to be a good gauge of how well the political system is actually performing. In other words, confidence questions are likely to provide an accurate thermometer of public life. Second, there are significant implications for public policy. The theory suggests that if public institutions earn little public esteem, the remedy for political leaders lies in either lowering public expectations of performance (politicians can promise less) or in improving institutional effectiveness (politicians can deliver more).

Third, the model also posits a relationship—albeit an indirect one—between confidence in political institutions and social trust. While we would not expect to find a strong *individual*-level relationship between the two, we would expect to find a stronger set of relationships at the *aggregate* level of societies or nation-states. This is because confidence in political institutions is the product of governmental performance in much the same way that estimations of the trustworthiness of others, and willingness to trust them, are based on the experience of how others behave

(Hardin 1996). Moreover, governmental performance affects individuals regardless of their particular personality or social type. Not all citizens are equally affected by government performance, but things like inflation, economic growth, government corruption, or foreign policy failures have an impact on all citizens to a greater or lesser extent. This explains why political trust and distrust tend to be more or less randomly distributed among people with different individual characteristics such as education, income, religion, age, or gender (Newton 1999).

At the same time, there may be a significant indirect relationship between social trust and confidence in political institutions. If social trust helps build social capital and social capital, in turn, helps strengthen political institutions, then governmental performance may improve, inspiring citizens' confidence. Conversely, if social trust declines and stores of social capital diminish, then political institutions will perform less well, governmental performance will suffer, and citizens' confidence in government will fall. Although effective political institutions do not guarantee good governmental performance, they can help. It is possible to imagine a government performing unsatisfactorily in spite of good institutions; it is difficult to imagine satisfactory governmental performance without effective institutions for making and implementing policies.

The institutional performance model is neither a psychological nor a social-cultural one, but a *systemic* one to be tested with aggregate data for nation-states. It does not predict a very strong relationship between social trust and confidence in institutions at the individual level. On the contrary, it leads us to expect that the relationship will be nonexistent at the individual level yet important at the aggregate level.

TESTING THE MODELS

If the social-psychological model is correct and trust is a personality trait that people do or do not display, then we would expect to find a strong association at the individual level between social trust and confidence in public institutions. Table 3.4 displays simple correlations between the measures of social trust and institutional confidence in the World Values Surveys when data for all 17 Trilateral democracies are pooled. Because this includes data on many countries in each wave with at least a thousand individuals in each national sample, the total number of individuals surveyed is very large (around 47,000). What matters, therefore, is less the statistical significance of the correlations than the substantive strength of the coefficients. The first column demonstrates that social trust is indeed positively related to confidence in public and private institutions (except for the education system); people who trust each other also do tend to have more confidence in public and private institutions. It should be stressed, however, that the association, while statistically significant, is

TABLE 3.4
Individual-Level Correlations between Social Trust, Voluntary Activism, and Institutional Confidence

	Individual-Level Correlations with Social Trust	Significance	Individual-Level Correlations with Voluntary Activism	Significance
Public Institutions	.09	**	.03	**
Parliament	.09	**	.07	**
Legal system	.09	**	.03	**
Police	.07	**	.03	**
Civil service	.06	**	.04	**
Armed forces	.01	*	−.03	**
Nonprofit/Private				
Institutions	.06	**	.04	**
Education system	−.04	**	−.02	**
The church	.07	**	.46	**
Major companies	.03	**	.01	*
The press	.06	**	−.01	N/s
Trade unions	.06	**	.06	**

Note: Individual-level correlations between social trust, voluntary activism, and confidence in institutions in 17 advanced industrial democracies with pooled data for both waves of the WVS. *p < .05. **p < .01.

Social trust: "Generally speaking, would you say that most people can be trusted (1), or that you can't be too careful in dealing with people (0)?"

Voluntary activism: Whether respondent belonged to any of a range of 16 voluntary organizations such as unions, sports groups, or religious organizations. Scale ranged from 0 to 16.

Institutional confidence: See Table 3.1 for details.

Sources: World Values Survey 1980–84, 1990–93. N = 46,502.

generally very weak. These results are consistent with previous research that found weak correlations between social trust and confidence in political institutions on the individual level (Wright 1976, 104–10; Craig 1993, 27), and they confirm Kaase's (1997, 15) conclusion that "the statistical relationship between interpersonal trust and political trust is small indeed."

According to the social-cultural model trust in people and confidence in institutions are associated with characteristics related to an individual's social position, cultural identity, and personal life experiences. In particular, we would expect to find that those citizens who are most active in voluntary organizations and community associations would develop the social trust and cooperative habits that lead to confidence in public institutions. Table 3.4 also allows us to examine the simple association between voluntary activism (as measured by membership in a range of 16

TABLE 3.5
The Effects of Social Background and Political Attitudes on Institutional Confidence at the
Individual Level

	All Public Institutions	Parliament	Civil Service	Legal System	Police	Military	Private Institutions
Gender	− .03	N/s	− .04	− .02	− .04	N/s	− .02
Class	.06	.02	.06	N/s	.05	.05	.09
Age	.14	.08	.10	.05	.12	.13	.12
Social trust	.08	.07	.05	.08	.06	.02	.06
Voluntary activism	N/s	.03	.02	N/s	N/s	− .05	.04
Life satisfaction	.13	.07	.09	.08	.13	.07	.12
Left-right self-placement	.20	.09	.09	.10	.17	.24	.11
Political interest	.04	.10	.02	.05	N/s	− .03	N/s
Adjusted R^2	.10	.04	.04	.03	.08	.09	.06

Note: The figures represent standardized (Beta) coefficients using OLS regression models. Both waves of the WVS data in the 17 countries are pooled. All coefficients are significant at the .05 level or higher.
Gender: Male (1), Female (0).
Class: Nine-point scale based on the respondent's occupational group from employed/manager with 10+ employees (1) to unskilled manual worker (9).
Age: Years.
Social trust: "Generally speaking would you say that most people can be trusted (1), or that you can't be too careful in dealing with people (0)?"
Voluntary activism: Whether respondent belonged to any of a range of 16 voluntary organizations such as unions, sports groups, or religious organizations. Scale ranged from 0 to 16.
Life satisfaction: "All things considered, how satisfied are you with your life on the whole these days?" Ten-point scale.
Left-right self-placement: Ten-point scale.
Political interest: Four-point scale.
Sources: World Values Survey 1980–84, 1990–93. N = 46,502.

different types of groups such as churches, sports groups, and arts associations) and institutional confidence. Once again the correlations prove to be statistically significant but quite weak. The exception is confidence in the church. One possible explanation is that people who are most active in their local community are often strong supporters of the church, so religious organizations may play a special role in this relationship.

To explore these relationships in greater depth, we used a series of ordinary least squares (OLS) regression models. Consistent with the classic "funnel of causality" logic, we first entered the social background variables that are most commonly associated with social and political attitudes (i.e., gender, social class, and age); then the cultural variables of social trust and voluntary activism; and finally measures of satisfaction with life, left-right self-identity, and political interest. We regressed these eight independent variables on confidence in public and private institutions in 17 Trilateral nations with the World Values Survey data pooled across waves. As with the earlier analysis, given the size of the pooled data source, we need to pay as much attention to the substantive strength of the coefficients as to their statistical significance.

As shown by the adjusted summary R^2 coefficient, the regression models in each case explain only a limited amount of variance in institutional confidence. The overall pattern by gender, class, and age displays a consistent but weak relationship across each model: institutional confidence tends to be marginally higher among women, the middle classes, and older people. As revealed by the simple correlations, social trust is significantly but weakly associated with institutional confidence even after controlling for social background. Contrary to many cultural accounts, the link between social trust and institutional confidence was not strongly or consistently mediated by voluntary activism, however. Membership in voluntary organizations proved to be an insignificant predictor of institutional confidence in three of the models, and a significant but weak predictor in three other models. Regarding confidence in the military, the relationship actually proved to be negative. In other words, being a member of a voluntary group was associated with less, not more, confidence in the armed forces. Among the remaining attitudinal variables the respondent's position on the left-right self-placement scale proved to be the strongest predictor of institutional confidence, with those people reporting themselves to be furthest to the left reporting the least trust.[4]

It is clear from these regressions that people's confidence in public institutions is only weakly associated with social trust, and its association with voluntary activism is even weaker. Whatever voluntary associations may or may not do for social capital, they seem to hold little importance for political capital. In contrast, the only political variable in the equation—the left-right measure—is fairly consistently the best predictor of confidence levels. Moreover, many of the standard social and economic variables so often used in the social sciences to explain individual attitudes and behavior, like age and class, provide little leverage for this analysis. It appears that institutional confidence is fairly evenly distributed within different social and economic groups in society, supporting the hypothesis that confidence in public institutions is the result of specifically political factors rather than general social or economic circumstances.

---

[4] It is worth noting that the poor results in Table 3.5 are not due to the fact that national data are pooled or that the figures represent the results from two surveys. The same analysis was carried out for separate countries in the same survey year with almost identical results. Not only were the R^2's very low in each country (less than 2 percent), but no independent variable was closely associated with institutional confidence or consistently significant in a majority of nations.

As a whole, then, these results offer little support for either the social-psychological or cultural theories of institutional confidence. On the contrary, the correlations and regression coefficients in Tables 3.4 and 3.5 are generally so weak that they suggest the need to look elsewhere. We will therefore turn our attention to political explanations related to institutional performance.

INSTITUTIONAL PERFORMANCE: SOCIAL TRUST AND VOLUNTARISM

Much of the work that has focused on social trust implies the existence of a significant relationship among levels of social trust, voluntary activism, and confidence in public institutions. Although the relationship between social trust and confidence in government has been of central interest, membership in voluntary associations is also thought to be important. The reasoning is that voluntary and community groups bring people together to work on local problems and public affairs, so high social trust should be associated with a dense and vibrant network of social capital. Social capital, in turn, is thought to lead to effective public institutions that are responsive to public needs and demands. The groups and organizations of civil society mediate between citizens and the state. As noted, this theory focuses not on individual-level data, but rather on national-level data. Thus, we can analyze the correlation between levels of social trust and institutional confidence aggregated at the national level. The World Values Survey data are pooled so that we can compare 34 cases (the 17 nations at two time points).

Most strikingly, the results presented in Table 3.6 do indeed confirm a strongly positive and significant relationship at the national level between social trust and confidence in four out of the five public institutions being compared. The exception is the armed forces; this may be because the military is the only public institution whose performance can be expected to operate and be evaluated according to standards different from those of civic life. The aggregate-level correlations are far stronger than the individual-level ones observed in Table 3.4, suggesting that there is an important systemic effect. Although the number of countries included in the pooled data is relatively small and the figures do not meet tests of statistical significance, most of the correlations between social trust and nonprofit/private institutions are also fairly strong. A comparison of the top and bottom halves of Table 3.6 suggests that at the national level social trust is more closely related to confidence in public institutions than to confidence in nonprofit and private ones.

The positive associations between social trust and confidence in the police ($R = .61$) and the legal system ($R = .51$) are particularly strong, which may have important implications for citizens' willingness to obey

TABLE 3.6
National-Level Correlations between Social Trust, Voluntary Activism, and
Institutional Confidence

	National-Level Correlations with Social Trust	Significance	National-Level Correlations with Voluntary Activism	Significance
Public Institutions	.56	**	.13	
Police	.62	**	.21	
Legal system	.51	**	.06	
Armed forces	.24		−.12	
Parliament	.38	*	.25	
Civil service	.40	*	.27	
Nonprofit/Private Institutions	.37	*	.29	
Education system	−.30		.04	
The church	.11		.53	**
Major companies	.22		.26	
The press	.09		−.09	
Trade unions	.51	**	.41	*

Note: National-level correlations between mean social trust, voluntary activism, and institutional confidence in 17 advanced industrial democracies with data pooled for both waves. *p < .05. **p < .01.

Sources: World Values Survey 1980–84, 1990–93. N = 34 societies.

the law. When people trust each other, they also tend to have faith in the authorities who enforce the law. This relationship is shown more clearly in a scattergram (see Figure 3.1), which shows that in countries like Norway, Denmark, and Canada high social trust is accompanied by considerable public confidence in the police. Most of the Nordic nations in particular tend to be clustered in the top-right corner of the graph. In contrast, countries like France, Belgium, and Italy display the opposite tendency, with suspicion of other citizens going hand-in-hand with minimal confidence in the police. Most countries, such as Japan, the Netherlands, and Britain, are predictably scattered along the middle of the diagonal. Similar patterns are found for confidence in the legal system.

Figures 3.2 and 3.3 show a similar but slightly weaker relationship at the national level between social trust on the one hand and confidence in parliaments and the civil service on the other. Again, the scattergrams confirm that most countries fall into a fairly predictable pattern, with Italy at one extreme, in the bottom-left corner with little interpersonal trust or confidence in the institutions of representative democracy, and

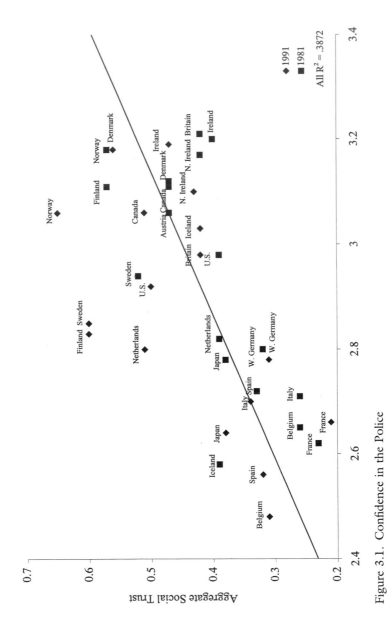

Figure 3.1. Confidence in the Police

Sources for Figures 3.1–3.3: World Values Surveys 1980–84, 1990–93.

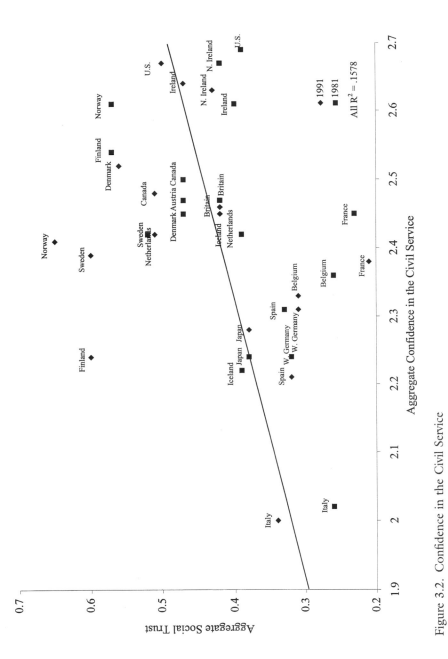

Figure 3.2. Confidence in the Civil Service

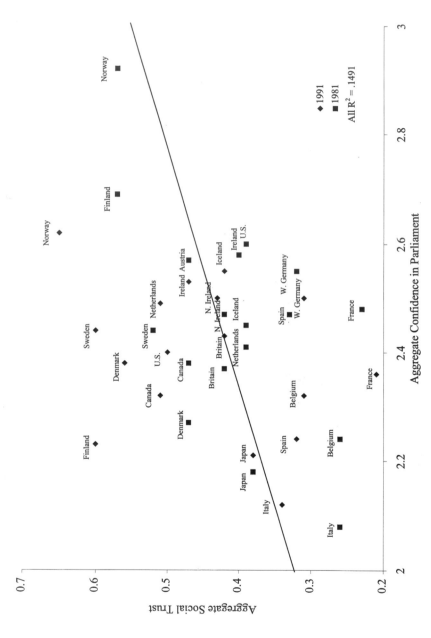

Figure 3.3. Confidence in Parliament

many of the Scandinavian nations located at the opposite end of the spectrum.

The overall pattern confirms our hypothesis that the relationship between social trust and institutional confidence operates largely at the societal rather than at the individual level. The reason for this association remains a puzzle, however, particularly in light of our findings that the relationship between social trust and institutional confidence is not mediated by social capital. As Table 3.6 showed, the national-level relationships between levels of voluntary activism and institutional confidence were not significant except for confidence in the church and trade unions; there was no significant link between membership in voluntary associations and confidence in key public institutions: parliament, the civil service, and the legal system. The association between social trust and institutional confidence clearly needs further exploration. A number of chapters in this volume offer possible explanations for the relationships, but further research is obviously required. Case studies comparing countries like Norway and Italy or aggregate-level cross-national models of policy performance would help illuminate this relationship.

CONCLUSIONS

The central institutions of the Trilateral democracies witnessed declines in public support in the 1980s. The available survey evidence suggests that social trust is not experiencing a long-term, secular decline in the Trilateral nations, although it certainly seems to be in some particular countries (Newton 1999); neither is there an across-the-board loss of confidence in all the major institutions of society. The evidence presented in this chapter (especially Tables 3.1, 3.3, and 3.6) suggests that public and private institutions have been regarded in rather different ways by the general public. While confidence in nonprofit and private institutions remained fairly constant or in some cases increased during the 1980s, confidence declined in public institutions—in parliament, the legal system, the armed forces, the police, and the civil service.

Even so, confidence in parliament did not fall in all Trilateral countries. In this sense the nature of the problem is far more specific than some alarmist claims about a general crisis that affects the whole of Western society. At the same time if we are correct that confidence in institutions is a good thermometer of malaise, then declining confidence in public-sector institutions is a serious matter. Although it may not herald a crisis, it surely is cause for concern.

What is the source of this loss of confidence in public institutions? We find little evidence that trust or confidence is a feature of basic personality types. Social trust is not strongly associated with measures of confidence in institutions at the individual level; socially trusting people are not necessarily politically trusting, and vice versa (Newton 1999). Nor is confidence in public institutions at all well explained by the social and economic variables usually associated with attitudes and behavior. Life satisfaction, education, income, gender, age, and membership in voluntary associations explain little of the variance in confidence in parliament, the civil service, or the police. These findings lead us away from social-psychological models as well as from social and cultural explanations of loss of confidence in public institutions. We also find little support for general theories that explain what is ailing the Trilateral democracies in terms of problems like heightened economic competition, postmodern society, increasing individualism, declining levels of social trust, or the disintegration of social and community life. Instead, our research provides substantial support for theories that focus on the performance of governments and political institutions to explain citizens' declining confidence in them.

Beyond this general finding, our research sheds light on a topic at the center of a maelstrom of debate in recent years, namely the complex relationship between social trust on the one hand and confidence in government and political institutions on the other. As we and others have demonstrated, the two are significantly but only weakly related at the individual level. This finding, however, is wholly consistent with the position adopted by most of the authors in this volume that it is primarily governmental performance that determines the level of citizens' confidence in public institutions. Political trust and confidence are more or less randomly distributed among various personality and social types in a given country because, after all, government policies and performance affect everyone, even if they do not necessarily affect everyone equally. Few people can escape at least some of the consequences of national economic failure, foreign policy disasters, government corruption, or increased taxes. In this sense "the rain falls on the just and unjust alike," so disillusionment or, alternatively, satisfaction with government is likely to be widespread among people, independent of whether they are high or low in social trust (see Introduction, this volume).

But when we step back and look at a nation as a whole, the story is quite different. At this aggregate level social trust and confidence in government and its institutions are strongly associated with each other. Social trust can help build effective social and political institutions, which can help governments perform effectively, and this in turn encourages confidence in civic institutions. Thus, Trilateral nations that enjoy a high level of social trust also tend to enjoy a relatively high level of confidence in political institutions. Conversely, countries with low levels of social trust are less likely to build the kind of vibrant civil society that spurs strong government performance, and the result will be low citizen confidence in government and public institutions. It may also be possible, as Donatella della Porta's chapter suggests, that the relationship also runs in the opposite direction: poor government performance as manifested, for example, in rampant political corruption may create a cycle that contributes to widespread social distrust. However, this question along with the important question of which measures of government performance matter most to citizens in determining their confidence levels lies outside the scope of this inquiry.

FOUR

Distrust of Government: Explaining American Exceptionalism

Anthony King

WHENEVER AMERICANS and Europeans meet to talk politics these days, the conversation almost invariably turns to the mass public's declining trust in government. The Americans and Europeans usually have little difficulty in agreeing that public trust in government has indeed declined in recent years, but from that point onward they are likely to find themselves talking at serious cross-purposes. When Europeans use the phrase "declining trust in government," they typically have in mind the dishonesty of specific politicians or parties or the mismanagement and incompetence of specific governments or government agencies; but what Americans have in mind, as we shall see, is something at once more profound and more diffuse. Politically aware people on both sides of the Atlantic use the same language, but what they mean by it is often quite different.

The purpose of this chapter is to explore the particular meaning given to the phrase "declining trust in government" in the United States, to argue that there has indeed occurred in the United States a quite exceptional decline in the amount of public trust enjoyed by the federal government, and, finally, to suggest some explanations of that exceptional decline—explanations that should serve to distinguish sharply between the American experience and the European. The phenomena to be explored are complicated, and the interconnections among them still more complicated. The approach used here will therefore be less Occam's razor, more Swiss army knife.

"GOVERNMENT"

In order to understand the phenomenon of declining trust and confidence in government, we obviously need to understand both of the two key concepts in the phrase: confidence or trust on the one hand and government on the other. The preceding chapters have focused, rightly, on confidence; but a comparison between Europe and the United States requires that we also look at the concept of government. A case can be made for the proposition that Europeans and Americans conceptualize government in ways that are subtly, but significantly, different.

Ask any European to free-associate about "government," and he or she is likely to look merely blank or puzzled.[1] Government? What is that? Europeans can easily grasp the concept of *the* government, meaning whichever partisan administration—Tony Blair's Labour government or Lionel Jospin's Socialist government—currently happens to be in power. In addition, most Europeans, though not the British and the Irish, can grasp the concept of "the state," meaning the legally constituted authorities, whoever they may be. But for most Europeans the state is a highly abstract concept, without corporeal existence. Ordinary Europeans frequently talk about "the government." Of course they do. But, unless they happen to be political theorists or lawyers, they almost never talk about "the state." Among Europeans, the tiny minority of anarchists are probably the only people who conceive of government as an entity that may or may not exist or as an activity that may or may not be carried on.

The same point can be made another way. People like political scientists and sociologists often juxtapose what they conceive of as two separate entities: government and society. The former cannot be imagined without the latter, but the latter can, if with difficulty, be imagined without the former. But there is no reason to think that this academic distinction, useful though it is for academics, has any resonance whatsoever in the minds of most ordinary Europeans. When they think of government, it is not as any kind of entity, let alone a single entity, juxtaposed to society. Rather, they think of it as the government of the day (as in the Blair government) or else as the specific governmental agency that they are currently dealing with. Europeans do not think of "government." They think of the pensions office, the passport office, the post office, or whatever. The distinction between state and nonstate is probably lost on most of them, especially in an era when the railways are owned by the government in some European countries but not in others and when the Dutch post office, traditionally a state agency throughout Europe, has lately been privatized.

Americans, so far as one can tell, think differently. For them government—as distinct from the government—is a reality, something almost tangible: out there, to be thought about, to be felt about, to be conjured with. Indeed, when Americans talk about *the* government, as of course they frequently do, they typically do *not* have in mind the Bush administration or the Clinton administration; rather, they have in mind the powers that be in Washington, the federal bureaucracy, "the feds." A

---

[1] The observations that follow are based on the writer's travels and conversations in Europe and the United States rather than on survey data. Relevant survey data do not exist. It would probably be hard to find funding for an international research project on such a recondite topic.

specific federal agency is likely to be seen as an outpost or an agent of *them*, the government back there in Washington. What Europeans typically fragment in their minds—the various agencies of government—Americans typically knit together to create a much more unified conception of "government" and "the government."[2] This more unified conception may not be terribly well articulated in the minds of most Americans. It probably is not. But a conception does not have to be clearly articulated to have a considerable impact on thinking and behavior.

Strangely enough (or is it strange?), the American conception of government—as a "thing," something unified, but also separate, distinct, detached—actually does assume a physical form in many American cities. In most European towns and cities government offices are widely scattered. The tax office is on one street, the social security office is on another; the vehicle licensing department is probably across the river somewhere. But in many American cities the offices of a number of federal agencies have been brought together under one roof. As a result, massive Federal Buildings, often imposing, seldom beautiful, dominate the business districts of cities like Chicago and Philadelphia, bearing in some cases a disconcerting resemblance to the headquarters of an occupying power. Any American who, like Timothy McVeigh, wants to vent his wrath against "the government" or "Washington" knows precisely what to target.

But that, for the moment, is not the point. The point at this stage is simply that Americans—ordinary Americans, not political scientists—appear to have a special way of thinking about government; and this special way of thinking means that, when Americans are asked whether or not they trust "government" or "the government," they are being asked a question that is, for them, intelligible. For Americans government in general is something separate, something distinct, something identifiable. It is much less clear what ordinary Europeans have in mind on the (admittedly rare) occasions when they are asked about their level of trust or confidence in government or the state.

Loss of Confidence in America and Elsewhere

That there has been a decline in trust and confidence in government in the United States is not in dispute and has been amply documented in

---

[2] It is worth noting that what is being claimed here is the precise opposite of what is usually supposed, namely that, whereas Europeans can and do conceptualize an entity called "the state," Americans do not. See, for example, Nettl (1968). But Nettl and the others who make this point are referring to the discourse of the intelligentsia, in which connection they are absolutely right. They are not referring to the discourse of ordinary people.

this book and elsewhere. Less attention has been focused on whether the decline in trust in the United States has been more or less in line with any declines that have taken place in other comparable countries or whether the American decline has been significantly larger than elsewhere. America may be typical, or it may be an outlier. In the latter case, one would need to try and identify the factors that have eroded trust and confidence in the United States to an exceptional degree.

The available evidence comparing the United States with other countries is not substantial and is not always easy to interpret (not least for the kinds of reasons given above); but it does suggest that the decline in confidence in America is indeed more "real" than in most other comparable countries. For example, when Dalton (1999) explored a variety of indicators of confidence in politicians and government in a number of developed countries, he found that, while confidence had declined in almost all of them, the declines in the United States were among the most marked; the impression created by the limited body of relevant survey data is reinforced by reading the American press and by listening to the rhetoric of American politicians—as well as by the rise in America of anti-government militia groups and episodes like the Oklahoma City bombing. Government as such has remarkably few defenders in the United States, and "the government" does seem to be perceived by a remarkably large number of people as an alien and hostile force. A foreign journalist (Esler 1997) suggests that the "red scare" of the 1950s has been replaced by an equally virulent "fed scare." Why should this be so? Why does the United States stand out in this way? The question becomes all the more puzzling when one remembers that, as the world goes, the United States is a well-governed country, its justice impartial, its taxes low, and most (though not all) of its political leaders tolerably honest.

Moreover, several of the explanations that Americans themselves offer for the decline of confidence in America—rising rates of violent crime, mounting pressures on the welfare state, the disintegration of the nuclear family, the stagnation of real disposable incomes and the increasing intrusiveness of the mass media (Nye, Zelikow, and King 1997)—seem unsatisfactory, because these phenomena are occurring in almost all other developed countries without producing the same effects, or at least without producing them to anything like the same degree. It follows that, in order to explain yet another instance of American exceptionalism, we need to focus on factors that appear to be specific to the United States. We also need to focus on factors that have been at work in America since about the mid-1960s because, all the evidence suggests, that is when the long-term decline in trust and confidence from which the United States still suffers first began to appear. In other words: Why the United States? And why the United States principally over the past three decades?

I begin, however, by considering two factors that are indeed specific to the United States but that go back a long way in American history, certainly far beyond the 1960s. The argument here is that, while these factors by themselves cannot account for the post-1960s decline in trust and confidence in the United States, they can help to explain why the decline has been greater in the United States than elsewhere and why it has persisted for so long. If a person succumbs to a virus and then suffers from a prolonged illness, the fact that he or she has a weak immune system cannot by itself account for the onset of the illness, but it can certainly help to explain why the individual in question was struck down when others were not and also why, in his or her case, the illness was prolonged. Predispositions are important.

One of the two longer-term factors is wholly familiar and can be discussed briefly. The other may be less familiar, at least in the present context.

SUSPICION OF GOVERNMENT IN AMERICA

The more familiar of the two factors is simply Americans' long-standing and well-known proneness to be suspicious of government. Americans are almost certainly suspicious of government today because Americans have always been suspicious of government; or, more precisely—since there have been periods when government in the United States has been held in higher esteem than now—they have always been liable to be suspicious of government. We tend to think of the recent period of distrust of government in the United States as an aberration; but perhaps, on the contrary, it was the apparently more trusting era of the 1940s and 1950s that was really the more unusual phenomenon.[3]

There is no reason whatever to doubt the importance of this factor. On the contrary, precisely because it figures in almost every political science textbook and is almost a cliché of American historiography, there is a danger of not taking it seriously enough and of not taking fully on board how sharply its historic distrust of government distinguishes the United States from other countries. Europeans take it for granted that, for better or worse, there has always been government and always will be. In con-

---

[3] It is a pity that relevant survey data—notably those of the type set out in Figure 4.1—are not available for a much longer time period. It would be fascinating to be able to compare levels of trust and confidence in government in the United States during, say, the Harding-Hoover era (1921–33) with levels during the Roosevelt-Eisenhower era (1933–61) as well as with levels over the past three decades. Were levels of trust and confidence high in the United States during the 1920s? It seems doubtful.

trast, Americans are still apt to wish, in a vague sort of way, that the whole business of governing could be dispensed with.

In the case of most European countries and Japan the history of the country in question and the history of the government of that country have been inextricably intertwined. In many cases a country's governmental institutions came into being before the country and actually created the country. France developed from the preexisting French kingdom, Germany from the preexisting Prussian kingdom, modern Italy from the preexisting Piedmontese kingdom (with help from Garibaldi, Mazzini, and others); Spain is likewise the product of the dynastic marriage of the monarchs of Aragon and Castile; and so on. In other cases, such as the English and the Japanese, the country and its governmental institutions grew up together over an extended period. In all these cases it is virtually impossible to imagine the countries in question without government.

Needless to say, the American experience was completely different. In the first place, many of those who emigrated to the American colonies did so precisely to escape from the oppression to which they had been subjected by governments in Europe: "the continent was peopled by runaways from authority" (Lipset 1977, 58). In the second place, the peoples of the United States did not inherit their government; they invented it. Whereas the French monarchy preceded France and the English monarchy and England largely grew up together, the United States—formed initially merely as a loose grouping of colonies to fight the British—actually preceded its political institutions. The Founding Fathers in Philadelphia had thus both to shape an entirely new form of government and to do so in a political climate suffused with anti-government feeling—feeling that had been reinforced by the former colonists' recent experience of British rule.

The consequences of this unusual, perhaps unique, experience have been twofold. First, as we remarked earlier, the conceptual map of most Americans still contains a separate zone or region demarcated as "the government" or "government." This conceptual zone simply does not exist in most Europeans' mental maps. Second, because of their early historical experiences, most Americans still see this conceptual zone as being occupied, potentially at least, by alien, even hostile forces. Government in Americans' minds still exists as a discrete entity, and, although it may well be necessary, it is still thought of as potentially dangerous. That was the view of the Founding Fathers, and that is still the view of most Americans today. As Huntington put it a generation ago (1981, 33), "The distinctive aspect of the American creed is its antigovernment character. Opposition to power, and suspicion of government as the most dangerous embodiment of power, are the central themes of American political thought." Latent distrust of government is thus a constant of American politics.[4]

GOVERNMENT'S LIMITED CONSTITUENCY IN AMERICA

The other long-term factor that suggests itself as one tries to explain the abnormal and surprising levels of distrust in the United States may well be less familiar. It has to do with the specific tasks that the U.S. federal government does, and does not, perform. The suggestion here is simply that the federal government in the United States provides fewer services and benefits for its citizens than do the national governments of most other countries, with the result that Americans have a much smaller stake in their national government and its activities than do the citizens of most other countries in theirs. In a strange way the U.S. government has failed to develop a sufficiently broad-based constituency for itself.

The basic facts about the range of government services in the United States and elsewhere are well known. The federal government in the United States provides its citizens with highly efficient armed forces, with a somewhat less efficient national postal service, with reasonably generous old-age pensions—and not with much else. There is no system of universal national health insurance. There is little in the way of government-provided housing. There are few subsidies for the arts. There is no national broadcasting service. Income support for the poor is set at low levels, with only a narrow range of potential beneficiaries. For better or worse, the United States does not have anything approaching a welfare state in the European sense, and much of what it does have, notably education, is organized and delivered at the state and local levels, with the federal government remaining in the background.

The fact that the U.S. government delivers services and benefits on such a limited scale has important political consequences (even if in sample surveys American citizens express their usual distrust of government and their usual preference for limited government). It means that government in the United States is not seen as a large and mostly benign presence in the lives of most Americans. "The government" in America may be the monthly Social Security check and whoever delivers the mail, but it is not, as it is in much of Europe, the radio or television news in the

---

[4] Europeans who find the idea of pervasive distrust of government in the United States hard to grasp should perhaps consider public attitudes toward the emerging institutions of the European Union (EU). Large numbers of European citizens undoubtedly regard the institutions of the EU as distant, alien, and potentially dangerous. The words "Europe" and "Brussels" could easily come to figure in European political discourse in much the same way that the word "Washington" already does in the United States.

morning, the train to work, the teacher, the doctor, the district nurse, the home-help, the distributor of meals on wheels, the provider of disability benefits and the provider of heavily subsidized seats at the opera. Europeans may complain about this or that specific government, and they will certainly grumble about administrative unfairness and long waiting lists. They will also criticize waste and inefficiency (and sometimes corruption). But the thought of complaining about "government" will never occur to most of them. Government in Europe, in other words, does have a constituency—a big one, embracing, in most European countries, the whole population.[5]

Moreover, there is another respect in which government in the United States has failed to develop a constituency—or, more neutrally, in which a constituency for government has failed to develop. There are few countries in the world whose collective ideology is more pro-business than that of the United States and where the climate of opinion is more favorable to free-enterprise capitalism. Yet American businesspeople—an immensely influential force in American society—do not love their government. On the contrary, in Vogel's words (1978, 45), "the most characteristic, distinctive and persistent belief of American corporate executives is an underlying suspicion and mistrust of government." This underlying suspicion and mistrust extends beyond the large corporate sector and is also deeply embedded in the small-business and entrepreneurial psyche.

Here, as elsewhere, the contrast with Europe is striking. A minority of British businesspeople sound exactly like their American counterparts in the generality of their anti-government rhetoric, and many Italian businesspeople feel they have good reason to distrust the Italian authorities; but, by and large, the relationships between business and government in Europe are close, continuing, and even cordial. Businesspeople and government officials have often been to the same schools. When they meet together, as they often do, the atmosphere is usually friendly and infor-

---

[5] A piece of survey evidence from Britain may illustrate the point. From time to time the British Gallup Poll asks a sample of the British public which of three statements about taxation and government spending comes closest to their own view. In April 1997, on the eve of the 1997 British general election, the responses were: "Taxes should be cut, even if it means some reduction in government services, such as health education and welfare," 7 percent; "Things should be left as they are," 18 percent; "Government services such as health, education and welfare should be extended, even if it means some increases in taxes," 72 per cent; "Don't know," 3 percent (Gallup 1997). These figures have changed little over the past decade or so. To some extent they undoubtedly represent altruism and a concern for social solidarity, but they probably also represent, to an even greater extent, a consciousness on the part of Gallup's respondents that they themselves and their families are heavily dependent on the very services, notably the National Health Service, that the question refers to.

mal; not least, they mostly share a sense that what both sides are doing is "good for Britain," "good for Germany," or wherever. Petty frictions abound, of course, and the imperatives of politics and business frequently diverge; but in Europe there is no generalized sense of alienation between the two communities, government and business. Indeed, there is seldom any generalized sense of their *being* two communities.

Although, as is well known, American business profited enormously from government backing in the early days of the republic, and indeed throughout the nineteenth century, there nevertheless developed in the United States a powerful sense that government and business were two separate entities—two entities that, moreover, were in a relationship of perpetual antagonism. However hard individual American firms competed with one another and however divergent American business interests often were, American business at a very early stage developed a strong sense of corporate identity—a sense of identity that was in large part defined by across-the-board opposition to, and resentment of, governmental interference in business affairs. The relationship, always uneasy, was put under further strain in the 1930s when Franklin D. Roosevelt enormously expanded the federal government's scope while at the same time denouncing anti–New Deal capitalists as "economic royalists." Unlike their European counterparts American businesspeople still see the autonomy of business as a bastion continuously under attack, continuously having to be defended.

There are two other features of government in the United States that have had the effect of prolonging this unique business-government estrangement. One is the contempt of American business for the American civil service. In Europe the norm—certainly in Britain, France and Germany—has been for the government to attract to its service some of the ablest young men and (recently) women from every generation. European administrative elites have indeed been elites: intelligent, well trained, and drawn from the most prestigious schools and universities. They have typically been held in high esteem in the wider society (and have typically held themselves in high esteem). In Japan, the phenomenon has gone, if anything, even further. Japanese civil servants are said to "descend from heaven" when they retire; but they can only descend from heaven if they have been in heaven in the first place.

More or less the opposite is true in the United States. To be sure, able public servants are to be found in Washington, but there is no sense in which American civil servants, even in the upper echelons, are an elite, think of themselves as an elite or, more to the point, are thought of by their fellow Americans in general and American businesspeople in particular as an elite. The civil service is a much newer institution in the United States than in Europe and Japan, and, although occasional attempts have been made, it has never attracted men and women from elite schools, people generally acknowledged to be of outstanding ability. In the United States, "The private sector rules, OK?" Both the quality and the social standing of the American civil service have suffered as a result. When businesspeople and civil servants meet in Washington, there can never be any doubt about which of the two groups enjoys the higher status (as well as the higher income). It is no accident that the term *bureaucrat*, with its ineffably negative connotations, is the term most Americans use to denote civil servants.

A second factor prolonging the estrangement of government and business in the United States may be less familiar. It is the extreme difficulty that American businesses and businesspeople have in relating to government. Even though businesspeople in the United States, like most Americans, lump together all the branches and agencies of the federal government as "the government," they know that in reality the U.S. government is not one thing but a myriad of things: the Supreme Court and the rest of the court system, the two houses of Congress and their individual members and committees, the White House, mainline cabinet departments, noncabinet departments, regulatory commissions, and so on.

In most European countries there tends to be one point of contact, or a very limited range of points of contact, between business organizations and those in government whom they seek to influence or learn from. In the United States government is not so much an institution as an arena. As a consequence, dealing with the American government on a matter of any importance or complexity is almost invariably a hazardous, expensive, and time-consuming affair—hard to avoid but best avoided if possible. Weir and her colleagues (Weir, Orloff, and Skocpol 1988, 22) note that in any conflicts between different business sectors in the United States, "the losers can always go to court—or back to the legislatures [plural], or to a new bureaucratic agency—for another round of battle in the interminable struggles that never seem to settle American policy questions." They add, and this is the crucial point for our purposes: "To American capitalists the U.S. state has seemed neither coherent nor reliable."

This long-standing estrangement of business and government in the United States has been made worse in recent years by the American government's characteristic regulatory style. Efforts to regulate business are not unique to the United States; on the contrary, the regulation of business in Europe and elsewhere often extends considerably further than in the United States, into such areas as land-use planning and workers' rights. But what is unique to the United States (or has been until recently) has been a heavy reliance on the regulatory style that Kagan (1991) has dubbed "adversarial legalism." In Europe the tendency in such areas as environmental regulation and health and safety at work has been to grant decision-making authority to a single government agency and to empower that agency to develop policies and make judgments largely free from judicial supervision. In practice, such agencies in Europe have usually sought to develop informal, consensual relationships with the various affected interests. The aim has been to achieve the objectives of policy with minimum cost and hassle to all concerned. In the United States, by contrast, the approach has been one of developing highly complex legal rules and then of seeking to enforce them by means of highly complex and formal—and adversarial—legal procedures. The rules and procedures change frequently, the legal sanctions are often punitive, and ample opportunities are provided for litigation and appeal. The outcome is a regulatory regime that, more often than not, is costly, cumbersome, and slow.

The effect, needless to say, is further to alienate American business from the American government. In their study of the effect of different countries' regulatory regimes on American-owned multinational corporations, Kagan and Axelrad (1997) report case after case of American firms suffering more in the United States than they would have in other countries from legalistic regulatory enforcement, from the risks arising out of American liability law, from the pervasiveness of legal unpredictability in the United States, and from the high costs of both American litigation and American litigiousness. One lawyer for a foreign vehicle manufacturer told Kagan and Axelrad (1997, 161) that "no country in which his firm sells vehicles comes close to the United States in terms of the incidence and cost of product liability legislation." A regulatory compliance official from a U.S. chemical plant was amazed when a British civil servant who had come across a nonwillful violation of a rule on the recording of chemical shipments said only, "Oh dear, I think I'll have to do something about that"—meaning that he would do as little as he reasonably could (Kagan and Axelrad 1997, 160). The cumulative effect on business-government relations in America can be imagined. Kagan is reminded of a *New Yorker* cartoon depicting a waiter who, when asked by one of his customers for advice about the menu, replies, "You won't catch me recommending *anything*, sir. I have a lawsuit on my hands right now."

The importance of this continuing and possibly intensifying business alienation from government should not be underestimated in a country whose "business is business" and in which businesspeople and the free-enterprise system are held in such high esteem. If businesspeople from the top of the corporate ladder to the humblest streetcorner retailer do not love their government, the rest of America is unlikely to. Popular distrust almost certainly mirrors, in part, corporate distrust. Throughout Europe and Japan business is an important part of government's constituency. In the United States it is not—and seems unlikely ever to be.

So much for the two long-term factors: Americans' abiding proneness to be suspicious of government and American government's failure to build a large and supportive constituency for itself, not least, but not only, in the business community. What of the more immediate factors that can help to explain why the downturn in trust and confidence in the United States occurred in the 1960s and why there has been no sustained upturn since? There are a number of such factors, and, again, some are more familiar than others.

GREAT EXPECTATIONS

To understand what has happened in the United States since the 1960s, one needs to begin by noticing a paradox that lies at the heart of Americans' attitudes toward government. On the one hand, as we have seen, Americans are suspicious of government and are inordinately disposed to be anti-government; but, on the other hand, as everyone who visits the United States quickly realizes, they are also inordinately proud of their government, or at least of their *system* of government. Far more than people in other countries, Americans are brought up to idolize, almost literally, both their governmental system, as embodied in the Declaration of Independence and the Constitution, and the heroes of American political history. If people are to be disillusioned, they must previously have had illusions, and America's present discontents probably owe something, possibly a great deal, to many Americans' overidealized view of their country's history and their exaggerated pride in American democracy. Great expectations are always in danger of leading to great disappointments.

Certainly, the available survey evidence suggests that Americans, for all their latent distrust of government, are strikingly proud of their system of government as a whole. As long ago as the late 1950s, Almond and Verba (1963, 102) found that, when respondents to their Civic Culture study in five countries were asked to list the aspects of their country of which they were most proud, Americans were far more likely than people in other countries to mention some aspect of their political system (the Constitution, freedom, democracy, or whatever). The proportion of Americans who spontaneously mentioned some aspect of United States governmental and political institutions was 85 percent, compared with 46 percent in Britain, 30 percent in Mexico, 7 percent in Germany, and a minuscule 3 percent in Italy. The specific data have changed since then, but not the overall pattern. Americans remain especially proud of their political system, if only in the abstract.[6]

This pride in the system manifests itself in a wide variety of ways. The

[6] In 1996 ABC News asked a sample of American adults whether they agreed or disagreed with the statement that "Whatever its faults, the United States still has the best system of government in the world." Fully 83 percent agreed; only 15 percent disagreed (Ladd and Bowman 1998, 114).

American capital, Washington, D.C., is a national shrine. Millions flock to the city every year to tour the White House, admire the Capitol dome, and gaze up at the inscription over the portals of the Supreme Court. The visitor's tour of the city also takes in, almost compulsorily, the Washington Monument, the Jefferson Memorial, and the Lincoln Memorial. The significance of all this devotion should not be overlooked. No European country begins to accord either its governmental buildings or its defunct political leaders anything like such respect. Hardly anyone in London notices the statue of Winston Churchill in Parliament Square. Few in France bother to visit Charles de Gaulle's home village of Colombey-les-deux-Églises. Almost no German ever travels to Bonn except on business. It is doubtful whether the average Roman—let alone the average Italian—knows the way to the Palazzo Chigi, the Italian prime minister's official residence.

This iconography of America's worship of government and politics even extends to the currency. The banknotes and coins of most countries depict either abstract symbols or else famous writers (Shakespeare in Britain, Goethe in Germany), painters (Delacroix in France, Caravaggio in Italy), musicians (Clara Schumann in Germany, Debussy in France), or mathematicians and scientists (Faraday in Britain, Gauss in Germany, Volta in Italy). Only in the United States are banknotes and coins adorned almost exclusively with pictures of politicians and government buildings (including a remarkably gloomy one of the U.S. Treasury).

Against this background one is forced at least to conjure with the idea—in the absence of any direct evidence—that Americans, who are brought up to revere their country's political system and Constitution and to venerate such great political leaders of the past as Washington, Jefferson, Hamilton, Madison, Lincoln, the two Roosevelts, and John F. Kennedy, are constantly liable to being dispirited and even outraged by the performance and characters of their real-life present-day politicians. Europeans expect relatively little from their political leaders; they are delighted when they behave well and not terribly surprised when they behave badly. Americans give the impression of hoping for more, of having higher ideals and of therefore being more vulnerable to being let down. If so, they have certainly been let down—frequently—in recent years.

VIETNAM, WATERGATE—AND AFTER

The American National Election Study has asked samples of American adults at intervals since 1958 the straightforward question "How much do you think you can trust the government in Washington to do what is right—just about always, most of the time, or only some of the time?" Figure 4.1 sets out the responses over the past four decades. As can be seen, a steady downward trend in the proportions replying either "just about always" or "most of the time" has been interrupted only twice, during the first half of the 1980s and again, briefly, in the mid-1990s. Between the late 1950s and the mid-1960s the proportions saying they trusted the government in Washington averaged 75 percent. During the 1990s they averaged considerably less than half of that, 30 percent.

But what is most striking about the data set out in Figure 4.1 is that most of the fall is concentrated in the first half of the period, between the beginning of the Vietnam War in 1964 and President Nixon's resignation a decade later. The proportion of respondents saying they trusted the government in Washington fell by nearly a third during the course of the Vietnam War, between 1964 and 1972, and by nearly another third as the Watergate scandal played itself out between 1972 and 1974. It is impossible, of course, to be sure precisely which aspects of the Vietnam War and Watergate caused such sharp falls in public trust, but they must have owed a good deal, probably a great deal, to Americans' belief that they had been systematically lied to. They had been deceived; they had been betrayed. Their topmost political leaders—the heirs of George ("I cannot tell a lie") Washington, Abraham Lincoln, and Franklin Roosevelt—had proved untrustworthy.

The fact that the decline in public trust and confidence has been so much greater in the United States than in most other countries can almost certainly be attributed to these two traumatic events, especially against the background of Americans' proneness to distrust and their higher—and, as they see it, legitimate—expectations of their political leaders. There has been no event remotely comparable to the Vietnam War in any other established democracy since the early 1960s, and only in Italy and Japan have there been events at all similar to America's Watergate scandal. In Italy the bribery and corruption scandals of the 1990s led to the collapse of the entire party system and to the repudiation of almost all the existing political class. In Japan, as Pharr (this volume) shows, public distrust is largely a function of reports of official misconduct. Watergate produced a considerable number of such reports.

Unfortunately for the United States, although nothing has happened quite to rival Vietnam and Watergate since the early 1970s, the experience of the American people with their presidents since Nixon has not been altogether happy. Most Americans put, or at least would like to put, their presidents on pedestals. Few presidents over the past four decades have seemed worthy of such an exalted position.

The contrast with other countries in this connection needs to be underlined. In the first place, expectations in other countries are far lower than in the United States. The American president is not only head of government but head of state. He is, in effect, America's monarch, its

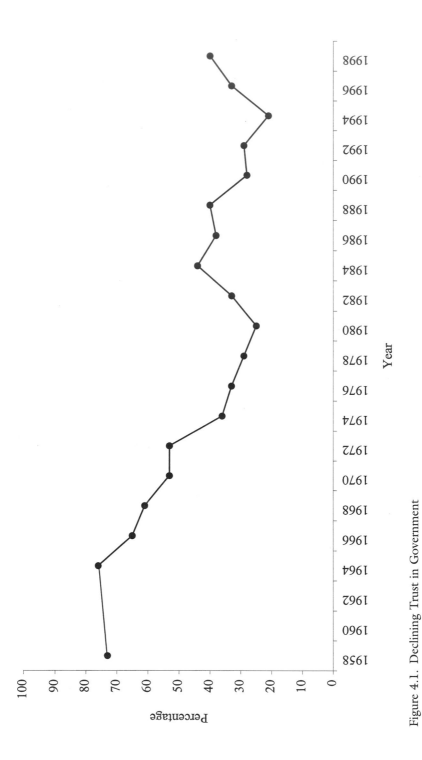

Figure 4.1. Declining Trust in Government

Note: Respondents were asked, "How much of the time do you think you can trust the government in Washington to do what is right—just about always, most of the time, or only some of the time?" The above figures traces the percentage who said that they trust the government "always" or "most of the time."

Source: American National Election Studies, 1958–98, University of Michigan.

most visible symbol. Thus, when a president besmirches his own reputation, he besmirches America's. In letting down the American people, he lets down his country. By contrast, political leaders in most other democracies are not monarchs or quasi-monarchs; they are not expected to have charismatic personalities or to be moral exemplars.[7] They are merely hired hands, expected to do a job of work, and are typically thought of as officeholders rather than leaders in any grand sense. A Churchill or a de Gaulle is rare—and is expected to be so.

In the second place, not only are expectations lower elsewhere than in the United States, but very few leaders of other democratic countries in recent years have come spectacularly adrift. Political leaders in Europe and the other major democracies tend, like American presidents in the nineteenth century, to be solid professionals, old political hands, people who have been around for a long time and who have usually held a number of other senior positions before reaching the top. By the time they get there they know what the rules are; they know how to behave. As a result, British prime ministers, German chancellors, French presidents and prime ministers, and so on almost invariably leave office because they have chosen to retire or because they have lost an election. With the usual exception of Italy, almost no major European country in recent years has seen its head of government embroiled in a major scandal or forced to leave office under a cloud. Few European heads of government since the 1960s have been outstanding (though some have), but few have disgraced themselves or been complete failures.

The United States—probably partly as a result of the way it chooses its presidential candidates—has not been so fortunate. Gallup asks a sample of Americans every month: "Do you approve or disapprove of the way [the incumbent] is handling his job?" Table 4.1 sets out the average approval rating accorded each president since the early 1950s, his highest monthly rating during his period in office and his lowest monthly rating. The figures in the table tell a somewhat doleful story. Three of the seven presidents since Eisenhower have had average approval ratings of below 50 percent, and Reagan's and Clinton's ratings have not been much above 50 percent. Moreover, all seven presidents' lowest ratings have been very low indeed: none above 40 percent and two below 30 percent.[8]

---

[7] The partial exception to this general rule is, of course, the president of France. He is not expected to be a moral exemplar, certainly not in sexual matters and probably not in financial matters either; but he is expected to be a dignified and forceful representative of the French nation, especially abroad.

[8] The only other country for which similar-seeming figures are readily available is Britain, but the figures, despite their surface similarity, are not really comparable. First, the British question is different: "Are you satisfied or dissatisfied with [the incumbent] as prime minister?" Second, there is almost certainly a larger purely partisan component in British voters'

TABLE 4.1
Presidential Approval Ratings, 1953–99

	Average	*High (month, year)*	*Low (month, year)*
Kennedy	70%	83% (Apr. 1961)	56% (Sep. 1963)
Johnson	55	79 (Jan. 1964)	35 (Aug. 1968)
Nixon	49	67 (Jan. 1973)	24 (Aug. 1974)
Ford	47	71 (Aug. 1974)	37 (Mar. 1975)
Carter	45	74 (Mar. 1977)	28 (Jun. 1979)
Reagan	53	65 (May 1981)	35 (Jan. 1983)
Bush	61	89 (Mar. 1991)	29 (Jul. 1992)
Clinton*	55	73 (Dec. 1998)	37 (Jun. 1993)

Note: Percentages are those approving of the way the incumbent was handling his job. Figures accurate to July 1999.
Source: Gallup.

But in a sense these Gallup ratings, although telling in their way, are beside the point. A person can approve of the way a president is handling his job—for example, his handling of the economy or the way he is dealing with foreign affairs—while at the same time thinking ill of him as a human being and not regarding him as an individual who should be respected or looked up to, let alone revered. The president of the United States, like the British king or queen, is expected to look the part, to comport himself with dignity and to be the embodiment of what the nation considers its best values. Failure to play the role of head of state with due dignity and decorum invites contempt (as several members of the British royal family have discovered).

Unfortunately, survey data bearing directly on presidents' performance of their head-of-state role, and on the extent to which the American people trust and respect them, are lacking; but it seems likely that, if they did exist, they would suggest that since Kennedy's sudden death in 1963 the only president in whom Americans have been able to take positive pride has been Reagan—and then during only part of his first term, following the 1981 assassination attempt.[9] Johnson bared his post-operative

---

responses to the question than in Americans'. Third, the fact that the American president is head of state as well as head of government undoubtedly has the effect of boosting all presidents' average ratings as compared with those of British prime ministers. For example, the highest average rating for any postwar British prime minister between Clement Attlee and John Major—that of Sir Anthony Eden (1955–57)—was only 55 percent compared with an American high—that of John F. Kennedy (1961–63)—of 70 percent. (The British figures have been calculated from British Gallup Poll data.)

[9] Again it is a pity that relevant survey data are not available for an extended time period. The American Gallup Poll in 1993 began to ask American citizens whether they thought

scar for the cameras and deceived the American people over Vietnam. Nixon was to all intents and purposes a criminal. Ford and Carter were, in their different ways, mediocrities. Reagan's integrity, as well as his attention to detail, were called into question by Iran-Contra. Bush was another mediocrity and broke his "Read my lips" pledge. Clinton is a philanderer and self-confessed liar with question marks hanging over his pre-presidential financial dealings. It seems doubtful whether most Americans would welcome the carving of any of these men's portraits on Mount Rushmore. The contrast between them and men like Roosevelt and Eisenhower (though not Truman) could hardly be more vivid.

In short, a major reason for declining trust in government in the United States since the 1960s has almost certainly been that a significant proportion of those at the head of the government have proved untrustworthy. They have cumulatively deprived the American presidency of much of its dignity. There is no evidence of a comparable decline in the quality of national leadership in any other democratic country (even in Italy and Japan).

INCOMPREHENSIBILITY

The factor just mentioned is probably the main one, but two others may also have played a contributory role. In connection with both factors, no hard data relating to the United States, let alone to other democratic countries, are available. The following observations should therefore be regarded as no more than hypotheses. But they do seem plausible ones.

The first is that the American people have lost confidence in their government and come to distrust it partly because they have ceased to understand it. It has become largely incomprehensible to them. Other things being equal, most of us are liable to distrust most that which we understand least, and since the 1960s the American political system has almost certainly spun well beyond the comprehension of all but a tiny minority of American citizens. Things happen in Washington, but most of what goes on in that remote city makes no sense at all to the overwhelming majority of people, who live their mental and emotional lives outside the Beltway. Small wonder that they shrug their shoulders and turn away, often in disgust.

It should be made clear that what is being referred to here is not what

---

the phrase "honest and trustworthy" did or did not apply to Bill Clinton. When the question was first asked, in April 1993, only 35 percent of people thought that it did not. In the immediate aftermath of Clinton's confession that he had had an "inappropriate" relationship with a White House intern, Monica Lewinsky, the proportion of respondents who thought the phrase "honest and trustworthy" did not apply to Bill Clinton was 67 percent (data supplied by the Gallup Organization). Nixon might well have fared even worse.

government *does*, the outputs of government, but rather the system of government, the institutions, procedures, and arrangements that produce the outputs. It is not to America's space program, for instance, which is as intelligible (or unintelligible) as it ever was, but to the congeries of institutions—the president, the National Aeronautics and Space Administration, the National Science Foundation, the Department of Defense, the Department of Energy, the House of Representatives Science Committee, the House of Representatives Space and Aeronautics Subcommittee, the Senate Commerce, Space, and Transportation Committee, the Senate Science, Technology, and Space Subcommittee, the Appropriations Committees in both houses, and both houses' Veterans Affairs, HUD, and Independent Agencies Subcommittees (to name but a few)— whose activities and interactions result in there being a space program.

The American political system was probably hard for most ordinary people to understand when it was first designed in the 1780s. Alexander Hamilton himself acknowledged in *Federalist* no. 82 (Madison, Hamilton, and Jay 1961, 491) that the new system proposed by the Philadelphia Convention originated many "questions of intricacy and nicety." These intricate and nice questions concerned the relations between the federal government and the state governments, between the president and Congress, between the House of Representatives and the Senate, between the executive and legislative branches of the federal government, between the federal courts and the state courts (the principal subject of *Federalist* no. 82), and so forth. Practicing politicians and political theorists designed the Constitution. One wonders how many other people really understood it, even in the 1780s.

The system became, if anything, a little simpler during the nineteenth century, with the rise of relatively strong national parties, which were able to provide ordinary voters with intelligible slogans and cues, and the nineteenth-century system survived more or less intact until well into the twentieth century. If anything, it became simpler still, with the rise to national prominence of the presidency, another institution to which ordinary voters could relate. Even so, and even during this period of the American system's relative simplicity, there must still have been millions of Americans who had difficulty understanding it.[10]

---

[10] One unobtrusive measure of the complexity of the American political system is the rise and the rapid growth of the political science profession in the United States. Political science, as that term is now understood, began in the United States, and in the 1990s there are probably as many political scientists in the United States as in the rest of the world combined. It is hard not to believe that political science's prodigious scale in the United States does not owe at least something to the enormous complexity of the principal object that American political scientists have available for study (though there are other reasons, of course).

If, however, the political system in the United States was already complicated by the middle of the twentieth century, it has become even more
complicated since then. The presidency has become almost a fourth
branch of government. Administrative agencies and regulatory commissions have proliferated (to the dismay of the business community). Lawyers and the courts have come to play an increasingly active role. Congress, with its pullulating committees, subcommittees, and staff agencies,
has become even more fragmented than the Founding Fathers meant it
to be. Not least, the national political parties, the cement that once
helped to bind the whole system together, have largely lost that capacity.

Moreover, and significantly, two of the most striking developments
rendering the American system more complex and therefore harder to
understand date from the late 1960s and early 1970s, the very period
during which distrust of government in the United States began to set in.
One was the spread of presidential primaries, which had the effect of
greatly prolonging the presidential nominating process and of greatly increasing the number of candidates involved. After the spread of primaries
what for most voters had once been a simple choice between Truman
and Dewey or Eisenhower and Stevenson became an altogether more
complicated—and almost certainly baffling—affair. On the Democratic
side the number of presidential primaries more than doubled between
1968 and 1992, rising from 17 to 40. On the Republican side the figures
were virtually identical (Stanley and Niemi 1994, 148). The spread of
primaries and candidate-centered campaigning had the further effect of
reducing the political parties' capacity to provide American voters with
meaningful symbols and cues. In the minds of voters the parties once
brought order out of chaos. Their ability to do that is now substantially
reduced.

The other post-1960s development that has made the American system more complicated and therefore harder to understand is the rise of
divided government, with different parties controlling the presidency and
either the House of Representatives, the Senate, or both. During the
three decades before 1968, the United States experienced divided government for a total of only eight years. During the three decades after
1968, the United States did *not* experience divided government for a
total of only six years. Divided government has one consequence so obvious that it can be easy to overlook: it makes the simple question
"Who's in charge?" much harder to answer. Using data from the National Election Study, Bennett and Bennett (1993) have shown that millions of Americans have no idea who is in charge. In 1990, for example,
52 percent of the National Election Study sample did not know which
political party had controlled the House of Representatives prior to that
year's congressional elections (even though the same party, the Demo-

crats, had been in control of the House for the whole of the previous 35 years and still were), and 59 percent did not know which party had controlled the Senate. Ignorance and incomprehension on this scale seem bound to fuel distrust.[11]

Two additional points are worth making in this connection. The first is that, while all democratic systems are complicated, few are remotely as complicated as the American. Most European systems, as well as the Japanese, focus on the executive rather than the legislature. In only a few do the courts play a significant role. Very few European systems are federal (though the German has been since the war and the French and the Italian now contain quasi-federal elements). Perhaps most important of all, the European democracies still boast strong political parties, parties that are still capable, as America's parties once were, of giving voters some guidance through the political maze. To be sure, most European voters would probably have trouble passing anything more demanding than a basic civics test, but they probably still have some grasp of how their country's political system works. It is doubtful whether many Americans have.

The second point is closely related to the first. Precisely because they have strong political parties and legislatures that are not detached from the executive, most European systems provide their citizens with at least a modicum of electoral accountability. If the voters are minded to "throw the rascals out," they at least know who the rascals are and how they can be thrown out. To take an admittedly extreme case, the majority of British voters in 1997 wanted to throw the rascals out; they knew who the rascals were, John Major and the Conservatives; and all they had to do was go to the polls and vote Labour (which they did, in large numbers).

[11] Interestingly, American voters turned out to be much better informed when the same questions were asked in 1996. In that year, according to the National Election Study, 75 percent of respondents knew that the Republicans had controlled the House of Representatives before the November elections; only 9.5 percent said they thought the Democrats had been in control. An additional 15.5 percent admitted they did not know who had been in control. The fact that the proportion giving the correct answer was higher in 1996 than in 1990 probably owes a great deal to the well-publicized disputes that took place in 1996 between President Clinton and the Republican-controlled Congress. A majority of voters knew who the two parties to the disputes were, but that did not, of course, enable them to answer any better the question "Who's in charge?" Moreover, to the 9.5 percent who thought the Democrats had controlled the House before the elections and the 15.5 percent who did not know probably needs to be added another 9.5 percent or so of people who, because there are only two major political parties in the United States, simply guessed right. If that calculation is made, the proportion of respondents who were truly well informed falls to about 65 percent. The figures for the Senate in 1996 were broadly similar. Further evidence of many Americans' limited knowledge of their own political system is provided by Delli Carpini and Keeter (1996, 70–71). For example, they cite a 1991 survey that found that only 25 percent of respondents knew the length of a U.S. senator's term.

German voters were confronted with almost as simple a choice when they elected Gerhard Schröder and the SPD in the following year.

But American voters are seldom offered choices that are anything like so straightforward, especially in an age when weak parties and divided government make the pinpointing of responsibility in the United States almost impossible. Clinton was elected in 1992 on a platform that included a commitment to introducing universal national health insurance. He signally failed to do so. But who was to blame? The president? His wife? The Republicans in Congress? Conservative Democrats in Congress? The private health insurance lobby? Even the experts cannot agree on the answers to these questions; no wonder ordinary voters are baffled. It can only be speculation, but it would be surprising if the high levels of distrust in government in modern America did not owe something to this quite awesome deficit of accountability.

POLARIZATION AND THE DECLINE OF COMITY

The other factor that has probably contributed to the decline in trust and confidence in the United States in recent years is the increased polarization of political conflict in America and the corresponding decline in the good humor, good manners, and general civility of American politicians (Dionne 1991). In the late 1990s there were signs that a new "era of good feelings" might be about to dawn; but, if that was so, it was only because of American voters' negative response to the era of bad feelings that immediately preceded it.

Although Americans may not have noticed it, politics in Europe nowadays tends to be rather humdrum and ordinary, even a little gray. The end of the Cold War and the sidelining of the once-powerful French and Italian Communist parties have virtually put an end to ideological conflict, and, at least in Western Europe, serious nationalist and religious conflicts are to be found only in Belgium, Northern Ireland, and the Basque country of Spain. The politicians in their little worlds are frequently excited, but the majority of citizens seldom are. This tranquillity is reflected in the way most European political leaders and parties campaign. Election campaigns in Europe are vigorous and hard fought, but they also tend to be relatively low key and decorous. Personal attacks are rare. Indeed, politics in general in Europe is usually conducted with considerable civility, partly, though not only, because most European governments are coalition governments, and people who are political opponents today know they may be coalition partners tomorrow.

Although American politics has always tended to be more rumbustious in style than European, it has only intermittently been ideologically polarized, and it is probably fair to say that for most of the postwar period there were quite high levels of comity in the American system, with personal friendships extending across party lines, with the party lines themselves remaining blurred and with personal rivalries and antagonisms kept mostly within bounds. Some of the Republican denunciations of Truman were savage, and the McCarthy period had a temporary polarizing effect, but until the 1980s politicians in the United States seemed to obey a tacit set of Queensbury Rules, toning down their rhetoric and limiting their conflict. Their obedience to the rules probably owed something to the fact that, while the personal stakes in American politics were often high, the ideological stakes seldom were. Most American politicians, like most American voters, held centrist opinions.

Now all that has changed (whether permanently or not it is too early to say). King (1997) has shown in detail how, over the past three decades, the central ideological tendency in the Democratic Party has become more liberal while that of the Republican Party has become more conservative, but with the bulk of American voters remaining steadfastly in the center, where they have always been. As the extreme views of activists and primary voters have led both major parties to take up positions remote from voters', large numbers of Americans have come to feel left out as well as let down. "It is not simply a question of which politicians are closer to you as much as how far away they are from your basic concerns," King writes (1997, 174). He remarks at another point (1997, 156) that "the public's mistrust of government is unlikely to be reversed unless and until politicians and their parties stage a concerted return to the sensible center. The politics of polarization *is* the politics of mistrust." The contrast with Europe is again striking. Albeit with exceptions (like the National Front and Jean Marie Le Pen in France), most European parties and politicians are now considerably more centrist, not less, than they were a generation ago.

With ideological polarization in the United States has come an intensification of partisan conflict and an altogether rougher and more uncouth political style, a style symbolized for more than a decade by the Georgia representative Newt Gingrich. This change in style has manifested itself in both the House of Representatives and the Senate—likened by Uslaner (1993, 5) to "day care centers in which colicky babies get their way by screaming at the top of their lungs"—and in the growth of negative political advertising. No one seems to have monitored the growth of negative advertising on television, but Ansolabehere and Iyengar (1995, 10) estimate that it accounts for roughly half of all political advertising. They are emphatic about its effects. "Our experimental data suggest," they report (1995, 105), "that the tone of political campaigning contributes mightily to the public's dwindling participation and growing cynicism." Those among their experimental subjects who were exposed to negative advertisements were significantly less likely than those exposed to positive advertisements to express confidence in the political process as a whole (1995, 104). The effect is what one would expect. If bankers spent half their time inveighing against other bankers, a crisis of confidence in the whole banking system might be expected to follow. There has, as yet, been no comparable development of negative campaigning in Europe.

CONCLUSION

This chapter has identified a number of factors that may help to explain why Americans, more than Europeans and Japanese, have lost confidence in government over the past three decades. Two of the factors—Americans' long-standing suspicion of government and the failure of the federal government to establish a large and supportive constituency for itself— were identified as predisposing factors. Distrust of government, it was argued, is always latent in the United States, far more than elsewhere.

The chapter went on to identify three further factors that would seem to have activated this latent distrust and intensified it over the past three decades: the lack of dignity and honesty of many recent American presidents (especially against the background of most Americans' high expectations of their "chief magistrates"); the increased complexity, opacity, and unintelligibility of the political system to large numbers of ordinary American citizens; and the polarization and loss of comity that have taken place among the American political elite. None of these developments has a close analogue in the other advanced industrial democracies.

It is worth noting that all these factors—both the long- and the short-term—have one thing in common: they all relate in one way or another to politics and government. This chapter's task has been to explain why trust and confidence in government have declined in America in recent decades and why they have declined further and faster in the United States than in other countries. Because the phenomena to be explained concern politics and government, it seemed best to concentrate on factors that also concern politics and government; and because these factors, especially when taken together, seem more than adequate to explain the phenomena in question, there seems no need to go further. Other factors—having to do, for example, with more general declines in social trust or the role of the mass media—may well be in play, but if they are, they would seem to be mediated through opinions and sentiments that are more directly relevant to politics.

One mystery, however, remains. It is one thing to explain Americans' current distrust of government. It is quite another to account for the extreme intensity with which many Americans feel this distrust and to account for the fact that these extremely intense feelings—of anger, frustration, and betrayal—are directed to such a large extent at government, especially the federal government. For those looking for scapegoats, there are always large numbers of candidates available. Why pick on the U.S. government? A generation ago Hofstadter delivered a lecture entitled "The Paranoid Style in American Politics." American political life, he noted (1967, 3), has served again and again "as an arena for uncommonly angry minds." It certainly does so today. But the deep sources of that paranoia, and the reasons why the paranoids' delusions focus on the objects that they do, remain mysterious.

ACKNOWLEDGMENTS

For research assistance in connection with the writing of this chapter, I am grateful to Jack Kneeshaw. For their helpful comments on an initial draft, I am particularly grateful to Samuel P. Huntington, Peter J. Katzenstein, Susan J. Pharr, and Robert D. Putnam.

PART II

Sources of the Problem: Declining Capacity

FIVE

Interdependence and Democratic Legitimation

Fritz W. Scharpf

THE PREMISE of this volume is that Western democracies have in recent decades come to suffer a decline of popular trust or confidence in, or satisfaction with, the performance of their representative institutions, and that this decline needs to be taken seriously as a potential threat to the viability of democratic government (see Introduction, this volume). The terms used here also suggest that the volume starts from an implicit principal-agent model in which citizens-as-principals have grown dissatisfied with the performance of their political agents. If we assume that this is empirically true and that the change does reflect a deterioration of perceived performance rather than the increasing (or increasingly conflicting) expectations of citizen-principals, there are still two fundamentally different working hypotheses that one might advance. Growing dissatisfaction could be caused by a reduction in either the *fidelity* of agents—that is, their willingness to act in the interest of their principals—or the *capacity* of agents to achieve the outcomes expected by their principals. My chapter will focus on one particular type of constraint on capacity: growing international economic interdependence. I will not review the empirical evidence regarding changes in the levels of popular satisfaction except to note the high degree of variance among countries (Newton and Norris and also Katzenstein, this volume). Instead, I will examine the analytical and normative arguments that could link interdependence to citizen satisfaction and, ultimately, to democratic legitimacy. I will argue that one should indeed expect such links to exist, but that their effect on legitimacy is strongly mediated by the distinctive characteristics of national political discourse.

INTERDEPENDENCE AS A CHALLENGE TO DEMOCRATIC LEGITIMACY

From the Athenian city-state to the modern nation-state, democratic self-government has been defined by reference to the territorially based constituencies of local, regional, and national governments. There do exist democratically self-governing associations with a geographically dispersed membership—professional associations, labor unions, some clubs, and perhaps some nongovernmental organizations like Amnesty International or Greenpeace come to mind—but the authority that such associations can exercise over their membership is either very limited, essentially depending on voluntary compliance, or exercised "in the shadow of the state," on whose laws and enforcement machinery they must rely when voluntary compliance is not forthcoming. The monopoly of legitimate coercion, at any rate, on which the problem-solving capacity of democratic self-government continues to depend, has been achieved within territorially defined units alone.

However, if democratic self-government is defined by reference to territorial units, it must be vulnerable to increasing military, economic, technical, ecological, and communicative interdependence under which choices made by any one unit will create, and suffer from, external effects. Spillouts may reduce the effectiveness of domestic choices, and spill-ins may produce domestic outcomes that have not been chosen internally. In the following sections I will explore the reasons why the lack of congruence between the constituencies of democratic governments and the populations that are affected by their decisions poses a major problem for democratic legitimacy.

Input- and Output-Oriented Democratic Legitimacy

"Democracy" has a variety of meanings, but when we speak of "democratic legitimacy" we refer to arguments that justify the exercise of governing authority, that is, the authority to adopt collectively binding decisions and to implement these decisions with resources taken from the members of the collectivity and by resort to the state's monopoly on legitimate coercion. Legitimating arguments, then, must establish a moral duty to obey these collectively binding decisions even if they conflict with individual preferences.[1] In the modern era the concept of democracy has become the major foundation of such legitimating arguments. Its basic appeal was most succinctly expressed in Abraham Lincoln's Gettysburg Address by reference to the triple identity of the *governed* ("government of the people"), the *governors* ("government by the people"), and the *beneficiaries of government* ("government for the people"). But how does Lincoln's formula create a moral duty to obey government?

Leaving aside for the moment the first element, which defines the collectivity that is to be self-governing ("government of the people"), the formula points to two analytically distinct dimensions of democratic legitimation, one input-oriented, the other output-oriented (Scharpf

---

[1] The presumption, of course, is that governments that lack legitimacy and rely purely on the exercise or threat of superior force will achieve only low levels of governing efficiency.

1970). On the input side, "government by the people" implies that collectively binding decisions should derive from the authentic expression of the preferences of the constituency in question. Legitimate government, in other words, is *self*-government, and compliance can be expected because laws are self-determined rather than imposed exogenously. On the output side, "government for the people" implies that collectively binding decisions should serve the common interests of the constituency. Obedience is justified because collective fate control is increased when government can be employed to deal with those problems that members of the collectivity cannot solve individually through market interactions or voluntary cooperation.

However, by using a singular term for the plural originators and beneficiaries of democratic government, both of Lincoln's criteria avoid the critical question of how the exercise of governing authority and the duty to obey its commands should be legitimated if "the people" is not an organic unity or an aggregate of homogeneous individuals but an association of individuals and groups whose preferences may diverge and whose interests may conflict. From a purely input-oriented perspective, there are two possible solutions to this problem. The first postulates that government should be consensual, based on the widest possible agreement among the individuals and groups affected; the second justifies decisions based on the expressed preferences of a majority of the membership (Lijphart 1984, 1991).

From an input perspective, consensual democracy has first-rate credentials, resting ultimately on the Roman law maxim of *volenti non fit iniuria* (i.e., if you have consented, you cannot claim damages). Its weakness lies on the output side: in the face of divergent or conflicting preferences, the search for consensus may prevent the adoption of any effective solution. Thus, output-oriented concepts tend to favor majoritarian democracy because of its greater problem-solving efficiency (Buchanan and Tullock 1962), but they must then face the problem of assuring that majoritarian policies will indeed serve the public interest. I will return to that point shortly.

To justify majority rule from a purely input-oriented perspective is more demanding than is often assumed.[2] As I have tried to show else-

---

[2] The general assumption is well stated by Michael Greven, who postulates: "The crucial idea from which the legitimacy of government in democracies derives is the possibility of participation by all citizens, based on the mutual recognition of their civic and political equality. . . . Precisely because and if this is true, democratic theory implies that the outcome of political will-formation has a claim to recognition and legitimacy even among those whose arguments failed in the discussion and whose preferences were defeated in a vote" (Greven 1998, 480; my translation). But why should the mere opportunity to participate on an equal basis have the force of legitimacy? At bottom, the argument seems to rest

where (Scharpf 1997a, ch. 7), it must ultimately presuppose that the preferences of the majority will somehow include the welfare of the minority—an assumption that rules out both hostile majorities (e.g., Nazi Germany or Bosnia) and the bloody-minded pursuit of rational self-interest. At bottom, therefore, notions of democracy that rely exclusively on the "will of the people" as a source of political legitimacy must assume the existence of a strong collective identity and a pervasive sense of common fate that will override divergent preferences and interests. Only if these Rousseauan assumptions are fulfilled is it possible to treat the preferences of the majority as a true expression of the *volonté générale* that the minority would be wrong to oppose.

In light of the totalitarian potential of the Rousseauan tradition (Talmon 1955) and of pervasive misgivings about the cognitive and normative shortcomings of "populist democracy" (Sartori 1965; Riker 1982), modern democratic theory rarely derives legitimacy primarily from the belief that "the people can do no wrong." Where input elements dominate, theorists take care to restrict the domain of "participative democracy" to the microlevel of local or shopfloor decisions (Lindner 1990) to emphasize procedural safeguards against the dangers of "direct democracy" (Luthardt 1994) or to insist that policy inputs should arise from public debates that have the qualities of truth-oriented deliberations and discourses (Manin 1987; Dryzek 1990; Schmalz-Bruns 1995; Habermas 1996). In effect, the ideal of "deliberative democracy" links input- and output-oriented arguments by insisting on specific input procedures that will favor qualitatively acceptable outputs by regulating "the flow of discursive option- and will-formation in such a way that their fallible results enjoy the presumption of being reasonable" (Habermas 1996, 301). I will return to this point below.

In any case, input-oriented justifications of majority rule are everywhere complemented by output-oriented criteria with a negative and a positive thrust. In addition to requiring that governments achieve effective solutions to collective-action problems, output-oriented criteria must also specify what governments should *not* be allowed to do if they are to be considered "government for the people." The emphasis here is on institutional arrangements that are meant to protect against the danger that the governing power of the majority will be used to the detriment of minorities or individuals, and to assure that these powers will be used only to further the common interests of the constituency rather than the

---

on the assumption that you have no reason to complain if you have fought and lost in a fair fight. Under the conditions of modern mass democracies, this logic may indeed be relevant for political candidates, but it is harder to see why it should persuade individual citizens.

special interests of officeholders and their clienteles. These institutional arrangements include constitutional guarantees of individual rights, an independent judiciary, and checks and balances as well as the mechanisms of representative democracy, which provide opportunities for public debate, reflection, and criticism that are thought to discriminate against self-serving policy choices (Habermas 1962; Elster 1986) and that also attempt to ensure the accountability of office-holders to the electorate.[3]

Countries differ greatly in the extent to which their institutions emphasize the negative requirements of output-oriented legitimacy by creating vetoes and electoral vulnerabilities that make it more difficult to coordinate and employ the policy resources available to government as a whole in the pursuit of coherent and effective policy choices (Tsebelis 1995). The differences between, say, the concentration of power in the British "Westminster Model" and the dispersion of power in the present German constitution (with coalition governments, an opposition veto in the federal chamber, an activist constitutional court, and an independent central bank) are rooted in historical experiences and path-dependent courses of institutional evolution, and there is no reason to expect convergence (Pierson 1997).

By contrast, regarding the positive dimension of problem-solving effectiveness, democratic theory has generally built on the foundations of the sovereign "Westphalian" state. It is taken for granted that the democratic state, like its absolutist predecessor, is potentially omnipotent within its own territory and able to control its borders. There are physical constraints on internally available resources, of course, and boundaries may be violated by outsiders, but within these limits, the democratic state is as capable as its nondemocratic predecessors and competitors of taxing its residents, regulating their actions with the force of law, requisitioning their property and services, and requiring them to risk their lives in its defense. Any limits on these capabilities are thought to be self-imposed, whether by constitutional norm or political choice. In principle, then, the state has the means to achieve all normatively and constitutionally acceptable domestic purposes, and governors are held accountable for failing to do so.

---

[3] Representation and accountability based on general elections have been thought to counteract the dangers of self-interested majorities since the Federalist Papers (Cooke 1961). The argument can be restated in rational-choice terms if it is first assumed that, for any individual voter, voting is a "low-cost decision" (Kirchgässner 1992), meaning that the probable effect on individual self-interest is so low that it is reasonable to think that at least some voters will be motivated by public-interest considerations (Brennan 1989). If that is granted, the anticipation of a public-interest-oriented swing vote creates strong incentives for office-holders to select policies that can be publicly defended as serving common rather than special interests (Scharpf 1997a, ch. 8).

Interdependence and the Loss of Congruence

If this now seems an unrealistic ideal in light of growing international interdependence, it is one that was closely approximated in the recent past. In the first three decades following the Great Depression and the Second World War, Western democracies finally learned to control the cyclical crises of their economies, and they were able to meet the aspirations of their citizens with full employment, growing incomes, rising levels of education, reduced inequality, and enhanced social security in times of unemployment, sickness, and old age. It is only now realized, however, to what extent this "Great Transformation" (Polanyi 1957) depended on the fact that, after the rampant protectionism of the 1930s and the Second World War, capitalist democracies were for a time able to control their economic boundaries. Goods and services that did not conform to domestic regulations or threatened the survival of domestic producers could be excluded, capital outflows could be prevented, and immigration was tightly controlled. Under these conditions, nations could choose among a wide range of options, and while the Scandinavian welfare states differed greatly from the German social-market economy or post–New Deal America, all were equally viable economically and legitimated by broad political support.

During these golden decades, interdependence increased only slowly under an American-led international regime of "embedded liberalism" (Ruggie 1982), and pre-1914 levels of international integration in product and capital markets were not surpassed until the 1980s (Hirst and Thompson 1995; Bairoch 1997).[4] In the meantime, however, the nation-state has once again lost control over its economic boundaries. This is most obvious within the European Union, where the completion of the unified market for goods, services, and capital has now been topped off by monetary union. Beyond Europe repeated rounds of GATT and WTO negotiations have drastically reduced tariff and nontariff barriers to trade in goods and services, and the explosive increase of transnational money flows has eliminated any chance of protecting national capital markets.

Consumers are thus free to buy goods and services regardless of their national origin; firms are free to produce anywhere without endangering

---

[4] These data are often cited to suggest that, because "globalization" is nothing new, there is no reason to be concerned about its political impact. But that argument forgets that international capitalism before 1914 and again in the 1920s was characterized by deep economic crises. Before 1914 political democracy was underdeveloped in most countries, and the level of political aspirations—and hence the potential impact of economic performance on political trust—was much lower than it is now. In the interwar period, however, the crises of international capitalism had serious, and in the case of Germany catastrophic, consequences for the viability of democracy.

access to their home market; capital is free to take advantage of profitable opportunities for investment or speculation around the globe and around the clock; and workers are free to choose where they work, at least within the European Union. Because they are held accountable for the economic and social welfare of their constituents, however, governments must be concerned about the potential loss of jobs when demand for locally produced goods and services declines, firms relocate production to other countries, capital owners prefer the investment opportunities offered elsewhere, high-skilled workers emigrate, and taxpayers or their taxable resources leave the nation.

The Impact of Regulatory Competition

Because of the mobility of economic actors and factors, there is now a much greater degree of interdependence not only among the formerly compartmentalized national economies, but also among national policy choices that affect the economy. If one government cuts its social security contributions, that reduces the competitiveness of products from countries that have not done so, and if one country cuts its rate of corporate taxation, that creates incentives for firms to relocate. Thus, it is wrong to think that only firms are in competition with each other. Under economic interdependence, nation-states find themselves competing for market shares, investment capital, and taxable revenues, and that competition constrains their choices among macroeconomic, regulatory, and tax policy options.

From the perspective of democratic legitimacy, therefore, economic interdependence raises two problems. On the one hand, the growing importance of external effects undermines the congruence between "the people" who are being governed and "the people" who are supposed to govern. Choices that may be legitimated in one country (e.g., the interest-rate policy of the German Bundesbank) may have a direct impact on the economy of another country (e.g., unemployment in France) in which this choice was not, and would not be, democratically legitimated. In effect, this reduces the ability of all governments to achieve the purposes that are salient for their citizens. On the other hand, the competition for mobile factors of production and taxable assets imposes a redistributive bias on national policies that shifts burdens from mobile actors and the owners of mobile assets onto immobile actors and the owners of immobile assets. Again, there is no reason to expect that these policy shifts would necessarily be legitimated by corresponding shifts in the authentic preferences of citizens in the competing countries.

Both of these changes are widely interpreted on the normative level as a loss of democratic legitimacy, and on the empirical level they may generate dissatisfaction with the government of the day and perhaps a more general disaffection with the democratic political system as such that would be reflected in political abstention, alienation, or growing support for system-critical movements and radical political parties. Increasing economic interdependence is thus thought likely to generate problems for democratic legitimacy on the national level. Before I examine this conclusion more closely, it is necessary to examine whether international or supranational solutions might avoid, or at least alleviate, the problems faced on the national level.

SUPRANATIONAL REMEDIES?

If territorially limited government is considered ineffective in the output dimension as well as unresponsive in the input dimension, territorial enlargement and functional centralization would seem to address the problems of interdependence. This, at any rate, is the standard prescription of fiscal federalism (Oates 1977); it is the logic behind the long-standing recommendation to overcome the deficiencies of joint decision-making in German federalism by merging several *Länder* to create larger units with fewer externalities (Scharpf 1988); and it is, of course, the logic driving European political integration.

Centralization is generally justified in output-oriented terms, but that is plausible only if it is also assumed that decisions at the higher level are taken under majoritarian or hierarchical rules and cannot be blocked by constituent governments. By contrast, from an input-oriented perspective, centralization appears problematic even within the nation-state, where a central government acts with clear democratic legitimacy. If citizen preferences differ but policies must be uniform, centralization will necessarily reduce the goodness of fit between preferences and policies (Buchanan and Tullock 1962, ch. 6).[5] It is at the supranational level, however, at which the centralizing solutions that are justified by output-oriented arguments become truly problematic. In the following sections I will discuss these problems by reference to the European Union.

---

[5] Both the assumption and the conclusion can be questioned. In the Jacobin tradition of French democracy, centralization is considered desirable precisely because it imposes uniformity and hence civic equality (V. Schmidt 1990). Conversely, centrally imposed policies might at least in theory provide for differentiated solutions that would fit the differing conditions or preferences of subgroups or regions within the larger constituency or territory. One example is the Spanish constitution, which grants differing degrees of autonomy to different regional units. In general, however, the empirical association between centralization and uniformity seems to be quite strong.

The Preconditions of Majority Rule

Governing systems that can overrule dissenting interests need to be legitimated, and before it is meaningful to talk about either input- or output-oriented arguments with regard to the European Union, it is necessary to discuss a precondition that is usually taken for granted in a national context: the definition of the constituency that is to be governed by majority rule. In Lincoln's triad this is "government of the people" that I skipped above and that Giovanni Sartori (1965, 26) found to pose "insoluble problems of interpretation." The difficulties are well illustrated by countries in which ethnic, linguistic, or religious divisions seem to undermine the legitimacy of majority rule (e.g., Canada, Belgium, the former Czechoslovakia, Bosnia). In other countries cleavages of a similar nature do not have nearly the same delegitimating effects (e.g., Switzerland, the Netherlands, the United States). Regardless of the main criterion of sameness or difference, it seems obvious that a "we-identity" (Elias 1987) that is shared by the members of the community is a logically necessary precondition of democratic legitimacy.

On the input side we-identity is necessary to justify "my trust in the benevolence (and perhaps even solidarity) of my fellow citizens" (Offe 1998, 17), which implies that the welfare of the minority must also be included in the preference function of the majority. On the output side we-identity is necessary to define membership in the community whose common interests are thought to justify governmental action even if it should entail individual sacrifices. In neither dimension is it possible to name a single set of necessary and sufficient criteria for what constitutes an effective we-identity; common language, culture, religion, history, and institutions play important but varying roles. There is also no reason to assume that only one specific type of group can be invested with a collective identity. Individuals may identify with different frames of reference— religious, partisan, territorial, local, regional, national, European, and so on—in different contexts or for different reasons. Moreover, collective identifications may differ greatly in their intensities and thus may legitimate rather different levels of sacrifices and involuntary redistribution.

Although the willingness to accept sacrifices for the purpose of solidaristic redistribution seems remarkably high at the level of established nation-states (Hicks and Swank 1992), it also seems clear that no political unit above the national level has as yet developed a we-identity of comparable intensity. This is true even of the European Union, which has gone further than any other supranational or international organization toward establishing institutions that resemble those of constitutional democracies on the national level. But even if further institutional reforms invested the directly elected European Parliament with the full range of competencies of a national parliament, there is no reason to think that its majority decisions could legitimate heavy sacrifices imposed on a dissenting minority. As Joseph Weiler (1996, 523) succinctly observed, "Democracy does not exist in a vacuum. It is premised on the existence of a polity with members—the Demos—by whom and for whom democratic discourse with its many variants takes place. The authority and legitimacy of a majority to compel a minority exists only within political boundaries defined by a Demos. Simply put, if there is no Demos, there can be no operating democracy." To drive the point home, Weiler constructs a counterfactual:

> Imagine an *Anschluss* between Germany and Denmark. Try and tell the Danes that they should not worry, since they will have full representation in the Bundestag. Their shrieks of grief will be shrill not simply because they will be condemned, as Danes, to permanent minorityship (that may be true of the German Greens too), but because the way nationality, in this way of thinking, enmeshes with democracy is that even majority rule is only legitimate within a Demos, when Danes rule Danes.

Turning to Europe, he concludes that "it is a matter of empirical observation that there is no European Demos not a people, not a nation."

It is hard to deny this conclusion, and with each territorial expansion the hope that the multiple peoples of Europe will soon develop a common political identity and a common space of political communication has receded further into the future. This is not meant to discourage efforts that could advance political integration.[6] For the time being, though, the European Union cannot yet rely on the foundation of a collective identity strong enough to legitimate majority rule.

The Limits of Supranational Legitimacy

If Europe has yet to meet the preconditions of a majoritarian democracy, that severely limits its capability to act in the face of politically salient disagreements. The European Union is now relying for the legitimation of its policy outputs on a combination of hierarchical and consensual

---

[6] Jacques Delors recently made a plausible proposal. It would require European parties to nominate their own candidates for the office of president of the European Commission in European elections. This would not only force governments to nominate the winning candidate for confirmation by the European Parliament, but it would also focus public attention in all member states on the competition for a highly visible European office, and it would put European issues on the agenda of the European election campaign, which has been dominated by purely national concerns. Although this option could be realized without revising the treaties, European parties have yet to respond.

decision-making processes. Hierarchical authority is most clearly exemplified by the European Central Bank (ECB), which, under the rules adopted in the Maastricht Treaty, was designed to be even more independent of political pressure and accountability than the German Bundesbank, which it will replace as the author of monetary policy for the members of the European Monetary Union. But whereas the formal independence of the ECB and the scope of its hierarchical authority were legitimated by the explicit and highly politicized decisions of national governments and parliaments, much less political attention has been paid to the expansion of the authority of the European Court of Justice (Weiler 1982). Nevertheless, the authority of the Court, together with the active use of independent enforcement powers granted to the European Commission, has been used to define and enlarge the reach of "negative integration," that is, the laws that restrict the capacity of national governments to interfere with the free movement of goods, services, labor, and capital throughout the internal European market (Scharpf 1996). The most important extension of authority was achieved through the application of European competition law to formerly protected services like telecommunications, air, road, and rail transport, and energy supply, which had been exempted from full competition in practically all European countries (S. Schmidt 1998). Even though this step might have strained the authority of the law to its limits, the legitimacy of judicial law-making has not been seriously undermined.[7]

By contrast, European processes of "positive integration," or active regulation of the economy, depend on broad political agreement. Admittedly this cannot be equated with the classical model of intergovernmental negotiations. The European Parliament is rapidly approaching the point at which its veto cannot be overruled in most important fields of European legislation, and the practical importance of the European Commission's monopoly on legislative initiative (in addition to its unilateral enforcement powers) can hardly be overestimated. Nevertheless, the approval of national governments represented in the Council of Ministers is ultimately decisive for the adoption of European legislation, and even though decisions by qualified majority are possible in an increasing number of areas, the requirements are so steep that small groups of governments with similar interests cannot be overruled. Most Council decisions are adopted by broad consensus.

If European legislation thus avoids the threat to political legitimacy that would be posed if substantial interests could be overruled by self-

---

[7] In the face of growing political unease, however, the Court and the Commission themselves have recently become more sensitive to the limits of negative integration (Scharpf 1999).

interested majorities, one of two consequences is likely to follow: either policy choices are blocked by disagreements among national governments, or the burden of legitimating European policy solutions is shifted back to the member states. In either case, the outcome adds to the difficulties of democratic legitimation on the national level: either problem-solving deficits persist, or policies must be accepted that may not, on the input side, conform to the authentic preferences of national constituencies or that may not, on the output side, be optimal solutions when judged in terms of the national interest. Because there are, in fact, areas where EU policy-making is highly effective, and others where the problem-solving capacity of the Union is very low (Scharpf 1997b), both types of legitimacy problems must be dealt with on the national level. I will begin with an examination of the input-oriented problems that arise on the national level precisely because European policy-making does succeed in producing effective outputs.

INTERNATIONAL PROBLEM-SOLVING AND NATIONAL PREFERENCES

To clarify the implications of internationally agreed upon policies for national democracies, I will refer to a highly simplified model of intergovernmental negotiations (see Figure 5.1). Assume that three countries, A, B, and C, face a problem that none of them can solve nationally, but that can be solved by means of international cooperation among all three countries. Although all of them dislike the status quo (located at SQ = 0), each country prefers a different solution, located (in a unidimensional and interval-scaled utility space) at points A = 1, B = 3, and C = 5, respectively. Assume also that these "ideal points" are determined, *ex ante* and by means of strictly input-oriented procedures, by the citizens (i.e., the median voter) in each country. If we further assume that negotiators from each country are strictly bound by citizen preferences, it is clear that none of the cooperative solutions can win the agreement of all three countries and that the undesirable status quo will continue. Thus, if negotiations are to serve any purpose at all, the governments must be allowed to agree to solutions that diverge from the *ex ante* preferences of their citizens—provided that the solution chosen increases the welfare of the country (i.e., reduces the distance from the country's ideal point) in comparison with the status quo.

SQ = 0   A = 1   B = 3   C = 5

Figure 5.1. Negotiations in Single-Issue Space

If only the *ex ante* positions of each country are considered, the sole acceptable solution would be point A, which represents the lowest common denominator outcome. It satisfies the preferences of the most "conservative" country A and is still preferred to the status quo by B and C. However, the famous Coase Theorem tells us that negotiations could do better. In the absence of transaction costs, they should be able to achieve an overall welfare maximum (Coase 1960). If distances from each country's ideal point are interpreted as welfare losses, this welfare maximum (i.e., the minimum aggregate loss) is located at point B rather than at point A. But because that solution is less attractive to country A than the status quo, it needs to be bought off by side payments, say, one unit each from countries B and C, which they could well afford to pay from the gains that they would achieve if the agreed-on solution is point B rather than A.

So far, so good. For each country, this outcome is the best that it can reasonably expect to reach in a world in which solutions cannot be unilaterally imposed but depend on the voluntary agreement of all parties involved.[8] In that sense the output-oriented legitimacy of the negotiated outcome would be assured. But what about input-oriented legitimacy? To appreciate the difficulties here, it is useful to consider the preconditions for achieving Coasian outcomes in the real as distinguished from the model world.

In order to achieve the welfare-maximizing outcome, the parties must somehow overcome the "Negotiators' Dilemma" (Lax and Sebenius 1986; Scharpf 1997a, ch. 6) that arises from the simultaneous presence of common interests (in finding the best overall solution) and competi-

	SQ	A	B	C
Loss for A	-1	0	-2	-4
Loss for B	-3	-2	0	-2
Loss for C	-5	-4	-2	0
Joint Losses	-9	-6	-4	-6

Figure 5.2. Welfare Losses in Negotiated Agreements

[8] The negotiated solution would not necessarily be the one preferred by the median voter in a larger country because negotiations tend to equalize the bargaining powers of the participating countries regardless of differences in the size of their populations.

tive interests (in maximizing one's share). This implies that all aspects of the situation—available policy options, their likely effects, and all participants' valuations of these effects—would have to be transparent to all of the parties involved. In addition, the parties would need to agree on a normative rule for distributing the costs and benefits of cooperation. These are extremely demanding preconditions. They depend to a large degree on the development of mutual trust, or at least mutual understanding, among the negotiators.[9] If these preconditions are not met, the Negotiators' Dilemma will induce self-serving negotiating strategies that produce inferior outcomes or frustrate agreement altogether.

With regard to input-oriented legitimacy, this analysis seems to lead to two dismal conclusions. First, it is clear that negotiations cannot reach their optimal outcome (i.e., the outcome maximizing total welfare for the group of countries as a whole) without systematically departing from *ex ante* citizen preferences in most or all countries. Second, and more important for our purposes, the specific reasons for these departures cannot be fully communicated to the constituencies in each country. If mutual understanding and trust among negotiators is an essential precondition for negotiating optimal solutions, it follows that intergovernmental negotiations are unlikely to succeed in the glare of publicity, and if that is so, there will inevitably be a communication gap between the international and national levels of this two-level game (Putnam 1988).

It is this systematic gap that poses the most serious threat to democratic legitimacy. Where it exists the opposition in each country can claim not only that the outcome does not conform to *ex ante* citizen preferences, but also that the national interest was sold short by incompetent or disloyal negotiators.[10] To rebut this claim credibly, a government would have to argue that this was the best that could be obtained under the circumstances and disclose inside information about feasible options and its informed guesses about the true preferences and options of the other governments—none of which could be fully scrutinized and verified in public or parliamentary debates.

Moreover, given the difficulties of renegotiation, governments can no longer afford to be responsive to criticisms and suggestions raised in pub-

---

[9] The difficulties of reaching agreement are reduced, and the approximation of Coasian outcomes is facilitated, if negotiations are "embedded" in stable networks, and conditions can be further improved by means of institutional arrangements that increase transparency, provide for the good services of an "agenda setter," and generate mutual trust through the evolution of normative regimes (Scharpf 1997a, ch. 6).

[10] In the early years of the Federal Republic of Germany, when Konrad Adenauer had to defend the disappointing outcome of negotiations over the "occupation statute," he was attacked by the leader of the opposition as being "the chancellor of the Allies."

lic debate, even if agreements need to be approved by parliament or referenda. Instead, they must present each agreement as a fait accompli, a take-it-or-leave-it proposition whose rejection will cause the collapse of the international effort. In addition, given the joint responsibility of all negotiating governments, no single government can in truth be held accountable for the ultimate outcome.[11] Thus, intergovernmental negotiations disable the institutional mechanisms that link government action to the expressed preferences of constituents or to the scrutiny of parliaments, political parties, and public debate.[12]

The need to discipline domestic preference formation has always frustrated demands for a "democratic" foreign policy (except under hegemonic conditions when one government can impose its domestically generated preferences on external partners). What is new is that increasing transnational interdependence now inflicts the same compulsion on ever larger areas of what used to be purely domestic policy choices. In effect, then, the more policy choices move from the national level to the level of intergovernmental negotiations, the more the institutions designed to assure input-oriented influence and accountability lose their effectiveness.[13]

LEGITIMATE DEMOCRACY WITHOUT OMNIPOTENCE

We seem to confront a dilemma. As interdependence increases, the nation-state finds its range of policy options exogenously constrained, and some previously legitimated policies become less effective, more costly, or downright unfeasible—which must be counted as a loss of democratic self-determination even if new options are added to the policy repertoire. It is true, however, that constraints do not rule out choice, and it may be possible to achieve former (or newly agreed upon) policy objectives by means of new policy instruments (Scharpf 1999). In that event output-oriented legitimacy may be maintained, but the new policy instruments must be adopted either through domestic processes that are extremely sensitive to international constraints or through international negotiations. Either way, the increase in output effectiveness seems to carry a high price in terms of input-oriented legitimacy.

---

[11] Exactly the same criticism is directed at interstate and federal-state negotiations in the joint-decision system of German federalism (Scharpf 1988).

[12] The same argument, without democratic-theory pretensions, supports the proposition that European integration is strengthening national governments in relation to other national and subnational political actors (Moravcsik 1993, 1994).

[13] For an early recognition of the problem, see Kaiser (1971).

The Inevitable Corruption of Input-Oriented Legitimacy?

On the input side the growing importance of external economic and institutional constraints directly challenges conventional notions of popular sovereignty and expectations that governments should carry out the "will of the people." Governments must increasingly avoid policy choices that would be both domestically popular and economically feasible out of respect for GATT rules and European law or as a result of decisions made by the WTO, the European Commission, or the European Court of Justice. Other policy choices that would be both legally permissible and domestically popular must be ruled out because they could have disastrous consequences for the international competitiveness of national producers, the confidence of investors, or the stability of the national currency.

In addition, as external legal and economic constraints multiply under conditions of growing international interdependence, the role of experts and specialized knowledge will increase to an extent that may render the role of authentic but untutored popular preferences practically insignificant. This is all the more true if solutions must be achieved by means of international negotiations. In short, citizens' approval is becoming ever less sufficient for assuring, or even for justifying, policy choices, so input-oriented legitimating arguments will become less plausible, and national governments must increasingly depend on output-oriented legitimation alone.

This is already happening. As more and more domestic policy areas have become internationally interdependent, governments are ever more tempted to rely on the argument that foreign policy should override domestic political considerations to immunize policies with an international dimension against the demands and criticisms of domestic public opinion, political parties, parliaments, and other democratic input processes. To the extent that they succeed, legitimating arguments take on a paternalistic and technocratic character, asserting that under difficult circumstances and in a dangerous environment, any demands for more direct participation and control would only make the government's difficult job even more difficult. When that argument is accepted, partisan controversies and political attention at the national level are likely to be diverted in two directions: toward personalities and scandals on the one hand, and policy outcomes (rather than policy choices) on the other hand. Elections will revolve around either candidates and their personal qualities and deficiencies or the performance of the stock market, the level of unemployment, the rate of inflation, the size of the public-sector deficit, or even natural disasters like floods and earthquakes, without regard for whether the government was in fact responsible for these outcomes. In

other words, input-oriented politics in general, and political accountability in particular, will lose their connection to, and their disciplining
effect on, policy choices.

Toward Internationally Embedded Policy Discourses?

Can it be otherwise? A positive answer requires a reconsideration of the
role that input-oriented mechanisms can and should play in the democratic process. I begin by returning to the discussion of intergovernmental negotiations. The objections made above from an input-oriented direction are compelling only when they are raised against negotiated
solutions for problems that could just as well have been dealt with at the
national level. In German federalism we have indeed identified instances
in which the practice of joint decision-making went far beyond the "objective" need for coordination in the face of interdependency (Scharpf
1988), and the same may be true in some European policy areas as well.
But as economic interdependency increases, these instances will become
rarer, and the input-oriented critique of intergovernmental negotiations
will be weakened. As for problems that cannot be solved within the
boundaries and means of the nation-state, the relevant criterion for judging solutions cannot be conformity to the particularistic preferences of
citizens of that state. Any country that is not a hegemon must also consider the interests of necessary partners in a cooperative solution. Preferences formulated within a national frame of reference are relevant for
defining the "ideal points" of a country's negotiators, but it is not reasonable to expect that negotiated outcomes should conform to these national aspirations. Instead, the most for which one can legitimately ask
within a national frame of reference is that the outcome be better than
the "best alternative to the negotiated agreement" (BATNA), and that it
approach nationally defined aspirations as closely as possible, given bargaining conditions and the BATNA positions of the other countries.

This implies that democratic theory can no longer treat popular preferences as exogenously given. To be normatively relevant, they must relate
to policy outcomes that are feasible within the international context
in which the choice must be made. Thus, "democratic decisionism"
(Greven 1998) and the assumption of omnipotence associated with popular sovereignty are no longer theoretically viable options. Within the
context of input-oriented theories, these requirements are met by concepts of "discursive" or "deliberative democracy," which insist on procedures of "will-formation" that are supposed to lead to "reasonable"
conclusions (Habermas 1996). In trying to avoid the pitfalls of unrefined
populism, however, Habermas and others tend to insist on extremely
demanding procedural preconditions that would assure a very high de-

gree of moral and intellectual sophistication in public debates. In the tradition of critical theory, these demands are not necessarily meant to be practicable; if they could be approximated, political discourse would be restricted to a small elite of philosopher-kings.

The policy-oriented discourses that are going on within existing Western democracies are, indeed, largely elite affairs. They are conducted by politicians, interest group representatives, prominent experts, and journalists under the filtering, amplifying, and distorting conditions of the media. Discussion takes place in policy communities with specialized publics of interested nonelites, and these specialized discussions are linked to the more general political discourses carried on among policy generalists in governments, parliaments, political parties, associations, and the media on issues that could potentially catch the attention of the wider public and affect electoral outcomes. It is in these interwoven patterns of communication among specialists, generalists, and communicators that problem definitions are proposed and rejected, policy options are presented, criticized, and justified, political performance is evaluated, and political trust and, ultimately, legitimacy are generated, eroded, or destroyed.

These communications surely will not approximate the ideal debates of philosopher-kings: they are often polemical in style and motivated by self-interest rather than by a search for truth. What matters, though, is that they are conducted in public and allow statements to be supported and contradicted in ways that may catch the attention of nonelites. The importance of these two conditions—publicness and contestation—can hardly be overstated. Publicness works as a powerful censorship mechanism (Elster 1986), discriminating in favor of public-regarding communications. It simply would not do to justify publicly a political demand or policy proposal on purely self-regarding grounds. Although that does not rule out self-serving communications, self-interest is forced to masquerade as public interest, at whicn point the possibility of contestation allows competing interests or public-interested critics to challenge such claims.

From the perspective of democratic theory, public discourses can serve two critical mediating roles in the relationship between governors and the governed (V. Schmidt 1997; 1998). On the one hand, they greatly reduce information costs for nonelites. Reasonably interested citizens have a chance to sort out the pros and cons of policy proposals and form an opinion of government performance either in terms of their own self-interest or in terms of the public interest, and these opinions may then enter into their electoral choices. On the other hand, public discourse provides a sounding board for governors to try out problem definitions and policy solutions, and an early warning system regarding issues that might achieve electoral salience. This is critical if the mechanism of anticipated reactions is to link policy choices to voter reactions (Scharpf 1997a, ch. 8).

What matters for input-oriented democracy is the quality of these public discourses. They can perform an orienting and legitimating function if they communicate the wider framework of ongoing policy controversies, the definition of the situation, and the political aspirations in light of which problems and options can be meaningfully considered. For the individual citizen, such discourses provide the context within which it is possible to make sense of what is happening and respond to specific policy. For the public as a whole, orienting discourses provide the stimuli in response to which the electoral expression of political support or opposition can indeed claim, and bestow, a maximum of democratic legitimacy.

But how would a practical reformulation of "discursive democracy" provide a promising perspective on the legitimacy deficits associated with increasing international interdependence? The answer lies in the connection between its orienting and legitimating functions. To maintain legitimacy even under conditions of international interdependence, national policy discourses must avoid the suggestion of omnipotence that still infects not only conventional notions of popular sovereignty but also mutual recriminations among governments and oppositions: governments claim exclusive credit for everything that seems to go well, while oppositions blame them for everything that seems not to. Instead, orienting discourses can provide a realistic picture of the country's present place and future options in an institutionally and economically integrating world, reassess policy goals with a view to their feasibility under international economic and institutional constraints, and emphasize the search for policy instruments that are still viable under these constraints.

When it is made clear that important goals can no longer be achieved through purely national action, the possibility of pursuing them through internationally coordinated or supranational action will be understood as a gain, rather than a loss, of collective fate control. If that is acknowledged, the national interest can no longer be defined in solipsistic terms, and policy options must be discussed in light of the relevant decision rules and constellations of actors at the international level with an empathetic understanding of the preferences, worldviews, and capabilities of the other countries involved. As a result, the information and communication gap discussed above will be greatly reduced. National policy discourses will shadow more closely the real choices that governments face at the international level, and governments will have fewer opportunities to escape from accountability by referring to fictitious external constraints.

Is this an impossible ideal? I think not. The economies of small European democracies have long been much more open than those of larger European states, let alone Japan and the United States, so they have never been able to control their policy environments or indulge in fantasies of omnipotence (Katzenstein 1984, 1985). Nevertheless, their economies have done very well, and some of them are also much more successful in coping with the current challenges of economic interdependence and systems competition than their larger, previously more self-sufficient neighbors. They also seem to enjoy higher levels of public confidence and political satisfaction than larger countries that have only recently felt the full thrust of international economic interdependence (Katzenstein, this volume).

It seems plausible, therefore, that the secret of the economic and political success of small and open countries like Switzerland, Austria, Denmark, or the Netherlands lies precisely in their ability to conduct policy discourses that are based on a realistic understanding of their own capabilities and constraints and to focus debates on those policy alternatives that might be feasible and effective in an international policy environment that is characterized by high degrees of institutional integration, economic interdependence, and regulatory competition (Visser and Hemerijck 1997). Under these conditions public opinion will not proceed from particularistic definitions of policy problems and goals, and when that is assured, the existence of international constraints and the need for international cooperation are not experienced as a delegitimating disappointment because they will have been taken into account from the start. For these countries democratic legitimacy does not presuppose omnipotence and is not challenged by awareness of their interdependence.

Although there is no reason why the larger democracies, too, cannot come to live with international interdependence, they need to learn from the successful small and open countries that orienting discourses require political leadership. They cannot merely reflect untutored popular preferences but must impose the discipline of Freud's "reality principle" on public policy debates. If they do not, international problem-solving will remain domestically vulnerable to populist appeals to wishful thinking, nostalgia for past national grandeur, resentment of foreign influences, or xenophobia. It is the responsibility of policy elites to communicate the extent to which international involvement, cooperation, and trustworthiness have become a precondition for effective pursuit of the national interest. If they succeed, policy discourses in even the larger countries should be able to maintain the tenuous linkage between the perceptions and preferences of nonelites and policy choices that are effective under the constraints of an increasingly interdependent international environment—and there will be no reason to fear that international interdependence will undermine democratic legitimacy.

SIX

Confidence, Trust, International Relations, and Lessons from Smaller Democracies

Peter J. Katzenstein

IT TOOK a long-time student of "il gioco delle bocce" to make "bowling alone" a compelling political metaphor (Putnam 1993; Putnam 1995a; Putnam and Yonish 1998). Robert Putnam's oft-cited paper helped frame arguments of New Democrats and old Republicans, communitarians and libertarians, pundits and scholars. Are Americans bowling alone? The answer to this particular question is clear. While the membership of bowling leagues has declined, the game is being reinvented by a younger generation. Even in Manhattan, America's sport is making a comeback. New Age bowling features Day-Glo pins, black lights, fog machines, disco music, same-sex deep kissing, and women bowling in bras. "Bowling is so retro, it's post-modern," writes Blaine Harden (1997).

Putnam (1993, 167) defines social capital as "features of social organization, such as trust, norms, and networks that can improve the efficiency of society by facilitating coordinated actions." While acknowledging that it is difficult to unpack causation, Putnam (1995b, 666) also argues that "people who join are people who trust . . . the causation flows mainly from joining to trusting."[1] According to Putnam (1995b, 665; 1993a, 36), the central insight of social capital theory is that "the more we connect with other people the more we trust them, and vice versa. . . . Social trust and civic engagement are strongly correlated" in the United States, Italy, and elsewhere. A decline in confidence may generate *a* crisis for democracy, but this differs from *the* crisis of democracy of which Michael Crozier, Samuel Huntington, and Jōji Watanuki (1975) warned when they examined the domestic causes of declining governability. With the end of the Cold War and deepening globalization, are democracies facing a corrosive process of institutional delegitimation that may ultimately be

---

[1] Inglehart (1990, 23) disagrees with Putnam when he writes that "interpersonal trust is a prerequisite to the formation of secondary associations." The model that Putnam, Pharr, and Dalton set forth in this volume modifies Putnam's earlier views in two respects. First, following Newton (1997c, 577), it distinguishes analytically between social capital and social trust rather than defining one in terms of the other. Second, it reverses the causal arrow between trust and social capital.

no less threatening than the "excessive" demands of democracy that were deplored two decades ago?

Public discussion of social capital and political confidence focuses on domestic causes in general and American causes in particular. Does an examination of international causes and comparative perspectives suggest that the American predicament is exceptional or prototypical? These questions raise some vexing conceptual and methodological issues that are addressed elsewhere in this volume. The first part of this chapter briefly characterizes the main developments in political confidence and social trust in the Trilateral democracies to belie the expectation, suggested by the exceptional case of the United States, that changes in one (social trust) foreshadow changes in the other (political confidence). The second and third parts of the chapter argue that neither the end of the Cold War nor the increasing internationalization of economic life have a strong, direct effect on political confidence. After dismissing the putative direct effect of social trust and international factors on political confidence, the chapter concludes with two plausible hypotheses. First, the welfare state and inclusionary politics are important sources of social trust and political confidence. Second, social movements offer democratic alternatives that are compensating for the weakening of attachments to national parliaments and political parties in many of the Trilateral democracies. Both arguments provide grounds for guarded optimism: Trilateral democracies are likely to resist far-reaching erosion of political confidence and social trust.

CONFIDENCE AND TRUST IN COMPARATIVE PERSPECTIVE

The social and political components of confidence are conceptually distinct yet empirically intertwined (Newton and Norris, this volume; Newton 1997a, 2–4). Political confidence is here defined as the public's confidence in representative democratic institutions, including political parties, parliaments, bureaucracies, the legal system, the police, and the armed forces. Social trust, on the other hand, consists of attitudes toward other citizens and thus may be helpful in solving collective action problems (Brehm and Rahn 1997; Stolle and Rochon 1996; Inglehart 1990, 23–24, 34–38, 172–74, 184–90; Nye, Zelikow, and King 1997, 259). Kenneth Newton (1997a, 15–19, 28; see also Kaase 1998, 10, 15–16) concludes in a careful and systematic analysis that political confidence and social trust are *not* closely related, and the data from Trilateral democracies support this assessment. Trend lines in political confidence differ in the United States (sharp declines from high levels), Japan (fluctuations around low levels followed by declines from the late 1980s), and Europe (slight declines around a trend line fluctuating at medium levels, followed by steeper declines in the 1990s). And America's secular decline in social trust is unique: Although it may have dipped in the 1990s, social trust increased gradually over the last several decades in all other Trilateral democracies.

United States

In the United States political confidence began its strong, secular decline in the early 1960s with the onset of the Vietnam War, and, reinforced by the Watergate scandal, that decline continued into the 1980s. After a temporary upswing in the first half of the 1980s, it continued as the Iran-Contra scandal dragged on and the U.S. economy turned anemic. From an all-time low in 1994, there has been a slight increase. In 1958 about 80 percent of respondents trusted the U.S. federal government; by 1996–98 that proportion had declined to the 30 to 40 percent range (*Washington Post* 10 March 1998, A15; *Washington Post* 3 March 1998, A15; *The Economist* 1998; Hamilton and Wright 1986, 361–73; Inglehart 1977, 305–7; Orren 1997, 81; Lawrence 1997, 129; Blendon et al. 1997, 206–16). Nevertheless, the United States still ranks in the upper third of Trilateral democracies in political confidence (Norris 1997, 219–20, 258). In fact, averaging scores for confidence in parliament and the civil service between 1981 and 1990 in the G-7 countries, the United States still ranks first, leading the bottom-ranking nation (Italy) by 50 percentage points.[2] It is difficult to conclude from these comparative rankings that the United States faces a particularly debilitating democratic crisis.

As Putnam and Steven Yonish have shown across a wide range of indicators, social capital and social trust have also declined sharply in the United States (Putnam 1995b; Putnam and Yonish 1998; Newton 1997a, table 4). Although the downward trend appears to be clear to most, though not all, observers,[3] it is by no means clear what to make of it. William Galston and Peter Levine (1997, 26), for example, echo common sense when they observe that in the United States "voluntary activities are on balance healthier than are formal political institutions and processes."

Despite its decline, social trust in the United States remains comparatively high, on a par with or higher than the levels found in the other Trilateral democracies and exceeded only in Scandinavia. Adverse trends

---

[2] McAllister (1998, 193 and table 9.1). These data are not unproblematic; although that finding is strongly contradicted by a large number of national polls, the 1990 World Values Survey score for trust in parliament for the United States recorded a substantial increase in the 1980s.

[3] Ladd (1996; 1998) offers a notable, strong dissent.

in social capital and trust in the United States, Putnam (1996, 24) acknowledges, must be viewed in the context of "undoubted increases in volunteerism in both Europe and Japan, as well as the proliferation of new social movements and citizens' groups." Social capital and trust have remained at comparatively high levels for several decades (Almond and Verba 1963; Curtis 1971 as reported in Curtis, Grabb, and Baer 1992, 139, 144; Wuthnow 1997b, 4; Skocpol 1996, 21; Ladd 1998, 137–61). Furthermore, the democratic history of the United States matters in public discourse. In the 1990s the United States and Germany have displayed almost identical levels of political confidence and social trust (Newton 1997a, table 4; Dalton 1999, table 3.4). Yet a surge of right-wing extremism in both countries led to worries about the stability of Germany's democratic institutions, not America's. In short, declining trends in political confidence and social trust in the United States are undeniable, but when viewed comparatively, the significance of these trends is open to debate.

Japan

In contrast to the United States, Japan has not seen political confidence plummet from high levels. "Disaffection with politics," Susan Pharr (1997b, 237) writes, "has been endemic in the postwar era." Together with Italy, Japan showed the lowest level of political confidence among Trilateral democracies in the 1970s despite its doubling of national income in the 1960s. A small, brief upturn in the 1980s was more than offset by subsequent declines. While declining confidence used to be reserved for party politicians and their institutionalized game of money politics, that mistrust has also begun to tar the elite civil service in the 1990s. In Japan, Pharr (1997b, 238) writes, the lack of political confidence "easily surpasses levels in the United States."

Public opinion surveys suggest that social trust is low in Japan; Japanese are not connected to one another. In comparative perspective they are dissatisfied with and place little trust in their social institutions, certainly much less than Americans do. Few Japanese belong to volunteer organizations; many Americans do. Japanese levels of satisfaction with and trust in a variety of social institutions are among the lowest by international standards; American levels are among the highest (Inoguchi 1997, 2–9; see also Curtis, Grabb, and Baer 1992, 142, note 4).[4] Experimental data confirm these conclusions (Inoguchi 1997, 9–11). In brief,

---

[4] On a standard question of interpersonal trust, it should be noted, Japanese respondents do not differ significantly from those in other countries. See Kaase (1998, table 5).

based on both survey and experimental data, we are safe in concluding that Japanese are playing *pachinko*—alone (Hayama 1994).

By most anthropological and sociological accounts, Japan is a high-trust society (Smith 1985; Fukuyama 1995), so there is something very paradoxical about these empirical findings. Takashi Inoguchi (1997, 14) suggests that the resolution of this paradox is methodological. Interviews and experiments are often context-free, inquire into hypothetical situations, pose questions about confidence in government (which is low) rather than confidence in state-society relations (which is high), and are conducted in artificial settings. In reviewing Japanese evidence, Newton (1997a, 19) comes to a similar conclusion when he writes that "it is difficult to know how to interpret figures for a culture which expresses so little but acts so much trust."[5]

In this instance, however, methodological difficulties do not constrain our analysis unduly.[6] Yutaka Tsujinaka's research has established that the number of interest groups and voluntary associations in Japan, a core indicator of social capital supportive of social trust as Putnam earlier argued, has increased sharply since 1960 (see Pharr, this volume). Based on different data sets, Inoguchi (1997, 15–16) similarly concludes that social capital increased somewhat between 1984 and 1994. In Japan the single most popular sports activity, bowling, boasts more than 37 million enthusiasts (see Pharr, this volume). Thus, it is thus not surprising that social trust rose sharply between 1978 and 1993, from 26 to 38 percent (Newton 1997a, 12). In contrast to the United States, then, social capital and trust in Japan have increased from low levels in recent decades.

Europe

Establishing secular trends in political confidence in Europe is more difficult. Confidence has fluctuated around a trend line whose decline has probably been less steep than in the United States until the 1990s, and whose level has been considerably higher than in Japan. Unfortunately the survey questions posed in Western Europe have often differed from those asked in the United States (Nye, Zelikow, and King 1997, 254, 263, 279). The analytical distinctions that Pippa Norris (1999) and her colleagues have drawn are helpful in circumventing some problems.

[5] Inoguchi and Newton both appear to refer to social and not political trust, and they would probably accept Pharr's insistence that survey results on political trust can be trusted. See Pharr (1997, 244–45).

[6] The limits of cross-national survey research are numerous. Meanings and connotations of concepts vary across nations, even though values and perceptions may not. Answers to identical questions will differ depending on how questions are framed, and high no-response rates can skew results.

Norris distinguishes between political confidence in the political community, the principles and processes of democratic regimes, the performance of democratic regimes,[7] democratic institutions, and democratic politicians.

Scholars differ in the relative importance they attach to these dimensions, particularly the middle three. In contrast to American scholars, European scholars, for example, tend to regard institutional factors as embedded in broader political arrangements. The growing strength of the public's commitment to democratic processes and principles counts for a great deal in a region that, unlike the United States, experienced catastrophic democratic crises and breakdowns in the twentieth century. Generally speaking, surveys in Europe show high and increasing support for and confidence in both the national political community and the principles and processes of democracy; fluctuating and, in the 1990s, declining confidence in democratic performance; variable, and recently declining, trends in institutional confidence; and declining confidence in politicians.

Focusing specifically on support for democracy and satisfaction with democratic performance, Dieter Fuchs and Hans-Dieter Klingemann (1995, 419–43) found little empirical evidence to support the notion of a secular decline in political confidence in Europe. Fuchs, Giovanna Guidorossi, and Palle Svensson (1995, 333) have demonstrated that Europeans' satisfaction with the working of democracy has fluctuated in a trendless way.[8] Similarly, Max Kaase and Newton conclude on the basis of numerous national and cross-national polls that "there is no pervasive or general trend towards decreasing satisfaction with the way democracy works in the member states of the European Union between 1976 and 1991" (Kaase and Newton 1995, 61).

The picture looks different for scholars who examine changing levels of confidence in political institutions. The divergence between increasing social trust and fluctuations or declines in political confidence observed in the German data appears to hold for Europe at large.[9] The 1981 and 1991 World Value Surveys point to a modest decline in political confi-

---

[7] Questions addressing this dimension are often ambiguous because they tap both support for democracy as a value and satisfaction with an incumbent government measured against either some ideal of democracy or the performance of a previous or imagined government. See Inglehart (1997b, 1–2).

[8] Fuchs and Klingemann (1995, 440–42) detect a more skeptical attitude among citizens in the early 1990s due perhaps to the end of the Cold War and rising unemployment.

[9] Newton (1997a, 23 and table 9). It is worth noting that EMNID time-series survey data give a figure of 60 percent for trust in parliament rather than the 29 percent reported in the 1996 World Values Survey, and they record a decline of 5 percent (from 65 to 60 percent) between 1990 and 1996 rather than the 22 percent (from 51 to 29 percent) reported in the World Values Survey. See Newton (1998, table 5), and Norris (1998a, table 11.2).

dence—an average of six percentage points across six political institutions—in the 1980s (Dalton 1997, 14; see also Norris 1997a, figure 3). Among the G-7 countries, however, confidence in parliament and the civil service declined slightly in the United States and France and remained unchanged in Germany, Canada, Britain, Japan, and Italy. "The results," concludes Ian McAllister (1999, 193 and figure 9.1), "demonstrate the wide variation in institutional confidence that exists across the G-7 countries."

Russell Dalton (1997, 19) insists, however, that in the mid-1990s, "the cross-national breadth and the magnitude of these changes is clearly much greater" than the changes that occurred in the 1980s (see also Kaase 1998, 13 and table 7; Nye 1997a, 2; Nye 1997b, 99; Nye and Zelikow 1997, 263). Based on six Trilateral democracies for which data are available between 1981 and 1996, Newton (1998, 10 and table 5) draws a different conclusion. While more figures decline (35) than increase (26), the pattern looks to him more like trendless fluctuations than strong secular declines, or, in his words, more like a Jackson Pollock than a Mondrian. It is noteworthy that Newton and Dalton agree that people have lost more confidence in public institutions in the 1990s than in private ones. Examining the most recent cross-national evidence on political confidence, Kaase (1998, 12–14 and table 6) nonetheless warns against drawing premature or alarmist conclusions based on data drawn from a short time period. Between 1992 and 1994 some European democracies experienced a significant decline in citizen satisfaction with the performance of democratic institutions. But aggregate figures conceal very large, country-specific swings, and in 7 of the 12 EU members levels of political satisfaction actually rose between 1995 and 1997. Kaase (1998, 14) thus concludes that "while there is not a major general decline in support for central democratic institutions in the OECD world, tendencies into this direction undoubtedly do exist. Whether they will develop into a pervasive trend or will continue to reflect, as argued above, a lot of country-specific ups and downs, at this point must remain a topic for further research."

The different tone in the conclusions of studies focusing on democratic institutions and performance as opposed to democratic principles and performance demands further investigation. Giving proper attention to short-term economic fluctuations, long-term value changes, objective conditions, and the wording of particular questions, Ronald Inglehart (1997b, 1–2) offers a number of plausible ways to reconcile different interpretations. Good cross-national data are rare, however. "The overall data situation, in longitudinal as well as in comparative perspective, is so desolate anyway," writes Kaase (1998, 4–5), "that hardly any of the theoretical differentiations in the literature can be empirically recovered" (see also Dalton 1997, 11). Unlike Putnam, Pharr, and Dalton (this volume), I conclude that scholarly assessments of changing levels of political confidence in Europe remain contested and that there is little prospect of convergent interpretations in the near future.

European data on social trust are less difficult to interpret and point consistently toward increases from relatively high levels. With the notable exception of Italy, the Eurobarometer surveys taken since 1976 show relatively high levels of social trust in such diverse countries as Germany, Belgium, Ireland, and Denmark. Now comparable to American figures, German data in particular record a strong and consistent upward trend between 1948 and 1994 (Newton 1997a, 23 and table 4; Kaase 1998, 9 and table 4; Offe 1997, 12, 19–20, 41). British data illustrate a very slight increase in social trust in the 1980s (Kaase 1998, 9 and table 4; Hall 1997). And with the exception of Northern Ireland, interpersonal trust increased in all seven small European democracies between 1981 and 1990 (Inglehart 1997c, 231).

Thus, while political confidence in Europe is either stable or in modest decline, social trust is either stable or weakly rising (Listhaug and Wiberg 1995, 302–6; see also van Deth and Scarbrough 1995, 534–35). According to Newton (1997a, 12, 27), there is no evidence of a general decline in social trust across Western Europe: "On the contrary, nine of the EU 12 show higher levels of trust at the end of the series than at the beginning. . . . Generally, the figures increase in the late seventies, fall in the late 1980s, but recover strongly in the early nineties. Most declines are reversed in time. . . . The Eurobarometer and World Values studies present a good deal of evidence that personal trust in Europe is rising." World Value Surveys yield convergent findings. Between 1981 and 1990 the figures for social trust rose in 14, declined in four, and remained unchanged in three states (Newton 1997a, 12; Newton 1998, 6 and table 1; see also Kaase 1998, 10). "Not only is personal trust more widespread in west Europe as a whole," writes Newton (1998, 7), "but the trend is generally upwards."[10]

Divergence between the trends in political confidence and social trust in the Trilateral democracies does not contradict Putnam's (1995a, 67) general claim "that social connections and civic engagement pervasively influence our public life," but it does undercut the presumption that their influence is direct. This is also Newton's conclusion (1997c). Focusing primarily on Europe and the United States, he concludes that the associations between social and political confidence, social trust and po-

---

[10] Newton notes that there is preliminary evidence in the World Values Surveys, but not in the Eurobarometer surveys, of stronger and more consistent declines in social trust in the 1990s.

litical behavior, and civic engagement and political attitudes and behavior are neither close nor consistent. Newton (1998, 11) further concludes that "we should not assume that the American pattern is universal, even less that it is typical of other western nations."[11] "In short," writes Norris (1999, 22), "Newton dashes cold water on social capital theory and stresses that political trust seems to be more a product of political than social factors." Diverging trend lines for political confidence and social trust outside the United States may also offer indirect support for Joseph Nye and Philip Zelikow's conclusion (1997, 259) that "Robert Putnam's alleged decline in voluntary association membership is probably not sufficiently strong to be a major cause of declining trust in government" in the United States (see also Newton 1997a, 5; Kaase 1998, 14–16).

This discussion of the diverging trends in the Trilateral democracies yields a first, important finding: there exists no direct relation between changes in social trust and political confidence. If not social trust, what about international factors like the Cold War and economic internationalization as major causes of declining political confidence?

GEOPOLITICS AND THE END OF THE COLD WAR

War is the father of all things—including different levels of political confidence. The United States won a war that Germany and Japan lost, and more than half a century later this difference is still clearly recognizable in public opinion. Declines in political confidence from what were extraordinarily high levels in the United States have been countered by substantial increases in the German and Italian figures and a slower rise in Japan (on Italy and Germany, see Newton 1998, table 1 and Kaase 1998, table 4). As was true of the decline of U.S. economic hegemony after 1945, the most dramatic drop in American confidence had occurred by the early 1970s.

Maybe, Nye (1997a, 16) proposes, the problem is not that confidence has been too low since the end of the Cold War, but that it was too high after the end of World War II. Putnam (1995b, 677) argues in a similar vein that in the United States, "the *Zeitgeist* of national unity and patriotism that culminated in 1945 might have reinforced civic-mindedness." Michael Schudson (1996, 19) agrees when he writes that the World War II generation that elected and reelected FDR may have been unique in supporting unequivocally what became universally accepted as an unquestionably good cause: "The 'long civic generation' had the advan-

---

[11] Going beyond the American evidence that first inspired the concept of "bowling alone," the different trends reported here suggest an important modification of Putnam's original formulation of social capital theory.

tages of a 'good war' and a good president. Later generations had no wars or ones about which there were less massive mobilization and much less consensus—Korea and, more divisively, Vietnam. They had presidents of dubious moral leadership—notably Nixon" (see also Putnam 1996, 44–46; Putnam 1995b, 673–77).

In contrast to the United States, the effects of World War II have not vanished in Germany and Japan. Their publics exhibit a lack of pride in their country that is striking in comparative perspective. In international surveys, they trail at the very bottom of a list of more than 20 states in the 1990s, a finding that is confirmed by their publics' very low support for their national political communities (Klingemann 1999, tables 2.3 and 2.5 and 39, 42; see also Dalton 1997, figure 3). The lingering effects of World War II could also explain why Germans and Japanese, in sharp contrast to Britons and Americans, judge the present to be better than the past by a significant margin (Pharr 1997b, 248). Differences in the historical origin of political confidence and a generational argument thus offer plausible explanations for some broad, cross-national patterns in political confidence.[12]

At first glance, the end of the Cold War and geopolitics more generally seem to provide a direct link between international politics and political confidence. In its early years the strong anti-communism spawned by the Cold War offered the United States, Germany, and Japan a collective identity and ideological glue that helped nourish political confidence. The institutionalization of a new national security state (in the United States) and the concealment of Nazi and militarist legacies under the mantle of anti-communism (in Germany and Japan) instilled confidence in political institutions. At the height of the Cold War citizens trusted their governments as visible guarantors of a preferred way of life that appeared to be threatened by a powerful enemy.

For the United States this was another chapter in what had been a complicated relationship with the outside world since the founding of the Republic. At the height of the first Cold War, Louis Hartz (1991, 285) wrote that America's "colossal liberal absolutism . . . inspires hysteria at home by generating the anxiety that unintelligible things produce." Growing familiarity with a world divided by the Cold War interacted with American political institutions that, in the words of Theodore Lowi (1969, 157–88), created systematic pressures to oversell both threats and

---

[12] They are problematic when applied to Germany and Japan, however. A plausible explanation must specify the relations between the direct experience and the institutionalized memory of victory and defeat in World War II; it is not history, but historical memory that matters politically. As Buruma (1994) has demonstrated, German and Japanese politics have dealt with and institutionalized the memory of defeat and guilt very differently.

remedies, over time helping to undermine political confidence. In the early 1980s, at the height of the second Cold War, Samuel Huntington pointed to the inherent tension between the liberal, democratic, individualist, and egalitarian American creed and the functional requirements of foreign policy institutions. According to Huntington (1982, 1), Americans have existed "in a state of national cognitive dissonance, which they have attempted to relieve through various combinations of moralism, cynicism, complacency, and hypocrisy." Declining confidence in government is a measure of how citizens have become more anxious about the unintelligible, less tolerant of political oversell, and exposed to tensions between ideals and institutions. It is a response evocative of what Robert Bellah and his colleagues (1985, 50, 250) call "the biblical and republican tradition in American politics," and consistent with a culture that views community and nation as inherently good and politics and government as necessary evils.

During the Cold War the desirability of active and assertive leadership in the world was a goal broadly shared by both elite and mass opinion. In sharp contrast, a substantial gap between mass and elite views marks foreign policy in the post–Cold War period. Traditional geopolitical conflicts perceived through the lens of "the national interest" matter less in the minds of Americans, and social and humanitarian issues such as the environment, health, drugs, immigration, international crime, and the loss of jobs to low-wage competitors matter more. In addition, although the American public strongly favors a multilateral approach and has a high esteem for the United Nations (Pew Research Center 1997; Kull, Destler, and Ramsay 1997; Kohut and Toth 1997; Crosette 1997), this diffuse support for an unconventional foreign policy agenda is largely disconnected from the foreign policy elites who wield power in Washington. The end of the Cold War has removed anti-communism as a collective frame of reference shared by both mass publics and political leaders, thus opening space for further declines in political confidence.

The United States is not alone in struggling with how it should relate to the outside world. In the twentieth century both Japan and Germany dealt with such complications by means of military expansion rather than political isolation. Military defeat, occupation, and full integration into the military and economic structures of the *Pax Americana* remade Germany and Japan into trading states (Rosencrance 1986). Initially the tender roots of democratic institutions and participatory practices were buried under the same virulent anti-communism that provided Americans with a collective identity. It helped create intimate political connections among domestic and international affairs that were only later superseded by strong economic links between national, regional, and global markets (Katzenstein 1996; Katzenstein 1997; Katzenstein and Shiraishi 1997).

Is it therefore true that with the end of the Cold War "things fall apart" (Nye 1997a, 15)? Did the Cold War eliminate "the principal philosophical and geopolitical challenge to liberal democracy and the market economy" and thus undermine political confidence (Putnam 1996, 2)? Both Nye and Putnam note that the existing survey data do not fit a Cold War explanation. "The decline of confidence in government," Nye (1997a, 15) argues, "starts in the mid-1960s. So unless one wants to date the end of the cold war from the mid- to late 1960s, the hypothesis does not fit very well" (see also Nye, Zelikow, and King 1997, 264, 269). With regard to social trust, Putnam (1995b, 677) concurs: "It is hard to assign any consistent role to the Cold War and the Bomb, since the anti-civic trend appears to have deepened steadily from the 1940s to the 1970s, in no obvious harmony with the rhythms of world affairs."

The Cold War explanation does not fit either German or Japanese survey data on confidence in the armed forces, one of the institutions most affected by the change in geopolitics. Both German and Japanese respondents have displayed a remarkable lack of confidence in their armed forces both before and since the end of the Cold War (Inglehart 1997b, table 2). This is not surprising. In Western Europe substantial fractions of the population (varying between 20 and 40 percent) had not heard of NATO, and another 10 percent did not know whether their country was a member or incorrectly believed that it was not. "Significant minorities of Western populations," Kaase and Newton (1995, 106) write, "even majorities, seem not to be armed with even the most basic information." Between 1976 and 1987 defense issues languished at the bottom of the list of popular priorities, ranking substantially lower than unemployment (Kaase and Newton 1995, 109). Low levels of information and the low political salience of defense issues among European mass publics limited the impact of the end of the Cold War on political confidence.

Changes in the material balance of power, rather than perceived threats or refashioned collective identities, offer an alternative test for the Cold War hypothesis, but it also yields negative results. A long-term, secular erosion of political confidence in some Trilateral democracies and fluctuation around a slightly declining trend in the 1990s in others are not easily explained by the rapid move in the structure of the international system away from bipolarity following the end of the Cold War. Only dramatic declines in political confidence in many of the former socialist states in the early 1990s point to a strong link.

The end of the Cold War transformed Europe much more than Asia. The Soviet Union's withdrawal from its Central and Eastern European empire, German unification, and the breakup of the Soviet Union all led to a fundamental change in the balance of power along the central front that had divided the Eurasian land mass. In sharp contrast, the continued division of Korea and unabated tensions between Taiwan and China indicate that the Cold War has not ended in Asia. Russia's bastion strategy led it to concentrate its navy, including its rapidly deteriorating nuclear-powered ships, on the Koala peninsula to the north of Norway and around Vladivostok, thus actually intensifying its threat to both Norway and Japan. For these two countries the end of the Cold War was clearly disadvantageous in terms of both Russian military capabilities close to their borders and their vulnerability to nuclear accidents. Yet their trend lines of political confidence have not been affected by this adverse change in international conditions. Japanese confidence in government has been low and relatively unchanging for decades. At a much higher level, Norwegian confidence has fluctuated around a slightly declining trend line (Listhaug 1995, 273–74; Listhaug and Wiberg 1995, 302–9; Holmberg 1999, figure 5.1). These trends in political confidence cannot easily be squared with the rapid deterioration in Norway's and Japan's security environments in the early 1990s.

Although the end of the Cold War had little in the way of direct effects, we should not belittle its potentially strong, indirect effect on political confidence. Hideo Ōtake (this volume), for example, argues that the Cold War lay at the root of the ideological polarization of the Japanese party system and was an important cause of the predominant position that the Liberal Democratic Party enjoyed for four decades. The large presence, gradual erosion, and reconstitution of a powerful communist party that imported international politics into domestic politics similarly shaped Italian politics. The indirect effects of international developments, including the end of the Cold War, on regime legitimacy is thus strong in both these countries. Political upheavals in Italy and Japan since the end of the Cold War testify to this. Judicial politics and the decomposition and realignment of political parties in each of these polities, it is safe to venture, would have been less far-reaching if international tensions had increased rather than abated.

More generally, Kaase and Newton argue that since the early 1990s the collapse of the communist bloc may have had strong effects on the decline in confidence because communist countries were previously the focus of critical attention as external enemies: "Now European citizens are free to look inward at the internal state of their own political systems" (Kaase and Newton 1995, 62). More generally, they suggest that an important era in Western politics came to a close in the early 1990s: "The political agenda of the future will be influenced increasingly by international trends, forces and considerations; national perspectives on democracy and decision-making will become less and less adequate for an understanding of its logic and outcomes" (Kaase and Newton 1995, 172).

Expanding our historical perspective, we could move from the suggested effects of the Cold War to the effects of the 30-year war in the middle of the century (1914–45) or examine the entire twentieth century (i.e., 1914–89) as what Raymond Aron (1954) once called a century of total war. In a recent essay Charles Maier (1994, 51, 54–55, 58–59) has pushed the historical comparison back even further back into the nineteenth century. Maier's historical comparisons are illuminating, but it is difficult, to say the least, to discern plausible connections between such broad historical reflections and the specific trends in political confidence that have characterized the Trilateral democracies over the last four decades.

Thus, the search for a single explanatory factor rooted in the international balance of power or a foreign threat that directly affects political confidence finds little empirical support. The indirect importance of international factors on political confidence appears to be more convincing, which turns attention back to more proximate, domestic causes.

Internationalization, the Loss of National Control, and Political Confidence

Although internationalization can take many different forms, virtually all analysts agree that the openness of national economies to a variety of cross-border flows (e.g., goods, services, capital, people, information) is its defining characteristic. Internationalization can lead to a loss of control and accountability as markets and social processes circumvent state borders and government policies, and there is no doubt that economic openness has increased greatly since the end of World War II, reaching or exceeding in the 1990s levels previously reached in the late nineteenth century (Berger and Dore 1996; Garrett 1998; Rodrik 1997).

A number of scholars have pointed to internationalization as a likely cause for secular declines in confidence. Putnam (1996, 2–3, 25), for example, writes that "international trade has grown faster than gross domestic product, and foreign investment has grown more rapidly than either. . . . Transnational trends increasingly escape control by any democratically constituted authorities. State boundaries no longer clearly define stable zones of political identity, economic activity, and military protection. National governments and the electorates to which they are responsible feel a very real 'loss of fate control.'" Nye (1997b, 104) also notes that "if people feel a loss of control over their lives because of larger competition in the world, that becomes a political reality in and of itself." Writing from a European perspective, Michael Zürn (1998) discusses at length how increasing global economic competition is creating problems of democratic legitimation. And the Japanese scholar Takashi Inoguchi (1997, 29) argues that "the market, further empowered by borderlessness, now reigns supreme. . . . The social and transnational forces that were inadvertently suppressed by the Westphalian framework of nation states have been unleashed." With economic performance slack in most of the Trilateral economies since the mid-1970s—high unemployment in Europe, declining growth and deepening financial crises in Japan, and record trade deficits and intractable poverty in the United States—have new international economic realities reduced political confidence?

Table 6.1 summarizes three conventional measures of the level of economic openness: trade, direct foreign investment, and government re-

TABLE 6.1
Different Levels of Economic Openness of the Trilateral Democracies

Country	Exports + Imports/GDP[a]		Multinationali- zation of Production FDI (% GDP)[b]		Gov't Restrictions on Cross-Border Capital Movements[c]	
	Average 1980–90	Rank	Average 1985 to Present	Rank	Average 1980–90	Rank
United States	19%	14	1.3	12	13.27	4
Canada	52	10	1.5	10.5	12.68	6
Japan	27	13	0.9	14	10.50	12
United Kingdom	53	9	5.1	3	14.00	1
France	45	11	2.6	6	10.77	11
Italy	43	12	0.9	14	10.95	10
Germany	61	7	1.5	10.5	13.95	2
G-7 average	43	10.9	2.0	10.0	12.30	6.6
Netherlands	110	2	5.3	2	13.72	3
Belgium	133	1	6.0	1	10.36	13
Sweden	64	6	3.4	5	11.18	8.5
Norway	83	3	2.0	7	9.63	14
Denmark	67	5	1.7	9	11.18	8.5
Finland	57	8	1.9	8	—	—
Austria	75	4	0.9	14	11.68	7
Switzerland	—	—	4.4	4	13.00	5
Small States Average	84	4.1	3.2	6.3	11.54	8.4
Trilateral Democracies Average	64	7.5	2.6	8.0	11.92	7.5

Sources: [a]Garrett (1988, 23). [b]Garrett (1998), table 1. [c]Based on *The Adjustment of National Employment and Social Policy to Economic Internationalization* (1998), table A6.

strictions on cross-border capital movements. Comparisons between the G-7 countries and the small European democracies show a strong inverse correlation between the size of a national economy and its openness to international trade (columns 1–4). Only in government restrictions on cross-border movement of capital (columns 5–6) are the G-7 countries more open than the small states, and there by only a slight margin.

In light of these data it is difficult to argue that economic openness undermines political confidence. In fact, the data suggest the opposite. The small Trilateral democracies are high-confidence polities that tend toward economic openness. Furthermore, the two largest economies in the world, the United States and Japan, are significantly less open than Europe, yet both countries' levels of political confidence are below those of many European states. These findings contradict the hypothesized effect of internationalization on political confidence.

A comparison of the United States with Germany points in the same direction. The German economy is more trade-dependent than America's, yet Germany's levels of political confidence are comparable to or higher than those of the United States. Eurobarometer surveys show that German levels of political confidence experienced no more than a minimal decline between 1979 and 1996 while economic openness increased very substantially. Newton (1997a, 23 and table 9) concludes that "there is no hard evidence of a long term decline in political confidence in West Germany." World Values surveys echo this finding. Between 1981–84 and 1990–93 support for West Germany's political system remained fairly stable (Newton 1997c, 20; but see Cusack 1997a for a more recent, pessimistic assessment).

Because Britain shares with the United States a long record of democratic government and an established liberal market economy and with Germany an economy quite open to global influences, it offers an additional test of the relation between economic openness and political confidence. As Newton and Ivor Crewe usefully remind us, a healthy degree of cynicism is not new to British politics; it dates back to the turn of the century, well before the onset of internationalization as it is now understood (quoted in Putnam 1996, 5; see also Newton 1997a, 23). Confidence has declined in Britain since the 1950s and especially since the mid-1980s (Newton 1997a, 24). In 1987 less than half of British respondents thought that the civil service, the national government, or local councils could be trusted to serve the public interest (Dalton 1997, 14). A differently worded question revealed that the British public had become even more skeptical a decade later (Newton 1997a, tables 10 and 11). In their levels of economic openness Britain and Germany are broadly comparable, but their data on political confidence are not. A secular erosion in political confidence makes Britain more comparable to the United States even though the two countries differ greatly in their degree of economic openness. Either way, in light of this evidence, any hypothesis that links economic internationalization to political confidence finds little support in the British data.

What is true of Germany and Britain appears to hold more generally for Western Europe. The authors of a massive, five-volume project exploring European public opinion conclude that satisfaction with democracy, here taken as an indicator of political confidence, has displayed a trendless fluctuation over time rather than a steady secular decline (Fuchs and Klingemann 1995). Increasing openness to the international economy did not cause a decline in political confidence.

Because they are even more exposed to global markets than Germany, Britain, and their other large neighbors, the smaller Northern and Western European democracies illustrate this general proposition well. In Europe the smaller states rank ahead of the larger ones in political confidence precisely *because* of their greater internationalization (Katzenstein 1985; Garrett 1998). World Value and Eurobarometer surveys support this conclusion. In 1994–97 support for one's political community and willingness to fight for one's country—which have remained high in all of the Trilateral democracies—were higher in Scandinavia than in the United States, and Switzerland's scores were about 50 percentage points higher than West Germany's (Klingemann 1999, tables 2.2 and 2.5; see also Norris 1997, 20). In 1994–97 Norway, Switzerland, and Sweden ranked ahead of the United States, Germany, and Japan in their citizens' evaluations of democratic performance. Only Finland fell below the U.S. mark, and even Finland surpassed Germany and Japan (Klingemann 1999, table 2.8). In 1990–93 a rank order of institutional confidence by state size generated a higher score for small (6.2) than for large (8.7) states (Norris 1997, figure 2). Confidence in political institutions is comparatively high in the small European democracies. In Scandinavia confidence in parliament is greater than in the United States, Germany, or Japan, for example (Klingemann 1999, table 2.11). And satisfaction with the democratic process is greatest among the small European states; German scores cluster at the midpoint of those of eight smaller European states, while France and Britain trail far behind (Klingemann 1999, table 2.13).

Ola Listhaug's analysis of time-series data for Denmark, the Netherlands, Norway, and Sweden supports the inference derived from cross-sectional data. Listhaug concludes that there is no uniform trend in these four countries. Political confidence in Norway and Denmark was at roughly the same level in the late 1980s as in the late 1960s and early 1970s while it declined sharply in Sweden and rose sharply in the Netherlands. The data, concludes Listhaug (1995, 294), "do not justify . . . a uniformly pessimistic—nor an excessively optimistic—picture of developments in trust." Sören Holmberg (1999) has updated Listhaug and Wiberg's data and extended the analysis to Finland and Iceland. He concludes that the development of political confidence has differed dramatically in these established, parliamentary, multiparty, unitary, welfare state democracies. Confidence has increased in Norway and the Netherlands, remained roughly constant in Denmark, and fallen from previously stable rates in Iceland in the 1990s. Taken together, this evidence undercuts the claim that internationalization reduces political confidence.

Why have the smaller European states not experienced a secular decline in political confidence? Two answers are plausible. First, greater exposure to international markets requires generous social buffers and welfare policies and large public sectors to soften the costs of adjustments to global changes that small states cannot influence (Katzenstein 1985). Under these conditions international exposure does not undermine political confidence. A second answer points to the politics of institutional inclusion (Katzenstein 1984). "People don't just come to politics," Richard Valelly (1996, 26) writes, "politics also comes to the people. The institutional setting affects who participates and how." The secular decline in electoral turnout in the United States, Rosenstone and Hansen's data suggest, was due primarily to a decline in institutional mobilization and only secondarily to the erosion in political confidence (Rosenstone and Hansen as summarized in Valelly 1996, 26; see also Holmberg 1999).

Anderson and Guillory (1997, quoted in Norris 1997a, 8) have argued that political winners enjoy more political confidence than losers do. This "hometown hypothesis" receives very strong support from the low scores of political confidence recorded in polities with long-term, one-party dominant regimes, such as Mexico, Italy, and Japan (Norris 1997, 21; Pempel 1990); strong support from cross-national data (Norris 1997, figure 4); and modest support from Swedish pre- and post-electoral polls taken in the 1990s (Holmberg 1999, 117–19). Majoritarian systems based on the winner-take-all principle tend to produce few winners and little political confidence. Electoral systems that are based on the principle of proportional representation and the need for governments to consist of politically encompassing coalitions, as in the small European states, tend to produce more winners and more political confidence. Norris (1997, 19–24) has found considerable evidence supporting this proposition in cross-national survey data. Prompted in part by their exposure to international markets, the small European welfare states have institutionalized the principle of social inclusion; they give their citizens both the resources and the sense of efficacy that sustain political confidence.

As has been frequently noted, Sweden is the only exception to this general conclusion. Between 1968 and 1988 Sweden experienced a long-term decline in political confidence of about 20 percentage points, with the major part of that decline occurring in the 1970s (Newton 1997a, 22–23). "Sweden," writes Putnam (1996, 7), "once widely considered to have invented the consummate welfare state and to have found a happy 'middle way' between the free-for-all of free enterprise and the oppression of state socialism, is emblematic of the newly troubled public mood." Based on his comparative analysis of six small welfare states, Holmberg (1999, 104–5) comes to the same conclusion without inferring, as Putnam does, that Sweden's decline is somehow more emblematic than the rising trends of the five other states: "Sweden is the only country among the six which, like the U.S., shows a long-term and sizeable downturn in the level of political trust among the public" (see also Dalton 1997, 11–12; Norris 1997, 3; Newton 1997a, 22–23, 29). Among a sample of 11 states for which data are available in 1990, "perhaps it is most surprising," write Arthur Miller and Ola Listhaug (1997, 3), "to find Sweden among this bottom group of countries, especially given that its Scandinavian neighbor, Norway, enjoys the highest level of political trust among all these countries."

What is the source of Swedish exceptionalism? Like the other small European states, Sweden ranks high on various measures of national pride, and between the early 1960s and early 1980s it ranked together with the United States at the top of the class in voluntary, multiple group memberships and various measures of sociability (Curtis, Grabb, and Baer 1992, 141–43, 145; see also Hallenstvedt 1974). Bo Rothstein (1998, 20–24, 33–39, 40–41) has made a compelling case that across a broad array of indicators such as membership in voluntary associations, participation in the nonprofit sector, and volunteer work, social capital has increased in Sweden over the last two decades. And in sharp contrast to confidence in political institutions, trust in social institutions is not declining (Holmberg 1999, 114–15). Participation in Sweden's civil society is high relative to other Western European states and has been increasing since the early 1980s. Defying expectations about how a large welfare state might have a "crowding out" effect on civil society, "the overall picture of Sweden," Rothstein (1998, 51) concludes, "is that of a rather vital, growing and changing civil society."

Two explanations might account for this disparity between declining political confidence and increasing social trust and associability. One explanation focuses on the same set of 17 factors that Nye, Zelikow, and King used to analyze the case of the United States. In general, Holmberg (1999, 115, 121) argues, a secular shift in sociocultural attitudes away from traditional authority has been accentuated by the extraordinarily high levels of social trust and political confidence achieved after World

War II and the trend toward individualism that the 1968 generation helped establish. If Holmberg is correct, this poses a profound challenge to the internationalization hypothesis. Because Sweden is much more exposed to the international economy than is the United States, Holmberg's analysis points to the strong effect of a common domestic cause, not a dissimilar international context.

If viewed from the perspectives of the other small European welfare states, Holmberg's analysis looks less compelling, however. The causal mechanism suggested for Sweden should presumably work for Norway or the Netherlands, but it does not, so the Swedish pattern requires a more idiosyncratic explanation. Sweden's democratic corporatism does have a distinctive feature that sets it apart from the variants of liberal and social corporatism that characterize all the other small states in Northern and Western Europe. In Sweden power was not in the hands of either an internationally oriented business community (as in Switzerland, the Netherlands, or Belgium) or of a nationally oriented union movement (as in Norway, Denmark, and Austria) (Katzenstein 1985). Instead, the Wallenbergs and the Swedish trade union movement were sharing power in Sweden, and over time they strengthened what Rothstein (1998) calls "organized trust." It was organized rather than individualized trust that provided the foundation for peak association bargaining conducted in the shadow of the state that affected wages, prices, and a range of other issues. This Swedish Model rested on a limited role for government.

Growing opposition from employers, politicization of the economy, and the breakdown in peak association bargaining arenas and institutions ended the Swedish Model and weakened the policy performance of the Swedish polity along a number of different dimensions, leading to declining political confidence. The Swedish Model "did not expire," argues Rothstein (1998, 60), "because of changes in technology or in the international economy; it broke down because the organized social capital upon which it was built evaporated. . . . The political system in Sweden is distrusted because the political hubris of the trade unions and the Social Democratic party during the 1970s led them to abandon the Swedish Model." Rothstein's explanation focuses on the specific strategy of the Swedish union federation in the early 1970s rather than the diffuse generational effect of 1968. Supported by data that point to great stability in support for the welfare state (Svallfors 1995), Rothstein's analysis, unlike Holmberg's, explains the Swedish case without creating new anomalies. It also lends no support to the internationalization hypothesis.[13]

---

[13] This argument may explain the sharp deviation between the decline in political confidence in the Netherlands and that in other European states that surprises Dalton (1999, 9). Dalton speculates plausibly that the Dutch time-series data began too late (1971) to cap-

TABLE 6.2
Rates of Change in the Economic Openness of the Trilateral Democracies

Country	Exports + Imports/GDP[a] Change (1980–90) Minus (1966–79)	Rank	Gov't Restrictions on Cross-Border Capital Movements[b] Change (1980–90) Minus (1970–79)	Rank
United States	6%	11	0.47	11
Canada	8	7	0.53	10
Japan	4	13	2.25	2
United Kingdom	6	11	4.95	1
France	12	6	0.23	13
Italy	6	11	0.55	9
Germany	16	3.5	0.10	14
G-7 Average	8	8.93	1.30	8.6
Netherlands	19	2	1.62	5
Belgium	44	1	0.46	12
Sweden	14	5	0.93	7
Norway	−4	14	2.03	3
Denmark	8	7	1.73	4
Finland	8	7	—	—
Austria	16	3.5	1.23	6
Switzerland	—	—	0.80	8
Small States Average	15	5.6	1.26	6.4
Trilateral Democracies Average	12	7.3	1.28	7.5

Sources: [a]Geoffrey (1998, 23). [b]Based on *The Adjustment of National Employment and Social Policy to Economic Internationalization* (1998), table A6.

Focusing on the rate of change rather than the absolute level of international openness does not alter any of the arguments advanced here (see Table 6.2). A comparison of the 1980s with the period of 1966–79 shows that the small European democracies continued to lead the G-7 in their dependence on trade by a ratio of about 2 to 1 (columns 1 and 2).

---

ture the effects of dealignment that accompanied the end of the system of discrete electoral pillars in the 1960s. Alternatively (or complementarily), to focus on organized social capital, within a few years of the onset of "the Dutch disease" and the supposed end of Dutch welfare corporatism, economic and political leaders agreed in the late 1980s to a series of corporatist bargains that introduced greater labor market flexibility and more part-time jobs, two innovations that created the "Dutch jobs miracle" of the 1990s and may have increased the confidence of the Dutch in their political institutions (see Visser and Hemerijck 1997).

And government restrictions on cross-border capital movements (columns 3 and 4), which the smaller states still had on the books in greater numbers in the 1970s, were eroding rapidly in the 1980s. Yet this decade saw trendless fluctuations in political confidence and continued increases in social trust in the small European democracies. Contradicting notions widely held among scholars of social capital and democracy, the small Trilateral democracies in Northern and Western Europe demonstrate that political confidence can correlate positively with both the level and rate of change in national openness to the international economy.

Social capital theory has focused on the United States. This book, for example, starts from the premise that what ails the United States may well ail the other Trilateral democracies. It is thus worth underlining the fact that the continued decline in U.S. political confidence after the mid-1970s proceeded well ahead of that of the other Trilateral democracies while the internationalization of the U.S. economy lagged well behind (table 6.2, columns 2 and 4). It would seem that the complex causes that are eroding political confidence in the United States are domestic rather than international.

In any case, it would have been very surprising if a single, international explanation yielded a satisfactory explanation of changes in political confidence and social trust that diverge so widely among the Trilateral democracies. This is not to deny the possibility that international factors play a more prominent role in some parts of the Trilateral world than in others. Fritz Scharpf, for example, argues in this volume that the EU is institutionalizing international economic interdependence and thus may be contributing to Europe's democratic deficit. Although it is true that European integration is an elite-driven process that may further erode the power of national representative institutions like parliaments, the EU is not the major cause of the highly variable and, until recently, slight decline in confidence in European political institutions. Strong evidence drawn from opinion surveys stretching back more than two decades does not support the view that the EU is creating a legitimation crisis for European democracies (Niedermayer and Sinnott 1995). And it is worth remembering that the EU deals with more issues and is more intrusive than other global or regional institutions of governance that affect the United States, Canada, and Japan. Thus, it is far from certain that institutionalized international governance is a major cause of variations, fluctuations, and, in the 1990s, declines in political confidence in the Trilateral democracies.

Considering the limitations of comparable, valid survey data, it is difficult to come to a definitive conclusion about the relationship between economic internationalization and political confidence, but the preponderance of evidence cuts against any strong claim about the harmful effect of internationalization. By most measures, the most open of the Trilateral democracies, the small European democracies, are high-confidence polities. Internationalization is not a major cause of decline in political confidence.

CONCLUSION

This chapter has argued that social trust has increased while political confidence has decreased or fluctuated, and that there have been no direct international effects on political confidence. Both findings are relevant for an evaluation of the framework that Putnam, Pharr, and Dalton outline in the introduction to this volume. That model posits that the major cause of declining confidence is the declining performance of representative democratic institutions.

Table 6.3 summarizes five indicators of governmental performance that reveal the small, open, high-trust Trilateral democracies to be consistently outperforming the G-7 nations. Because they could free-ride on the defense expenditures of larger states, the small states have defended their security at relatively low cost (column 1). Superior economic competitiveness made their currencies appreciate faster against the dollar than did the currencies of larger states (column 2). The misery index, which simply adds the rates of unemployment and inflation, was on average lower in the small states than in the G-7 nations (column 3), while social expenditures as a share of GDP and an index measuring honesty-in-government were higher (columns 4 and 5). These indicators and the quality of the data are far from perfect. They do not, for example, measure general policy failures (e.g., the Vietnam War for the United States, the excesses of money politics for Japan, unification for Germany) that have reduced levels of political confidence, so we should be cautious about drawing strong inferences from the consistent differences in the average scores reported in Table 6.3. But the governments of the smaller democracies do appear to have outperformed those of the G-7 nations. They are also relatively high-confidence polities that have withstood, until recently, the erosion of political confidence and social trust better than the G-7 nations. This finding reinforces the cautionary note that Putnam, Pharr, and Dalton sound against alarmist interpretations. The decline in political confidence is "less visible" or "almost wholly absent" in fully half of the Trilateral democracies, mostly those located in Northern and Western Europe. Furthermore, this finding tends to support the framework set forth in the Introduction: internationalization is *not* a direct cause of fluctuations or declines in confidence; domestic politics shaping government performance is.

This chapter has emphasized two aspects of domestic politics, welfare

TABLE 6.3
Government Performance in the Trilateral Democracies

Country	Military Expenditures as Percentage of GDP[a]			Appreciation of Currency Against Dollar[b] 1985–93	Misery Index[c]		Total Social Expenditures as Share of GDP[d]		Honesty in Government 1996[e1]
	1975	1985	1995		1983–85	1993–95	1985	1993	
United States	5.8%	6.1%	3.8%	N/d[2]	11.7	8.9	N/d	N/d	7.66
Canada	1.9	2.2	1.7	−0.07	15.9	11.7	N/d	N/d	8.96
Japan	0.9	1.0	1.0	+7.45	4.7	3.5	N/d	N/d	7.05
United Kingdom	4.9	5.1	3.0	+0.91	16.5	12.0	21.0	23.4%	8.44
France	3.8	4.0	3.1	+4.15	17.0	13.6	27.0	28.7	6.96
Italy	2.5	2.2	1.8	+0.29	21.1	15.9	21.6	25.0	3.42
Germany	3.6	3.2	1.9	+5.18	10.5	11.1	25.5	28.3	8.27
G-7 Average	3.3	3.4	2.3	+3.0	13.9	11.0	23.8	26.4	7.25
Netherlands	3.2	3.0	2.1	+5.22	14.3	9.1	29.0	30.2	8.71
Belgium	3.0	3.1	1.7	+4.89	19.2	14.8	28.5	27.0	6.84
Sweden	3.3	3.0	2.8	−0.18	11.2	11.3	31.6	38.0	9.08
Norway	3.3	3.1	2.7	+1.18	9.8	7.5	N/d	N/d	8.87
Denmark	2.5	2.3	1.8	+4.44	15.0	10.4	26.5	31.0	9.33
Finland	1.5	1.7	2.0	−0.28	12.8	19.1	N/d	N/d	9.05
Austria	1.1	1.3	0.9	+5.18	7.9	7.3	24.2	25.8	7.59
Switzerland	1.9	2.4	1.6	+4.23	4.1	5.6	17.4	20.6	8.76
Small States Average	2.5	2.5	2.0	+3.1	11.8	10.6	26.2	28.8	8.53
Trilateral Democracies Average	3.0	3.0	2.2	3.1	12.9	10.8	25.0	27.6	7.89

Sources: [a]U.S. Arms Control and Disarmament Agency. World Military Expenditures and Arms Transfers 1972–1982 and World Military Expenditures and Arms Transfers 1996. [b]Garrett (1998), table 7. [c]Based on The Adjustment of National Employment and Social Policy to Economic Internationalization (1998), table A3. [d]Based on The Adjustment of National Employment and Social Policy to Economic Internationalization (1998), Table C2. [e]Transparency International (http://www.transparency.de).

Notes: [1]Corruption score represents a "poll of polls" of executives of multinational firms on perceived levels of corruption using ten different sources. A score of 0 represents "perceived to be totally corrupt"; a score of 10 represents "perceived to be totally clean." [2]N/d = no data

states and a politics of institutional inclusion, as important institutional pillars of political confidence and social trust. Going beyond this chapter's analysis, inclusionary politics are also shaped by the growing strength of social movements as arenas for political participation as the public's attachment to parties and hierarchical voluntary organizations is weakening in the Trilateral democracies.

Among OECD countries, the correlation between social trust and the size of the governmental sector was positive in the early 1990s (Putnam 1995b, 671). This chapter has argued that the same is true of political confidence. The generous welfare policies that most European states have adopted since the mid-1950s extend from institutional to social inclusion across class, ethnic, and regional lines. In Germany, for example, it is not the down and out who are bowling alone (Offe 1997, 112), and although they have been living for most of the decade through their country's most serious economic recession in the postwar era, the satisfaction of Japanese with their lives has actually increased (to 85 percent) in the 1990s. "Material, spiritual, personal, and social contentment rose through 1993," writes Ōtake in this volume. Although Japan's welfare state is publicly funded, it is a relatively egalitarian, high-performance polity that has brought to the vast majority of its citizens a measure of affluence that would have been scarcely imaginable only three decades ago.

Where inclusionary policies are viewed with suspicion, as in the United States, or systematically undermined by government policies, as in the United Kingdom in the 1980s, this is an important cause of declining political confidence and social trust. In the United States, for example, the loss in political confidence is comparable among economic winners and losers (Nye 1997b, 105; Nye, Zelikow, and King 1997, 258, 263). After a careful investigation of the data, Robert Wuthnow (1997b, 51) concludes that "to the extent that social capital has declined in the United States over the past two decades, a significant share of this decline has occurred among marginalized groups whose living situations have become more difficult during this period" (see also Wuthnow 1997b, 9). In a similar vein Newton concludes that "social trust seems to be most strongly expressed by the winners in society, insofar as it correlates most strongly with education, satisfaction with life, income, class and race. For that matter social trust is the prerogative of the winners in the world" (Newton 1997a, 28; Inglehart 1990, 37; Inglehart 1997a, 174). British data also support this view. "For the most part," Peter Hall (1997, 26) concludes, "political activism and the associational life that sustains it have remained middle class phenomena in Britain and the preserve of those in middle age."

In all of the Trilateral democracies mass publics show a weakening attachment to political parties. Dalton (1998 and 1999) has documented pervasive partisan dealignment in impressive detail and has empirically assessed some of its main causes.[14] One is the rise of new forms of participatory democracy. Kaase (1998, 7, tables 1 and 2, 16–19), for example, writes that "the extension of the citizens' political repertory is probably one of the most pervasive changes in the political orientations of democratic mass publics over the last thirty years." Partisan dealignment and democracy may go hand-in-hand. The rise of social-movement democracy was spurred by opposition to the Vietnam War and symbolized by the student movements of 1968. What to Crozier, Huntington, and Watanuki looked like a grave threat to democracy in 1975 turned out to be an important source of indirect support for democratic government. Political conflicts over international affairs have at times bypassed party politics. Opposition to the war in Vietnam and nuclear arms in the United States, to the deployment of Euromissiles in Germany, and to a military buildup in Japan have been among the issues in which movement politics became normal. So have environmental protection, feminism, and a host of other domestic issues. Partisan dealignment has *not* undermined historically unprecedented levels of support for democratic political processes, democratic principles, and national communities in the Trilateral democracies (Dalton 1999).

Some astute observers have criticized the conclusions that scholars and policy-makers have drawn from the alleged decline of social capital, social trust, and political confidence in the United States as overly pessimistic and one-sided.[15] In the words of Michael Schudson (1996, 19–20), rather than bemoaning the loss of a mythical golden age that was defined among other things by institutionalized social exclusion based on race, gender, and sexual preference, it is "better to conceive the changes we find as a new environment of civic and political activity with altered institutional openings for engagement." "Less likely to find civil society in neighborhoods, families, and churches, Americans are more likely to find it at the workplace, in cyberspace, and in forms of political participation that are less organized and more sporadic than traditional political parties," concludes Alan Wolfe (1997, 12) on the basis of substantial field research. "If we listen carefully both to those who worry about civil society's decline and to their critics, we ought to come away impressed by the capacity of Americans to reinvent their worlds."

As Sidney Tarrow reminds us in this volume, this process of reinven-

---

[14] Unfortunately, the cross-national data do not permit us to distinguish between declining confidence in parties and in the institution of party government.

[15] Most foreign scholars have also been reluctant to embrace the view that the Trilateral democracies are in crisis.

tion may require conceptualizations, types of data, and styles of analysis that are typically neglected in the existing literature on social capital and political confidence (see also Newton 1997c, 581–83). Theda Skocpol (1996, 22) observes perceptively about Putnam's work that "ironically for a scholar who calls for attention to social interconnectedness, Putnam works with atomistic concepts and data." In the words of Wuthnow (1997a, 31), "trust is far more complicated than surveys have managed to capture. It requires paying attention, not only to the social conditions that may reinforce it, but also to the ways in which it is understood." Wolfe (1997, 12) concurs while writing that changes in social relations that affect trust and confidence—cooperation, altruism, or intimacy— "can best be understood as qualitative rather than quantitative in nature." People bring different frames to how they think about trust and confidence that are related to how they interpret their own behavior and that of others. "The diagnosis of moral crisis," argues Maier (1994, 55), "is highly self-reflective."[16]

Throughout the Trilateral democracies, citizens are taking a more skeptical look at political institutions for reasons that this book develops, and many citizens are expanding their understanding and repertoire of what it means to be political. Not only is the personal political: so is the professional and occupational. Social-movement politics is becoming an institutionalized complement to party politics (Tarrow 1998; M. Katzenstein 1998). In the words of Tarrow (this volume), it may well create unenduring commitments of critical citizens. In modern democracies "politicians are less likely to be trusted because they are 'one of us' (Catholic, black, southerner, farmer, gentleman), but because of their policy record and personal performance and appearance. This," writes Newton (1997a, 20), "is not necessarily better or worse, but it is different."

Lacking a well-developed welfare state and experiencing a secular decline in social trust that is unique among the Trilateral democracies, the United States suffers a lagging confidence in representative institutions that is more pervasive than that of any of the other Trilateral democracies. In his chapter in this volume Anthony King sees in the American distrust of government one more instance of American exceptionalism. At the end of World War I the United States sought to make the world safe for democracy—and failed. At the end of World War II the United States attempted to force Germany and Japan to be free (Montgomery 1957)—and succeeded. After the Cold War, in an era of globalization, is

---

[16] Most studies of social capital, political confidence, and social trust lack a sustained discussion of the behavioral power of attitudes in different political contexts (see Nye, Zelikow, and King 1997, 279–80).

the United States exporting its declining institutional confidence to other Trilateral democracies? Or are social movements creating a new-style democratic politics that, like New Age bowling, is revitalizing democratic politics and regenerating political confidence in the Trilateral democracies? At the end of the last century the German sociologist Werner Sombart asked, Why no socialism in America? At the end of this century, we are asking, Why no trust? History does not repeat itself. But does it rhyme?

ACKNOWLEDGMENTS

For their critical comments on earlier drafts I would like to thank Hans-Dieter Klingemann, Takashi Inoguchi, Max Kaase, Mary F. Katzenstein, Joseph S. Nye, Susan Pharr, Fritz Scharpf, Sidney Tarrow, and the participants in the Ford Foundation and American Academy of Arts and Sciences workshop on "Public Trust and Governance in the Trilateral Democracies," Bellagio Conference Center of the Rockefeller Foundation, June 29–July 3, 1998.

SEVEN

The Economics of Civic Trust

Alberto Alesina and Romain Wacziarg

MANY OBSERVERS have argued that the advanced industrial countries are undergoing a crisis of democracy. In spite of the expansion of democracy worldwide (Huntington 1991) and increased confidence in this system of government, some of the established democracies in Europe and North America are experiencing declines in both civic participation and confidence in the institutions of government. In the United States a secular trend of declining confidence can be found in poll data (Dalton 1999) as well as in shifts of voter turnout over time. In other countries trends in confidence as measured in polling data are both more varied and more difficult to establish because of a lack of reliable time-series data.

The most convincing and general evidence for a decline in voter confidence comes from the United States.[1] Dalton (1999) finds a large and statistically significant decline in popular confidence in the institutions of government in the United States between 1952 and 1994. Although there is some recent evidence that the decline may have stopped and perhaps even reversed itself since the early 1990s, other sources confirm this finding. The 1996 Survey of American Political Culture indicated that in 1966, 41 percent of the population had "a great deal of confidence" in the presidency; this figure had fallen to 23 percent in 1976 and 13 percent in 1996. For Congress the figures are 42 percent in 1966, around 15 percent in the 1970s, and only 5 percent in 1996. Only 32 percent of Americans now have "a great deal" or "quite a lot" of confidence in the federal government as a whole. Similarly, the Pew Research Center for the People and the Press (1998) reports that "just 20 percent of Americans are satisfied with the state of the nation and only 34 percent basically trust the government."

Surveying data from various sources, Dalton (1999) found that confidence in government in many other advanced industrial democracies displays, if anything, a downward trend (see also Introduction, this volume). Outside of the United States, available poll data are less directly concerned with confidence per se, but rather with questions such as "Do

---

[1] Throughout this chapter we will use the terms *voter satisfaction* and *public confidence* interchangeably.

politicians care?" In all 14 OECD countries surveyed except the Netherlands, the proportion of negative answers to this type of question has
risen over time, indicating, in Dalton's words, that "there is clear evidence of a general erosion in support for politicians and political institutions in most advanced industrial democracies" (Dalton 1999, 63). The
most striking examples of these trends are Germany and Britain, where
declines in confidence are both large and significant statistically.

Another clear example of decline in voter satisfaction is France, where
the number of alternations of power between parties of the left and right
has recently increased: after 20 years of Gaullist and conservative rule in
the 1960s and 1970s, there have been five major shifts in political orientation since 1981. Although alternations of power are not in themselves
undesirable in a democracy, this increase in instability demonstrates the
impatience of voters, who are constantly sanctioning incumbents. This
change has coincided with a decline in voter turnout and a growing perception that no clear policy alternatives are being offered. Several other
countries in Europe are experiencing similar situations. In Italy the collapse of the so-called First Republic was accompanied by a decline in
citizens' confidence in their government. It is probably too early, however, to establish any trends for the Second Republic.

We can interpret these shifts as a sign that people in many OECD
countries feel less and less confident in their governments. Although the
data needed to establish this fact conclusively are hard to gather, a growing body of evidence supports this conclusion. The decline in confidence
is probably larger for the United States than for other OECD countries,
for which the evidence is more varied both across countries and over
time. Both time-series and cross-country variations in the decline of confidence in government may allow the identification of some of its causes.
And as suggested by Norris (1999), there are two different ways to assess
this trend: either the nature of public policy, public action, and government performance has changed in such a way that the declining confidence reveals a true "crisis of democracy," or voters are becoming more
mature, and their loss of confidence in government is a healthy expression of a more critical electorate.

THE MEANING OF VOTER DISSATISFACTION

As noted above, voters in many advanced industrial democracies express
increasing discontent about their governments. Before discussing possible
economic explanations for this phenomenon, we address two questions:
Can we formally define voter dissatisfaction and its change over time?
When is the level of voter dissatisfaction "too low" or "too high"?

Voter Satisfaction and the Median Voter

Regarding the first question, one can think of three different ways in which citizens' satisfaction may decrease. First, voters may perceive politicians to be less competent and/or more corrupt than before. In other words, governments are now perceived as less able than in the past to deliver the same set of policies. Keeping voter preferences and the capacity of the political system to respond to those preferences fixed, we can equate this with a decline in the quality of policy.

To illustrate the other two types of voter dissatisfaction, it is useful to recall some simple notions of voting theory and rational choice. One of the most famous results in social choice theory is the "median voter theorem" of Black (1956) and Downs (1957). According to this theorem, under certain specific conditions, majoritarian voting will lead to the adoption of the policy preferred by the median voter. In the context of general elections the median voter theorem holds when two candidates (or parties) face each other and care only about winning; that is, they do not have policy preferences of their own. Under these conditions both parties will adopt the median voter policy platform preferred by the median voter, and full convergence of platforms and policies ensues.

This result holds regardless of the distribution of voters' preferences. Figure 7.1 illustrates three different preference distributions, all of which share the same median. In all three cases, the equilibrium policy is the same. In case A the distribution is relatively tight around the median. In case B the distribution is much more spread out. Comparing B with A, it follows that on average, two randomly drawn individuals from distribution B will be farther from the median voter, thus farther from the chosen policy. As a result, voter dissatisfaction will be higher in case B. Analogous arguments apply to case C. Here the distribution is bimodal, but, once again, relative to case A, the median distance of a randomly drawn individual from the median voter will be higher.

The point is that the second characterization of citizen satisfaction can be identified with median distance from the median voter (while keeping fixed the position of the median voter).[2] In cases B and C the "median distance from the median" is higher than in case A. As a result, people's preferences are more spread out, and it is more costly for voters to agree on a common set of policies and pool their resources to achieve a given objective.

---

[2] Alesina, Baqir, and Easterly (1997a) formally develop a voting model in which the median distance from the median voter is a critical determinant of people's willingness to cooperate by pooling resources needed to produce useful public goods.

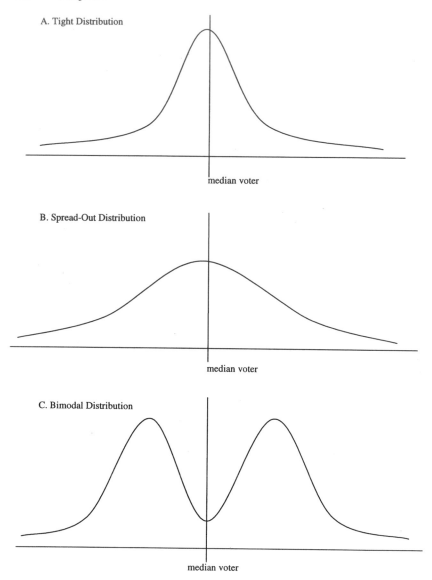

Figure 7.1. Distributions of Voter Preferences over a Single Policy Issue

This analysis has two implications. In the context of cross-country comparisons, it suggests why the average level of confidence in government may be different in countries with different voter populations. In more homogeneous citizenries, which are closer to case A, the level of confidence is highest. In countries with preferences distributed as in cases

B or C, the level of confidence is lower. In this chapter, however, we are more concerned with a second, dynamic implication. If, *within a country*, the distribution of voter preferences evolves over time from a case similar to A toward a situation more like B or C, then the average level of citizen confidence will decrease. There are two reasons why the political equilibrium might move from case A to case B or C. First, the distribution of voter preferences may have changed. Second, the issues at the forefront of the government's agenda may have changed, moving from those for which the distribution of voter preferences is like case A to other issues for which the distribution is like case B or C. Needless to say, these two sources of change are not mutually exclusive and may well operate simultaneously. In this chapter we argue that changes in the nature of government intervention in the economy may indeed have changed the public preferences from type A distributions to type B or C distributions.

The third way in which dissatisfaction can increase has to do with how the political system translates the preferences of the median voter into actual policy goals. Consider Figure 7.2, which reproduces case A of Figure 7.1. For whatever reason the policy choice does not reflect the median voter's preference. Obviously, if the median policy were feasible, one of the two candidates would choose it, win the election, and this case would not emerge as an equilibrium. But if supra-national constraints, for example, rendered the median policy unfeasible, then policy P of Figure 7.2 may represent the only possible equilibrium. If this is the case, then in moving from case A in Figure 7.1 to Figure 7.2, the median distance from the policy choice increases, and the level of confidence in government policies correspondingly decreases.

In this case, too, one can think of two nonexclusive reasons why the electorate may perceive the political outcome to be characterized by Figure 7.2. First, within the set of feasible policies, the policy choice is differ-

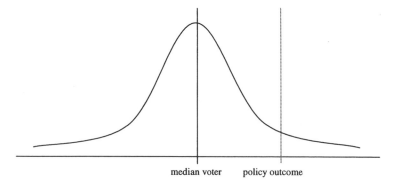

median voter   policy outcome

Figure 7.2. Bias in the Transmission of Voter Preferences into Political Choice

ent from the one preferred by the median voter. Second is a problem of perception and complexity of policy. In a world where governments do more and more and the various constraints on policy imply a growing complexity of government action, voters may find it more and more difficult to perceive adequately the relationship between government policy choices and the electorate's desired outcomes. In other words, voters face greater uncertainty about whether government policy really reflects their goals.

Finally, a word of caution about the model. The median voter result is very stylized and does not always provide a realistic characterization of the complexities of multiparty democracies. The point here, of course, is not to develop a realistic model of multiparty democracies, or even of a two-party political system. We are well aware that this task would require much more.[3] The point of using the median voter model is simply to characterize different ways of explaining the decline in confidence.

Indeed, the basic implication of our discussion carries over beyond the median voter model. Consider, for example, the case of two parties that have ideologies and care about their policies. For instance, in Figure 7.3 (which reproduces the preference distribution of case A in Figure 7.1), we have two parties, "Left" and "Right," with corresponding ideal policies. Under certain realistic conditions the two parties will adopt partially convergent policies; namely, they will converge toward each other, but not completely.[4] If the distribution of voter preferences becomes more polarized, the average distance of a randomly drawn voter will be higher *for*

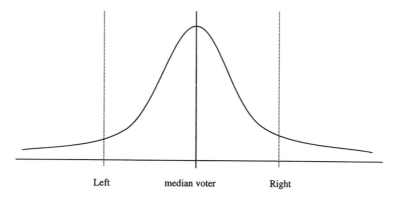

Left   median voter   Right

Figure 7.3. Partially Convergent Party Platforms

(In all figures, preferences refere to preferences regarding feasible policy outcomes.)

[3] As a matter of fact, much of the work of one of the authors of this paper is very critical of the median voter theorem as an unrealistic characterization of two-party democracy. See Alesina and Rosenthal (1995) and Alesina, Roubini, and Cohen (1997).

[4] See chapter 2 of Alesina and Rosenthal (1995) for a discussion of this type of model.

given parties' ideal policies. The implication here is that it may be unreasonable to assume that the two parties' policies will remain the same if the distribution of voters' preferences changes, because, at least up to a point, party policies must reflect the electorate's distribution of ideal policies.

This two-party model with polarized policies can be used to make another point that the stricter interpretation of the median voter model does not encompass. Suppose that, for a given distribution of voter preferences, say the case of Figure 7.3, the policies advocated by parties become more polarized. A larger fraction of the voters, those in the middle of the political spectrum, will become increasingly dissatisfied with the two parties as they move away from the median. We argue below that this phenomenon may help explain the fall in voter satisfaction in the United States.

In summary, we posit three types of voter dissatisfaction: first, dissatisfaction originating from the government's incompetence and the lack of honesty among elected officials (the *policy quality hypothesis*); second, dissatisfaction originating from greater polarization of preferences (the *heterogeneity hypothesis*); third, dissatisfaction originating from the deviation of policies from the electorate's median (the *representation hypothesis*). We discuss evidence for all three arguments. Before doing so, however, it is worth addressing our second question, namely, whether voters' satisfaction with their governments was "too high" in the past or is "too low" now.

The Optimal Level of Voter Satisfaction

The question of an optimal level hinges on how one interprets voter satisfaction. If one views it as a measure of government performance, it can never be too high. This interpretation, however, is incomplete at best. Voter satisfaction reflects not only an evaluation of government performance, but also a comparison with voters' prior expectations, standards, and ability to monitor government. A change in voters' expectations about what governments can and should do would change voter satisfaction for a given level of government performance. Similarly, an increase in the ability to evaluate government activity (thanks to greater flows of information or enhanced human capital, for example) would lead to changes in voter satisfaction. Within this more articulated view of voter satisfaction, it is meaningful to ask whether the level of confidence in government at any given time is too high or too low.

From an empirical point of view, this question is almost impossible to answer. From a theoretical point of view, the optimal level of confidence in government depends on one's conception of government. Neoclassical economists think of governments as social planners, namely, benevolent agents who maximize social welfare. An extreme Chicago version of this argument would be that inefficient governments will not survive and will be replaced by better ones. Thus, a high level of voter dissatisfaction should be a temporary phenomenon: in a steady-state equilibrium, the electorate should be happy with its social planners. At the opposite extreme, one can think of the public choice view of government as a Leviathan. In this case voters should deeply mistrust their governments. In fact, mistrust would a very good starting point for citizens wishing to defend themselves against the Leviathan. Trusting and satisfied voters would simply be gullible voters.

The point here is not to offer a complete treatment of the role of government, but simply to argue that antithetical views of the economic role of the public sector lead to diametrically opposed conclusions about the "correct" attitude of voters toward government. The simple fact that voters' confidence in government may be falling is thus insufficient for drawing a pessimistic conclusion. Perhaps electorates are achieving a more realistic view of their governments. Of course, this view still leaves us with the task of explaining why the level of confidence was too high in the past.

GOVERNMENT COMPETENCE

In this section we explore how government policy, especially macroeconomic policy, has failed since 1974 to perform as well as in the preceding three decades. We interpret this as an example of how our policy quality hypothesis can sometimes explain declines in civic confidence: for a given policy objective of the median voter, for a given distribution of voter preferences around those of the median voter, and for a given ability of the political process to translate these preferences into policies, we argue that governments have been less able to deliver outcomes of the same quality as in the past.

Macroeconomic Policy Outcomes

A vast literature suggests that government popularity depends on basic macroeconomic variables, in particular income growth, unemployment, and inflation. The evidence is extremely solid and clear-cut for the United States, a bit murkier for other OECD countries.[5] For the United States the evidence suggests that the rate of GDP growth is the best

[5] On the United States see Kramer (1971), Fair (1978), and Alesina and Rosenthal (1995). On other OECD countries see Lewis-Beck (1988), Powell and Whitten (1993), and Alesina, Perotti, and Tavares (1998).

predictor among economic variables of the electorate's level of satisfaction. Inflation and unemployment are also important, but less so. For other OECD countries, the results vary depending on the institutional framework, the nature of government (e.g., a two-party or multiparty system), and the economic structure. While sweeping generalizations are difficult, broadly speaking, the evidence suggests that inflation, growth, and unemployment do affect electoral results, although in different ways and to a different extent in different countries. This is not the place for an in-depth analysis of the effects of economic conditions on voting behavior in a cross section of OECD countries; for this the reader is referred to Lewis-Beck (1988), Powell and Whitten (1993), Paldam (1991), and Alesina, Perotti, and Tavares (1998), among others. Here we are simply starting with the rather uncontroversial premise that voters in any country prefer higher to lower growth and lower to higher unemployment and inflation. Obviously there can be trade-offs among these variables, although only in the short run, and voters may disagree on the optimal trade-offs, but the assumption is that a voter cannot be happier with, say, higher inflation *and* higher unemployment.

In this chapter we are not particularly interested in cyclical fluctuations of popularity, but rather in secular trends in confidence in government, where by "secular" we mean movements over the last three or four decades. If voters react at the cyclical frequency to these three variables (unemployment, inflation, and growth), and if these same variables exhibit secular trends, then perhaps these long-term trends are correlated with secular trends in voter satisfaction. Table 7.1 summarizes the evidence on these three variables for the United States, Japan, the European Union average, and the OECD average. All variables deteriorated in all samples: average growth fell, average unemployment rose, and average inflation also rose from the pre-1974 to the post-1974 period.

Admittedly, using the first oil shock as the watershed between periods conceals some important differences in the two decades following 1974. In fact, the 20 years following the first oil shock displayed a marked deterioration of macroeconomic performance before the mid-1980s and an improvement thereafter. Improvement over the last decade has not been even, however. Unemployment has worsened in Europe, for example, and the average rate of growth has been much lower in Europe than in the United States. Recent events in Southeast Asia as well as a major recession since 1992 have undermined the prospects for a continuing miracle in Japan. The variability of macroeconomic outcomes has unquestionably risen since the early 1970s, and insofar as people care about the volatility of their environment (in addition to the absolute level of economic indicators), this also helps explain shifts in civic confidence.

TABLE 7.1
Deterioration of Macroeconomic Performance

	1961–73 Average	1974–93 Average*
Growth of GDP		
OECD average	5.030%	2.481%
EU15 average	4.941	2.280
United States	3.842	2.346
Japan	9.170	3.825
Germany	4.234	2.179
France	5.268	2.362
Unemployment Rate		
OECD average	2.354	6.139
EU15 average	2.338	7.148
United States	4.899	6.920
Japan	1.251	2.270
Germany	0.563	4.599
France	2.014	7.852
Inflation Rate**		
OECD average	4.903	9.845
EU15 average	4.533	8.589
United States	3.158	5.606
Japan	5.904	4.299
Germany	3.329	3.459
France	4.663	7.164

Notes: OECD and EU15 averages are unweighted. *1974–91 for Germany. **Defined as the growth rate of the consumer expenditure deflator.
Source: OECD.

Government Size

Although the macroeconomic performance of the last two decades has not been stellar relative to the previous period, government involvement in the economy has increased tremendously. Table 7.2 demonstrates that for the OECD sample, the share of government spending in GDP has basically doubled between 1960 and today, from 25 percent to almost 50 percent. Tax revenues lagged behind expenditures in the 1970s and early 1980s, increasing more rapidly thereafter. As a result, budget deficits remained high in many countries between 1975 and 1985. The last decade or so has witnessed several major attempts on the part of OECD governments with large public-sector deficits to balance their budgets. In many cases these adjustments were motivated by a desire to join the European

TABLE 7.2
Revenue and Spending as a Percentage of GDP

	1960	1997
Total Revenue		
OECD average	27.09%	45.45%
EU15 average	28.16	46.55
United States	26.36	31.98
Japan	18.77	33.05
Total Spending		
OECD average	25.73	46.66
EU15 average	26.86	49.90
United States	25.70	31.98
Japan	16.86	34.72
Primary Spending*		
OECD average	24.03	41.47
EU15 average	25.16	44.07
United States	24.40	30.13
Japan	16.33	30.96

Notes: OECD and EU15 averages are unweighted. *Excludes interest payments on the public debt.
Source: OECD.

Monetary Union. Even during periods of fiscal adjustments, however, expenditures kept increasing with very few exceptions, and taxes increased even more as a percentage of GDP. With lower macroeconomic performance and higher government involvement in the economy, the least one can say is that the productivity of government intervention in terms of its ability to deliver stable and favorable economic outcomes has fallen dramatically.

Although it must be conceded that some of the increase in government size was used for redistributive or insurance purposes in the face of economic shocks like the oil crisis, it is hard to deny that it has played a part in reducing performance. It is not surprising that its social marginal product should shrink as government grows.[6] Furthermore, as the public sector commands a larger and larger share of GDP, the electorate holds it more and more accountable for the state of the economy because its

[6] On the optimal size of government from a growth perspective, see Barro (1990). This paper identifies an optimal size of government beyond which government consumption results in reduced growth. The optimal size of government is derived from a trade-off between the productive aspects of certain government expenditures and the distortionary effects of the taxes needed to finance them.

actions are rightly perceived to have a growing impact on economic outcomes. If, as we argued earlier, these outcomes have become less favorable as government has expanded, it is only natural that satisfaction with government should have declined.

It is interesting to compare the United States and Europe with respect to government size and macroeconomic performance. While average economic performance since 1974 has deteriorated in both places, growth has been higher and unemployment lower in the United States than in the European Union in the last decade or so. How is this consistent with the fact that voter satisfaction seems to have decreased more in the United States than in Europe? One possible answer is that a more extensive welfare state in Europe may have dispersed the costs of unemployment to a broader base of taxpayers. In other words, high unemployment is more tolerable in the presence of social protection, even when the fiscal costs of that protection may in fact contribute to keeping unemployment high. Although a generous welfare state may lessen the costs of unemployment, it also expands redistributive flows that generate political conflicts, which is the topic of the next section. In the United States the deterioration of the macroeconomic environment has led to increased income inequality rather than higher unemployment, and this may have helped reduce civic confidence by means of the polarization mechanism described above. A further indication that this may well be the case is that the prolonged expansion of the U.S. economy since 1992 has coincided with a stabilization—if not a slight reversal—of the downward trend in civic confidence.

In summary, citizens of a typical OECD country have observed a massive increase in government economic intervention and a deterioration in macroeconomic conditions in the last few decades. Several observers, including the authors of this chapter, would argue that the massive increase in government intervention is at least partially responsible for some of our current macroeconomic ills. This is certainly the case in many European countries, where the burdens of taxation and extensive government regulation, particularly of labor markets, are generally viewed as the main culprit for persistently high levels of unemployment. As we argue in the next section, however, while an increase in the size of government is observable in all OECD countries, the dimensions of the increase and the composition of government spending differ quite significantly in the United States and many European countries.

Corruption

The degree of honesty of politicians and bureaucrats is another measure of the quality of policy. Is there any evidence that corruption has increased in OECD countries? Italy, Japan, and South Korea are examples of countries in which, for a variety of reasons, voters became less tolerant of persistent corruption, and this became a crucial issue over the last two decades. It is hard to establish whether the actual level of corruption rose sharply in Italy and Japan in recent years, however.

On the one hand, it is extremely difficult to assemble time-series data on objective measures of political corruption in OECD countries. By its very nature, objective measurements of corruption are hard to obtain, so one has to rely on subjective measures, namely, surveys in which people are asked about their perceptions of corruption. Furthermore, most available data on corruption across countries rate OECD countries very close to one another, so there is very little variance from which to draw inferences. Finally, although these measures of corruption may be reasonably useful for the purpose of cross-national comparisons, they are not useful in establishing time trends within each country because they lack time-series variation.

On the other hand, even if objective measures of observed corruption were available, this would be of little help in assessing the true degree of underlying corruption. Perhaps the detection technology for such activities has improved over time. If that is the case, then a rising level of observed corruption would be perfectly compatible with a reduction in its true level because improved detection is likely to deter bureaucrats and politicians from breaking the law. Rational voters would not lose confidence in government as a result of this. But it is difficult to establish whether it is the true level of corruption that has increased in some OECD countries or whether it is detection that has improved, so it is difficult to ascribe the decline in civic confidence to this phenomenon. One is left with the weaker conclusion that, for a given level of corruption, citizens may have grown less tolerant of corrupt acts, but it would be difficult to provide anything but anecdotal evidence for this.

POLARIZATION

Redistribution and Polarization

Increasingly, governments in OECD countries are becoming redistributive machines; that is, they tax someone in order to redistribute to someone else. In fact, transfers account for virtually all of the increase in government size documented in Table 7.3. As a share of GDP, government consumption of goods and services is roughly stable, and government investment is declining. Thus, while governments were mainly providers of public goods and infrastructure in the 1950s, today they are primarily involved in redistribution. The other component of government outlays

TABLE 7.3
Composition of Expenditures as a Percentage of GDP

	1960	1997
Transfers		
OECD average	7.95%	19.74%
EU15 average	8.85	21.34
United States	5.58	13.71
Japan	3.98	15.08
Government Wages		
OECD average	8.04	11.95
EU15 average	8.37	12.48
United States	9.01	9.73
Japan	5.91	7.24
Public Investment		
OECD average	3.35	2.77
EU15 average	3.03	2.49
United States	5.36	2.80
Japan	3.88	5.72

Notes: OECD and EU15 averages are unweighted.
Source: OECD.

that has increased is government wages. It is likely that a portion of public wages is also used as an instrument of redistribution toward politically powerful groups. In Italy public employment has been widely used to redistribute fiscal resources from the North to the South, for example.[7] Similarly, Alesina, Baqir, and Easterly (1997b) document the use of public employment for redistributive purposes in U.S. cities. They find that public employment per capita is higher in cities with greater income inequality and ethnic fragmentation.

An extended welfare state has two effects. First, as discussed above, it provides social insurance, removing some economic risks against which the market cannot adequately insure. Second, it also generates a complex web of redistributive flows. The more governments redistribute, the more they generate winners and losers: while everyone can take advantage of public goods and infrastructures, which are generally of a nonrival nature, it is necessarily the case that somebody gains and somebody loses in redistributive schemes. Given that redistribution is inherently conflictual, it may polarize the interests of voters. In other words, the median distance from the median voter increases. Forced to support overex-

[7] For an excellent discussion of the distortions and inefficiencies of public employment and the welfare system in Italy, see Rostagno and Utili (1998).

tended welfare states, taxpayers become more vocal as the tax burden continues to increase. Recipients of net transfers, on the other hand, become accustomed to government generosity, and any attempt to reduce their benefits also invites vocal complaints. Thus, the more governments become redistributive machines, the more they generate direct conflicts between winners and losers, and the more difficult it becomes to reverse the trend of increasing redistribution.[8] If it is assumed that losers are more vocal than winners, this increased conflict will result in increased dissatisfaction with government.

A particularly important example of this phenomenon is the case of pensions, one of the largest components of government transfers. As the population ages and pension systems start to face financial difficulties, governments try either to reduce the benefits of current or prospective retirees or to increase payroll taxes. The first option riles those who feel that the rules of the game are being changed just as they are about to benefit from them. The second option generates dissatisfaction among the relatively young, who feel that they bear an ever-increasing tax burden to support preceding generations. Similar arguments apply to public employment. Public employees are very vocal in their outrage when faced with attempts to reduce their benefits. Taxpayers, on the other hand, are losing tolerance for increasingly large and inefficient bureaucracies.

The Cases of Europe and the United States

The size of the welfare state varies from country to country. It is larger in Europe than in the United States, and larger within certain European countries than in others; it is much larger in Nordic countries than in Britain, for example. As Table 7.3 demonstrates, however, transfers as a share of GDP have more than doubled between 1960 and 1997 in both the European Union and in the United States, while they have nearly quadrupled in Japan. We argue that this increase helps explain the decline in public confidence, especially in the United States.

In countries with growing welfare states, such as many European nations, the growth of government is self-sustaining, leading to an excessive and ever-increasing tax burden.[9] As the welfare state expands, a growing segment of the population receives more and more of its income from the government, that is, from other taxpayers. These recipients of public monies include pensioners, whose share in the total population is increasing for demographic reasons, beneficiaries of long-term unemployment

[8] See Olson (1982) for a similar point.
[9] Meltzer and Richards (1981) were the first to formulate the idea of a political equilibrium that generates a self-sustaining increase in the welfare state. See also Alesina and Rodrik (1994).

compensation, public employees, and recipients of income-support programs. In addition, a fraction of these groups, especially pensioners, are relatively wealthy and have the time to engage in political activities, so their weight in public policy-making may be greater than their weight in the electorate. Furthermore, it may be rational for each taxpayer or constituency individually to insist on preserving the transfers they receive even if it would be collectively optimal to overhaul the welfare state. In other words, the economy suffers from a coordination problem. As a larger constituency comes to support the welfare state, it too becomes larger, inducing a vicious cycle. As this political equilibrium develops, taxpayers become increasingly unhappy. When governments attempt to reduce the weight of the welfare state due to mounting constraints on their finances, those people whose income depends on it are particularly vocal in their disapproval.

In the United States the political equilibrium is quite different, and in some ways precisely the opposite. In this country the welfare state is narrower and public nonmilitary expenditures much lower than in the average European country. A large majority of the American electorate views government as a burden and an impediment to market activities. But if the increase in the size of the welfare state has something to do with increasing voter dissatisfaction, why has public confidence fallen more in the United States than in Europe when the American welfare state is smaller than its average European counterpart?

Three details of the American case may help resolve this apparent contradiction and explain why a given increase in the size of the welfare state may have led to a larger decline in public confidence in the United States than in Europe. First, the welfare state and racial problems are deeply interconnected in the United States. Wilson (1996, 193, 202) eloquently puts it as follows: "Many White Americans have turned against a strategy that emphasizes programs that they perceive as benefiting only racial minorities. Public services are identified mainly with Blacks, private services mainly with Whites." Poterba (1997) convincingly demonstrates that the elderly object to increasing local taxes used to finance education, and this effect is much stronger when these funds are used to support public educational programs in which minority children are perceived to be the main beneficiaries. Alesina, Baqir, and Easterly (1997a, 1997b) examine a large body of evidence on spending programs in U.S. localities and conclude that ethnic fragmentation is a major determinant of the allocation of public funds: public goods are less abundant in ethnically fragmented cities. In this context a smaller expansion of the welfare state than has occurred in Europe can result in a greater decline in voter satisfaction.

A second peculiarity of the American case has to do with the degree of polarization of its two main parties, especially their most vocal activists, vis-à-vis the position of the median voter. This is particularly relevant to the size of the welfare state. Although a large majority of the American public probably favors limited welfare programs, the two parties offer polarized choices: While Democratic activists champion a large expansion of welfare, many Republican activists advocate drastic cuts. Similar examples of party polarization can be found on such issues as abortion and school prayer. Poole and Rosenthal (1984) have amply documented the increased polarization of American political activists. In fact, according to polling conducted by the Pew Research Center for the People and the Press (1998), excessive partisanship is one of the main reasons Americans give for distrusting the government.[10] This suggests that the excessive polarization of the two parties has much to do with voter dissatisfaction.[11] American voters feel discontented because they face only extreme choices, the flip side of our earlier argument regarding the increased polarization of voter preferences themselves (which may apply more directly to Europe).

Third, culture, traditions, and social norms also play a role. In the United States much more than in Europe, the idea of the "self-made man" is pervasive: Citizens are expected to be masters of their own fortunes with little help from others, especially the government. Thus, while European governments are often criticized for inadequately protecting some group of potential beneficiaries, America's federal government is often criticized on opposite grounds, for trying to do too much. For a given increase in the size of the welfare state, the resulting decline in satisfaction due to heightened distributional conflict is thus likely to be greater in the United States than in Europe.

This implies a paradox. In Europe, where governments occupy a larger share of the economy, they are often criticized for doing too little, particularly by those who are already well protected by government programs. In the United States, on the other hand, where the government is smaller, it is often criticized for doing too much. This observation points to the possible existence of two polarized equilibria. In the first, an increasing fraction of the population relies on government support and provides the backing for increasing the scope of the welfare state. In the second, a shrinking fraction of the population takes advantage of government services and provides shrinking support for taxation.

---

[10] More generally the survey reports that "When asked to say in their own words why they do not like government, 40% of those with an unfavorable opinion of the government offer complaints about political leaders or the political system as the reason for their negative view."

[11] As argued by Fiorina (1992) and Alesina and Rosenthal (1995), divided government is the result of voters' attempt to implement moderate policies by splitting control of government institutions between polarized parties.

SOVEREIGNTY

We argued above that growing voter dissatisfaction could also originate from increased discrepancies between the preferences of the median voter and the policies actually implemented, keeping fixed the distribution of voter preferences and the quality of policy.[12] This idea provides a good framework with which to understand the effects of international economic integration on voters' confidence in government. Globalization challenges democratic institutions in two distinct ways. First, the international environment reduces governments' latitude to implement preferred policies. Second, certain policy prerogatives tend to be transferred to supra-national institutions without a concurrent transfer of sovereignty, reducing democratic control over policy outcomes. This point is especially valid in the case of Europe.

Rising International Constraints on Policy

Even if policy-makers and the median voter seek to maximize the same objective function, a tightening of the constraints on policy will lower voter satisfaction. Since World War II economic integration has risen sharply. As measured by the ratio of imports plus exports to GDP averaged over a sample of 61 countries, the volume of trade has increased from 43.2 percent in 1950 to 60.6 percent in 1992. But economic integration is not limited to trade: financial markets have become more tightly linked as the share of domestic assets owned by foreign entities has increased sharply in most industrial countries. These trends have been supplemented by a move toward "deep integration" in most developed nations, the breaking up of the process of production into different stages, each potentially occurring in a different country. Falling transportation costs permit a slicing up of the value-added chain: multinational firms can "produce a good in a number of stages in a number of locations, adding a little bit of value at each stage" (Krugman 1995). This allows producers to locate each step of the production process in the most advantageous location.

The flip side of this development is to undermine governments' ability actively to monitor and direct industrial activity. And whatever the objective desirability of active industrial policies (it may not be great), this limitation on governments' potential influence is sufficient to drive a

---

[12] A Rasmussen Research poll published in April of 1998 found that only 9 percent of American adults believe that U.S. politicians represent the American people. The polling agency also reports that "34% of Americans believe that the government reflects the will of the people. Half (47%) say it does not, while 20% are not sure."

wedge between the preferences of the median voter and feasible policy outcomes.

The impact of globalization on public policy is not limited to industrial policy, of course. International constraints also affect macroeconomic policy, for example. It has often been pointed out that capital market integration across the OECD has reduced the effectiveness of monetary policy; countries face the threat of capital flight and devaluation if they do not maintain a strict anti-inflationary stance. This was especially true in Europe during the 1980s, when many countries such as France would immediately have been sanctioned by global financial markets had they not closely followed the same monetary policy as the German central bank. Thus, in this dimension, too, globalization has reduced the ability of governments to conduct autonomous policies as prescribed by the domestic system of political decision-making. And while these constraints may have led to more virtuous policies in the long run, they have also put a growing range of potentially important economic decisions under constraints that lie outside of the control of nation-states. Indeed, there is mounting evidence that the average European voter is and has for some time been less enthusiastic about European integration and monetary union than his or her leaders. Germany provides a good example of this point, with Chancellor Helmut Kohl actively supporting monetary union despite the objections of a majority of voters.

The Declining Authority of Nation-States

Beyond the constraints that globalization imposes on domestic policies, international economic integration has also required some explicit transfers of political prerogatives to supra-national institutions, often without a concurrent transfer of sovereignty. In other words, as powers are transferred further away from citizens, the objective functions of the median voter and relevant policy-makers are becoming more and more distinct.

The prime example of this shift is the European Union, where policies decided in common now range from agricultural policy to monetary matters and competition regulation.[13] Because the European Parliament has a very limited ability to control the actions of the European executive branch, these transfers have occurred without a corresponding transfer of popular sovereignty. Executive decisions made at the Council of Ministers result from negotiations among representatives of member nations, each presumably representing the preferences of a different median voter. It is very unlikely that these decisions could effectively reflect the choices

---

[13] See Alesina and Wacziarg (1998) for a recent discussion of European political integration.

favored by the median voters of each country, and it is unlikely that the European median voter (defined as the median voter obtained by pooling the electorates of member states) would see his or her preferences implemented either.

Although they are still the basic units in which democratic sovereignty operates, the authority of nation-states is thus threatened from above by the rise of supra-national institutions. But they are also threatened from below by the rise of separatist and regionalist movements in Europe.[14] Alesina, Spolaore, and Wacziarg (1997) argue that globalization in the form of a liberalization of the trade regime provides heterogeneous groups with access to large markets without their having to share institutions with other groups. Indeed, if the optimal size of countries is determined by a trade-off between the gains from scale and the costs of ethnic, cultural, and linguistic heterogeneity, trade liberalization should result in a multiplication of countries because the benefits of country size, in terms of returns to scale, are reduced when access to foreign markets is assured. In other words, economic integration leads to political disintegration. In fact, there is considerable empirical evidence to support this claim. In the interwar years, a period of increasing protectionism, practically no countries were created. But in the aftermath of World War II, when global trade started to rise sharply as a result of liberalization and falling transportation costs, the number of countries exploded from 74 in 1945 to 192 in 1997.

The problem with these tendencies toward greater autonomy is that they take time to result in actual secessions. In fact, most episodes of country creation have occurred in lumps as the result of a major political event like the end of a war. The end of World War II resulted in a first wave of decolonization, and the end of the Cold War brought an explosion in the number of countries in Eastern Europe and the former Soviet Union. The process of country formation is far from smooth, largely because of centers' resistance to letting go of their regions. When the fundamental conditions determining the optimal number of countries change, as happens when the world becomes increasingly integrated economically, yet there is resistance to secessions or mergers, there will be heterogeneous groups that would like to secede but cannot. In such a situation these groups are likely to voice growing dissatisfaction with the nation-state from which they would like to secede.

Even if these demands for political autonomy do not always take the form of explicitly separatist movements, as is increasingly the case in Europe, they may take the form of more subdued demands for greater de-

---

[14] In the United States this takes the form of greater demands for decentralization by individual states.

centralization and local empowerment, as in the United States. The bottom line is that, in many cases, the nation-state does not seem to be the optimal unit for decision-making anymore. For a wide range of economic issues, the optimal unit for decision-making lies above the nation-state, at the supra-national level, and for a growing range of political or local issues the optimal unit lies below the nation-state, at the regional level. Until *both* sovereignty and political prerogatives are transferred to these new units of political and economic decision-making, voter satisfaction and confidence in the traditional institutions of the nation-state are likely to decline further.

Finally, discrepancies between voter preferences and governmental policy can arise from the increased complexity of public policy. A global economy, supranational institutions, national entities, and local governments interact in ways that give rise to a complex division of political prerogatives, conflicts among levels of government, and difficulties in assessing who should be held accountable for which policy outcomes. One can argue that the multiplication of levels of government, the rapidly expanding amount of information that voters need to process in order to understand the actions of government, and the increased expertise needed to exercise governmental power have all led to more complex political systems. One response to this trend is that governments have had to become more technocratic, which is another way of saying that the distance between citizens and policy has increased. This certainly explains much of the decline in confidence in a country like France, where complaints about the excessive technocracy of ruling elites is a recurring theme at election time. This is another way in which the objective functions of policy-makers and voters can come to differ.

CONCLUSION

This chapter has suggested three possible interpretations for the decline in public confidence in the advanced industrial democracies. First, the quality of government policy may have declined. Second, the distribution of voter preferences may have become more polarized. Finally, the ability or willingness of political actors to deliver the policies favored by the median voter may have been reduced. For each of these explanations we have provided examples illustrating how recent economic shifts could help explain the drop in public confidence. Comparing the economic performance of OECD countries before and after the 1974 oil shock, we showed that growing voter dissatisfaction may be due in part to the weaker performance of the last 25 years in terms of average inflation, economic growth, and unemployment. Although the decline in performance is not necessarily attributable to inappropriate government activities, we argued that the observed correlation between government approval ratings and measures of economic performance indicates that governments are generally held accountable by voters for the state of the economy.

We then argued that the rise of the welfare state has polarized voter preferences. In Europe each constituency is happy to receive government handouts and reduce other constituencies' share of the public-sector pie. This struggle among pressure groups has resulted in an upward spiral of government transfers, leading to increased discontent with the privileges of others and a diminished willingness to surrender one's own. In the United States the game has been played out differently: the unwillingness of voters to be taxed in order to finance transfers to certain constituencies has limited the government's ability to expand the welfare state, and this tendency is increased by the influence of racial conflict on welfare politics. This explains why a given rise in the size of the welfare state has resulted in a greater fall in public confidence in the United States. It is the increased polarization of America's main parties over the proper extent of government involvement rather than the polarization of voter preferences themselves that has irked relatively moderate voters.

Finally, we argued that globalization tends to drive a wedge between the preferences of the hypothetical median voter and the actual policies being implemented. First, globalization sets limits on the set of feasible policies. Second, economic integration has resulted in transfers of powers to supra-national institutions as well as demands for local autonomy. This has not, however, led to corresponding transfers of sovereignty. Because it is increasingly viewed as "too big to run everyday life and too small to manage international affairs" (Newhouse 1997), the nation-state may be the real target of voter dissatisfaction. The organization of public life among local, national, and supra-national governments has been undergoing profound transformations, especially in Europe. In this context declining voter confidence may result from natural worries about a rapidly changing polity.

ACKNOWLEDGMENTS

This chapter was prepared for the Conference on Public Trust and Governance in the Trilateral Democracies, at the Rockefeller Study and Conference Center, Bellagio, Italy, June 29–July 3, 1998. We thank our discussant Peter Katzenstein as well as Susan Pharr, Robert Putnam, and many other conference participants for their useful comments, but all errors are ours alone.

PART III

Sources of the Problem:
Erosion of Fidelity

EIGHT

Officials' Misconduct and Public Distrust: Japan and the Trilateral Democracies

Susan J. Pharr

ITS TWENTIETH-CENTURY TRIUMPH over rival political systems has not spared democracy some lingering ills. Foremost among these is widespread citizen distrust of government across the Trilateral countries. From Washington to Paris, from Tokyo to Milan, public disaffection is an everyday reality. According to recent work on the subject, declining confidence in government and the institutions of representative democracy marks recent decades in Austria, Belgium, Britain, Canada, Finland, Germany, Ireland, Italy, Japan, the Netherlands, Norway, Spain, Sweden, and the United States (see Introduction, this volume; Dalton 1997; Nye, Zelikow, and King 1997). Attempts to explain it abound, as this volume attests.

In the litany of candidate causes, two explanations stand out. The first points the finger at society, arguing, in effect, that confidence in government can be kindled in citizens only when social capital is in good supply and, conversely, that it diminishes when stores of social capital run low. Though more sophisticated formulations of this thesis posit a complex, indirect relationship between social capital and political trust (see Introduction, this volume), much of the contemporary debate over social capital assumes that a direct relationship exists. The second explanation points to the policy performance of leaders, notably their handling of the economy, and holds that good times boost citizens' confidence in government while economic downturns erode it. This chapter tests both of these theories by examining the experience of Japan. Neither one, it shows, can explain low levels of citizen satisfaction with politics and government in Japan over the past 20 years. It then offers a far more compelling explanation. Leadership has two distinct dimensions: policy performance and "conduct in office." Although both are obviously important, a preoccupation with the former leads us to discount the importance of the latter in liberal democracies. This chapter demonstrates that in Japan, at least, officials' misconduct has been by far the single best predictor at any given point in time of citizen confidence in government over the past two decades. In the conclusion the chapter considers the broader relevance of these findings for other Trilateral democracies.

THE JAPANESE SETTING

Disaffection has distinctive features that vary by country. Unlike the United States and a number of other Trilateral democracies, Japan has not seen public trust plummet from more halcyon days. In the 1950s and 1960s, when Americans were exuding faith in their political institutions and processes, Japanese were far more skeptical. The experience of losing rather than winning a war almost surely accounts for some of the difference in outlook during the early postwar period. In place for more than a century, American political institutions, after all, had carried the country to victory and global preeminence; Japan's prewar political institutions had brought the nation ignoble defeat and seeming economic ruin, and democratic institutions that had been imposed from outside were not as yet fully tested.

The basic pattern in Japan has been relatively low levels of confidence in government over all of the last 40 years, with distrust reaching near-record levels in the 1990s. After weighing available evidence for the 1950s and 1960s, Richardson (1974, 232) concluded that "majorities of respondents showed either little satisfaction or outright dissatisfaction with the way politics is conducted." Even after national income doubled during the 1960s, Japan, along with Italy, featured the lowest levels of trust in politics among seven industrial nations (see Table 8.1).

Nor did the trend change appreciably in the 1980s, after the country attained the status of economic superpower. A majority of respondents reported dissatisfaction with politics in 18 out of 22 *Asahi Shimbun* surveys conducted between 1978 and 1996; only in the mid-1980s and once again in 1991 did less than a majority report dissatisfaction (see Table 8.2). Long periods of one-party rule have sometimes been associated with popular malaise, and this was certainly true of Japan, where the

TABLE 8.1
Political Trust and Orientation in Seven Trilateral Countries, 1976

	Japan	Britain	Germany	Netherlands	Austria	U.S.	Italy
Trust in politics[a]	27%	45%	69%	58%	71%	31%	22%
Interest in politics[b]	49	45	63	58	54	69	21
Efficacy[c]	27	37	27	44	28	59	28

Notes: [a]Respondents answering that "the people" rather than "big interests" run politics. [b]Respondents answering that they were interested in politics "all of the time" or "sometimes"; missing data are excluded from calculations. [c]Respondents answering that people have a "say" in what government does.

Sources: Adapted from Richardson (1991, 25), table 1.3. Data are from JABISS 1976 Japan survey and ICPSA "Political Action" Study code book.

Table 8.2
Dissatisfaction with Politics in Japan, 1978–96

Date	Dissatisfied	Somewhat Satisfied	Satisfied	Don't Know/ N/a
12/79	61%	25%	5%	9%
12/79	61	19	5	15
12/80	50	30	6	14
12/81	54	30	7	9
12/82	56	25	6	13
5/83	53	29	6	12
12/83	58	27	6	9
3/84	52	29	9	10
12/84	48	31	10	11
12/85	40	31	12	17
12/86	47	32	9	12
12/87	47	29	11	13
12/88	57	25	8	10
3/89	68	19	5	8
12/90	50	34	10	6
9/91	48	33	10	9
12/92	53	29	9	9
4/93	66	21	5	8
12/93	51	29	8	12
12/94	61	24	5	10
12/95	65	21	5	9
12/96	74	15	5	6

Notes: The question was "In general, are you satisfied with politics today, or are you dissatisfied?" All figures are percentages. First stage: 345 national statistical areas were classified by age structure, industrial structure, and population. Second stage: persons were randomly selected from one randomly selected election district in each area and were interviewed in person by university student volunteers. Response rate: around 75 percent. N = 3,600 individuals nationwide who were chosen by means of a two-stage, stratified, random selection method.

Sources: Asahi Shimbun, Tokyo Morning Edition, selected years.

conservative Liberal Democratic Party (LDP) was in power continuously from 1955 to 1993. Although one might thus have expected confidence in government to surge with the LDP's fall in 1993, that was not the case. Despite a major overhaul of the electoral system and other political reforms,[1] citizen dissatisfaction with government soared to 65 percent at

---

[1] Until 1994 Japan had a system of medium-sized, multimember electoral districts that weighted rural votes over urban ones and, critics held, drove up campaign costs by pitting members of the same party against one another for the multiple seats available. A major

mid-decade.[2] Indeed, according to one survey conducted in December 1995, only 29 percent of respondents subscribed to the view that democracy was functioning well in Japan, while 61 percent disagreed (*Nihon Keizai Shimbun*, December 19, 1995, 1).

IS JAPANESE DEMOCRACY DIFFERENT?

The pattern just described is, of course, subject to various interpretations. Some observers might argue that disaffection in Japan is not deeply held. Thirty-eight years of one-party rule, some people hold, established a pattern in which voters sounded off about the LDP, secure in the knowledge that it would remain in power. Voicing disapproval of both the party and the political system with which it was synonymous may have been a reasonable way to check LDP excesses, but it makes survey evidence of disaffection suspect, or so the argument goes. This logic is not compelling, however. If signals of disaffection and dissatisfaction were deliberate voter strategies in a system of one-party rule, then we would have expected to see satisfaction with politics rise after 1993, particularly in the wake of reforms that voters themselves had sought, but there has been no such upswing. Indeed, dissatisfaction has grown.

Other critics might question whether expressions of disaffection in Japan, an Asian nation with a relatively short liberal democratic tradition, mean the same thing as they do in Western countries in which democracy has deeper roots. A quarter of a century ago *The Crisis of Democracy* saw Japan as something of an outlier: because Japanese citizens were somewhat less efficacious and active in their orientation toward politics than their counterparts in other advanced industrial societies, democracy there was somewhat more fragile, the report implied (Crozier, Huntington, and Watanuki 1975). The so-called revisionist school, which first appeared in the late 1980s, also regards Japan as unique rather than West-

---

political reform package passed on January 29, 1994 introduced a new system that combines redrawn and smaller single-member districts with proportional representation. A new law provided public campaign funds for the first time; it made available ¥ 30.9 billion ($283 million) to be distributed among parties. Furthermore, in a frontal attack on "money-power politics," the reform package set limits on company donations: companies can contribute no more than ¥500,000 ($4,600) per politician per year, and the law virtually phased out corporate contributions to candidates over a five-year period. (See Hayano, Sone, and Uchida 1994; also *Economist*, February 5–11, 1994, 27.)

[2] The survey data presented here are from *Asahi Shimbun*, one of Japan's four national, mass circulation dailies. Although it is considered to be on the liberal-progressive end of Japan's political spectrum, it is the daily most widely read by opinion leaders. The two-decade trend revealed in the *Asahi* data is mirrored in NHK data as well as other data sources (Pharr 1997). Unfortunately, most surveys relevant to this inquiry have asked about "satisfaction" (*manzoku*) with politics rather than about "confidence" or "trust."

ern and casts similar doubts on the state of Japanese democracy (Fallows 1994; van Wolferen 1989). Survey data fail to support such a conclusion, however, showing instead a steadily deepening acceptance of the values associated with democracy. In Japan, for example, a key index is whether people are prepared to defer to authority, as in the prewar era, or adopt a more participatory stance. Data collected over 50 years by the Clean Election League reveal that citizens have steadily moved away from a belief that leaving things to leaders is preferable; far more than in the past, they believe that they should be active ("debating among themselves") in making policy choices rather than passively accepting what leaders do. Similarly, following from top-down patterns of authority in prewar Japan, early postwar generations saw voting as a duty rather than a right. Younger people today, however, overwhelmingly view voting as a right: in the 25- to 29-year-old age group, for example, 57 percent of respondents in one study saw voting as a right, while only 35 percent called it a duty (Kabashima 1987). In this sense Japanese democracy has matured, and any lag that may have existed has virtually disappeared.

Japan, then, is a liberal democracy that like many others, including the United States, has suffered a decline in citizen confidence in government and politics. While Japan has no "golden age" to hark back to when ordinary people radiated support for the nation's politics and political institutions, the persistence of high levels of dissatisfaction in the face of spreading prosperity and an upturn in distrust dating from the late 1980s call for an explanation. In the remainder of the chapter, I first consider two common candidate causes of citizen distrust of government and political institutions in the Trilateral democracies and, finding them wanting, offer my own. I take up where the previous chapter left off by focusing first on economic explanations.

POLICY PERFORMANCE AND EMPTY POCKETS

No explanation for citizen disaffection with politics has greater currency in the media today than economic malaise. When times are good, the theory holds, citizens credit their leaders with wise economic policies. And deservedly or not, the public also holds leaders responsible for poor economic performance and registers their dissatisfaction with government. Undergirding this popular interpretation is a wealth of research that establishes the existence of significant links between key economic variables and political behavior and attitudes. On the one hand are theories that link citizen opinions and behavior such as voting to "pocketbook" reasoning, that is, people's estimates of how government actions affect their personal finances; and on the other hand are theories that focus on "sociotropic" assessments, that is, citizen evaluations of how the economy is performing overall (Kinder 1981; Kinder and Kiewiet 1979, 1981; Meehl 1977).

On the face of it, looking to the economy for clues as to why citizen satisfaction with government and politics may have declined makes sense for Japan. Since 1992 the country has endured the longest recession in its postwar history. Furthermore, economic tensions were also present in the 1980s, ranging from fear of a "hollowing out" of the economy as Japanese firms moved to low-wage countries in the face of a rising yen to a reactive nationalism triggered by market-opening pressure from Japan's trade partners. At the level of individual lives, signs of a modest economic ratcheting-down can be detected long before the recessionary 1990s. Although more than 90 percent of Japanese have routinely classified themselves as "middle class" since 1970, perceived relative prosperity within that class has undergone subtle change. According to surveys conducted by the Prime Minister's Office, the percentage of respondents who said they considered themselves "middle" middle class as opposed to "lower" middle class increased markedly prior to 1970 as the benefits of high growth filtered down. By the late 1970s, however, the trend began to reverse itself, and this shift accelerated as the "bubble era" of the late 1980s inflated the value of land and stocks, creating a perceived gap between those people who owned these assets and those who did not. Although these differences have been fairly small,[3] if people's relative sense of economic well-being affects how they judge their government and leaders, then even relatively minor shifts of this kind might matter.

Other evidence points in the opposite direction, however. Where one is coming from should affect assessments of one's current economic situation (Samuelson 1955, cited in Nye, Zelikow, and King 1997, 124). In the United States and many other advanced industrial democracies, for example, a golden era of past productivity casts a shadow over the present. As Robert Lawrence (Nye, Zelikow, and King 1997, 125) observes after comparing America's post-1973 record of economic performance with the previous 150 years, "Americans who are using history as their benchmark have every right to feel disappointed." For a country like Japan, where real prosperity dates only from the 1970s, historical comparisons look very different. Japanese respondents in a 1995 study were almost twice as likely as Americans (60 percent versus 35 percent) to

[3] The percentage of people considering themselves middle-middle class fell from 60.6 percent in 1979 to 53.6 percent in 1992, while the percentage who considered themselves lower-middle class correspondingly rose from 22.2 percent to 26.2 percent. The difference in income between these two groups is quite small. The most significant difference is in the floor space of their homes: an average of 50 square meters for the self-identified lower-middle class versus 75 square meters for those who thought of themselves as middle-middle class (NHK 1995, 229–33).

compare their own situation favorably with that in which their parents grew up (International Gallup Poll, April 1995; "no opinion" responses are excluded). Perhaps for similar reasons the same survey found Japanese to be less pessimistic about the future than the people of any other Trilateral country included in the survey except France.[4] These data provide a basis for speculating that in Japan any subjective sense of economic reverses in recent decades due to a minor erosion in economic circumstances or trade tensions is offset by a strong and widely shared perception that things used to be much worse.

Against this background I consider the fit between economic performance and citizens' satisfaction with politics and government. Most research on how economic variables affect political behavior and opinion focuses on election outcomes and the popularity of particular governments (the so-called vote-popularity, or VP, functions). According to Lewis-Beck, "all but a handful" of over 100 studies conducted before the late 1980s in Britain, France, Germany, Italy, Spain, and the United States found economic conditions "significantly related to electoral outcomes"; such research establishes that economic factors accounted for roughly one-third of the change in the vote for the government (Lewis-Beck 1988, 29; Nannestad and Paldam 1994, 237). Looking at the years 1960 to 1976, Inoguchi (1980, 147) also found that economic conditions significantly affected public support for the government and the party in power in Japan. Extending the same logic, one may ask whether economic conditions matter when it comes to more basic feelings about politics and the political system.

To explore this question, I looked at the economic variables that have been standard in prior research, namely, unemployment, inflation, and income growth, along with several others, over the years 1978 to 1996 (see Table 8.3).[5] I also included a political variable—strength of the Liberal Democratic party as measured by its number of seats in the Lower House of the Diet—to test the proposition that a strong LDP majority would be associated, whether positively or negatively, with trust.[6] The

[4] Fifty-eight percent of Japanese believed that the next generation would be worse off compared to 56 percent of French, 70 percent of Germans, 64 percent of Canadians, 63 percent of Britons, and 60 percent of Americans (International Gallup Poll, April and May 1995).

[5] The "Big Three" economic variables in VP work are widely agreed to be inflation, unemployment, and income growth (Fair 1978, 164; Lewis-Beck 1988, 29; Nannestad and Paldam 1994; Schneider and Frey 1988, 243). In Australia, Britain, Denmark, Germany, New Zealand, Sweden, and the United States unemployment typically trumps inflation or income growth in importance for electoral outcomes; in Japan, however, inflation and income growth have been found to matter more (Schneider and Frey 1988, 247).

[6] See discussion of this explanation later in the chapter.

TABLE 8.3

LDP Strength, Economic Conditions, and Dissatisfaction with Politics in Japan, 1978–96

	Correlation with Dissatisfaction	Spearman's Rho	Pr > |t|
LDP strength	−0.303	−0.347	0.145
Income per capita	0.342	0.256	0.29
GDP	0.327	0.294	0.222
Income	−0.231	−0.194	0.427
Inflation	−0.218	−0.14	0.568
Unemployment	0.209	0.23	0.344

Notes: Political dissatisfaction: The percentage of respondents who answered "dissatisfied" in reply to the question "In general, are you satisfied with politics today, or are you dissatisfied?" in surveys conducted by *Asahi Shimbun* at fairly regular intervals over the period in question. See Table 8.2 for details.

LDP strength: Percentage of Lower House seats held by the Liberal Democratic Party.

Income per capita: Real national income (at factor prices) per capita; base year of 1990.

GDP: Real gross domestic product; base year of 1990.

Income: Percent annual change in real gross domestic product; base year of 1990.

Inflation: Percentage change in the consumer price index from the preceding year.

Unemployment: Annual change in percentage of the work force that was completely unemployed.

Sources:

Dissatisfaction and LDP data: Asahi Shimbun (morning edition), 1978–96.

National income data: Ministry of Finance, *Financial Statistics of Japan, 1997.* Data on price deflators used to calculate real national income come from the Prime Ministers' Office, *Japan Statistical Yearbook, 1998.*

Unemployment and inflation data: Bank of Japan, *Economic Statistics Annual,* selected years through 1995, and for 1996 from the Economic Planning Agency, *Pocket Statistical Indicators, 1998.*

GDP data: International Monetary Fund (IMF), *International Financial Statistics* [CD-ROM], January 1998.

results support the conclusions of Lawrence (1997) and a great deal of other research: while the state of the economy may significantly affect electoral outcomes and the popularity of particular governments, it appears to have little bearing at a more fundamental level on people's feelings about their government and politics. In Japan the economic variable that is most strongly associated with political satisfaction is per capita national income (with a correlation of .342), but the relationship is not in the expected direction: as per capita income increases, so does dissatisfaction.[7]

---

[7] Although none of the economic variables meet tests of significance, this finding (paralleled by a similar finding of a positive relationship between GNP growth and dissatisfaction) raises at least the possibility that economic prosperity in Japan—and with it the spread of

Despite widespread media claims to the contrary, pocketbook issues appear to have remarkably little to do with people's confidence in their government and leaders.

SOCIAL CAPITAL AND EMPTY LIVES

Civicness, a wide variety of scholars, pundits, and politicians alike now say, is fundamental to social trust and attitudes of cooperation that in turn promote and sustain good government. Looking at the United States, Putnam (1995a) has argued that "social connections and civic engagement pervasively influence our public life" and that civic disengagement—a lack of social connectedness and involvement in associational life—has profound and wide-ranging effects on society and politics. A major concern of much recent research is whether civicness fosters political trust, and thus whether the widespread decline in confidence in government is linked to an erosion of social capital (Newton 1997a; Hall 1997).

The search for civicness and for ways to know when there is a lack of it has been far-ranging, sending scholars sleuthing to discover how citizens spend their leisure time and transforming British pubs, the bouling greens of Italy, and Americans' backyard decks into social science laboratories (Putnam 1995a; Hall 1997). A basic measure of civicness, however, is citizens' participation in associational life. The nature of the group is thought to matter. Putnam observes, for example, that in Italy, belonging to a political party is common in both the most and least civic regions, and he and others tend to discount the potential value for building social capital of membership in political parties, labor unions, and other groups to which members belong automatically or as a by-product or extension of work (Putnam 1993, 109). In general there is agreement that horizontally organized, or voluntary, groups are more likely to be building blocks for social capital. Although his view has been challenged, Putnam holds that hobby groups should be optimal generators of social capital (Putnam 1993; Putnam 1995a; Levi 1996, 47). For other measures of social capital and its absence, the spotlight has fallen on television viewing on the grounds that it pulls people away from nourishing forms of civic engagement and other culturally configured settings in which social networks operate (Putnam 1996; Patterson 1993).

Applying the "civic disengagement" thesis to Japan as a possible explanation of declining public trust is a relatively recent enterprise, but a focus on social networks and group associations as a key to understand-

---

education—has, if anything, helped create a more skeptical citizenry rather than inspire public trust.

ing Japanese social, economic, and political life is not at all new. As it operates in the workplace and organizes leisure activities outside of it, social capital by other names has been at the heart of many analyses of the Japanese economic model. Indeed, Japan's "communitarian capitalism," the dense network of "wet" social relations within the firm that binds workers and brings them together after hours for baseball, golf, mahjong, or karaoke, has, along with other social network attributes, triggered a raft of Western management theories (Thurow 1993; Vogel 1987; Fukuyama 1995, 28). Social capital explanations were also at the core of many analyses of Japanese politics long before the term came into vogue. It is widely agreed that at least among conservative voters, a "social network model" best explains voting behavior in Japan, and that both formal and informal groups operating around opinion leaders have been critical not only for mobilizing the vote, but also for shaping basic political attitudes (Flanagan et al. 1991, 85, 152–53; Richardson 1997; Richardson 1974). Indeed, political science research on Japan has tended to discount political ideology and class as bases for voting behavior, instead assigning the greatest importance to the mix of values and social networks that lie at the center of social capital research today.

The distinction recent research makes between horizontal and vertical interest associations—the "good" and "bad cholesterol" of social capital, as it were—is also a familiar one in Japanese studies. Prewar Japan was rife with interest groups that were "organized by elites for elites" (Allinson and Sone 1993, 26). Prominent examples were prewar residential associations (*chōkai,* or *chōnaikai*). Tracing their origins to castle towns in the Tokugawa era, these were originally administered by landowners and house agents as omnibus religious, recreational, occupational, and residential units. In the twentieth century such community associations became the basic unit of daily life for most people, organizing local festivals and carrying out a variety of grassroots activities, and although they elected their leaders, they were routinely used by the state as a means of administrative control and, later, mobilization for war (Hastings 1995, 70–79; Watanuki 1977). Organizations like this, in which membership is mandated by work or some other affiliation, are thought to be different from voluntary associations, which are modern, horizontally organized, and more participatory (McKean 1981). Even types of associations that are discounted in much social capital research have been credited with fostering dense social networks in Japan. Political parties frequently offer a clubhouse environment, for example. Among the recreational and social activities provided to members of individual LDP politicians' support groups (*kōenkai*) are "baseball games and marathon races for the youth division, chess tournaments and golf outings for the middle-aged, cooking classes for the housewives, volleyball for the women, kimono-wearing lessons, tea ceremony and flower-arranging classes, and on and on" (Abe, Shindo, and Kawato 1994, 179).

The task, then, is to move beyond these types of evidence to explore more systematically how stores of social capital may have changed over recent decades. The results of our research demonstrate that changes in social capital have remarkably little explanatory power with regard to levels of confidence in Japan, for by almost any available measure social capital has been on the rise over recent decades. Indeed, by the most common metric, the number of interest groups in general and of voluntary associations in particular, it has soared in Japan.

The gains have been steady. According to leading experts, interest groups proliferated in Japan over the first two decades of the postwar period (Muramatsu, Itō, and Tsujinaka 1986, 72–76). Since then, the most ambitious study to date concludes, Japan's interest groups have moved toward "greater participation and pluralization"; indeed, the number of interest groups *almost tripled* between 1960 and 1991 (Tsujinaka 1996, 11; see also Tsujinaka 1986) (see Table 8.4). By contrast, the number of interest groups in the United States, though significantly higher than in Japan, has remained flat. And in Japan's near neighbor Korea, the number actually declined over this period.

The data in Table 8.4 present problems for distinguishing between voluntary and nonvoluntary associations, at least initially. The figures for Japan, unlike those for the United States, do not include a category for civic associations as opposed to business, labor, political, professional, and academic groups. The data do reveal dramatic growth in every category, however, including the large and intriguing category "other," which in-

TABLE 8.4
Interest Groups in Japan, the United States, and Korea, 1960–91

	1960	*1975*	*1986*	*1991*
Japan	11.1	18.4	27.7	29.2
United States	34.6 (1962)	37.5 (1976)	35.4	35.5 (1990)
Korea	—	12.8 (1981)	13.5	9.5

Notes: Number of interest groups per 100,000 people.

Source: From Yutaka Tsujinaka, "Interest Group Structure and Regime Change in Japan," Maryland/Tsukuba Papers on U.S.-Japan Relations, November 1996: 12–13. Data are for nongovernmental, nonprofit organizations and associations. Japan: Management and Coordination Agency, Bureau of Statistics, *Census on Establishments*, selected years; United States: Bureau of the Census, *County Business Patterns*, selected years; South Korea: National Office of Statistics, *Report on Census of Establishments*, selected years. Categories include business, labor, political, "civil," professional, academic, and "not elsewhere classified."

cludes civic associations along with foundations and quasi-official bodies (Tsujinaka 1996, 21, 37, and personal communication with the author), and which soared *411 percent* over three decades. Collectively, these facts support the conclusion that all types of interest groups, including voluntary associations, are dramatically multiplying (see Table 8.5). Other sources provide additional evidence of the growth of horizontal organizations. Between 1965 and 1975, for example, citizens' grassroots groups organized to press for solutions to environmental problems mushroomed (Krauss and Simcock 1980, 187; Pharr 1990, 2–3). The number of people in consumer cooperatives—organizations owned and operated by consumers to improve their daily life—almost quadrupled between 1970 and 1995, leaping from 12.7 million to 45.2 million people (*Asahi Shimbun* 1999, 195). Furthermore, hobby groups of the kind championed by Putnam scored impressive gains. In a 1996 government survey 36.6 percent of respondents rated leisure and leisure activities as their highest priority in life—a doubling of the 18.1 percent who gave that answer in 1976—with group activities figuring prominently among people's recreational interests. Bowling, the most popular sports activity, boasted 37.3 million enthusiasts (*Asahi Shimbun* 1998, 268, 272). The enormous popularity of foreign travel, which Japanese typically undertake in groups as an extension of the activities of clubs and other preexisting social collectivities, is yet another sign of deepening social networks and enriched stores of social capital. Such travel has increased so dramatically over recent decades that Japan's "tourist deficit" was responsible for 39.2 percent of the country's trade surplus in 1996; more than 13.5 million Japanese traveled abroad for sightseeing that year (*Asahi Shimbun* 1998, 273).

TABLE 8.5
Growth of Interest Groups in Japan by Type, 1960–91

	1960	1975	1986	1991	Percentage Increase between 1960 and 1991
Business	4,698	10,027	13,386	13,798	294%
Labor	1,572	2,268	4,816	5,116	325
Political	169	532	790	828	490
Academic	147	455	679	878	597
Other	3,771	7,332	13,997	15,520	411

Note: Figures indicate number of interest groups.

Sources: From Tsujinaka (1996, 12–13). Data are for nongovernmental, nonprofit organizations and associations. Japan: Management and Coordination Agency, Bureau of Statistics, *Census on Establishments*, selected years; United States: Bureau of the Census, *County Business Patterns*, selected years; South Korea: National Office of Statistics, *Report on Census of Establishments*, selected years.

In exploring claims that social capital may be eroding in the United States, television viewing has come in for scrutiny on the grounds that spending hours in front of the screen diminishes time for building social networks (Putnam 1996). The average number of hours Japanese spend watching television certainly merits attention because it surpasses even the U.S. level: while 53 percent of Americans watched two or more hours of television per day in 1995, the figure was 59 percent in Japan (Inglehart 1996). Nevertheless, television watching is an unlikely explanation for the low levels of satisfaction with government and politics seen in Japan over many decades and for the rise in dissatisfaction witnessed in the 1990s. Low levels of political trust precede the television era, and heavy television viewing has actually *declined*: whereas 34 percent of respondents watched more than three hours a day in 1976, that figure had dropped to 24 percent by 1996 (Inglehart 1996; Flanagan in Pharr and Krauss 1996, 281).

To give the social capital explanation its due, I finally examined cross-sectional data from the 1996 Japan Election and Democracy Study (JEDS). If associational life is directly related in some fashion to confidence in politics and government then people embedded in dense social networks by means of multiple group memberships should have higher levels of satisfaction with politics. But this is not the case: belonging to three or more groups of any kind or to several voluntary groups had no significant effect on one's level of political trust (see Table 8.6). Belonging to sports or hobby groups also made no significant difference. The only type of membership that was positively associated with satisfaction with politics was belonging to farmers' cooperatives, a type of "nonvoluntary" association found in the rural stamping ground of Japan's conservative politicians. Perhaps it is no surprise that farmers, who constitute the core of the LDP's support, would enjoy higher levels of satisfaction than most people with a political system that has been almost synonymous with that party. Indeed, the relationship between membership in farmers' groups and satisfaction with politics became statistically insignificant once we controlled for political ideology.

At the other end of the continuum, membership in a residential (*jūmin*), consumer, citizens', or women's movement was inversely related to satisfaction levels. This finding, too, is not surprising. As Tarrow points out in this volume, it is reasonable to expect that citizens who join social movements are less trusting of government and politics than people with more conventional types of group membership (see also Hall 1997). It is nevertheless troubling that members of citizens' movements, which are widely interpreted as a bellwether of grassroots civicness in Japan, should be less satisfied with politics than members of other groups. Although the number of people in this type of group was small,

TABLE 8.6
Social Capital and Satisfaction with Politics in Japan, Controlling for Age, Sex, and Education, 1996

	Logistic Regression Coefficient[a]	P Value
Group Memberships of Any Type		
Belongs to no group of any kind (N = 409)	1.020	0.898
Belongs to 1 or more groups of any kind (N = 917)	0.887	0.389
Belongs to 2 or more groups of any kind (N = 447)	0.980	0.898
Belongs to 3 or more groups of any kind (N = 174)	0.820	0.327
Belongs to 4 or more groups of any kind (N = 53)	1.141	0.695
Voluntary Associations		
Belongs to 1 or more voluntary associations (N = 437)	0.981	0.885
Belongs to 2 or more voluntary associations (N = 111)	1.198	0.430
Belongs to 3 or more voluntary associations (N = 27)	1.339	0.524
Belongs to a sports, hobby (*shumi*), or recreational (*goraku*) group (N = 247)	1.138	0.411
Belongs to youth, women's, or old people's groups and organizations (N = 137)	1.208	0.366
Belongs to a trade group or industrial organization (N = 73)	1.452	0.193
Belongs to a religious organization (N = 45)	0.562	0.083
Belongs to residential (*jūmin*), consumer, citizens', or women's movements (N = 18)	0.312	0.024*
Belongs to welfare or volunteer groups (N = 6)	0.969	0.914
Nonvoluntary Associations		
Belongs to 1 or more nonvoluntary associations (N = 796)	0.977	0.859
Belongs to 2 or more nonvoluntary associations (N = 209)	0.858	0.397
Belongs to 3 or more nonvoluntary associations (N = 26)	0.869	0.757
Belongs to a township, local autonomous, or district organization (N = 659)	1.035	0.781
Belongs to a labor union (N = 144)	0.693	0.073
Belongs to consumer cooperatives (*seikatsu kyōdō kumiai*) (N = 139)	0.691	0.058

TABLE 8.6 (*continued*)

	Logistic Regression Coefficient[a]	P Value
Belongs to farmers' cooperatives (*nōkyō*) or other organizations for farmers or forest workers (*hoka no nōrin*) or fishermen (*gyogyō*) (N = 93)	1.700	0.043*

Notes: N = 1,326. *p = 0.05.

[a]Logistic regression in an equation of age, education, and sex. A logistic coefficient greater than one increases the odds of a respondent's being satisfied with democracy, while a coefficient of less than one decreases the odds. All coefficients were calculated controlling for age, sex, and education level. In each regression examining the effects of one, two, or three or more memberships, the results were in comparison to the effect of zero memberships for that category. For each regression examining the effects of no membership in voluntary, nonvoluntary, or any type of group, the results were in comparison to the effects two or more such memberships. For each row in the table N represents the number of respondents out of the original 1,326 who answered about group memberships who met the criterion described in that row. Note, however, that the number of observations used in any given regression was usually less than the total number of 1,326 observations because of the elimination of respondents who did not provide information about their sex, age, and/or education level.

Satisfaction with politics: Response of "somewhat satisfied" or "satisfied" when asked, "To what degree are you satisfied with the way Japan's democracy works?"

Voluntary associations: Residential movements, consumer movements, citizens' movements, women's movements, youth organizations, women's organizations, old people's clubs, welfare or volunteer groups, sports and hobby groups, religious groups, trade groups, and industry organizations.

Nonvoluntary associations: Labor unions, farmers' and livelihood cooperatives, township organizations, local autonomous organizations, district organizations, or other organizations for farmers, forest workers, or fishermen.

Other groups: Respondents were also able to denote memberships in groups not listed above. A total of 955 respondents were in this group.

Source: Japanese Elections and Democracy Survey (JEDS) 1996, surveys administered before and after the October 20, 1996 Lower House Elections. N = 1,535.

their dissatisfaction raises especially serious doubts about a direct relationship between social capital and political confidence. Indeed, when we combine this finding with the fact that voluntary group membership was a better predictor of dissatisfaction than satisfaction with politics (even though it did not approach levels of statistical significance), then any kind of a claim of a direct link between an individual's social capital and civic engagement on the one hand and political confidence on the other seems especially suspect.

These findings are consistent with the work of *Crisis of Democracy* coauthor Jōji Watanuki. For Watanuki embeddedness in dense social relationships and membership in traditional nonvoluntary associations meant social capital, but of the "bad cholesterol" type. To him, like many other scholars, "dense social networks" have been virtually synonymous with clientelism. He has seen the kind of political trust generated within such social networks as a remnant of anti-democratic attitudes and behavior associated with "traditional" as opposed to "modern" behavior. Though such social capital was associated with high political trust, the result was bad for democracy. In contrast, membership in modern voluntary associations—of which citizens' groups and movements are an optimal example—translates into social capital of the "good cholesterol" variety. His "modern man" of the kind most desired in liberal democracies stands apart from traditional social networks, enters more new, vibrant, civic ones, and has "less trust in politics at all levels of government" (Watanuki 1977, 92).

An individual's degree of civicness, then, appears to have relatively little to do with that person's satisfaction with politics. Furthermore, the data presented earlier on the rise of interest groups in Japan challenge even the "rainmaker" hypothesis (see Introduction and also Newton and Norris, this volume) that overall low or declining levels of social capital and social trust produce poor government, which in turn lowers political trust and confidence among all citizens. The logic of the "rainmaker" hypothesis would lead us to predict better government in Japan as a consequence of the rise of associational life and increasing social trust, which in turn should translate into higher levels of satisfaction with politics. But this has not occurred. Low levels of satisfaction with and confidence in the political system have persisted at a time when interest groups of all kinds have been exploding on the scene, embedding Japanese in new kinds of social networks. Nor is the trend toward greater stores of social capital likely to subside. An "NPO [Not-for-Profit Organizations] Law" that went into effect in December 1998 is expected to spur the growth of new civic groups by providing them with a long-sought avenue to legal status.[8]

---

[8] Under the new law, which took effect in April 1999, the government will grant corporate status to groups whose activities fall within 12 areas: health and welfare; social education; community development; culture, arts, and sports; environmental protection; disaster relief; community safety; human rights and peace advocacy; international cooperation; gender equality; youth programs; and groups providing aid to citizens' groups that fall in one of the other categories. Official status will make it easier for groups to rent space, order phone service, and open bank accounts. On the basis of an April 1997 Economic Planning Agency survey, it was anticipated that over 10,000 civic groups would apply for corporate status under the new law (*Japan Times Weekly* International Edition, March 30–April 5, 1998, 4).

THE PROBLEM IS POLITICAL

Thus, one can conclude that the source of low satisfaction with politics, at least in Japan, lies neither in depleted coffers of social capital nor in the government's recent or past mismanagement of the economy, but in politics itself. The question is where.

The first and most obvious possibility is that levels of political satisfaction have varied with the strength of the ruling party. Voters consistently returned the Liberal Democratic Party to power between 1955 and 1993, and once again from 1995. If party politicians are agents of voters, then it should follow that when an election results in a strong majority for the ruling party, a correspondingly large portion of voters should be satisfied with this outcome, and this in turn should translate into higher overall levels of political satisfaction. Inversely, a weak LDP majority should translate into lower levels of satisfaction. Despite the compelling logic of this hypothesis, numerous observers of Japanese politics challenge it. In the absence of a better alternative, they argue, voters may have returned the LDP to power, but they still fear its excesses. If this line of reasoning is correct, then a strong LDP majority should mean lower overall citizen satisfaction with politics. As it turns out, the evidence supports neither hypothesis (see Table 8.3). LDP strength was in fact positively correlated with political satisfaction (or, as stated in Table 8.3, it was inversely related to political dissatisfaction), but the relationship was not strong enough to be statistically significant.

Performance of Another Kind: Misconduct in Office

This investigation has brought us full circle, to focus once again on the performance of public officials. Although performance in managing the economy is a surprisingly poor predictor of satisfaction with leaders, as this chapter has demonstrated for Japan and numerous scholars suggest in their work on other countries (Lawrence 1997; McAllister in Norris 1999), leaders' performance still remains a logical place to look. As Inglehart (1997a, 294–95) notes, it "seems inconceivable that governmental performance *would not* influence public evaluations" of the political system and government (emphasis in the original). Thus, we should step back to consider leaders' performance more broadly.

This explanation is all the more compelling because of the close correlation in most Trilateral countries between low satisfaction with government and politics and negative evaluations of specific institutions of government, including the prime ministership, legislature, and bureaucracy (see Introduction and also Newton and Norris, this volume). Over postwar decades marked by low levels of satisfaction with politics, distrust of politicians has been a regular feature of Japanese survey results. Although bureaucrats previously fared better, as overall levels of public distrust reached their highs in the 1990s, citizens reported little trust in bureaucrats as well. In a December 1995 survey, for example, 70 percent of respondents answered "no" when asked if they had confidence in legislators, and 65 percent distrusted central government bureaucrats (*Nihon Keizai Shimbun*, December 19, 1995, 1). In contrast to leaders at the national level, prefectural and local officials have enjoyed more trust, and this overall trend continues: the closer to the voter, the greater the trust (surveys conducted by the Clean Election League). Trust in local leaders dropped precipitously in the 1990s, however. Only 12 percent of respondents in one survey judged local government to be "quite responsive" or "somewhat responsive" to people's opinions and wishes (*Nihon Keizai Shimbun*, December 19, 1995, 1).

Some would argue that negative evaluations of public officials reflect a gradual increase in more general anti-authority attitudes that result from broad socioeconomic transformations (e.g., rising educational levels) in the advanced industrial democracies (see Dalton, this volume; see also Inglehart 1997a). Such an explanation is not very applicable to Japan, however. Asked to rate the trustworthiness of various domestic institutions in 1995, Japanese reported far more favorable impressions about the courts (29 percent), police and prosecutors (42 percent), hospitals (35 percent), and newspapers (34 percent) than about the prime minister (3 percent), the legislature (6 percent), central government offices (4 percent), and local government offices (9 percent). The Japanese public, in other words, makes distinctions when awarding trust, as did citizens in the United States, Britain, Germany, and France in response to the same survey (Gallup-Yomiuri Poll, May 1995, reported in *Yomiuri Shimbun*, June 22, 1995).

To advance the inquiry, I argue that the performance of public officials involves two dimensions: policy performance and "conduct in office." By the latter term, I mean conduct, or deportment, with respect to handling the duties and privileges of public office. A great deal of research has focused on how leaders perform in policy roles and how this affects a whole range of public responses, from voting to issue support. But as was shown above, policy performance even in the crucial area of the economy appears to explain little about levels of public confidence or satisfaction with politics in Japan or elsewhere. In the remainder of this chapter I argue that a perceived leadership deficit in the second performance dimension, conduct in office, is the single best explanation for people's satisfaction with government and politics, at least in Japan.

This thesis flies in the face of much of the political science literature, in which citizens' judgments of conduct-in-office issues have been regarded as less durable or stable over time than the public's issue preferences (Page and Shapiro 1992). Despite the maelstrom of media furor and public debate that frequently greets corruption and other ethical lapses on the part of officeholders, the public reaction is thought to be epiphenomenal, in contrast to its views on policy issues. Some scholars treat corruption and other ethics scandals as socially constructed, implying that they have no real or lasting weight (Giglioli 1996, 381–93). Others claim, in the absence of any particular evidence, that low evaluations of politicians are a cause rather than an effect of officials' misconduct: negative judgments of officials supposedly give license to officials' wrongdoing, or, alternately and more cynically still, such wrongdoing should be taken as a given and comes to light only when citizens register low evaluations of leaders in general (Mortimore 1995, 579). Anthony King's call (1986, 173–222) for research that would link issues of official misconduct with larger characteristics of political systems was met with a deafening silence punctuated only rarely by serious investigations (e.g., Markovits and Silverstein 1988). And indeed, political science research grounded in economic theory, with its assumptions about self-interested, rent-seeking utility maximization, in effect treats corrupt government as normal and makes it hard to explain how the impulse to constrain corruption could arise (Miller 1992; Miller forthcoming; Bicchieri 1999). Although studies of individual corruption and political ethics cases go forward, and corruption itself, its causes and cures, attracts research, the deeper significance of conduct-in-office issues for relations between mass publics and leaders in democracies goes largely unexplored.

The frequency with which politicians charged with major ethics violations are returned to office reinforces the assumption that conduct in office is secondary to other dimensions of job performance (Peters and Welch 1980; Dolan, McKeown, and Carlson 1988). The view that conduct in office is of little importance to the Japanese public has been a persistent feature of research. Periodic corruption scandals have so flooded the political landscape that elections have even been named for them (e.g., the Lockheed Election of 1976, the 1983 Tanaka Verdict Election, the 1989 Recruit Election), leading to the conclusion that "structural corruption" prevails and is thus tolerated (Johnson 1986; MacDougall 1988; Reed 1994). Throughout the postwar era, much of this research maintains, citizens readily accepted politicians' corruption in exchange for porkbarrel benefits and high growth (Ramseyer and Rosenbluth 1993). As in the United States, the high reelection rate enjoyed by Diet members implicated in corruption scandals seemed to support such claims. Although Reed (1996, 5) shows that scandal-tainted Diet members have incurred a significant vote penalty (an average of 15,000 votes in 1976, for example), the simple fact that they were frequently reelected was taken as sufficient evidence that citizens accepted a Faustian bargain with the LDP: high growth in exchange for tolerance of corruption. Indeed, 38 years of uninterrupted rule by the LDP was taken as proof positive of citizen acceptance of conduct-in-office lapses.

This perspective, I hold, overlooks the many reasons why corruption and ethics scandals—whether socially constructed or not, and regardless of the forces that bring them to light—have to make a difference in the bond between the governed and those who govern them in the moral universe of liberal democracies. After all, the basis for that bond involves a covenant between leaders and followers that is based on some level of trust. Indeed, it is mainly in liberal democracies that scandals over political ethics lapses on the part of leaders arise in the first place; elsewhere they are generally suppressed. Although there are obvious exceptions,[9] the basic argument is highly persuasive, for modern liberal democracy fuses antithetical traditions: liberalism distrusts authority over the individual, while democracy celebrates equality and participation, even if this sometimes means sacrificing individual freedom as a result of state actions taken in the name of the common good (Markovits and Silverstein 1988, 5–6; Huntington 1981; Sandel 1996). The result is continuing tension over the uses of political power, which is addressed—but never fully resolved—by sharply differentiating the public and private realms and relying on due process and public scrutiny to contain the secrecy and arbitrariness inevitably involved in the exercise of power. Given this ideological tension, the exercise of power is inherently suspect, and legitimate only when it occurs in public (Markovits and Silverstein 1988, 6). In countries with recent histories of massive abuses of authority, like Japan, Germany, and Italy with their legacies of fascism, it is reasonable to believe that such suspicion is greater still.

Conduct-in-office issues always involve activities of public officials that occur in secrecy outside the public realm and, in effect, extend political power arbitrarily, at the expense of rules and procedures designed to check abuse of privilege. Given the deep suspicion inherent in liberal democracy toward something as basic to government as the notion of delegating power to leaders, it seems obvious that violations of trust in the leader-follower bond potentially have an important bearing on the public's overall confidence in, and satisfaction with, liberal democracy per se and the institutions it comprises.

---

[9] Prewar Japan is an obvious example. In the "transcendental" democracy established after adoption of the Meiji Constitution in 1889, corruption scandals involving politicians were commonplace. A prominent example was the Siemens scandal of 1913, which brought down a prime minister.

Despite what many political scientists may say, there is abundant evidence to support the claim that mass publics take conduct-in-office charges seriously. Studying trends in American public opinion and policy preferences over a 50-year period, Page and Shapiro found that official misconduct and corruption were among the very small number of triggering events for abrupt but enduring shifts in public opinion. Among other things, the Watergate revelations "led many people to conclude that campaign finances needed closer regulation . . . and that the presidency itself should be restrained"; similarly, reports of corruption in labor unions "contributed to increased support for strict regulation of labor" (Page and Shapiro 1992, 337–38). Even in Japan, where the public is widely thought to be inured to misconduct on the part of officeholders, public opinion surveys routinely show that citizens rate political ethics violations as one of the most important issues that need to be addressed. In the Japanese Elections and Democracy Survey study of 1996, 20 percent of respondents ranked political ethics among the top problems facing Japan, and an additional 40 percent listed administrative reform, which to many people means downsizing bureaucracy and reducing its discretion as a response to recent cases of wrongdoing by officials (Pharr 1998). Furthermore, there is substantial evidence that the quality of politics is of considerable importance to citizen's lives. In a 1987 survey, when asked whether improving politics had any relation to their lives, 65 percent of respondents said that it did; only 15 percent saw no meaningful connection between the two (Yamamoto 1995, 93).[10]

There is ample evidence that what people do, as well as what they say, is affected by their perceptions of official misconduct. The presumption that voter disapproval of scandal-tainted candidates can be measured only by whether they lose or win by a reduced margin of victory has been strongly challenged; it has been argued that the total movement of votes is a far more accurate measure (Lodge, Steenburgen, and Blau 1995). By analyzing the results of three major Lower House elections in Japan in which major corruption cases figured prominently, Reed calculated both the "scandal penalty" to incumbents and the vote gain to alternative new party candidates as a result of vote-switching, and he concluded that the 1993 defeat of the ruling LDP is best interpreted as a delayed response to these corruption scandals and the lack of significant political reform in their wake. Japanese voters routinely penalize incumbents who are implicated in conduct-in-office lapses by switching votes away from them

[10] Data are from the Akarui Senkyo Suishin Kyōkai (Clean Election League) national survey conducted in March 1987. Fourteen percent of respondents said they saw "no relationship between politics and our lives," and another 15 percent said, "We do not count on politics to improve our lives."

when a new alternative candidate appears (Reed 1996, 8–9). Watershed conduct-in-office cases such as Watergate in the United States are widely agreed to have major, long-term effects on voter turnout. If conduct-in-office cases can have these kinds of effects on citizen behavior, then it is reasonable to explore their effects on more basic orientations of the kind reflected in citizens' level of confidence in, and satisfaction with, politics and government.

Misconduct Reports

There are formidable obstacles to testing the hypothesis that officials' misconduct has important consequences for public confidence in government and that changes in this dimension help explain changes in confidence levels. Because the absolute amount of misconduct is unknowable, our assessments must be based on reported wrongdoing, but the level of reported misconduct in a country can increase for two reasons. First, the amount of wrongdoing may have actually increased. Second, it is possible that more wrongdoing is being reported than in the past irrespective of the actual level of misconduct; this may occur because the legal environment has become more restrictive or because of increased media attention to cases of misconduct.

For the purpose of investigating the relation between reported misconduct and citizen confidence, I take the position that which of these reasons applies is not really relevant. A given report of misconduct is a fact, a data point, in that it records a specific occurrence in which a public official is accused of wrongdoing. Obviously it matters a great deal to democracy and the quality of political life whether an increase in the number of such reports represents an objective increase in official misconduct or an increase in information about such misconduct. The remedies for the former (e.g., increasing the penalties for wrongdoing, raising the salaries of public officials to reduce incentives to misbehave) are not the same as those for the latter (e.g., changing the nature and amount of media coverage). The immediate issue for us here, however, is not what remedies are in order, but simply whether reports of misconduct have increased, and if so, whether this change affects citizens' satisfaction with politics.

To test for this relationship over recent decades in Japan, I first compiled an Asahi Corruption Report Database for the years 1948 through 1996. The database consists of all stories that appeared in *Asahi Shimbun*, one of Japan's four leading, mass circulation daily newspapers, on the subject of corruption, categorized as political, bureaucratic, subnational, and other. Selecting one newspaper might be a problem in some countries such as the United States, where almost all newspapers are local. In Japan, however, the major newspapers are national, and though research does reveal modest ideological differences among them, a number of characteristics of the Japanese news media assure relative uniformity of coverage (Freeman 1995; Pharr 1996). Stories that dealt with corruption occurring in other countries were excluded unless they involved Japanese nationals, in which case they were classified as "other." The resulting database consisted of over 15,000 corruption reports (see Figure 8.1).

A number of features stand out in the pattern that emerges. An obvious one is the importance of a single watershed conduct-in-office case, the Lockheed scandal of 1976. Like the Watergate scandal of a few years earlier in the United States, no scandal since that time has attracted comparable media coverage.[11] But if the Lockheed case is in a league of its own in the number of corruption reports it generated, there has been a dramatic racheting-up since then in the average number of corruption reports per year. Thus, between 1948 and 1975 the annual number of misconduct reports exceeded 200 in only five years; in contrast, for the years 1976 through 1996, the number of such reports exceeded 200 in *all but* five years. Furthermore, compared with the previous decade, the annual average jumped significantly in the 1990s. In the first half of the 1990s, for example, the average annual number of misconduct reports implicating bureaucrats increased by 27 percent over the annual average in the 1980s.

The Asahi Database provides a starting point in our analysis; the next step is to explore the relation in recent decades between misconduct reports and levels of citizen satisfaction with politics. If, as many scholars have claimed, conduct-in-office issues are of little real importance to citizens or if citizens discount them in various ways, then the number of misconduct reports in the media should have no bearing on something as fundamental as people's overall satisfaction with politics and government.

To determine whether conduct-in-office issues matter, I conducted a time-series analysis of the relation between the level of misconduct reports and the level of dissatisfaction with politics over the years 1978 through 1996 in Japan and plotted the result (see Figure 8.2). The result is quite striking. Not only do confidence levels mirror to a remarkable

---

[11] According to preliminary work on a similar database for the United States that uses a Lexis-Nexis search of *The New York Times* for the years 1969–96, the nearest rival to Watergate (which resulted in 6,874 reports in 1973) was Whitewater (with 727 reports in 1994). The other leading conduct-in-office cases in the United States for this period (and the number of reports for each) were Ellsberg Break-in/Pentagon Papers, 1971 (661); Abscam, 1980 (555); Wedtech, 1987 (409); Tongsun Park, 1977 (266); Vesco, 1973 (215); Keating, 1990 (117); House banking scandal, 1993 (113); FBI files ("Filegate"), 1996 (43); and the White House Travel Office, 1993 (42).

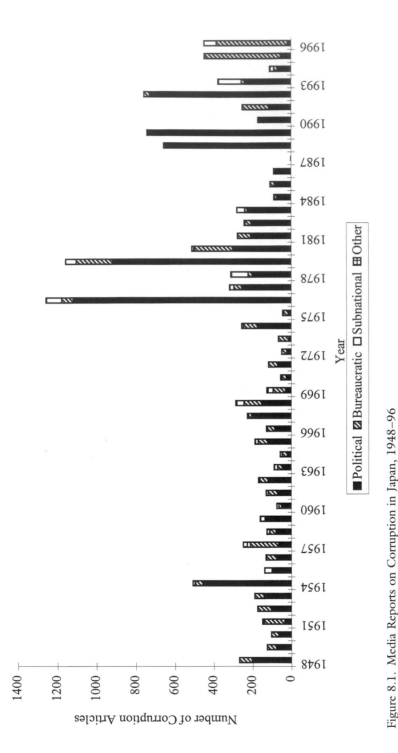

Figure 8.1. Media Reports on Corruption in Japan, 1948–96

Note: Number of corruption-related articles per year, classified according to the four categories political, bureaucratic, subnational, and "other," which includes corruption occurring outside Japan but involving Japanese public officials and general articles on corruption.

Sources: The annual number of stories on corruption in Japan as reported in the *Asahi Shimbun*, one of Japan's top four daily national newspapers, in the years 1948 through 1996. The Asahi Corruption Reports Database 1948–96, was compiled by the author using optical-disk indexed storage files, clipping counts, and, for updating, keyword searches of the *Asahi Shimbun*.

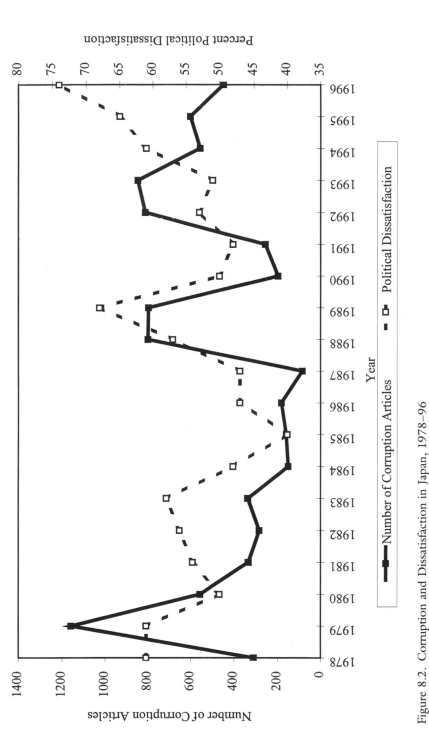

Figure 8.2. Corruption and Dissatisfaction in Japan, 1978–96

Notes: Political dissatisfaction: percentage of respondents answering "dissatisfied" when asked, "In general, are you satisfied with politics today, or are you dissatisfied?" See Table 8.2 for details. Corruption reports: the annual number of stories on corruption in Japan reported in *Asahi Shimbun*. See Figure 8.1 for details.

Sources: Political dissatisfaction data: *Asahi Shimbun*, Tokyo Morning Edition, selected years.

degree swings in the number of misconduct reports over the period in question, but causation is strongly implied by the fact that a spike in citizens' dissatisfaction with politics follows closely on the heels of a spike in misconduct reports. The pattern is especially dramatic over the years 1988 and 1989. The Recruit scandal broke in 1988, sending the number of corruption stories soaring, and soon after, levels of citizen dissatisfaction reached a record high.

To explore the relationship with somewhat greater precision and take into account other explanations for changes in levels of citizen confidence, I ran a Cochrane-Orcutt regression that included LDP strength and the most promising of the many economic variables tested earlier. The result offers exceedingly strong evidence of a positive relationship between reports of officials' misconduct and citizen dissatisfaction (see Table 8.7). The tepid correlations for the "Big Three" economic vari-

TABLE 8.7

The Effect of Corruption Reports, LDP Strength, and Changes in Economic Conditions on Political Dissatisfaction in Japan, 1978–96

	Coefficient	Standard Error	T-Statistic	$P > T$
Number of corruption articles in *Asahi Shimbun*	0.017	0.007	2.23	0.050
Dissatisfaction, preceding year	0.524	0.336	1.56	0.149
GDP, annual change	−1.45	1.48	−0.986	0.369
Inflation	0.073	1.35	0.054	0.958
Unemployment	11.6	7.47	1.55	0.153
LDP strength	0.767	0.581	1.32	0.216
Constant	−45.7	50.5	−0.905	0.387
Adjusted R^2	0.46			
Number of observations	17			

Notes: Cochrane-Orcutt regression correcting for serial auto-correlation.

Political dissatisfaction: The percentage of respondents who answered "dissatisfied" to the question "In general, are you satisfied with politics today, or are you dissatisfied?"

GDP, annual change: annual percent change in real gross domestic product; base year of 1990.

Unemployment: percentage of the work force that was completely unemployed.

Inflation: annual percentage change in the consumer price index; base year of 1995.

LDP strength: percent of total seats in the Lower House held by the Liberal Democratic Party.

Sources:

Dissatisfaction data: Asahi Shimbun, Tokyo Morning Edition, selected years. See Table 8.2 for details.

Corruption reports: Asahi Shimbun. See Figure 8.1 for details.

Unemployment and inflation data: Japan Management and Coordination Agency.

GDP data: International Monetary Fund (IMF).

ables of unemployment, inflation, and income growth (see Table 8.3) pale beside the robust correlation (.58) between misconduct reports and citizens' dissatisfaction with politics. Misconduct reports are the one and only variable that rises to the level of statistical significance (p ≤ .050).

CONCLUSION

In explaining people's satisfaction or dissatisfaction with their leaders and government, many observers assert, "It's the economy, stupid." Meanwhile, an outpouring of scholarship in recent years posits that social capital holds the key for taking the measure of democracy and, by extension, for shaping public orientations toward political life. This chapter has demonstrated that neither explanation has much relevance for understanding and interpreting changes in citizens' basic level of satisfaction with government and politics over the past two decades. That economic explanations do not apply is supported not only by the results presented in this chapter for Japan, but also by the mounting evidence presented elsewhere for numerous countries (Lawrence 1997; McAllister in Norris 1999). The finding that stores of social capital have little bearing on citizen satisfaction with politics and government in Japan echoes the conclusions of a great deal of recent research on a variety of Trilateral countries (Hall 1997; Newton 1997a). Some recent evidence suggests that for the Trilateral nations as a whole, social trust may be correlated with political confidence levels (see Newton and Norris, this volume). But the evidence for Japan poses a particularly strong challenge to theories of such a link. Low satisfaction with government—which fell lower still in the 1990s—has characterized decades over which Japan's stores of social capital have increased by a wide variety of measures.

Governmental performance holds the key for illuminating citizens' confidence in their government. But policy performance—at least in the all-important economic domain—explains little when it comes to public trust. I therefore shifted the focus to a second dimension of leaders' performance, which I call conduct in office, their deportment in carrying out their duties on behalf of the citizens they serve. This chapter has demonstrated that in Japan, at least, reports of officials' misconduct are by far the single best predictor at any given point in time of confidence in government over the past two decades. The more numerous the media reports of leaders' misconduct in office—as measured by the number of corruption stories between 1978 and 1996 in one of Japan's leading newspapers—the lower the public's confidence in government.

Reports of leaders' misconduct are obviously open to interpretation. Some observers would argue that in certain Trilateral countries—particularly Italy and Japan, given the scale and number of corruption cases that have come to light—the actual amount of wrongdoing by public officials may have increased over recent decades. Others would contend that changes in technology and in the political economy of the mass media in Trilateral countries are eroding the boundaries between the public and the private, thereby exposing officeholders to greater scrutiny and more charges of wrongdoing. The position we adopt is that whichever of these is true (and they are not mutually exclusive), this is basically irrelevant to an investigation of whether reports of misconduct matter to citizens.

The evidence presented here focuses on Japan, and the question thus arises as to how broadly our findings may apply in the Trilateral world. Compiling detailed data for all the Trilateral countries on officials' reported misconduct is a monumental task that could not be attempted here. Nevertheless, the evidence presented by della Porta (this volume, see Figures 9.3 and 9.4), who uses a readily available data source, suggests that for Italy, France, and Germany, and indeed for a wide range of Trilateral nations, there is a striking (albeit rough) correlation between citizen confidence in government on the one hand and perceived corruption on the other.

In closing, we may ask why reports of misconduct apparently matter so much to citizens in contemporary democracies. After all, leaders' policy performance has a far more direct effect on their lives than a great many types of misconduct by officials. Even in Japan, which has experienced a series of major corruption scandals implicating a significant number of politicians (if far fewer than was the case in Italy's Tangentopoli scandal of 1992), most incidents have involved illegal campaign contributions; in other words, citizens experienced no direct harm. In order to explain why all this matters, four factors stand out. First, given the premise that democracy depends on the accountability of public officials to citizens, misconduct reports represent information that is relevant to everyone, not just a select few (unlike many public policies). Second, officials' misconduct inevitably involves violations of the rules and procedures that are supposed to govern political life, and evidence of such misconduct thus gives rise to perceptions that the political system is basically unfair. A wealth of recent social psychology research establishes the central importance to people of procedural fairness in shaping their basic reactions to authority and the law. Lind and Tyler (1988; see also Tyler 1990) found that procedural fairness generally mattered more to people than actual outcomes, suggesting why policy performance may trail officials' misconduct in shaping basic orientations toward the political system. Third, compared to many other kinds of information about what the government does, misconduct reports are generally easy to understand, in part because they closely parallel ethical and moral dilemmas in everyday life or can easily be related to citizens' lives through media priming (Iyengar and Kinder 1987, 114–16). Fourth, because of the presumption of accountability in liberal democracies and also because of the often-strong moral content of the charges themselves, misconduct reports are likely to trigger what cognitive psychologists call "hot cognitions," judgments that carry powerful emotions, facilitating the retention of such reports (Zajonc 1980). And indeed, empirically speaking, we know that across class, educational, and age lines, people tend to be remarkably aware of major misconduct cases, often far more than they are about many other domains of government action or policy. For all these reasons, misconduct reports offer an important key for understanding declining citizen confidence in government.

ACKNOWLEDGMENTS

The research upon which this chapter is based was funded by grants from the Social Science Research Council's Abe Fellowship Program and the National Science Foundation. I would like to express warm appreciation to Robert D. Putnam, Russell J. Dalton, Paul Beck, Ellis Krauss, Steve Reed, Anthony King, Samuel P. Huntington, Donatella della Porta, Yasunori Sone, and an anonymous reviewer for Princeton University Press for their help and suggestions at various stages of preparation; to Christian Brunelli, Christina Davis, Shigeo Hirano, Emily Morris, Paul Talcott, and Jessica Wolf for their able research assistance; and to Bradley Richardson, Dennis Patterson, and Aiji Tanaka, fellow team members in the 1996 JEDS study.

Social Capital, Beliefs in Government, and Political Corruption

Donatella della Porta

THERE ARE THREE basic ways of thinking about social capital, trust in government, and governmental performance. First, the three variables may not be related to each other. That political corruption reduces confidence in government (and trust in general as a component of social capital) may be considered obvious. Why should citizens trust governors who mainly look out for themselves? In fact, citizens' dissatisfaction with corrupt officeholders should serve as democracy's main defense against political corruption; dissatisfied citizens should replace "bad" politicians with "good" ones by means of their votes. For many reasons, however, what appears to be a truism may not hold in reality. Corruption may remain hidden, invisible to the public. Even if it is visible, it may be tolerated. Political corruption may not seriously injure the "public good," or there may be a perception (cultivated by corrupt politicians) that in order to get things done, you have to "dirty your hands." Therefore, corruption may be regarded as the way things work, and corrupt politicians as those who are actually able to produce services and jobs—at least for their own constituencies. Corruption may be regarded as secondary to more serious issues, and citizens may therefore feel compelled to vote repeatedly for corrupt politicians whose politics they prefer to those of honest competitors. Social capital may vary independent of beliefs in government. Kenneth Newton and Pippa Norris's contribution to this volume presents evidence that at least one component of social capital—social trust—is related only weakly to public trust at the individual level (though the relationship is strong when aggregated data for the nation as a whole are considered). Governmental performance, too, has often been explained by variables other than social capital: modernization or institutional design, for instance.

Among analysts who do see a correlation between social capital, trust in government, and governmental performance, some take social capital to be the independent variable. Robert Putnam (1995a, 66) suggests that "the quality of public life and the performance of social institutions . . . are indeed powerfully influenced by norms and networks of civic engagements." Putnam (1993a) attributed differences in the performance of regional governments in Italy to differences in their levels of social capital. As he summarized later (1995a, 66), "the quality of governance [in Italy] was determined by long-standing traditions of civic engagement (or its absence). Voter turnout, newspaper readership, membership in choral society and football clubs—these were the hallmarks of a successful region." According to Putnam (1995a, 66), the presence of associations is a predictor of successful outcomes in many areas, including education, urban poverty, unemployment, the control of crime and drug abuse, and even health. Social capital produces good government insofar as it produces trust in others, including trust in government, by facilitating "coordination and cooperation for mutual benefit" and broadening citizens' "sense of self, developing the 'I' into 'we'" (Putnam 1995a, 67).

Building on this hypothesis, we should expect that a lack of social capital produces mistrust in government and, as a result, bad governmental performance, including corruption. This model was challenged on different grounds, however. First, social capital does not always improve public performance. According to Coleman, social capital includes all those social resources useful for getting things done, that is, those aspects of the social structure (e.g., obligations and expectations, information potential, norms and sanctions, authorities, and social organization) that facilitate action. In this sense social capital is neutral (Foley and Edwards 1997, 551; Greely 1997, 589). There is therefore such a thing as "bad" social capital: the social capital that was used by the Nazis to bring down the Weimar Republic, for example (Berman 1997), or that used by militias or the Mafia today (Levi 1996).

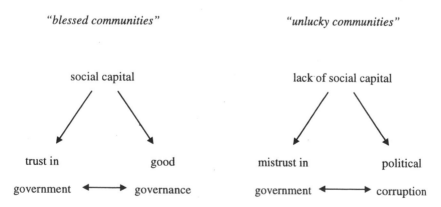

Figure 9.1. The Relationships of Social Capital, Trust in Government, and Government Performance with Social Capital as the Independent Variable

Second, not all types of associations produce trust and cooperation. According to Boix and Posner (1996), associations such as choral societies or bowling leagues do not produce public goods and therefore do not help overcome the tendency to free-ride. They do not provide norms of reciprocity, sanctions for defectors, or information, and the trust generated inside an association does not automatically extend to outsiders. As Levi (1996, 51) put it, "By themselves dense networks support localism, which is often extremely resistant to change. . . . Neighborhoods (and certain other networks of civic engagement) are a source of trust and neighborhoods are a source of distrust. They promote trust of those you know and distrust of those you do not, those not in the neighborhood or outside the networks." It is not always the case that "membership in one kind of society leads to overcoming the free-rider problem in another" (Levi 1996, 49).

Third, social capital may be produced by institutions located below associations, such as the family or workplace (Newton 1997c), or by institutions above associations, such as schools (Newton 1997; Younnis, McLellan, and Yates 1997), churches (Wood 1997), social movement organizations (Minkoff 1997), imagined communities (Edwards and Foley 1997), or even political parties (Tarrow 1996) or governments (on the role of institutions, see among others Sabetti 1996 and Cusack 1997b).[1] Huntington (1968) concurs that trust and cooperation are the result of effective government. Social capital may therefore depend on government performance: as Levi (1996, 50) noticed, "governments also may be a source of social capital. Policy performance can be a source of trust, not a result." In fact, "the obligations, expectations, norms, sanctions, and authority of the state—not to mention its functions as information provider and organizational resource—constitute the ultimate institutionalization of social capital à la Coleman" (Foley and Edwards 1997, 557).

In an alternative model government performance stands among the causes of public confidence and social capital. To explore the hypothesis of this new model, analysis must begin with an assessment of the extent to which corruption and confidence in government are related to each other. Although it does not affect all aspects of political participation the same way, the available data on corruption and beliefs in government in Italy, France, and Germany reveal that corruption is, in fact, inversely

---

[1] In fact, trust may derive from relationships that are not face-to-face (e.g., a broad sociopolitical sense of belonging, collective identities) and from nonhorizontal organizations (e.g., vertical chains of authority). The welfare state as well as the educational system explain the survival of a strong associational life in Britain (Hall 1997). City governments actively sponsor civic associations (e.g., Tarrow 1996; Portney and Berry 1997).

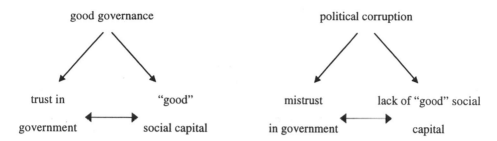

Figure 9.2. The Relationships of Social Capital, Trust in Government, and Government Performance with Government Performance as the Independent Variable

related with trust in government. What determines this relation? What is the causal direction, and how does it interact with the presence or absence of social capital?

This chapter uses research on political corruption to investigate the nature of these linkages. I will suggest that political corruption worsens governmental performance, thus reducing trust in the government's capacity to address citizens' demands. In addition, and less obviously, lack of confidence in government actually favors corruption insofar as it transforms citizens into clients and bribers who look for private protection to gain access to decision-makers. The relationship between confidence in government and political corruption is therefore not a causal one in which the direction of causality may be easily traced. On the contrary, corruption and mistrust feed each other, producing vicious circles.

The same can be said about social capital. Far from being the domain of anomic relationships, corrupt exchanges multiply when corruption become systemic, that is, when a system of norms and networks develops in which corrupted, corruptors, middlemen, clients, and the like can reduce the risks and costs usually attendant on participation in illegal activities. "Bad" social capital is needed to produce the reciprocal trust that is all the more indispensable for conducting deals in the shadows, where no formal laws, police, or judges are available to uphold agreements. Political corruption, in turn, reproduces this "bad" social capital, rewarding those who belong to the "right" networks and follow the "right" norms.

I shall refer in an illustrative way to research on political corruption in Italy based on judicial documents relating to 40 episodes of corruption, in-depth interviews with experts, reports of relevant parliamentary commissions of inquiry, requests for indictment of members of parliament, and the daily and weekly press.[2] Comparative remarks on the German and French cases are added on the basis of an analysis of the social science literature (della Porta and Mény 1997; della Porta and Vannucci 1998).

IS TRUST IN GOVERNMENT INFLUENCED BY POLITICAL CORRUPTION?

To test empirically the relationship between political corruption and confidence in government is no easy task. The construction of causal explanations is hampered by the difficulty of measuring the frequency of corrupt exchanges. As in any form of crime, official statistics include only the exposed fraction of the phenomenon. Not only do they underestimate the amount of corruption, but there is no reason to believe that the exposed part of the iceberg is representative of the submerged one. On the contrary, it is safe to assume that the distribution of discovered corrupt exchanges and their characteristics are influenced by both the investigative strategy of the state law-enforcement apparatus and the degree of tolerance of illegal activities among certain social groups or the public at large. These problems are even more serious given that corruption often has no visible victims, while the potential risk for those who denounce corruption may be quite high. Recent experiments with indexes of corruption based on experts' perception of the phenomenon face serious criticism as to their reliability, at least if they are expected to reflect the real amount of corruption.

Thus, any attempt at building an explanatory model of political corruption faces the difficulty of accurately measuring its dependent variable. Because I seek to investigate the effect of corruption on confidence in government, however, I can assume that some amount of corruption has been brought to light. Perceptions about corruption are, in this case, not a bad approximation for corruption itself. The data from Transparency International's Index on Perception of Corruption may constitute a starting point for cross-national comparison, and for confidence in government we can begin with an analysis of belief in government as measured by the Eurobarometer. I will focus on Italy as a case of widespread corruption versus France and Germany, as cases of medium to low and low degrees of corruption, respectively.[3]

---

[2] The results of this research are presented in della Porta (1992), Vannucci (1997), and della Porta and Vannucci (1994). Some results have been published in English in della Porta (1993), (1995), (1996a), (1996b); della Porta and Pizzorno (1996); and della Porta and Vannucci (1995), (1996), (1997a), (1997b), and (1998). For a comparative perspective, see della Porta and Mény (1996).

[3] The Transparency International Index is in line with other measures. According to an opinion poll run in 1993, for example, only 28 percent of German managers considered corruption among administrative officials to be commonplace, against 50 percent in France and 90 percent in Italy (cited in Seibel 1997, 86).

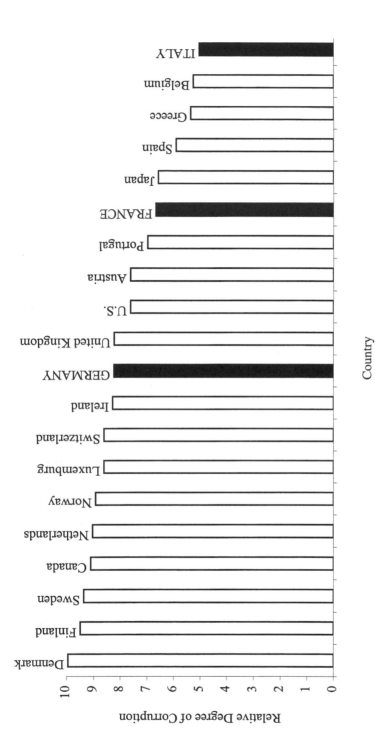

Figure 9.3. Corruption Evaluations of Germany, France, and Italy Compared to Other Trilateral Countries

Source: From the 1997 Transparency International (TI) corruption evaluations of 54 countries. TI evaluations report perceptions of corruption based on results of 10 surveys and other assessments conducted over the period 1993–96. Respondents in the surveys are international businesspeople and staff of international organizations. 10 = a corruption-free country.

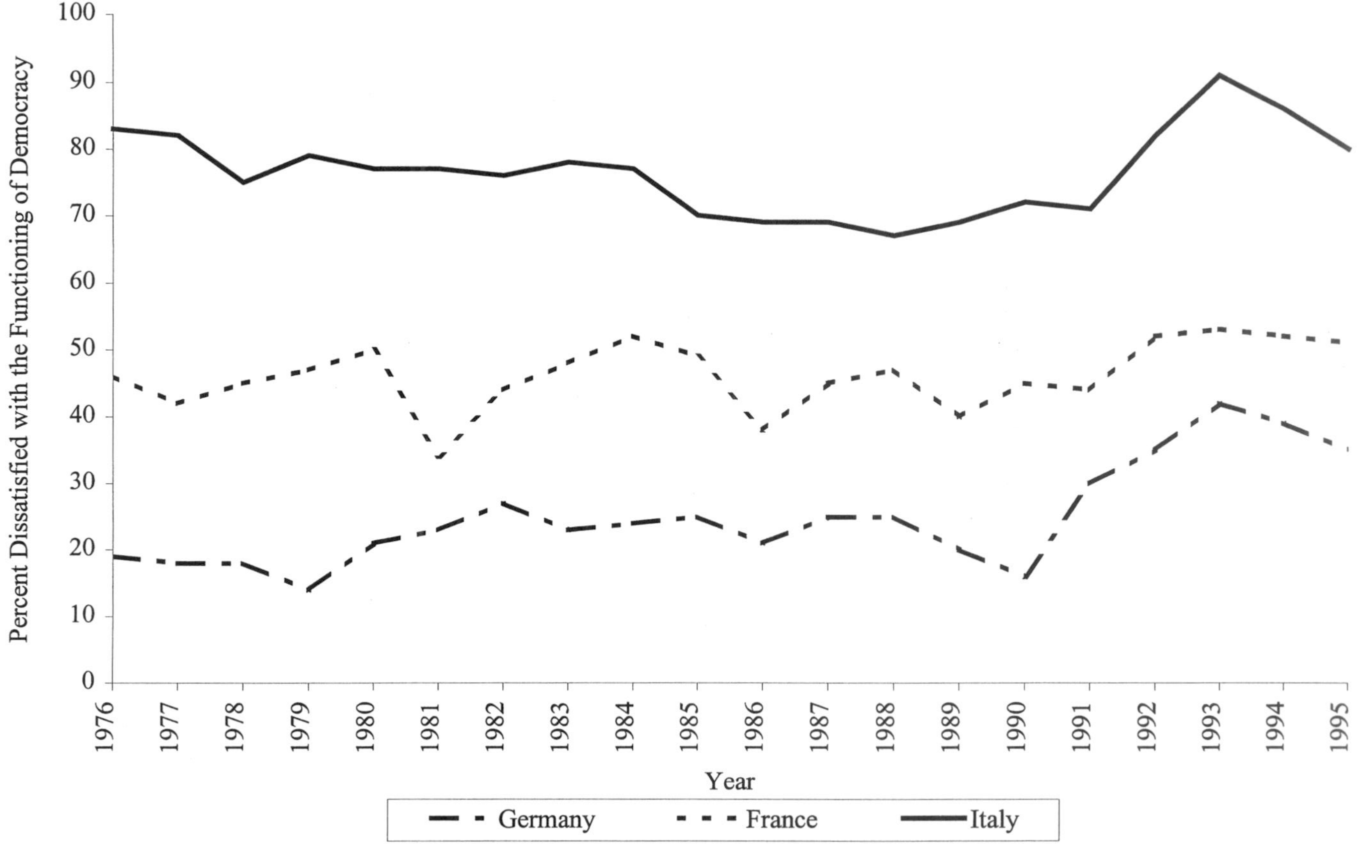

Figure 9.4. Dissatisfaction with the Functioning of Democracy

Source: My elaboration from Eurobarometer trends 1974–95, Brussels.

Comparing the data on perceptions of corruption (Figure 9.3) with the data about satisfaction with democracy (Figure 9.4), we can observe a rough correlation. That fraction of respondents who are dissatisfied ("not very satisfied" or "not at all satisfied") with the functioning of democracy between 1974 and 1995 fluctuates between 70 and 90 percent in Italy, between 40 and 60 percent in France, and 15 and 40 percent in Germany. In the Transparency International index Italy ranks as the most corrupt of the EU countries, followed by Belgium, Greece, Spain, France, Portugal, Britain, Germany, Ireland, Luxembourg, Finland, and Denmark. In turn, Eurobarometer data for 1995 indicate that the nations that are most satisfied with democracy (with the proportion of respondents who were very or fairly satisfied ranging from 70 to 83 percent) were precisely Denmark, Norway, Luxembourg, the Netherlands, and Ireland—that is, those countries that topped the cleanliness scale. Correspondingly, the lowest satisfaction with democracy was found in Italy, Greece, Spain, and Portugal—all countries that scored quite low on the cleanliness index.[4] In a cross-national analysis of perceptions of corruption and confidence in democracy in Southern Europe, Leonardo Morlino (1998, 315) observed that at least in Italy and Greece there is a close and consistent correlation between the level of dissatisfaction and with politics and media coverage of corruption. In general, "the review of the press sources gives strong empirical support to the relevance of news on corruption for the growth of dissatisfaction" in Southern Europe (Morlino 1998, 317). As Pharr demonstrates in this volume, the same is true of Japan, where there is a robust correlation between political dissatisfaction over the period 1978–95 and "discovered" corruption as indicated by the number of newspaper articles on the subject.

If we look at shifts over time, we find that confidence in government declined in the 1990s, when political scandals emerged. In Italy the proportion of citizens who were dissatisfied with the functioning of democracy rose above 80 percent in the 1970s, decreased to 70 percent in the 1980s (with the lowest ebb in 1988), and increased again after 1989, peaking in 1994. Their numbers declined thereafter, reaching in 1995 more or less the same level as 1976. If we look at trends in corruption as measured by Transparency International's (TI) indexes, which are based on the evaluations of international businesspeople and staff in international organizations, we observe that for both Italy and France the level of perceived corruption increased steadily over the period 1980 to 1996, with a drop for Italy in 1997 (see Figure 9.5). For Germany, in contrast,

---

[4] The rough correlation between ranking in the corruption index and satisfaction with democratic performance seems to hold true for Eastern European and Latin American countries, too (see Klingemann 1999, table 2.10).

the picture is one of stable "cleanliness." Comparing these patterns with levels of dissatisfaction with the working of democracy (see Figure 9.4), it is apparent that the relationship is hardly clear-cut. Thus, dissatisfaction in Italy declined somewhat in the 1980s—when, according to the TI data, corruption was actually increasing.

If we compare the Italian trend of dissatisfaction with the functioning of democracy with official statistics on corruption (as measured by the Italian Statistical Institute, or ISTAT), the relationship between "discovered" corruption and confidence in government turns out not to be an easy, "straight" inverse correlation (see Figure 9.6).

In fact, confidence in democracy rose in the 1980s, when the amount of corruption reported in official statistics was more or less stable, declined with the rise in reported corruption, then rose while corruption statistics peaked. Thus, dissatisfaction with democracy seems to vary with visible political corruption, especially when scandals emerge, while judicial activism against corruption (and the "forced" political reforms that can follow judicial investigations) boost confidence in democracy even if the number of crimes discovered is on the rise or remains high. After an initial shock, the public can regard the discovery of corruption as a positive sign, a sign that authorities are engaged in a struggle against it.

Although discovered cases of corruption increased in the 1980s in Italy, the curve of mistrust in government followed a different path. As Morlino and Marco Tarchi (1996, 54–55; see also Morlino 1998, ch. 7) indicated, there are in fact two types of mistrust that follow different patterns. *Ideological* mistrust in democracy tends to decrease, with democracy enjoying growing legitimacy even among the supporters of opposition parties. *Instrumental* mistrust in the actual performance of democratic government, on the other hand, increased, even among supporters of the parties in power. Although ideological dissatisfaction with democracy declined on the left in the 1980s, instrumental dissatisfaction increased in the 1990s among centrist as well as left-wing voters (Morlino 1998, 305–7).

A different picture emerges, however, if we examine the available data on media coverage, or the "scandalization" of corruption. According to Franco Cazzola's analysis of three Italian dailies over the years 1976 to 1992,[5] the number of cases of political corruption covered in the press started at 55 in 1976, remained stable the following year, declined to about 20 per year between 1978 and 1982, increased again to about 85 cases in 1984 and 1985, fluctuated around 50 to 60 cases between 1986

---

[5] The three dailies were *La Repubblica*, a national center-left newspapar; *La Stampa*, owned by the Agnelli family, which stands behind Fiat; and *L'Unità*, the official organ of the Italian Communist Party. See Cazzola (1988) and (1993) for more details.

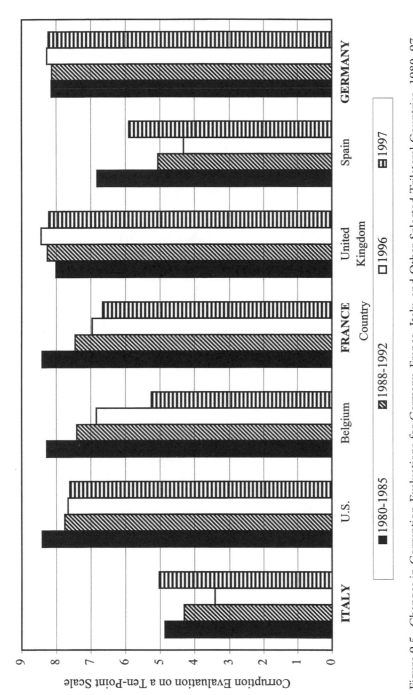

Figure 9.5. Changes in Corruption Evaluations for Germany, France, Italy, and Other Selected Trilateral Countries, 1980–97

Source: Elaboration from Transparency International and the University of Göttingen 1997.

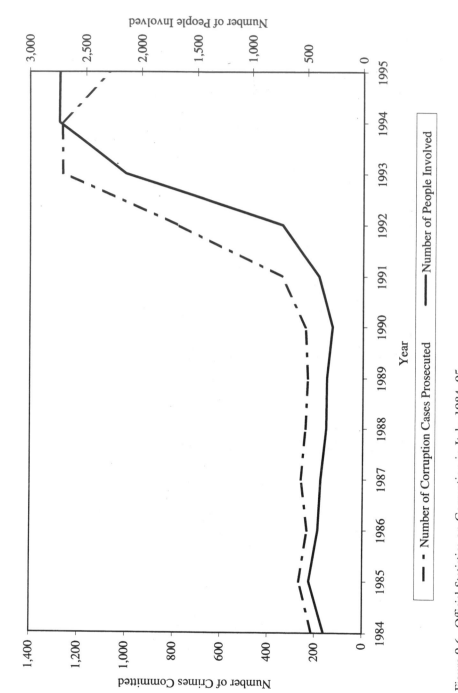

Figure 9.6. Official Statistics on Corruption in Italy, 1984–95

Source: Based on data from the Italian Statistical Institute (ISTAT), Rome.

and 1990, rose to 74 in 1991, and jumped to 268 in 1992. Following a similar trend (see Figure 9.7), dissatisfaction with democracy declined from over 80 percent in 1976 and 1977 to about 75 percent between 1978 and 1984. From 1985 it declined again to about or below 70 percent until 1991, only to rise to 82 percent in 1992. In the Italian case, as in the Japanese, confidence in government appears to vary with press coverage of political corruption.

A second caveat emerges if we look at trust in different institutions (see Table 9.1). Compared with the European average, Italy is characterized by low confidence in parliament, the civil service (stable in both cases), and its educational system (with a sharp decrease between the 1980s and 1990s). As for the educational system, not only has trust been low, but Italy's declining trend contrasts with a significant increase in both France and Germany. Italians are not mistrustful of all institutions: they trust (even more than Germans do) major companies, and they trust (more than the French and Germans do) the church. Japanese also reacted to political scandals by assigning different rates of trustworthiness to various domestic institutions; like the Italians, they penalized most representative institutions (see Pharr, this volume). Finally, according to the Eurobarometer, trust between citizens increased in Italy (from 2.20 to 2.57), West Germany (2.63 to 2.83), and France (2.29 to 2.85) between 1976 and 1993 in opposition to the trend of trust in government (see Newton and Norris, this volume). Thus, corruption clearly does not affect trust in different institutions in the same way. Corruption seems to reduce trust in representative institutions and political parties without necessarily influencing trust in private institutions or interpersonal trust.

The quality of trust may also differ. Italians do not feel particularly close to political parties compared to Germans (37.7 versus 59.7 percent), but they are not much different from the French (35.4 percent) in this respect. The quality of this relationship is peculiar: although very few Italians had a pragmatic attitude toward parties in 1989, many (more than in other countries) identified with or felt integrated into their party. This was particularly true for supporters of the Communist Party (Biorcio and Mannheimer 1995).

If we distinguish between attitudes and behavior, the diffusion of corruption may have coincided with increasing mistrust toward some institutions, but it did not affect political participation in the same way. Not only is voter participation higher in Italy than in Germany and France, but political participation beyond voting in Italy reaches levels very similar to France and Germany, and it increases (from a very low 10 percent in 1959) between 1981 and 1990 at a similar speed (see Table 9.2). Participation in unconventional political activity displays a similar pattern. Forms of peaceful protest such as signing petitions, joining boycotts, and

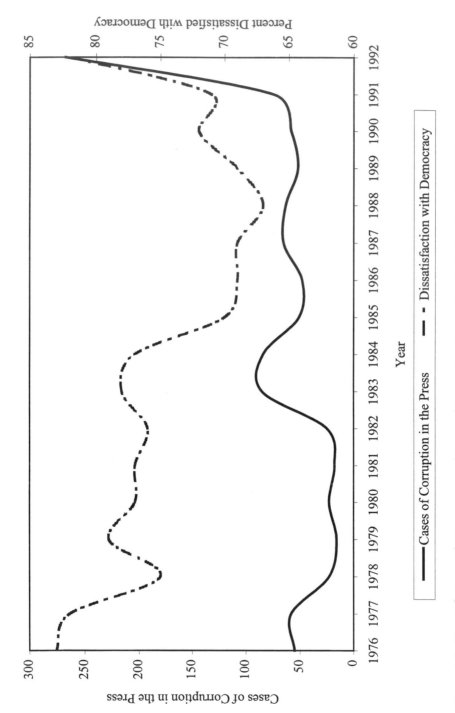

Figure 9.7. Dissatisfaction with Democracy and Cases of Corruption Reported in the Italian Press, 1976–92

Source: My elaboration on Cazzola (1993, 51).

TABLE 9.1
Confidence in Institutions in Italy, France, and Germany, 1981 and 1990

	Parliament	Civil Service	Educational System	Press	Trade Unions	Major Companies	Church
Italy 1981	30%	27%	56%	32%	29%	33%	58%
Italy 1990	32	27	48	39	34	62	63
France 1981	56	53	57	33	40	49	54
France 1990	48	49	66	38	32	67	50
Germany 1981	52	33	43	32	38	34	44
Germany 1990	51	39	54	34	36	38	40
Europe 1981	50	45	64	33	40	41	54
Europe 1990	48	44		35	41	50	50

Source: European Value System 1981 and 1990 as reported in Listhaug and Wiberg (1995, 304).

attending lawful demonstrations are very much on the rise. More disruptive forms of political participation such as occupying buildings achieve levels of support similar to those of France and greater than those of Germany. The union density rate is very high in Italy compared with Germany and especially France. If the union density rate steadily declined in France and remained stable in Germany, it increased in Italy after a decline in the 1960s and rose again in the 1970s and 1980s. Although party membership has been decreasing in Italy over the last few decades, especially since 1976 (see Morlino 1996, 14), this trend is not peculiar to Italy. In Italy the percentage of party members among voters fell from 12.7 percent in the beginning of the 1960s to 9.7 percent at the end of the 1980s, but the figure for Germany is much lower (4.2 percent at the end of the 1980s), and the decline was much more dramatic in other countries that were not hit by waves of scandals. In Denmark, for example, the proportion fell from 21.1 percent in the beginning of the 1960s to 6.5 percent at the end of the 1980s (Katz and Mair 1992).

Two different explanations might be offered for corruption's apparent lack of a precise effect on political participation. First, participation in parties, elections, or trade unions may carry a different meaning in clean and corrupt polities. In a clean polity, citizens vote or join a party to obtain a collective good; in a corrupt polity, citizens vote or join a party in exchange for a private benefit (see Putnam 1993a). A second explanation is that, because not all citizens are involved in corrupt activities, conventional and unconventional forms of political participation may express their discontent with the way the corrupt system works. This may account for the expansion of the Third (i.e., nonprofit) Sector in Italy and Japan in the 1980s and 1990s during a period of widespread political corruption (on Japan, see Pharr, this volume).

In summary, although political scandals do appear to influence confidence in government, political corruption does not affect confidence in all institutions in the same way. And if it can transform its forms and meanings, corruption does not affect levels of political participation as it does levels of trust.

How Political Corruption Produces Mistrust in Government

What explains the observed correlation between political corruption and confidence in government? First, political corruption reduces confidence in government insofar as it lowers the efficiency and efficacy with which public administration performs its official function of enhancing the public good. This is not a truism. The functionalist approach has long emphasized the positive effects corruption might have in "oiling" blocked bureaucratic and political mechanisms that would otherwise hinder devel-

TABLE 9.2
Political Behavior in Italy, France, and Germany

A. Average Participation in the Vote for the Lower House of Parliament, 1960–95

	Italy	France	Germany
Participation	90%	76%	86%

Source: Pasquino (1997, 49).

B. Political Participation beyond Voting

	Italy		France		Germany	
	1981	1990	1981	1990	1981	1990
Political participation	50%	56%	52%	57%	48%	57%

Source: European Value System 1981; World Value System 1990, as reported in Topf (1995, 69).

C. Participation in Unconventional Actions

	Italy		France		Germany	
	1981	1990	1981	1990	1981	1990
Sign petition	42%	44%	45%	54%	47%	57%
Join boycott	6	11	12	13	8	11
Attend lawful demonstration	27	36	27	33	15	21
Join unofficial strike	3	6	10	10	2	2
Occupy building	6	8	7	8	2	1

Source: European Value System 1981; World Value System 1990 as reported in Topf (1995, 88–90).

D. Union Density Rate

	1950	1960	1970	1980	1985
Italy	50%	35%	38%	54%	51%
France	21	19	21	17	15
Germany	35	38	38	41	39

Source: Visser (1990), as reported in Aarts (1995, 239).

opment, thus modernizing the political system, lessening the recourse to political violence, and favoring social integration and capital accumulation.[6] Research on Italy, however, indicates that corruption has reduced

[6] On the putatively positive functions of political corruption in developing countries, see Huntington (1968), Merton (1957), Leff (1964), and Nye (1967), among others, and a

the efficiency and efficacy of public administration. In fact, corruption distorts public demand; increases the cost, reduces quality, and delays the completion of public works; delays access to public administration for those people who do not pay bribes; and reduces the productivity of firms that interact with the state.

Corruption and the Distortion of Public Demand

The definition of public demand is a pivotal moment in the democratic process because it is here that the administrative system is confronted with the needs and demands of social groups. Political mediation is the filter through which interests are articulated and aggregated, and its task is "to identify and interpret the needs and desires of the population; select and generalize those which can be expressed in political terms; propose, justify and criticize policies and measures to achieve these ends or, when necessary, to explain why they cannot be satisfied" (Pizzorno 1992, 22). Corruption radically alters this function, privileging the satisfaction of so-called internal demand (Chevallier and Loshak 1983, 113). Corruption, and complicity among those who are corrupt, weakens the institutional restraints designed to protect the general interest, so public demands come to be decided by those people who participate in corrupt exchanges.

When political corruption is systemic, the discretionary management of public spending often becomes an objective in itself. Administrators aim to attract as many resources as possible to areas in which they have power in order to pocket a bribe in return for mediation and/or gain support as a result of the effects of public investment on employment (which is treated here as a sphere for clientelistic exchange). Public spending is therefore diverted to those sectors in which gains from corruption are greatest and the discretionary nature of procedures reduces the risks involved. In general, little attention is paid to whether the nation is served by these works or services. It is not even necessary that they be completed or brought into use. As noted in the case of the "Teardo Clan" of Savona in Italy, corrupt administrators can "radically and seriously distort administrative activity, with works being contracted exclusively for the function of exacting bribes more safely and easily and not on the basis of any actual technical requirement" (Court of Savona 1985, 155; see also Somogyi 1992, 80). Massive programs for events such as the Columbus Celebrations or the Soccer World Cup of 1990 brought public works to Italy that later turned out to be unnecessary, exorbitant, or simply impos-

---

number of recent economic analyses such as Beck and Maher (1986) and Lien (1986). For a critical review, see Cartier-Bresson (1997, especially 52–55).

sible to realize but that proved lucrative in terms of bribes for the administrators involved.

The Elevation of Costs

Research on contemporary democracy suggests that corruption only very rarely assumes the guise of extortion (della Porta and Mény 1997; della Porta and Vannucci 1994). In most cases entrepreneurs are not the victims of greedy politicians, but their accomplices. As such, they enjoy the advantages of voluntary corrupt exchanges as much as corrupt politicians do. Thus, bribes are not taken from the pockets of entrepreneurs; instead, they come from politically produced rents. Thanks to the protection of corrupt politicians, entrepreneurs obtain extra profits from their contracts with public administration: they are paid more than the exchange value of their product on the private market, or they pay less than the market value for services provided by the state. Italian judges have noted that "the damage to public administration caused by the need for entrepreneurs, drained for the profit of the accused, to make up the losses sustained from extortion and the consequent elevation of costs, poor execution of work, proliferation of price revisions, execution of non-contractual work, and the requirement of supplementary technical evaluation, has been very serious" (Court of Savona 1985, 434).

Both corruptor and corrupted share an interest in having the costs of bribery drawn from the public purse in order to widen their margin of gain. As Italian magistrates have observed, it is impossible by the end of the process to "distinguish between who in the dance is leading and who is following: the illegal demands of functionaries may have led suppliers to augment prices further while the former, accustomed to receiving a percentage as compensation, not only had no interest in enforcing the official price-list, but if anything had quite the opposite interest" (Court of Appeals of Catania 1991, 60–61). Bids far lower than the market would permit, the discretionary awarding of contracts, and continual revision of prices and modification of the services contracted permit corrupt actors to avoid legal and procedural obstacles, and as a result the public administration behaves (to use an expression frequently encountered in the course of research) "like the most irresponsible of private actors."

In Italy the uncovering of corruption normally coincides with a realization that public administration is paying too much for goods and services that often turn out to be of poor quality. The State Audit Court investigation of the prison-building program revealed cases in which the final cost was *20 times* the original estimate or in which the work had taken 20 years (*L'Espresso*, March 13, 1988, 11). Of 20 projects settled on in 1972, only four were complete on December 31, 1987. The variation in cost per inmate was extraordinary, ranging from 27 million lire in Bergamo to 320 million in Florence. Even after termination of the work, the final inspection was sometimes delayed for years (three and half years in the case of Salerno). Changes to projects led to the demolition of already completed buildings in Ascoli Piceno, among other places. Projects have been suspended or deferred for years: 1,019 days at Ivrea, for example, and 1,135 days at Vercelli. In addition, more than 40 percent of the plans for new prisons have since been abandoned because it was discovered that the necessary land was unavailable (State Auditors Department Report, vol. 3, 1988, 28). These examples of extremely overpriced and delayed work significantly overlap with the "golden prison" scandal that in 1988 revealed a vast bribery ring in which entrepreneurs who were awarded contracts had paid off functionaries, local politicians, and government ministers.

A similar story can be told of privatization in the former German Democratic Republic, in which kickbacks paid to public officials permitted corrupt entrepreneurs to buy public properties or licenses at much less than their actual value. Unlike the Italian case, however, the wave of scandals following German reunification focused on minor cases of misuse of public property (e.g., the use of an official car for private purposes) or the acceptance of favors from private firms (e.g., paid trips) (Seibel 1997). And as in the past, most political scandals (e.g., the Flick or the Neu Heimat affairs) ended without any corruption charges.[7]

Corrupt politicians often produce political rents for a protected firm by paying—with public money—for nonexistent services. The most intangible services, such as expertise or brokerage, are the most difficult to control and thus the services of choice for such exchanges. In Italy political parties themselves may unofficially create firms, frequently with no professional expertise, that participate in public bids. In France similar firms have been used to collect kickbacks from entrepreneurs. Often financed by the state, various associations receive money that they use to finance political parties. These associations provide salaries to party members with whom they enjoy relations, finance their campaigns, and pay for party activities (Becquart-Leclercq 1989, 9–10; Mény 1992). One of the scandals that pushed the Socialists out of power in France came with disclosure of the activities of Urba, a research bureau that collected illegal party financing for the Socialist Party and distributed it, in the word of its director (*Le Monde*, March 3, 1995), "according to the principle of 40-30-30, that is, 40 percent for the functioning of Urba, 30 percent for

---

[7] For an analysis of political scandals in Germany, see Noack (1985). On the scandal related to the Flick company's political contributions, see Kilz and Preuss (1983). On the bankruptcy of the trade unions related to the firm Neue Heimat, see Mehnert (1997).

the national headquarters of the party, and 30 percent for local elected politicians." Collecting bribes from local entrepreneurs and concealing them as compensation for services that were never rendered, Urba paid the salaries of functionaries in the central headquarter of the party as well as various political campaign expenses at both the local and national levels.

"Fast" Lanes and "Slow" Lanes

When long delays become the rule, a functionary can ask for a bribe simply to expedite his or her job, but when preferential treatment is bought through corruption, the rest of the public increasingly suffers the negative effects of bureaucratic inefficiency. Because the time and effort of functionaries represents a limited resource, a firm that expedites its own business slows down everyone else's. For example, the functionary in charge of payments for the Sicilian local health board, later found guilty of corruption, "left a great many invoices lying unattended to with the excuse that he could not sort out the dossiers, while he was quick in approving others, disregarding their chronological order" (Court of Appeal of Catania 1991, 58–59).

The "Inverse" Selection of Firms

Where corruption is widespread, it will not only be efficiency (i.e., the ability to perform the task at hand more quickly and at less cost) that is rewarded, but also the capacity to build relationships of friendship and trust with public decision-makers and the absence of moral scruples. Thus, efficiency is but one—and often not even the most important—of the factors behind the winning bid in a system dominated by corruption. In fact, the more efficient firms may be unsuccessful precisely because competitors that have no prospects of success in the private sector are willing to pay bribes and accept reduced profits in order to maintain a share of the public-sector market. As alternative sources of profit arise in the private sector or abroad, the efficient firms that become marginalized in this way abandon the public sector to be replaced by the less efficient. Given that the return on investment from privileged contacts with the state frequently exceeds that on investment in new technology, the incentive to pursue research and development diminishes for the firms that remain in the public sector, so they come to form a separate, inefficient clique.

In sum, political corruption results in the poor functioning of public administration, which is likely to reduce the "instrumental" component of public confidence. As the Italian case suggests, public scandals allow the blame to be targeted against politicians. In general, however, the poor functioning of public administration generates widespread criticism among citizens and entrepreneurs concerning the efficiency and impartiality of public procedures, that is, their equal access to rights formally sanctioned by law.

HOW MISTRUST IN GOVERNMENT FACILITATES CORRUPTION

Because it worsens the performance of public administration, corruption seems to reduce confidence in government. Conversely, individuals' mistrust of and low expectations regarding the efficiency and impartiality of government encourage corruption. As a Sicilian politician observed (*La Repubblica*, October 17, 1991), "Administrative paralysis transforms any right into a favor. If you need a certificate or a building permit and have to wait about two years to receive it, then you end up asking and paying for it as a favor." In France the development of political corruption has been related to a basic mistrust on the part of citizens that multiplies procedural controls and usually retards the administrative process (Mény 1997, 17).

Because they can then selectively offer protection from such inconveniences, corrupt politicians and civil servants have a positive interest in portraying public administration as inefficient and unpredictable. In exchange for bribes, they are willing to guarantee speedier consideration of particular cases, favorable interpretation of regulations, simpler procedures, or a positive outcome in clashes with the public administration. As a Milanese businessman complained (Federazione Italiana Pubblici Esercenti 1992, 54), "Because it is the best way to keep everyone over the coals, a lot of dossiers remain open under consideration."

When corruption reaches those centers of power that influence the rules agents must follow, irrational and contorted procedures multiply as the organizational structure comes to reflect the interests of those who are corrupt. The successful conclusion of a particular case comes to depend on the personalization of relations with the public bureaucracy. This encourages the creation of privileged channels of communication with the public administration to obtain profits, reduce time spent waiting, or forestall other potential corruptors.

Moreover, corrupt politicians use the inefficiencies they have produced to increase mistrust in the functioning of public administration. For example, the owner of premises in Florence was clearly told by an intermediary close to the local administration that "in the event he did not agree to pay [a kickback], the value of the premises would be irremediably depreciated because it would be sucked into an inextricable administrative maze." In short, "if you pay the bribe, you can sell it for a good price; the alternative is an endless torment against which a private citizen has, for all intents and purposes, no defense other than a court case that, as is well known, will take many years" (Court of Florence 1986, 338 and 342).

As corruption grows, people increasingly regard administration as arbitrary. Dissatisfaction with the functioning of public administration thus increases the propensity of those people who were initially excluded from the market of corruption to seek protection themselves. According to a shopkeeper in Rome (Federazione Italiana Pubblici Esercenti 1992, 7), "oiling the necessary wheels is like having to pay an additional tax. But it's worthwhile because administrative procedures that would take years get done in a few weeks. It costs. But I don't see any alternative for those people who want to work in this city."

How "Bad" Social Capital Favors Corruption

How does social capital enter into this picture? As in any exchange, political corruption requires norms of reciprocity. Corruption requires trust among the different actors who take part in illegal exchanges if it is to become systematic. Without the presence of "bad" social capital, of an alternative set of norms and relationships of trust embedded in special networks, corruption would not spread. In fact, corruption developed together with an alternative set of rules of the game that grows out of a patrimonial conception of the state and a disregard for bureaucratic, legalistic, and impersonal authority.

The relationship between the corruptor and the corrupted is regulated by a complex system of informal norms. As research on the French case indicated (Becquart-Leclercq 1989, 207), "Hidden norms regulate corruption. Thus, systemic corruption is not anomic, but it does seem like it because the norms are parallel and implicit. These norms are clear to those who are 'in' the game, however. They are the winners." For example, in the Grenoble judicial inquiry that led to the indictment of former Minister Alain Carignon, all firms involved in the system of corruption paid the same bribe percentage as a sort of "fair price" for the awarding of public contracts (*La Repubblica*, January 27, 1995, 18). In Italy the setting of bribes as fixed percentages for each kind of public bid became a "rule of the game," informal but well known to those involved. In these situations the payment of bribes was facilitated by the widespread conviction—emphasized by those seeking money—that it was unavoidable. The existence of precise rates of payment reduced the risk and transaction costs of negotiation between the corruptor and the corrupted. A complex system of values developed in order to neutralize any feeling of guilt about participation in the corrupt exchange. Officials justified accepting bribes as the way to give politics its due; paying bribes testified to one's understanding of how politics really works. Entrepreneurs justified the paying of bribes in the name of their paramount goal of making profits, which they frequently portrayed as flowing from their duty to protect employees' jobs. In an illegal system of exchange, a high degree of trust and reciprocity is necessary among participants, so the internalization of some rules of the game is therefore necessary. A good reputation for respecting the terms of the illegal exchange, which participants often call "honesty," is valued by the actors involved.

These norms and trust are embedded in special kinds of networks. Networks of power, whose official ends range from charity to the promotion of culture, serve the purpose of illicit lobbying and the negotiation of business. Different interests meet and illegal pacts are negotiated in the nodes of these networks. In Italy and France, for example, deviant Masonic lodges played an important role in the development of political corruption. Moreover, the Knights of Malta, the Club des Anysettiers, and the Knights of the Holy Sepulchre are more or less exclusive societies involved in Italian political scandals (della Porta 1992; for France, see Mogiliansky 1995, 2). The various participants in corrupt exchanges may feel the need to meet each other in a confidential environment in which they come to know each other, learn about their reciprocal availability, negotiate, and exchange promises and sanctions. By participating in the formal or informal associations that secretly bring together people of heterogeneous backgrounds and customarily decide the affairs of the city, they can also acquire the information necessary to identify occasions for corruption and corruptible people. To fulfill this function as a clearinghouse for particularistic interests, meeting places of the local elite must possess specific features: they must be protected from indiscreet attention or, in other words, have selective membership procedures; they must favor the development of solidarity and complicity among members; and they must bring together the various actors interested in, or necessary for, the exchange. Mistrust in visible, democratic institutions may therefore be paralleled by a strong trust in all the most hidden forms of power. As Norberto Bobbio (1980) indicated many years ago, political corruption in Italy as well as attempted coups d'état were both forms of "cryptocracy" that were often intertwined.

In sum, the presence of "bad" social capital in terms of an alternative normative system and hidden networks of power facilitates the spread of corruption.

How Corruptors Create "Bad" Social Capital

Political corruption, in turn, reproduces these norms and networks. In particular, the hidden structures of the political parties involved in Italian corruption played the important role of socializing participants into the rules in force (Sherman 1980, 480). As criminologists have long observed (Sutherland and Cressey 1974, 75), "criminal behavior is learned in interaction with other persons in a process of communication." In the case of political corruption in Italy, this process developed in particular inside political parties. Parties place their people in positions of responsibility in public bodies, and in return they demand that these people conform to the rules, utilizing those positions not only for personal enrichment, but also for (illegal) party financing.

Corrupt parties' assumption of this socializing role in corruption permits the system of covert transactions to expand. Politicians already introduced to the rules of the illegal marketplace introduce others in turn. Loyalty to the party serves to obtain appointments, which are then paid for by distributing the money acquired through corruption. Moreover, the creation of networks in which corruption could proliferate was an important task for corrupted politicians. Italian "business politicians" had other talents traditionally valued in politics: the abilities to network, form relations, create bonds of trust, and encourage mutual obligations and favors (Pizzorno 1992). Indeed, many of the corrupt politicians who were exposed spent a large part of their time creating webs of reciprocal links, instrumental friendship, and mutual trust. Similar mechanisms develop on the side of firms, too.

The Vicious Circle of Corruption and Mistrust of Government: Some Conclusions

Social capital, confidence in government, and governmental performance do appear to be related to each other. The data on Italy, France, and Germany indicate that confidence in government appears to decline when corruption is perceived to be widespread. Confidence in government was lowest in Italy, the country in which corruption appeared to be most widespread. It was highest in Germany, the country in which the governors appeared to be least corrupt. France occupies a medium position on both variables. The correlation between confidence in government and perceptions of corruption over time is not a linear one, however. In Germany confidence in government has declined without an increase in the perception of corruption. In Italy the fact that confidence in government and corruption both increased in the 1980s can be explained by the different dynamics of "ideological" versus "instrumental" trust. The relationship between beliefs and action was complex: notwithstanding a low degree of confidence in representative institutions, Italians have demonstrated high degrees of participation in both conventional and unconventional forms of politics.

Why and how are corruption and confidence in government related to each other? To return to the questions raised in my introduction, which one is the independent and which one the dependent variable? Does corruption produce mistrust, or does mistrust produce corruption? As indicated in Figure 9.8, the two phenomena appear to be interrelated, producing spirals and vicious circles more than clear paths of causation.

On the one hand, investigations have indicated that corruption produces maladministration through distortion of the demand for public works, arbitrary hikes in their price, delays in the provision of public services for those who do not pay bribes, and the inverse selection of firms. Maladministration due to corruption reduces the confidence in government of citizens who judge the functioning of democratic institutions on the basis of their actual performance. The emergence of scandals, with their evidence that maladministration is related to corruption, reduces confidence further. In this case the reaction seems to be a moral one more than an ideological or instrumental one. A more in-depth look at the Italian case indicates that a decline of confidence in some institutions can coexist with an increase in confidence in others.

On the other hand, a lack of confidence in government facilitates corruption. Maladministration (sometimes resulting from inertia, sometimes from able maneuvering) expands the discretionary and arbitrary power of administrators in each phase of the process leading to the "purchase" of public measures by bribery, from the creation of artificial demand to the contamination of the system of adjudication and the weakening of controls. In such a context the generalized inefficiency of public structures, for which functionaries themselves are partly responsible, permits them to privatize and sell the resources of their offices in exchange for bribes. The discretionary power accompanying administrative inefficiency can be used to further the interests of aspiring corruptors. Thus, corruption feeds on inefficiency. When long delays become the rule, even a functionary who

Maladministration → Mistrust in the Protection of Citizens' Rights → Search for Protection →

Propensity for Paying Bribes → (Demand for) Corruption → Selective Inclusion →

Increased (Perception of) Maladministration

Figure 9.8. Vicious Circle: Maladministration → Corruption → Maladministration

Source: della Porta and Vannucci (1998).

limits himself to performing his job within the time foreseen by regulations can demand a *tangente* in exchange for this now unanticipated service. Moreover, maladministration reduces confidence in public administration and expectations of enjoying rights sanctioned by law on the part of citizens and entrepreneurs. As a result, they seek privileged channels of access, and the need for such privileged channels increases their willingness to buy access by means of bribes or, in other words, the demand for corruption. As corrupt practices spread, those who are willing to pay are selectively included. If one of the objectives of functionaries is to collect bribes, they have an interest in fostering procedural delays and unpredictability that create the conditions for corrupt transactions, and corruption breeds inefficiency, recommencing the vicious cycle.

This pattern of interactions is related to another vicious cycle involving the production of "bad" social capital. Political corruption requires the presence of informal norms, reciprocity, and clandestine networks. In order for corruption to become systemic, moral as well as material costs (such as the risk of being denounced) must be lowered by a normative system in which corruption is regarded as normal. The spread of corruption itself ensures that those who respect illegal agreements will be rewarded, while politicians who do not ask for bribes and entrepreneurs who do not pay them will be slowly expelled from the political system and the public-sector market. In turn, the agents of political corruption help produce "bad" social capital, socializing others into the alternative normative system, enforcing respect for illegal pacts, and constructing hidden networks for corrupt exchanges.

These vicious cycles help explain the increase in corruption in Italy. Not only the number of judicial cases and newspaper articles (which are imprecise indicators of the true amount of corruption) but also the testimony of informants indicate that corruption increased dramatically in the 1980s. A "bad equilibrium" stabilized at that time, when these vicious cycles weakened all possible opposition to political corruption from inside and outside the political system. It was widely believed that corruption was nothing but "the way things work." In this situation corruption did produce mistrust in representative institutions, but mistrust fed corruption, rather than leading to a breakdown in the corrupt system.

The same example, however, indicates that the "bad equilibrium" of widespread corruption is ultimately unstable, destroying both material and symbolic resources in a futile attempt to buy a personalistic consensus. Like any illegal system, corruption needs more trust and reciprocity—"bad" social capital—than it is able to produce. Without formal institutions to enforce agreements among participants in corrupt exchanges, the temptation to "sell a lemon" is always very strong. By its very nature the corrupt system has to continue expanding to win the complicity of those who, if excluded, could denounce corrupt politicians and entrepreneurs. The more the system expands, however, the more difficult it becomes to maintain control within corrupt networks, and in this unstable situation external circumstances may act as a catalyst to upset the "bad equilibrium."

In Italy the vicious cycles that produced corruption were interrupted when the fall of the Berlin Wall definitively delegitimized those political parties whose raison d'être was the defense against communism. At the same time, market globalization as symbolized by the Maastricht Treaty increased citizens' impatience with the inefficiency of a state that consumed resources without producing the services needed to withstand foreign economic competition. These developments reduced the hitherto widespread complicity with the corrupt system, aiding the investigation of a judiciary that had become increasingly independent and increasingly keen to destroy the power of a corrupt political class. At the same time, the media (or at least part of it) launched a campaign against the immorality of politicians, changing the master frame in the definition of corruption. If corruption was perceived as a victimless crime in a situation of "bad equilibrium," with the development of the Clean Hands scandal in the 1990s, public opinion came to regard citizens as the victims of corruption and politicians as villains. It would be over-optimistic to think that the breakdown of the traditional political parties and the change in the political class that followed the political scandals has already set in motion a positive equilibrium of good government and good social capital. What is clear, however, is that Italy's peaceful revolution has indicated that, in a democracy, a negative equilibrium of bad government and "bad" social capital is inherently unstable. They can last for long—too long!—but not forever.

PART IV

Sources of the Problem: Changes in Information and Criteria of Evaluation

TEN

The Impact of Television on Civic Malaise

Pippa Norris

THE LAST DECADE has witnessed a new cycle of anxiety about democracy and civic malaise. The most recent review of evidence worldwide concluded that popular accounts of a "crisis of democracy" were greatly exaggerated (Norris 1999). The end of the Cold War has brought the triumph of democratic values. At the same time, however, as other chapters in this volume demonstrate, there is a systematic and pervasive pattern of declining confidence in representative institutions connecting citizens and the state. In light of these developments, this chapter explores how far television is responsible for civic malaise, as many assume.

The media are commonly blamed for the ills of the body politic. Recently the trickle of accusations has become a deluge. For Postman (1985) television is responsible for our "amusing ourselves to death." For Patterson (1993) journalism is "out of order." For Fallows (1996) the media are "undermining American democracy." Some critics blame television entertainment in general. Others indict television news. This critique has produced widespread hand-wringing within the journalism profession and debate about the virtues of a range of panaceas, including civic journalism and revised codes of professional practice (Hachten 1998). Some seem to want nothing but a steady diet of C-SPAN on all channels, like political cod liver oil, to educate the public in their democratic duties. But before we turn all the airwaves over to C-SPAN, is the chorus of complaints justified?

The first section of this chapter reviews the videomalaise literature and argues that the evidence supporting this thesis often remains problematic. I go on to compare the effects of television watching in nine advanced industrialized democracies based on the 1995–97 World Values Survey and then to a more detailed comparison of media use in the 1996 National Election Study and the 1997 British Election Study. The results suggest two primary conclusions. First, in many advanced industrialized democracies, the amount of time people devote to watching television is in fact associated with indicators of civic malaise (including lower levels of social trust, voluntary activism, and political participation). It is not possible to analyze the direction of causality based on cross-sectional data, but I demonstrate that the association between television watching and civic malaise is consistent in many different countries.

Yet this observation needs to be qualified in one important regard: my second conclusion is that it matters *what* you watch, as well as *how much* you watch. Those viewers who watch television *news* during British and American elections display greater civic virtue (indicated by higher-than-average political interest, efficacy, and knowledge). Although the most plausible explanation is that people with these political characteristics are more likely to turn on the news, that exposure reinforces these tendencies in a positive cycle. The picture is therefore complex, with television entertainment generally associated with apathy but television news with strengthened political engagement. The conclusion considers implications for the media's power to mobilize the public in the democratic process.

VIDEOMALAISE AND MOBILIZATION THEORIES

Videomalaise theories differ in many ways, but they all emphasize the corrosive effects of the news media on the body politic (for a discussion, see Newton 1997b). One school of thought contends that watching all forms of television programs reduces civic engagement. Putnam (1995b) analyzed the U.S. General Social Survey to demonstrate that the people who watched the most television were the least socially trusting and the most reluctant to become engaged in community life. Putnam argues that television saturation of American homes in the 1950s produced a post-civic generation. Citizens raised in this cultural environment were less likely than their parents to trust others, join voluntary associations, and vote. Three hypotheses are offered: television may displace other leisure activities and community involvement outside the home; watching prime-time television entertainment, with its emphasis on violence and crime, may produce a "mean world" syndrome (Gerbner et al. 1994); and television may have a particularly strong effect on childhood aggression. The assumption is that the amount of time devoted to watching the box has impoverished and privatized the public sphere.

A second school of thought focuses on television news. It is argued that when politics is covered on television, it is covered badly because of an excessive emphasis on the poll-driven horse race (Who's ahead, who's behind?), conflictual and negative news, and strategic game frames (Postman 1985; Jamieson 1992; Sabato 1991; Patterson 1993; Hart 1994; Fallows 1996; Schudson 1995). Tabloidization has resulted in a relentless pursuit of sensational, superficial, and populist political reporting as network news attempts to maintain eroding ratings. All this breathless flimflam, it is argued, comes at the expense of detailed and informed debate about policy issues and hard news. In an attempt to staunch the hemorrhage of viewers, recent years have seen the expansion of soft news, or a blurring of entertainment and news values, with endless coverage of Di, Lewinsky, and Viagra rather than the serious problems of health care, Indonesia, or Kosovo (see Klite, Bardwell, and Salzman 1997). Similar worries have been aired in Japan (Pharr and Krauss 1996) and Europe. Echoing Habermas, there is widespread concern that the displacement of public-service television by commercial channels has impoverished the public sphere (Dahlgren 1995; Langer 1998; Weymouth and Lamizet 1996; Holtz-Bacha 1990; Lull and Hinerman 1997).

There is nothing new in coverage of scandal. Newspapers have highlighted the moral peccadilloes and sexual proclivities of the rich and famous since the rise of yellow journalism. Think of Teapot Dome, Watergate, and Iran-Contra. But today routine and daily front-page headlines about government scandals seem more pervasive than in previous decades, whether on sleaze in Britain, Tagentopoli in Italy, Recruit and Sagawa Kyubin in Japan, or Lewinsky in America. This coverage is believed to corrode the trust that underpins social relations and political authority (Garment 1991; Markovits and Silverstein 1988; Lull and Hinerman 1997; della Porta and Mény 1997). Michael Robinson (1976) used American survey data from the 1960s to show that people who relied upon television news had lower political efficacy, greater social distrust and cynicism, and weaker party loyalties than those who relied upon newspapers, radio, or magazines. Miller, Goldenberg, and Lutz (1979) linked content analysis of newspapers, particularly critical political coverage, with feelings of political disaffection. More recently Ansolabehere and Iyengar (1995) demonstrated that watching negative or attack television advertising discouraged voter turnout. Other experiments (Cappella and Jamieson 1997) have found American network news guilty of sensationalizing and over-simplifying complex issues like health care, producing a spiral of cynicism among the public.

In contrast to these theories, the mobilization perspective suggests that the modern mass media have a largely positive role, sustaining and promoting civic participation. Traditional Michigan theories have always looked to newspapers to mobilize and reinforce voters (Campbell et al. 1960), and Downsian theories of rational voters hold that the news media can contribute toward enlightened or reasoned choices among the electorate (Gelman and King 1993; Lupia and McCubbins 1997). Societal modernization has increased the availability of a diverse range of specialized news media—newspapers, magazines, radio, television, and now the Internet—catering to different markets and providing a rich and dense information environment for citizens in advanced industrialized democracies. The costs of finding out about current affairs have been greatly reduced for interested citizens. Moreover, higher levels of literacy and education may have increased the ability of citizens to make use of this information. In many advanced industrial democracies, these developments have produced an electorate—particularly among the well-educated—that is better equipped to participate and more sophisticated about public affairs—if perhaps more skeptical and critical toward established authorities than ever before.

EVIDENCE FOR AND AGAINST THE VIDEOMALAISE THESIS

What is the evidence that television in general and television news in particular can influence either civic mobilization or malaise? Research on this issue raises difficult theoretical and methodological challenges. Sweeping claims about the ill effects of television—whether about the impact of violence on children, the commercialization of popular culture, or public disaffection with government—are often cast at such a high level of generality as to be untestable. This study explores the association between patterns of television use and indicators of civic malaise in nine established democracies included in the World Values Survey (WVS) of 1995–97: Australia, Finland, Japan, Norway, Spain, Sweden, Switzerland, the United States, and West Germany.[1] The comparison therefore includes different regions of the world, major powers as well as small states, and a variety of media systems. The WVS allows us to compare television habits in terms of how much time, if any, people say that they usually spend watching television on an average weekday (see Appendix). As Table 10.1 shows, the amount of time that people reported watching varied quite substantially among countries, with Australia, Finland, Japan, and the United States at the high end opposite Switzerland, Norway, and West Germany. For subsequent comparison, these data are recoded into two groups: light users (who watch no more than two hours of television per day) and heavy users (who watch at least two hours per day). We can test the association between this measure of exposure to television and six different indicators of civic malaise that tap levels of social trust, voluntary activism, regime support, institutional confidence, and political interest and discussion.

[1] I am most grateful to Ronald Inglehart for data from the third wave of the World Values Survey, without which this study would not have been possible, and to Sidney Tarrow, Susan Pharr, and Robert Putnam for helpful comments on an earlier draft.

TABLE 10.1
Hours of Television Watched per Day

Nation	Does Not Watch TV	One to Two Hours per Day	Two to Three Hours per Day	More Than Three Hours Per Day
Switzerland	6%	69%	18%	7%
Sweden	2	36	43	12
W. Germany	10	54	24	12
Norway	3	58	26	13
Spain	5	44	32	19
Japan	2	40	35	24
Finland	4	20	34	26
United States	3	43	27	26
Australia	2	41	27	30

Note: Q.228: "Do you ever watch television? IF YES: "How much time do you usually spend watching television on an average weekday?"
Source: World Values Survey 1995–97. N = 34,477.

SOCIAL TRUST AND VOLUNTARY ACTIVISM

If the Putnam thesis about the decline in social capital is correct, we would expect to find, as our first hypothesis, that watching television would be associated with low levels of trust between people. The standard question was used to gauge social trust: "Generally speaking, would you say that most people can be trusted, or that you can't be too careful in dealing with people?" The results in Table 10.2 confirm that a significant negative association exists between social trust and television use in every nation examined except Spain. As Putnam found in the United States, the more television people watched in most advanced industrialized democracies, the less likely they were to trust others. This pattern was most striking in West Germany, Switzerland, and Scandinavia, which showed a substantial and significant gap between heavy and light television viewers. Overall, while 50 percent of light users trusted other people, this was true of only 41 percent of heavy television users. Despite this finding, the direction of causality remains to be determined: in itself, this association does not tell us whether the experience of watching a television world dominated by crime, violence, and conflict gradually encourages us to distrust each other, or whether people who tend not to trust others choose to stay home and watch television.

If television also influences civic engagement and social capital, as Put-

TABLE 10.2
Social Trust and Television Viewing: Percentage Who Believe "Most People Can Be Trusted"

Nation	Light/No TV use	Heavy TV Use	Percentage Difference	Significance
W. Germany	50%	28%	−22%	**
Switzerland	44	31	−13	**
Sweden	68	56	−12	**
Norway	69	59	−10	**
Finland	56	46	−10	**
Japan	50	43	−7	**
Australia	44	37	−6	*
United States	38	34	−4	*
Spain	30	30	0	
All of the Above	50	41	−9	**

Notes: "Light/no TV use" is defined as less than two hours per day. "Heavy TV use" is defined as at least two hours per day.

Social trust: "Generally speaking, would you say that most people can be trusted, or that you can't be too careful in dealing with people?" The figures are the percentage responding "Most people can be trusted." Anova was used to test the significance of group differences. *p < .05. **p < .01.

Source: World Values Survey 1995–97. N = 34,477.

nam argues, then we would expect to find that exposure to television would depress activism in voluntary organizations. Engagement was gauged by asking respondents about their level of participation, if any, in various types of voluntary organizations. The results in Table 10.3 display a significant but modest inverse relationship between the use of television and activism in voluntary organizations, again confirming the Putnam thesis in this broader range of nations. In these countries people who watched more television were less likely to be active in voluntary associations like sports clubs, political parties, professional associations, labor unions, charities, and churches. Although it was statistically significant in every society, this relationship proved particularly strong in the United States, West Germany, Australia, and Switzerland. It is worth noting that activism in civil society remained relatively high in America in the mid-1990s despite heightened concern about the decline of social capital.

To explore this relationship further, we compared different types of voluntary associations to see whether the association with television use varies by category (see Table 10.4). The results confirm that light television users were more active in sports and recreational groups, churches, and arts, music, or educational organizations, which strongly suggests

TABLE 10.3
Level of Voluntary Activism and Television Viewing

Nation	Light/No TV Use	Heavy TV Use	Difference	Significance
United States	15.2%	14.2%	−1.0%	**
W. Germany	12.3	11.6	−0.9	**
Australia	13.7	12.9	−0.8	**
Switzerland	12.3	11.5	−0.8	**
Sweden	12.9	12.2	−0.7	**
Norway	12.7	12.1	−0.6	**
Spain	11.2	10.8	−0.4	**
Finland	12.4	12.1	−0.3	*
Japan	10.5	10.2	−0.3	*
All of the Above	12.6	11.9	−0.7	**

Notes: See Table 10.2 for definitions of media use.

Activism: "Now I am going to read off a list of voluntary organizations. For each one, could you tell me whether you are an active member (3), an inactive member (2), or not a member (1) of that type of organization?"

The figures are the mean activism scale (ranging from 9 to 27) summed from nine types of organizations such as labor unions, churches, sports or recreational clubs, political parties, and charitable organizations. Anova was used to test the significance of group differences. *p < .05. **p < .01.

Source: World Values Survey 1995–97. N = 34,477.

different patterns of leisure activities and lifestyles. For example, while 28 percent of light television users were active members of sports clubs, this was true of only 22 percent of heavy television watchers. Although they remained statistically significant, these differences became less marked in more explicitly political groups like parties or environmental organizations, and there was no difference among union members. The results confirm the association between television watching and lower activism within many of the local associations that are thought to create social community. Nevertheless, as noted earlier, the direction of the causal relationship can run both ways. Television may encourage people to watch sports at home rather than play with the local team. Alternatively, people who opt for a less active lifestyle may choose to stay home and watch Monday night football.

CONFIDENCE IN POLITICAL INSTITUTIONS

One of the most important claims of the American videomalaise literature is that watching television reduces confidence in governing institutions and support for the political system in established democracies.

TABLE 10.4

Percentage of TV Users Who Are Active Members of Voluntary Organizations

Type of Organization	Light/No TV Use	Heavy TV Use	Difference	Coefficient of Association	Significance
Sports or recreational club	28.3	21.9	−6.4	.14	**
Church or religious organization	19.4	15.4	−4.0	.06	**
Arts, music, or educational organization	17.6	12.0	−5.6	.19	**
Other voluntary organization	12.4	12.1	−0.3	.01	
Professional association	11.9	7.3	−4.6	.23	**
Charitable organization	10.4	8.8	−1.6	.11	**
Labor union	9.1	7.2	−1.9	.01	
Political party	5.9	4.6	−1.3	.10	**
Environmental organization	4.4	2.9	−1.5	.19	**

Notes: See Table 10.2 for definitions of media use.

Activism: "Now I am going to read off a list of voluntary organizations. For each one, could you tell me whether you are an active member (3), an inactive member (2), or not a member (1) of that type of organization?" The figures represent the percentage of each category of TV users who are active members in each organization. The coefficient of association and measure of significance is based on Gamma. *p < .05. **p < .01.

Source: World Values Survey 1995–97. N = 34,477.

Television coverage of politics is thought to encourage viewers to become cynical and disenchanted with their institutions of government because of its focus on exposing government scandals and corruption, revealing insider strategies, and dramatizing political conflict. To evaluate regime performance, respondents were asked to rate how well they thought things were going in their country's political system. To evaluate support for political institutions, they were asked how much confidence they had in their nation's political parties, parliament, civil service, and legal system.

The results presented in Table 10.5 suggest that in the advanced industrialized democracies under comparison, use of television was significantly associated with lower levels of regime support only in West Germany, Switzerland, and Sweden, and even there the relationship was very weak. Heavy television users tended to have slightly lower levels of confidence in governmental institutions like parliament, the legal system, and parties (see Table 10.6), but this difference approached significance (at

TABLE 10.5
Support for Political Regime and Television Viewing

Nation	Light/No TV Use	Heavy TV Use	Difference	Significance
W. Germany	5.1	4.7	−0.4	**
Sweden	4.7	4.4	−0.3	*
Switzerland	5.3	5.0	−0.3	**
Spain	4.7	4.6	−0.1	
Japan	4.1	4.0	−0.1	
Australia	4.4	4.4	0.0	
Norway	6.3	6.3	0.0	
United States	4.7	4.8	0.1	

Notes: See Table 10.2 for definitions of media use.

Regime support: "People have different views about the system for governing this country. Here is a scale for rating how well things are going: one means very bad and ten means very good. Where on this scale would you put the political system as it is today?" Anova was used to test the significance of group differences. *p < .05. **p < .01.

Source: World Values Survey 1995–97. N = 34,477.

the .10 level) in only two countries, Switzerland and Spain. Thus, watching television is not consistently associated with these indicators of political support, undermining the contention that broadcasting is to blame for the decline of confidence in the institutions of representative democracy that is discussed elsewhere in this book.

TABLE 10.6
Institutional Confidence and Television Viewing

Nation	Light/No TV Use	Heavy TV Use	Difference	Significance
Switzerland	6.66	6.34	−.32	
Spain	5.61	5.86	−.25	
Australia	5.94	5.81	−.13	
Norway	7.94	7.81	−.13	
Sweden	6.87	6.76	−.11	
United States	6.28	6.23	−.05	
Finland	6.30	6.28	−.02	
W. Germany	6.03	6.03	.00	
Japan	6.42	6.51	+.09	
All of the Above	6.50	6.38	−.12	

Notes: See Table 10.2 for definitions of media use.

Confidence in political institutions: A five-item scale was used to measure confidence in governments, parliaments, parties, the civil service, and the legal system. *p < .05. **p < .01.

Source: World Values Survey 1995–97. N = 34,477.

CONVENTIONAL POLITICAL PARTICIPATION

Even if television does not encourage cynicism about the political system, the videomalaise thesis argues that television produces alienation or apathy among viewers, influencing their behavior as well as their attitudes. If so, we would expect to find that exposure to television should reduce political interest and discussion. Respondents were asked about their level of interest in politics and how often they discussed politics with friends. These are among the most universal indicators of civic engagement because they are comparable across countries irrespective of the institutional context. The results (see Table 10.7) confirm that in six out of nine countries, people who watched more television were less likely to be involved in political discussions with friends or to display interest in public affairs. In Sweden, Finland, and Japan, no significant differences were associated with television use. On the basis of this comparison, we can conclude that television viewing in the advanced industrial democracies is associated with certain indicators of mild civic malaise.

To summarize, we have found few consistent differences between heavy and light television viewers in their attitudes toward the political system and core institutions of the state. We have established, though, that heavy viewers tend to be less socially trusting, less active in voluntary associations, and less engaged in politics. But is this pattern due to watching television, or may other factors be influencing the process, such as the type of people who watch television? To examine this issue, we can compare differences in the indicators of civic malaise by means of ordinary least squares regression models. We can first examine the significance of the direct relationship between indicators of civic malaise and television watching. We can then control for the social background variables that are most commonly associated with civic engagement and patterns of television use, namely gender, social class, education, age, labor force participation, marital status, and having dependent children. This will permit us to reexamine the significance of the residual effects of television watching on civic malaise.

Regressions (see Table 10.8) confirm that without any controls the amount of television viewing remains a significant predictor of civic engagement across all six indicators. In advanced industrial democracies, the more time spent watching television, the slightly greater the signs of malaise. The pattern changes once we add the social controls, however: the effects of television viewing become insignificant in four out of six indicators. The only exceptions are social trust and regime support. What this overall pattern suggests is that the association between civic malaise and the amount of time devoted to watching television is usually mediated by the type of person who is attracted to television. Heavy viewers

TABLE 10.7
Political Interest and Discussion and Television Viewing

Nation	Discussion			Interest		
	Light/No TV Use	Heavy TV Use	Significance	Light/No TV Use	Heavy TV Use	Significance
Switzerland	2.01	1.80	**	2.45	2.10	**
Spain	1.72	1.60	**	1.96	1.75	**
Australia	1.91	1.80	**	2.60	2.51	*
United States	1.93	1.83	**	2.75	2.64	*
W. Germany	2.18	2.10	**	3.07	2.89	**
Norway	2.10	2.03	*	2.77	2.68	*
Sweden	1.99	2.02		2.53	2.50	
Finland	1.79	1.82		2.29	2.31	
Japan	1.64	1.64		2.64	2.58	
All of the Above	1.95	1.83		2.59	2.44	

Notes: See Table 10.2 for definitions of media use. Anova was used to test the significance of group differences. *p < .05. **p < .01.
Source: World Values Survey 1995–97. N = 34,477.

TABLE 10.8
Regression Model of Indicators of Civic Malaise

	Social Trust		Voluntary Activism		Institutional Confidence	
Constant	.594	.280	13.6	9.6	6.92	4.68
Gender		−.05 **		−.02 *		−.03 *
Class		−.06 **		−.09 **		N/s
Education		.11 **		.29 **		.10 **
Age		.05 **		.04 *		.09 **
Marital Status		.05 **		.03 *		.06 **
Children		N/s		.09 **		N/s
Work Status		.09 **		.11 **		.05 **
TV Watching	−.09 **	−.04 **	−.09 **	N/s	−.05 **	N/s
Adjusted R^2	.01	.04	.01	.14	.01	.02

Note: See Appendix for questions and scale items. The figures represent standardized Beta coefficients using OLS regression models. Data from the nine advanced industrialized democracies are included in the analysis. *p < .05. **p < .01. N/s = not significant.
Source: World Values Survey 1995–97. N = 34,477.

are less likely to be engaged in community organizations, for example, but this association becomes insignificant once we control for other factors strongly related with voluntary activism such as education, employment status, and class.

We need to make some important observations about how to interpret these preliminary findings. First, the attitudinal differences associated with television exposure that we have documented usually remain very modest in terms of absolute size. In many ways this is to be expected. After all, even light viewers who watch just a little television each night can still be expected to be influenced by this process as well as by any systemic effects of coverage on the broader political culture. These findings are consistent with previous research, such as studies focused on knowledge gains from debates and campaign ads, which have usually found very modest learning from the news (Bryant and Zillman 1994, 139). The most important issue is whether we can establish an overall pattern in these findings that proves to be robust and persistent across the different indicators and countries.

Another important limitation is that the major findings established here concern differences in civic attitudes and behavior based on how much television people regularly watch. Using the WVS, we have so far been unable to determine whether this relationship is the result of viewing television entertainment in general (if there is a "mean world" effect from fictional images of violence, crime, and conflict), or whether this is the result of watching political coverage in news and current affairs in

TABLE 10.8 *(continued)*

	Regime Support		Political Discussion		Political Interest	
Constant	5.33	3.71	1.87	2.56	13.6	9.6
Gender		.08 *		.09**		−.07**
Class		.03**		.08**		−.10**
Education		.11**		.20**		.29**
Age		.05 *		.10**		.13 *
Marital Status		.05**		.03 *		N/s
Children		N/s		N/s		N/s
Work Status		.04 *		.11**		.11**
TV Watching	−.06**	−.03**	−.09**	N/s	−.07**	N/s
Adjusted R^2	.01	.03	.01	.09	.01	.14

particular, as many suggest. Using WVS data, we cannot explore *what* people watch, only how much. But someone viewing current affairs, C-SPAN, and the History Channel is likely to have an experience very different from that of someone else watching the daytime soaps, *NYPD Blue*, and violent movies. We obviously need to analyze the contents of what people view, as well as the duration of their viewing.

Finally, and most important, up to this point, we have been able to explore only the direction of the relationship between television viewing and civic malaise. None of the evidence allows us to draw any conclusions about the *causal effects* of watching television. Whether we choose to watch television or prefer to spend our time on charitable works, Parent-Teacher Association meetings, or environmental recycling projects is a matter of personal priorities. Which leads to which cannot be inferred from cross-sectional studies carried out at one point in time. What we need to monitor are changes in media habits (which are infrequent) or changes in attitudes using panel surveys over time.

COMPARING MEDIA EFFECTS IN THE UNITED STATES AND BRITAIN

To carry this analysis further, we can turn to a more focused comparison using the 1996 National Election Study (NES) and the 1997 British Election Study (BES) campaign panel surveys.[2] Both elections provide a suitable context to evaluate the videomalaise thesis because both were characterized by highly negative campaigns. Although the 1996 presi-

[2] The British Election Campaign Panel Survey 1997 was directed by Anthony Heath, Roger Jowell, John Curtice, and Pippa Norris as part of the British Election Study. I am most grateful to all my colleagues for use of this data. Further technical details about all the components of the BES can be found at http://www.ksg.harvard.edu/people/pnorris.

dential race did not plumb the depths of 1988, the tone of campaign coverage by network news was generally critical of both Clinton and Dole (Lichter and Smith 1996; Just 1998). In Britain Labour was given a relatively easy ride by the press in 1997, but the issue of Conservative sleaze, both sexual and financial, dominated the early stages of the campaign, while headlines over Tory splits and internal dissension over Europe eclipsed other news in the final weeks. The Conservatives received twice as much negative as positive press coverage during the campaign, while reporting on Labour and the Liberal Democrats was far more evenly balanced or neutral (Norris 1998). If the videomalaise thesis is correct, these campaigns provide suitable case studies.

A further advantage of this design is that it allows us to compare the effects of campaign coverage in two contrasting media environments. Obvious differences include such media structures as the predominance of a national, party-committed press divided sharply between tabloids and broadsheets in Britain, and a regional/local and more politically dealigned and middle-of-the-road press in the United States. Prior to the advent of digital broadcasting, British television news was dominated by the four major terrestrial channels, notably the public-service BBC, with relatively little competition from cable and satellite coverage. The United States, on the other hand, is characterized by the fragmentation of commercial channels and specialized audiences. The legal regulation of television election coverage also differs, with a proliferation of paid commercials in the United States versus free five-minute political party broadcasts in Britain. Most important, the public-service culture that influences British broadcasting on all channels provides saturation coverage during the six-week official campaign that is strictly regulated by considerations of party balance. This compares with far more limited political coverage during the equivalent period in the United States.

These structural differences have had a major impact on the respective news cultures in these two countries (Semetko 1996). Thus, if we can establish that patterns of media use in both countries are associated with similar patterns of civic mobilization or malaise, this helps us to test certain structural explanations. If American voters who pay attention to the news learn little about the policy positions of candidates, for example, then it can be claimed, as many commentators do, that this is because of the limited and superficial issue coverage found on network news. If Britain were to display similar patterns of learning from the campaign despite its extensive issue coverage on television news, then we must search elsewhere for reasons.

Certain qualifications should be noted. Because the British and American surveys often lack identical questions (for example, on questions on political trust and efficacy), we are mainly interested in whether we can establish differences in political attitudes between users of different media *within* Britain and *within* the United States, rather than comparing responses *between* nations. The best we can do is compare concepts and measures that are functionally equivalent (details are listed under each table). Although we are often unable to utilize fully the "pre-post" research design to monitor changes in political attitudes during election campaigns in both countries, these surveys allow us to compare different types of media users in terms of their political interest, efficacy, and knowledge, and social and political trust. Media users are classified on the basis of their reported use of television news and newspapers and their attention to political news in these sources (see Table 10.9 for the definitions used).

TABLE 10.9
Political Interest and Media Attention in Britain and America

| | Britain | United States | | |
	Pre-Election	Pre-Election	Post-Election	Change
All	2.6	2.0	2.2	+0.1
Attentive to TV news	3.5	2.5	2.6	+0.1
Not attentive to TV news	2.4	1.8	1.9	+0.1
Attentive to newspapers	4.0	2.6	2.6	0.0
Not attentive to newspapers	2.5	1.9	2.1	+0.1
Heavy use of TV entertainment	N/a	2.1	2.2	+0.1
Light use of TV entertainment	N/a	2.0	2.2	+0.1

Notes: Only respondents in pre- and post-waves are included.
Britain:
   Attentive to TV news: Respondent claimed in Wave B to pay "quite a bit" or "a great deal" of attention to stories about politics in yesterday's TV news.
   Attentive to newspaper news: Respondent claimed in Wave B to pay "quite a bit" or "a great deal" of attention to stories about politics in yesterday's newspaper.
   Political interest: "How much interest do you have in politics? A great deal (5), quite a lot (4), some (3), not very much (2), or none at all (1)."
United States:
   Attentive to TV news: Respondent claimed to pay "quite a bit" or "a great deal" of attention to stories about the campaign in TV network news.
   Attentive to newspaper news: Respondent claimed to pay "quite a bit" or "a great deal" of attention to stories about the campaign in newspapers.
   Political interest: "How interested are you in the political campaign? Very much interested (3), somewhat interested (2), or not much interested (1)."
   Use of TV entertainment: Scale based on how often respondent claimed to watch six different TV shows such as *ER, Frasier,* and *Friends.*
Sources: British Election Campaign Panel Survey 1997. N = 1,422. American National Election Study 1996. N = 1,714.

The results reveal two major findings that are deeply damaging to the conventional wisdom about videomalaise (see Tables 10.9–10.13). First, if we compare media users within each column, these tables display a persistent pattern: *attention to television news in Britain and America was consistently and significantly associated with higher than average levels of political interest, efficacy, knowledge, and social trust.* On political trust, there was no difference between media users. The overall pattern among viewers of television news was very similar to, if a bit flatter than, the pattern of exposure and attention to newspapers. In itself this association cannot reveal the causal mechanism at work here. The most plausible interpretation is that people who are more politically engaged are more likely to turn on the evening news and read a newspaper. The process is interactive, however: in the long run, people who watch network news and read the paper are more likely to become interested, efficacious, and knowledgeable about public affairs. In other words, contrary to all the popular criticism, the association points to a virtuous circle between use of the news media and civic mobilization.

TABLE 10.10
Political Trust and Media Attention in Britain and America

| | Britain | United States | | |
	Pre-Election	Pre-Election	Post-Election	Change
All	2.6	2.3	2.3	0.0
Attentive to TV news	2.7	2.3	2.4	0.0
Not attentive to TV news	2.6	2.3	2.3	0.0
Attentive to newspapers	2.6	2.3	2.4	0.1
Not attentive to newspapers	2.6	2.3	2.3	0.0
Heavy use of TV entertainment	N/a	2.3	2.3	0.0
Light use of TV entertainment	N/a	2.3	2.3	0.0

Notes: Only respondents in pre- and post-waves are included. See Table 10.2 for definitions of media use.

Britain: Responses to how often respondents said that they trusted "British governments of any party to place the needs of the nation above the interests of their own political party. Just about always (4), most of the time (3), only some of the time (2), or almost never (1)."

United States: V960566. Responses to how often respondents said they trusted government, whether "Just about always (4), most of the time (3), only some of the time (2), or none of the time (1)."

Sources: British Election Campaign Panel Survey 1997. N = 1,422. American National Election Study 1996. N = 1,714.

TABLE 10.11
Political Efficacy and Media Attention in Britain and America

	Britain			United States
	Pre-Election	Post-Election	Change	Post-Election
All	6.8	8.2	1.4	8.1
Attentive to TV news	7.5	9.2	1.7	8.4
Not attentive to TV news	6.6	7.9	1.3	7.8
Attentive to newspapers	7.8	9.2	1.4	9.0
Not attentive to newspapers	6.7	8.1	1.4	7.8
Heavy use of TV entertainment	N/a	N/a	N/a	8.0
Light use of TV entertainment	N/a	N/a	N/a	8.1

Notes: Only respondents in pre- and post-waves are included. See Table 10.2 for definitions of media use.

Britain: Five-point agree/disagree responses to the following items:

"Generally speaking, those we elect as MPs lose touch with people pretty quickly."

"Parties are only interested in people's votes, not in their opinions."

"It doesn't really matter which party is in power; in the end things go on much the same."

(15-point political efficacy scale.)

United States: Four-point agree/disagree responses to the following items:

"People like me don't have any say about what the government does."

"Sometimes politics and government seem so complicated that a person like me can't really understand what's going on."

"People like me don't have any say about what the government does."

(12-point political efficacy scale.)

Sources: British Election Campaign Panel Survey 1997. N = 1,422. American National Election Study 1996. N = 1,714.

TABLE 10.12
Social Trust and Media Attention in America

	Pre-Election	Post-Election	Change
All	.39	.51	+.11
Attentive to TV news	.42	.53	+.12
Not attentive to TV news	.37	.49	+.12
Attentive to newspapers	.49	.61	+.12
Not attentive to newspapers	.37	.49	+.12
Heavy use of TV entertainment	.42	.54	+.12
Light use of TV entertainment	.38	.49	+.11

Notes: Only respondents in pre- and post-waves are included. See Table 10.2 for definitions of media use.

Social trust: "Generally speaking, would you say that most people can be trusted (1) or that you can't be too careful in dealing with people (0)?"

Sources: American National Election Study 1996. N = 1,714.

TABLE 10.13
Political Knowledge and Media Attention in Britain and the United States

	Britain			United States
	Pre-Election	Post-Election	Change	Post-Election
All	3.3	3.3	0.0	2.6
Attentive to TV news	4.1	4.1	0.0	3.1
Not attentive to TV news	3.1	3.2	+0.1	2.4
Attentive to newspapers	4.4	4.3	−0.1	3.3
Not attentive to newspapers	3.2	3.2	0.0	2.5
Heavy use of TV entertainment	N/a	N/a	N/a	2.9
Light use of TV entertainment	N/a	N/a	N/a	3.0

Notes: Only respondents in pre- and post-waves are included. See Table 10.2 for definitions of media use. Cell entries are mean scale scores.
Britain: Correct answers in Waves A and C to the following:
  "Which party would you say is most in favor of:
  Changing the voting system to a form of proportional representation?
  Reducing government spending in order to cut taxes?
  Schools' being under local authority control?
  Independence for Scotland?
  Letting private industry run the railways?
  Setting a minimum wage, below which no one can be paid?"
  The British knowledge scale ranges from 1 to 6.
United States: Correct answers in the post-election wave to the following questions:
  "What office does Al Gore hold?"
  "What office does William Rehnquist hold?"
  "What office does Boris Yeltsin hold?"
  "What office does Newt Gingrich hold?"
  Plus the correct identification of the names of up to three candidates in the respondent's district.
  The U.S. knowledge score ranges from 0 to 6.
Sources: British Election Campaign Panel Survey 1997. N = 1,422. American National Election Study 1996. N = 1,714.

Second, there is some evidence regarding the short-term effects of changes in civic attitudes during the campaign. We might expect public opinion to shift during the election campaign. Feelings of political efficacy might grow as voters feel that they can, at last, throw the rascals out should they so desire, for example. Knowledge about politicians and policy issues can also be expected to grow as people start to pay attention to the choices offered them. The key question here is whether political interest, efficacy, trust, and knowledge increase more than average during the campaign for those who are most exposed and attentive to the media. Although the panel surveys were taken at slightly different points in time, they permit a limited comparison of the effects of the long and short campaign in Britain (with BES panel waves in May 1996, April 1997, and after the election in May 1997) and the official campaign in the United States (with NES pre- and post-election waves).

If we compare the table rows for which we have pre- and post-election data, *the very modest short-term changes in the indicators of civic mobilization and malaise are not significantly associated with patterns of media attention, either positively or negatively.* Thus, knowledge about where the parties stood on a range of policy issues did not increase during the long British campaign despite the wall-to-wall coverage in the media and politicians' efforts to publicize their manifestoes. And it certainly did not increase more than average for regular users of the news media. Political efficacy did increase as polling day drew near, but again, this was a uniform effect, irrespective of patterns of media use (for more details, see Norris et al. 1999). In the United States we find a similar pattern: there was no difference in political interest between those who tuned in and those who tuned out campaign news.

CONCLUSIONS AND DISCUSSION

What are the implications of this study? Popular criticism of the media has been common, but in recent years the trickle of complaints has become a flood, particularly in the United States. The public seems to share many of these concerns (Kohut and Toth 1998). Popular commentators frequently blame television, and television news in particular, for political coverage that produces a more cynical and disenchanted public and a half-empty ballot box. The growth of tabloid television has often been singled out as a major threat to the health of modern democracy.

The first section of this chapter confirmed that the amount of time devoted to watching television was modestly but consistently associated with indicators of civic malaise in a range of Trilateral democracies. In these nations the more time spent watching television, the lower the levels of social trust, organizational activism, and political participation. The evidence does not establish whether this pattern is the effect or the cause of watching television. After all, if we do not trust other people, if we do not enjoy community meetings, if we are bored by politics, it makes sense that we might decide to spend our time in the company of Frasier, Oprah, and Seinfeld. This pattern often washed out once we included a battery of standard social controls associated with television use and civic engagement.

The more detailed comparison of Britain and America based on campaign panel surveys suggests that the short-term negative effects of watching television news have been greatly exaggerated, and the long-term effects of attention to television news are actually beneficial for civic engagement. People who regularly watched television news in Britain and America had greater than average political interest, efficacy, and knowledge. The most plausible interpretation is that people who tuned into *The Jim Lehrer News Hour*, ABC's *World News*, or CNN probably did so because they were more interested than average in public affairs, but televisions news reinforced this tendency as people learned more about Bosnia, the role of the Judiciary Committee, or the problems of health care. To explore this issue further, we need other sorts of research designs such as experiments and focus groups that more precisely match the contents of the media messages to their impact on audiences.

While far from conclusive, the evidence in this study strongly suggests that we need to look elsewhere than television news for the source of our political ills. If leaders in high office are increasingly rocked by financial sleaze and sexual shenanigans, if the public is increasingly disillusioned with government institutions, we should look more directly at the functioning of representative democracy and stop blaming the messenger.

APPENDIX. MEASURES AND CODING IN THE WORLD VALUES SURVEY 1995–97

Television Use

V228 "Do you ever watch television? IF YES: How much time do you usually spend watching television on an average weekday? (NOT WEEKENDS)" The responses were coded: "Do not watch TV or do not have access to TV" (1); "One to two hours per day" (2); "Two to three hours per day" (3); and "More than 3 hours per day" (4).

Social Trust

"Generally speaking, would you say that most people can be trusted or you can't be too careful in dealing with people?"

Support for Democratic Values

"I'm going to read off some things people sometimes say about a democratic system. Could you please tell me if you agree strongly, agree, disagree, or disagree strongly after I read each one of them."
V160 "In democracy, the economic system runs badly."

V161 "Democracies are indecisive and have too much squabbling."
V162 "Democracies aren't good at maintaining order."

Evaluations of the Performance of the Political System

"People have different views about the system of governing this country. Here is a scale for rating how well things are going. One means very bad and ten means very good."
V152. "Where on this scale would you put the political system as it is today?"

Regime Institutions

"I am going to name a number of organizations. For each one, could you tell me how much confidence you have in them: is it a great deal of confidence, quite a lot of confidence, not very much confidence, or none at all? The government in [your capital]; political parties; parliament; the civil service; and the legal system."
It should be noted that principle component factor analysis rotated by varimax confirmed that the above attitudinal items measuring support for the political system fell into these four distinct dimensions, explaining in total 60 percent of variance.

Membership in Voluntary Organizations

"Now I am going to read off a list of voluntary organizations. For each one, could you tell me whether you are an active member (3), an inactive member (2), or not a member of that type of organization (1)? Church or religious organization; art, music, or educational organization; labor union; political party; environmental organization; professional association; charitable organization; or any other voluntary organization?"

Political Interest

"How interested would you say you are in politics? Very, somewhat, not very, or not at all?"

Political Discussion

"When you get together with your friends, would you say you discuss political matters frequently, occasionally, or never?"

ELEVEN

Value Change and Democracy

Russell J. Dalton

A QUARTER CENTURY AGO, the authors of *The Crisis of Democracy* worried about the fragility of democracy in the Trilateral nations (Crozier, Huntington, and Watanuki 1975). Governments struggled with new issue demands, and political institutions had difficulty adjusting to calls for a more participatory democracy. This theme was repeated by other analysts (Huntington 1981; Kielmansegg 1976; Rose 1980). Michel Crozier and his colleagues borrowed a foreboding image of democracy's future from Willy Brandt, an otherwise enthusiastic supporter of democracy: "Western Europe has only 20 or 30 more years of democracy left in it; after that it will slide, engineless and rudderless, under the surrounding sea of dictatorship" (quoted in Crozier, Huntington, and Watanuki 1975, 2).

Fortunately, the dire predictions of Brandt, Crozier, and others did not come to pass. The era of student protest faded, and many of the new participatory tendencies were integrated into the democratic process. Governments responded to the problem of "overload" by reducing their activity in some policy areas and downsizing public expectations about government. Both governments and the public adapted. In a popular account of these developments Ben Wattenberg (1985) portrayed them as a positive example of how democracy functions: if democracy can generate political excesses, it also contains an equilibrium mechanism that encourages political balance. He argued that democracies had generally succeeded in retaining the benefits of the new ideas while avoiding the dire results predicted about the excesses of democracy (see also Dalton and Kuechler 1990). Furthermore, opinion research failed to uncover broad, cross-national evidence of diminishing public faith in the democratic process, which was central to the "crisis of democracy" thesis (e.g., Klingemann and Fuchs 1995). Subsequently, the end of the Cold War engendered a new euphoria about the democratic process that swept up some of the same commentators who had earlier trumpeted warning calls (Huntington 1991; Fukuyama 1992). In short, the good news was the bad news was wrong.

Even so, new doubts about the vitality of the democratic process have recently surfaced. Joseph Nye and his colleagues (1997) recently demonstrated that Americans still express political cynicism in the 1990s. Robert

Putnam (1995a) has written about the decline in social and political engagement in America and other advanced industrial democracies. Pippa Norris and her colleagues (1999) convincingly show that contemporary publics in most Trilateral democracies are more skeptical about politicians, less attached to political parties, and less trustful of democratic political institutions. The introduction to this book reviews some of the most prominent evidence of these changing public orientations. A new crisis of the democratic spirit—if not democracy itself—is upon us.

The underlying assumption of this chapter is that such general trends in public images of democratic institutions across such a diverse set of Trilateral democracies are unlikely to be explained by coincidental problems of performance deficits or scandal. Rather, such general trends more likely arise from broad forces of social and political change that are transforming the content and context of politics in these nations. This chapter argues that changing public values are an important factor in altering citizen expectations about the democratic process. This affects images of government, expectations of governmental performance, and expectations of democratic citizens. My goal here is to determine the impact of these changing values and their implications for the functioning of contemporary democracies.

THE ROLE OF VALUE CHANGE

It could reasonably be argued that over the last 50 years the Trilateral democracies have experienced the greatest change in the human condition in their histories. The horrors of World War II were followed by an age of unprecedented economic growth and social change. By most measures, the citizens in these nations are several times better off financially than any prewar comparison group. This economic miracle has transformed living standards and life references. No longer are the basic struggles for minimal sustenance and security a concern for most people. There have been concomitant changes in lifestyles, social stratification, and social relations as a result of this modernization process. In addition, this has been an age of profound technological change, most clearly represented by the expansion of the electronic mass media.

In writing about these developments, Ronald Inglehart (1977a, 1990, 1997a) has argued that these societal changes are transforming the values of contemporary publics. The social and political values of younger generations raised in the new postwar environment are shifting away from the material and security concerns of the past to a new set of *postmaterial* values. Postmaterial values emphasize goals like enhancing the quality of life, individual freedom, lifestyle choice, free expression, and participation. Surveys from the early 1990s indicate that the number of postmaterialists has grown to 20 to 30 percent of the public in most Trilateral democracies (Inglehart 1997a). Indeed, a large literature has developed on the nature and impact of these changing values on advanced industrial societies (for a review, see van Deth and Scarborough 1995).

If public values are changing as Inglehart and others posit, then this has direct, albeit complex, implications for the democratic process. Inglehart maintains that these younger, better-educated postmaterialists want governments to address a new set of political issues, such as environmental protection, women's rights, and lifestyle choices. Along with others (e.g., Offe 1985; Baker, Dalton, and Hildebrandt 1981), Inglehart holds that changing values are expanding the boundary of politics, providing new rights to women, protecting our health and national heritage through environmental conservation, and creating new opportunities for underrepresented groups—hardly developments antithetical to democracy. The rise of Green parties, for example, may have caused some initial consternation to conservative political leaders (and academics), but most now realize that the Green movement has added a positive element to democratic politics.

Postmaterialists are also calling for a new participatory style of politics (Inglehart 1990, chs. 10–11; Barnes and Kaase 1979). Reflecting their participatory and expressive values, postmaterialists favor elite-challenging forms of political action and are openly skeptical about social and political authorities. These pressures for participation take many forms. Although protests and direct confrontations strain the norms of democratic politics, their use has become less challenging to the polity since the initial protest wave of the 1960s and 1970s (see Tarrow, this volume). Changing public values also lead to a general expansion of democratic participation in new forms. New social movements and citizen action groups have steadily grown in size and influence and have provided a new channel of political action for an involved public (Dalton and Kuechler 1990). By many accounts, membership in such citizen groups now exceeds formal party membership in several Trilateral democracies.

Many of these same themes, albeit with a different emphasis, were presented in Crozier's (1975) chapter in *The Crisis of Democracy*. Crozier held that societal changes were transforming the values of contemporary publics. Economic growth, for example, both expanded the political skills and resources of the public and increased the new demands being made on government. Social mobility weakened the bonds between individuals and social institutions such as churches and unions. The mass media altered the relationship between governors and governed. Thus, changes in the values of democratic publics seemed to underlay the trends in governability and the political process that Crozier and his colleagues were describing. Crozier asserted (1975, 39): "Behind all these governability problems of modern Western societies lie some more basic *problems of values.* Participation, people's consent, equality, and the right of the collectivity to intervene in personal affairs, and the possible acceptance of authority seem to be the preliminary questions to debate" (emphasis added).

Crozier then detailed the role of changing values. He believed that changing orientations toward freedom, equality, order, and political opposition created new tensions that democracies were struggling to resolve. Increased public demands for political freedom and a diminished appreciation for public order and stability created governability problems for democracies. To a lesser extent Huntington (1975a) also argued that social and generational forces were transforming public values. Huntington, however, seemed to emphasize only the negative aspects of these changes. He believed that shifts in values were promoting governability problems by eroding respect for authority, trust in public officials, and bonds between the individual and political parties. At the same time value changes encouraged individuals to be more assertive in expressing their political preferences and less deferential to authority, another source of governability problems. Huntington (1975b, 37–38) saw these trends as creating a "democratic distemper":

> The problem of governance in the United States today stems from an "excess of democracy." . . . The effective operation of a democratic political system usually requires some measure of apathy and non-involvement on the part of some individuals and groups. The vulnerability of democratic government in the United States comes . . . from the internal dynamics of democracy itself in a highly educated, mobilized and participatory society.

Huntington (1974, 1981) thus painted a fairly dark picture of what the development of postindustrialism and the concomitant process of value change meant for the Trilateral democracies.

The main empirical goal of this chapter is to examine whether the process of value change has systematically altered public expectations of government and the democratic process, contributing to the feelings of dissatisfaction that now characterize public opinion in these nations. I will use Inglehart's measure of postmaterial values to tap the major dimension of change that concerned the authors of *The Crisis of Democracy* as well as those studying postmaterialism, explain different hypotheses about the effects of value change, and marshal a variety of empirical evidence to test these hypotheses. The results should provide a more accurate assessment of the impact of postmaterial value change and, by implication, yield better predictions about the consequences for the Trilateral democracies.

VALUES AND POLITICAL SUPPORT

Many discussions of political support intermix public orientations toward politicians and political institutions and the fundamental norms and values underlying the political system. As I have argued elsewhere (Dalton 1999), each set of orientations has different implications for the democratic process, and each has followed somewhat different empirical trends (see also Easton 1965; Fuchs and Klingemann 1995; Klingemann 1999). Thus, I will examine separately the relationship between postmaterial priorities and these various measures of political support.

Political Trust

Postmaterialism clearly represents a critique of the established political order. Postmaterialists and their representatives (e.g., Green parties, new social movements, and citizen action groups) have criticized contemporary democracies for their corporatist tendencies and the lack of representation for minorities and alternative groups. Similarly, postmaterialists have criticized the policy outputs of the Trilateral democracies for their emphasis on materialist goals and their inadequate attention to such postmaterial goals as environmental protection, women's rights, and international cooperation. Thus, there is a general consensus that postmaterialists should be less trusting of politicians and government.

As was discussed in the introduction to this volume, political trust has generally eroded in the Trilateral democracies over the past generation, raising the question of whether postmaterialists have contributed to these trends. Although it was included in only three nations (the United States, Spain, and Canada), the 1990–93 World Values Survey contained a standard item on political trust.[1] In each nation postmaterialists displayed significantly lower levels of political trust (United States r = −.12, Spain −.14, Canada −.07). In the United States, for instance, 48 percent of the most materialist respondents said one can always or mostly trust the government to do what is right, compared to only 26 percent of the most postmaterial respondents.

These results reflect a pattern common in other empirical findings. Oscar Gabriel (1995, 366–70) found that postmaterialists in most European nations were less trustful of government. Inglehart's research (1990) on political support underscores this conclusion. As postmaterialists find fault with contemporary governments, they also express less trust in the

---

[1] The question read: "How much do you trust the government in [Washington] to do what is right? Do you trust it almost always, most of the time, only some of the time, or almost never?"

politicians who hold office. Thus, postmaterialists' criticism of government actions has probably contributed to declining political trust in the Trilateral democracies. The question, however, is whether these feelings have been generalized to other objects of political support.[2]

Confidence in Political Institutions

If some citizens are dissatisfied with politicians, there are reasons to consider this a normal element of democratic politics that actually has positive benefits for the democratic process.[3] But as the object of dissatisfaction broadens to include political institutions, the implications multiply. A drop in public support for the institutions of democracy would signal significant doubts about the democratic process that transcend dissatisfaction with the incumbents or recent government actions. A variety of sources now provide clear evidence of such a general erosion in support for political institutions in most Trilateral democracies. The American decline is well known, its early trends documented in *The Crisis of Democracy* (Huntington 1975a). Now there is also strong evidence of falling confidence in political institutions, especially parliaments, in other Trilateral democracies (see Introduction, this volume).

What role has value change played in the recent drops in confidence in political institutions? The authors of *The Crisis of Democracy* regarded the young and better-educated as a major source of this erosion in political support. Similarly, Inglehart (1999) maintains that materialists value social order, structure, and hierarchy, generating support for the dominant institutions of politics and society; he argues that postmaterialists tend to reject authority, reducing support for the military, the police, churches, and other social and political institutions. Furthermore, materialists generally perceive political institutions to be more responsive to their interests, while postmaterialists fault dominant social actors for rejecting their alternative values. The result, according to Inglehart, is that "governing has become more difficult than it used to be: the tendency to idealize

[2] Because other chapters in this book are concerned with social or interpersonal trust, I should note that Inglehart (1999) found that postmaterialists are more likely than materialists to trust their fellow citizens. In the United States in 1990, for example, 63 percent of postmaterialists said "most people can be trusted," while only 43 percent of materialists expressed this opinion.

[3] People often become dissatisfied with political officeholders and act on these feelings to select new leaders at the next election. Thus, dissatisfaction with authorities is not usually a signal for basic political change in a democratic system, and negative attitudes about political officials can coexist with little loss in support for the office itself or the institutional structure encompassing the office. As Easton has written (1975, 437), "not all expressions of unfavorable orientations have the same degree of gravity for a political system. Some may be consistent with its maintenance; others may lead to fundamental change."

authority that characterized societies of scarcity has given way to the more critical and demanding publics of postmodern societies. Authority figures and hierarchical institutions are subjected to more searching scrutiny than they once were" (Inglehart 1999, 236). In other words, the decline in support for political institutions is regarded as due in part to the shift toward postmaterial values among contemporary publics.

To examine this issue, I use data for 17 Trilateral democracies taken from the 1990–91 World Values Survey.[4] The survey includes a battery of questions that test support for a variety of social and political institutions. These are some of the same data that led Inglehart (1999) to his conclusions about the impact of value change on political support.

Table 11.1 presents the correlation between postmaterial values and two indices of institutional support replicated from Listhaug and Wiberg

TABLE 11.1

Postmaterial Values and Confidence in Political and Social Institutions

	Political	*Social*
Austria	−.14	−.12
Belgium	−.16	−.07
Canada	−.12	−.04
Denmark	−.14	−.10
Finland	−.08	−.09
France	−.20	−.08
Germany	−.31	−.16
Great Britain	−.20	−.03
Iceland	−.13	−.22
Ireland	−.14	−.06
Italy	−.12	−.11
Japan	−.01	.09
Netherlands	−.06	.00
Norway	−.09	−.06
Spain	−.27	−.15
Sweden	−.04	−.06
United States	−.12	−.09
Average	−.14	−.09

Note: Table entries are the correlations between the 12–item postmaterial values index and confidence in political or social institutions.

Source: 1990–93 World Values Survey.

[4] These data were acquired from the Inter-University Consortium for Political and Social Research. Neither the original collectors of the data nor the archive bear responsibility for the analysis presented here.

(1995).[5] The political institutions index measures confidence in five political institutions: the armed forces, civil service, legal system, police, and parliament. The social institutions index includes churches, the press, trade unions, and major companies.

There is clear evidence of a link between postmaterial values and a lack of confidence in political institutions for most Trilateral nations. Among German postmaterialists, for example, only 16 percent express a lot of confidence in the civil service, as opposed to 51 percent among the most materialist category. Yet these results also suggest caution in generalizing about the impact of value change. Even though this is part of the syndrome attributed to value change, postmaterial values display a noticeably weaker relationship to confidence in social institutions. In addition, the correlation between values and confidence in political institutions varies substantially across nations, from a low of − .01 in Japan to a high of − .31 in Germany.

The variability of value effects is even more apparent in Figure 11.1, which displays the average correlation between postmaterialism and confidence in each specific political and social institution. Value priorities are most likely to lessen confidence in institutions that are identified with hierarchy, bureaucratic structures, and conservative political orientations such as the military, police, the church, and big business. These are the institutions of authority that Inglehart (1999) emphasized in his research. But the link between postmaterialism and other key institutions of democracy like parliament, the legal system, the civil service, and the press is quite weak.

Postmaterialists actually display greater confidence than materialists in the one clearly leftist institution on the list, unions.[6] And if we broaden our focus to include political movements and citizen groups, the pattern changes dramatically. On average, postmaterialists are *more likely* to support ecology groups (r = .10), women's groups (r = .08), human rights organizations (r = .16), and groups opposed to racial discrimination (r = .20).[7] Thus, some political organizations do earn the confidence of postmaterialists.

---

[5] The postmaterial values measure is a simple count of the number of postmaterial items ranked as most or second most important among the 12 value items (which were presented in sets of four). The scale runs from 0 to 6. Respondents lacking three or more responses were excluded from the measure.

[6] Preliminary data from the 1995–98 World Values Survey tends to underscore this point. There is not a significant relationship between postmaterialism and confidence in political parties, and the relationship to confidence in parliament is very weak and changes in polarity across nations.

[7] The 1990–91 World Values Survey included a different set of items to measure support for social movements and citizen groups. See Inglehart (1997, ch. 11).

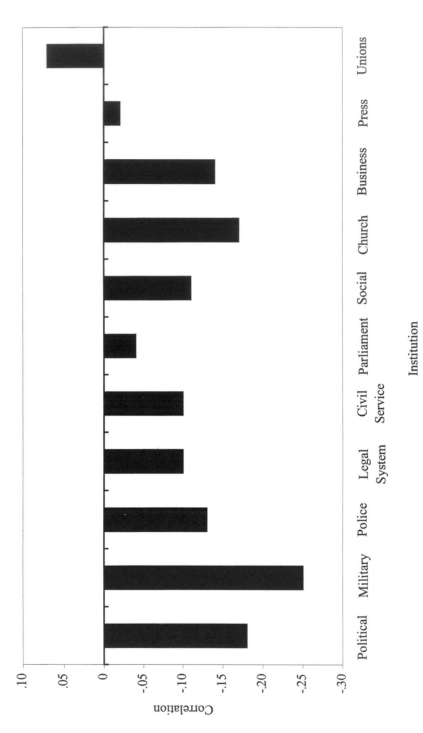

Figure 11.1. The Relationship between Postmaterialism and Institutional Confidence

In summary, these data yield our first qualification of presumptions about the impact of value change in the Trilateral democracies. The authors of *The Crisis of Democracy* and Inglehart (1999) have argued that citizens' changing values are eroding respect for authority and thereby reducing public confidence in political and social institutions. We believe the impact is not a general decline in confidence, but rather a shift in the criteria some citizens use to evaluate political and social organizations. In other words, it is not that political legitimacy is in question, but that the source of legitimacy for political and social institutions is changing. A Weberian-style legitimacy based on hierarchical authority is no longer sufficient; support for organizations based on such structures is systematically weaker among postmaterialists. Thus, confidence in the armed forces and police suffers among postmaterialists (although these institutions never were shining models of democratic values). At the same time postmaterialists display more confidence in their fellow citizens and in institutions that emphasize participation and the representation of public interests. *Legitimacy based on inclusion is replacing legitimacy based on hierarchical authority.* Would democracy really be in crisis if contemporary publics were more skeptical of the police and more supportive of grassroots citizen movements?

Support for Democracy

Declining confidence in political institutions may reflect eroding public faith in the democratic process or simply in how it currently functions. Thus, a basic question is whether this disenchantment has been generalized to the political system and the democratic norms that underlie it. The rise of radical leftist groups in the 1970s and 1980s represented a challenge to the political establishment in the Trilateral democracies, and postmaterialism and Green parties have often been portrayed as a threat to democracy (e.g., Huntington 1974). In the 1990s these groups have been joined by extreme rightist movements. Recent studies of political support have speculated once again about an emerging crisis of democracy (Nye, Zelikow, and King 1997; Clarke 1992; Norris 1999), echoing the earlier concerns of Crozier and his colleagues (1975).

Although none of them is ideal, various survey questions attempt to test public attitudes about democracy. A frequently used survey question asks whether democracy is the best form of government. There is not a long, cross-national time series for this question, but the current high degree of support suggests there has not been a major erosion in these sentiments (Dalton 1999; Klingemann 1999; Introduction, this volume).[8]

---

[8] The two questions were worded as follows: "Let us consider the idea of democracy without thinking of existing democracies. In principle, are you for or against the idea of

On average, more than three-quarters of the public in the Trilateral democracies feel that democracy is the best form of government. Another common question taps public support for the ideal of democracy. At the beginning of the 1980s, before the post–Cold War euphoria for democracy had caught fire, support for the idea of democracy was nearly universal in Western nations. Reviewing this evidence, Dieter Fuchs, Giovanna Guidorossi, and Palle Svensson (1995) concluded that these data and other measures of democratic values indicate that democratic legitimacy is still widespread.

We examined whether postmaterial values represent a challenge to democratic norms and ideals by calculating the relationship between these measures (see Table 11.2). In contrast to confidence in political institutions, postmaterialists are *more likely* to believe that democracy is the best form of government and to support democracy as an ideal. In nearly every instance, postmaterialism strengthens support for the democratic creed. To illustrate the magnitude of these differences, Figure 11.2 presents the differences in opinion averaged across the nine nations included in Table 11.2. Only 39 percent of the most materialist respon-

TABLE 11.2
Postmaterial Values and Support for Democracy

Nation	Approve of the Idea of Democracy	Democracy Is the Best Form of Government
Australia	.10	.06
Finland	.17	.13
Germany	.11	.14
Japan	− .02	.05
Norway	.12	.11
Spain	.10	.07
Sweden	.16	.09
Switzerland	.04	.06
United States	.08	.00
Average	.10	.08

Note: Table entries are the correlations between the 12-item postmaterial values index and the two measures of support for democracy (see footnote 8).
Source: 1995–98 World Values Survey.

democracy?" "Which of the following opinions about different forms of government is closest to your own? 1) In any case, democracy is the best form of government, whatever the circumstances may be. 2) In certain cases a dictatorship can be positive. 3) For someone like me, it doesn't make any difference whether we have a democracy or a dictatorship."

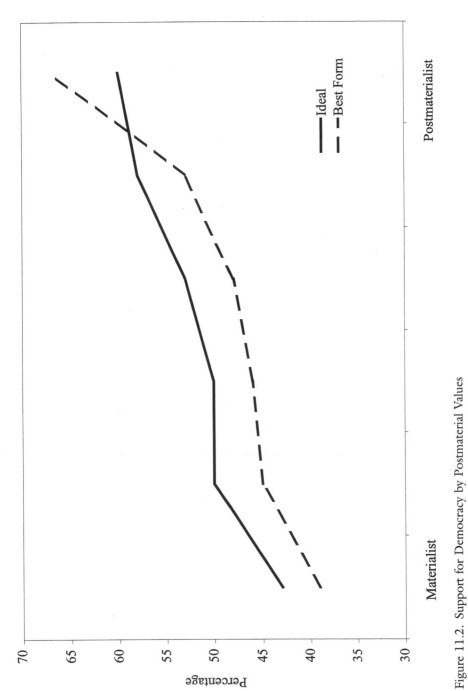

Figure 11.2. Support for Democracy by Postmaterial Values

Source: 1995–98 World Values Survey.

dents strongly agreed that democracy is the best form of government, compared to 67 percent of postmaterialists.

When tested with empirical evidence, it is difficult to sustain the argument that postmaterial value change is promoting a crisis of democracy in the Trilateral nations. Many members of the public are dissatisfied with incumbent office-holders and even with institutions of representative democracy, and these sentiments are more common among postmaterialists. At the same time, however, postmaterialists are more supportive of the principle of democracy. This is reminiscent of Huntington's (1981) concern about the "creedal passion" of the American public: he conjectured that democracy was threatened by the public's belief that democracy should function in line with its ideals. Such a creedal passion may create challenges for democracy when critical citizens expect government to live up to its ideals and act on their dissatisfactions and policy desires. But the emergence of a critical group of postmaterialists who want to expand democracy does not represent a democratic crisis.

VALUES AND POLICY DEMANDS

Another aspect of the debate on the implications of value change involves the policy expectations of young postmaterialists. The authors of *The Crisis of Democracy* were concerned that the changing priorities of contemporary publics were increasing the policy demands made on governments. Huntington (1975a, 64) succinctly summarized this position: "By the early 1970s Americans were progressively demanding and receiving more benefits from their government and yet having less confidence in their government than they had a decade earlier." Huntington blamed such excessive demands by the public for the policy overload thought to threaten democracy.

Similarly, popular accounts of changing social values have stressed the supposed hedonism of the "me" generation of the 1980s and the self-absorption of "Generation X" of the 1990s. Hedonism and self-centeredness are often attributed to postmaterialists' emphasis on self-expression and self-fulfillment. There is some support for this position in the academic literature on postmaterialism and the New Politics. Herbert Kitschelt (1989), for example, used the term *left-libertarian* to describe the advocacy of both traditional social democratic *and* new postmaterial issues by adherents of Green parties. Inglehart has also written that postmaterialists favor many traditional leftist policies while also advocating an expansion of government activity to embrace environmental protection, women's rights, and other New Politics issues.

There is little question that the scale of government activity has increased during the postwar period in all the Trilateral democracies. What can be debated is the public's responsibility for increasing demands made on governments, and specifically the idea that postmaterial values are a driving force of these developments.

The longest time series of public opinion data on government spending priorities is the General Social Survey opinion series for the United States. Reviewing these data, Dalton (1996, 116) concluded, "although specific spending priorities change over time, the average preference for increased government spending . . . has varied surprisingly little across six administrations." Across 11 policy areas, the average difference between those wanting more and those wanting less spending was 13 percent in 1973 and 17 percent in 1994. Other data indicate that contemporary publics do expect government to assume a greater role in some sectors that were once beyond the boundaries of conventional politics, but there are also other areas in which publics want the government to do less. Evidence from European surveys tends to present the same pattern of constancy in the overall level of governmental demands with shifts in the specific issues emphasized by the public (Kaase and Newton 1995).

I am specifically concerned with the question of whether postmaterial value change has been a major source of expanded public demands on government. Until now I have located only one cross-national survey that contains both the postmaterial values index and a battery of items on government spending. Eurobarometer 21 asked Germans and Britons about their spending preferences across a large number of policy areas.[9] The policy areas in which postmaterialists want the government to spend more are located at the top of Table 11.3, and the areas in which they want the government to spend less are located at the bottom. Although postmaterialists do want the government to spend more in many policy areas, this is not a universal rule. If we focus on the German results, postmaterialists want a decreased public role in some predictable areas: defense, public security, and assistance to trade and industry.[10] Instead, postmaterialists are more likely to emphasize government spending on education, foreign aid, the arts and culture, and European Union activities. Even for a typically postmaterial policy, such as environmental pro-

---

[9] Besides posing the spending question in only two nations, Eurobarometer 21 contains only the four-item postmaterial value index, which is much less robust than the 12-item index.

[10] Opinions on government spending are also strongly related to one's position on the left-right scale, so we attribute the stronger correlations in Britain to left-right polarization over Prime Minister Thatcher's budget cuts. If one enters both left-right position and postmaterial values into a regression, these effects are removed, and the preference for greater spending by postmaterialists is substantially attenuated. For that reason, the German results better illustrate the finding we would expect from broader cross-national analyses.

TABLE 11.3

Postmaterial Values and Support for Government Spending by Policy Sector

Policy	Germany	Britain
Aid to developing countries	.23	.13
Arts and culture	.17	.06
Higher education	.17	.07
EC policies	.15	.06
Primary and secondary education	.14	.09
Sports and recreation	.04	.12
Environmental protection	.03	.16
Technological development	.02	.06
Social security	.00	.19
Housing	.00	.12
Transport	−.01	.05
Health care	−.01	.12
Defense	−.02	−.04
Assistance to trade and industry	−.04	.06
Public security	−.10	−.11

Note: Table entries are the correlations between the four-item postmaterial values index and support for more or less government spending in each policy area.

Source: Eurobarometer 21 (1985).

tection, postmaterialists' support for greater public spending is not significantly greater than that of materialists.

In summary, these findings do not suggest that postmaterial value change has been driving a general expansion of government activity. It is more accurate to say that postmaterialists—like many other political groups—have different expectations of government. They want a change in the priorities of government rather than a wholesale expansion of its role. This might be obvious for policies related to security themes, but postmaterialists also display mixed support for spending on traditional social welfare issues. These patterns reflect the normal competition over policy priorities that might exist between political groups, whether partisan or sociodemographic groups, in a democracy. Indeed, it is a bit fanciful to imagine that postmaterialists who advocate more spending on the arts, foreign aid, and primary education are really generating a crisis of democracy.

THE FUTURE OF DEMOCRATIC POLITICS

These findings contribute to the ongoing debate on the vitality of democracy. *The Crisis of Democracy* was one of several studies that claimed that changing public values were leading to a weakening of democratic values and excessive public demands that were overloading the ability of government to perform, creating a crisis of democracy.

In retrospect, one must view the more strident voices in this debate as unnecessarily alarmist (e.g., Huntington 1974, 1975b, 1981). On the one hand, democracy has proven more resilient than these authors assumed. Governments have responded, and are continuing to adapt, to the public's changing preferences for policy outcomes and policy-making processes. On the other hand, some of the early analyses misstated the political challenges posed by changing public values (if these changes are treated as synonymous with Inglehart's theory and measurement of post-material value change).

Postmaterial value change is deeply affecting contemporary democracies, reinforcing many of the social and political changes that preoccupy us in this book. Value change is stimulating political action, shifting the sources of legitimacy, and changing citizen expectations of government—but postmaterial values do not threaten democracy. Although post-materialists may be more cynical toward political authority and institutions, especially certain institutions, this reflects changes in the basis of legitimacy rather than an outright rejection of political and social institutions or the democratic process. Is democracy really in crisis if post-materialists are more cynical about the police and more trustful of citizen-based movements? On the contrary, postmaterialists actually express more support for democratic principles and processes than do materialists and are more likely to trust their fellow citizens. Adherence to the democratic creed should not be seen as a threat to democracy. The "creedal passion" that so worried Huntington is actually a sign of the vitality of democracy, a force that can generate progressive political reform.

Similarly, postmaterialists are not calling for a wholesale expansion of government activity. Rather, they represent a new policy agenda that emphasizes such issues as education, environmentalism, the arts, and international cooperation. If there is a real challenge for democracy, it is finding a way to balance the divergent policy agendas embraced by different subsets of the public, in contrast to the consensual agenda that once dominated political discourse in the immediate postwar era. The advocacy of such alternative agendas is what democratic politics is supposed to resolve. Indeed, at one point, Crozier (1975, 47) summarized the forces that were first discussed in *The Crisis of Democracy* and have only strengthened in subsequent decades: "What is at stake, therefore, is not the democratic creed and the Christian ethos, which are less directly threatened than they were for example in the thirties, but the contradiction between these core political beliefs and the principles of action that could make it possible to implement them." The challenge of democracy is to advance the process of democratic reform in response to citizens' changing expectations of government.

To take one example, popular dissatisfaction with current democratic structures is fueling calls to reform the processes of representative democracy. Data from the 1996 British Social Attitudes Survey indicated that politically dissatisfied respondents were more likely to favor constitutional reforms such as changing the role of the House of Lords, judicial protection of human rights, and greater public access to government information (Curtice and Jowell 1997). These reforms were then taken up by the new Labour government. Similarly, recent elections have led to Green parties entering government in Germany and Sweden and pursuing postmaterial agendas from these new positions of influence. These political reforms are exactly the types of changes that democracies make to respond to postmaterialists' new political demands—and that advance the process of democratization.

Demands for political reform extend further. Some citizens are dissatisfied with representative democracy itself (Klingemann and Fuchs 1995, ch. 14; Dahl 1989). As noted, the recent increase in political dissatisfaction is focused on the institutions of representative democracy, not on democratic values and principles. Thus, another response to popular dissatisfaction has been a move toward participatory democracy that is more consistent with postmaterial values.

Traditional forms of representative democracy limit the potential for citizen participation, especially in Western Europe. In fact, the opportunities for electoral input are scandalously low for most Europeans. Casting a few votes during a multiyear electoral cycle leaves insufficient room for citizen input. Furthermore, declining voter turnout in the Trilateral democracies suggests growing disenchantment with this form of democratic participation. Although contemporary democratic institutions were developed in the nineteenth century, society has changed a great deal since then. Strengthened commitments to the democratic ideal and increased skills and resources among contemporary publics are leading to increased political participation outside the boundaries of representative democracy. Research documents the growth of protest and direct-action methods among Western publics, for example (Barnes and Kaase 1979; Jennings and van Deth 1989). Similarly, Sidney Verba and his colleagues (1995, 72) show that while Americans' participation in elections has been declining, their direct contact with government officials and work with community groups has been increasing. Participation in new social movements such as the environmental movement has also increased substantially over the past generation. These new patterns of participation are putting pressure on governments to consider new forms of policy-making and administration (e.g., Ingram and Smith 1993).

Institutional reform is not a sufficient response to the democratic challenges presented by postmaterial value change, however. Despite all the institutional change that has occurred in recent decades, political dissatisfaction continues to grow. At the heart of the problem may be a breakdown in the consensus over how democracies should operate and what they should provide their citizens. While postmaterialists want a more participatory democracy, materialists scoff at these demands as threats to representative democracy. While postmaterialists push an alternative political agenda, materialists want governments to continue playing their traditional policy roles. New styles of interest representation simply heighten these tensions.

In summary, the Trilateral democracies are facing new challenges that are rooted in the changing values and skills of their citizens. Democracies need to adapt to a new style of citizen politics and divided sentiments about the democratic process. But as aptly summarized by Ralf Dahrendorf (1975, 195) nearly a quarter century ago, this has always been the challenge for democracy:

> What we have to do above all is to maintain that flexibility of democratic institutions which in some ways is their greatest virtue: the ability of democratic institutions to implement and effect change without revolution—the ability to react to new problems in new ways—the ability to develop institutions rather than change them all the time—the ability to keep the lines of communication open between leaders and the led—and the ability to make individuals count above all.

The challenge to democracies is to evolve, guarantee political rights, and increase the ability of citizens to control their own lives.

TWELVE

Mad Cows and Social Activists: Contentious Politics in the Trilateral Democracies

Sidney Tarrow

> Without common purpose, there is no basis for common priorities, and without priorities, there are no grounds for distinguishing among competing private interests and claims. . . . The system becomes one of *anomic democracy,* in which democratic politics becomes more an arena for the assertion of conflicting interests than a process for the building of common purposes.
>
> (Crozier, Huntington, and Watanuki 1975, 161; emphasis added)

OVER THE PAST two decades some scholars (e.g., Norris 1999) have noted a marked decline of trust and confidence in government, institutions, and political leaders in the so-called Trilateral democracies of the United States, Western Europe, and Japan. Is this decline of confidence a bad thing? If it is connected to anomic democracy—which is what the authors of *The Crisis of Democracy* feared—then it probably does sap democratic trust and erode citizen confidence. There are contrary signs, however. As W. Lance Bennett (1998, 749) writes: "Despite the outpourings of academic and journalistic concern about the decline of civic culture, 'dissatisfaction with government and politics' barely registers on lists of the most important problems facing the [United States] today." What *has* changed, according to Bennett (1998, 747–49; see also Inglehart 1997a), is that while trust in government has declined, volunteer activities have not, and interest in national affairs and local politics, political discussions with friends, petition signing, support for boycotts, demonstrations, and other forms of direct action have increased.

Bennett's observations can be generalized: throughout the Trilateral democracies we see a growth not only of volunteerism, but also of shifting networks of social activists, many of them overlapping with interest groups and parties and working partly within established institutions. While their discourse and actions are contentious and uncivil, they nourish vigorous communities—often quite critical of powerholders—

whose effects may prove more of a boon than a burden to democracy. Let us begin with a story about unperforming government, distrustful citizens, and social activism. We will turn from there to a reexamination of contentious politics and its hypothetical effects on the dynamics of the Trilateral democracies.

MAD COWS . . .

Between 1988 and 1996 an epidemic of bovine spongiform encephalopathy (BSE) swept through Britain's cattle herds. As unease rose among Britain's beef-loving population and its cattle-raising farmers, the Tory government appointed the blue-ribbon Spongiform Encephalopathy Advisory Committee (SEAC) to investigate what became popularly known as "Mad Cow Disease." The commission's report was far from sanguine. Losses of cattle had continued to mount, and the government admitted that the source of contagion was probably cow feed that included animal detritus. This was bad enough, but in March 1996 Britain's secretary of state for health announced that ten cases of a new form of Creutzfeldt-Jakob Disease (CJD) had been diagnosed in human patients. CJD is a fatal disease caused by a rampant protein that eats away the brain cells of its victims, causing madness and then death. On the same day the ten cases of CJD were announced, SEAC scientists held a press conference at which they explained that there might be a connection between the human disease and BSE. Were Britons eating themselves to madness and death? What made the news so appalling was not just the idea that beef, a staple of the British diet, could be fatally contaminated. That aside, as Sheila Jasanoff (1997, 222) writes, "since 1988, the government and some of its advisers had repeatedly stated that beef was safe. . . . If government officials had deliberately misled the public, then how could anything they now said be trusted?"

Accompanied by gallows-humor cartoons, explosions of rage from Britain's EU partners, and savage criticism of the government by publicists and Labour Party opponents, the BSE affair marked what Jasanoff (1997, 223) calls "an unprecedented breakdown of communication between British citizens and their public institutions." A cartoon in the usually staid *London Times* "showed Rodin's famous Burghers of Calais, one gagging, the rest looking pained and scornful, all tossing hamburgers off their pedestal; the caption read 'The Burgers of Calais'" (Jasanoff 1997, 222). Domestic humor was followed by international humiliation. As consumers across the European Union stopped buying beef—whatever its provenance—Britain's Tory government was forced to bow before the demand of its EU partners that virtually all the country's cattle be slaughtered. And in widely publicized polemics the British government saw itself lambasted by EU officials, Continental farmers whose products were avoided by consumers for fear that they came from British slaughterhouses, and its own citizens. It eventually cost some $6 billion to shore up failing businesses and compensate farmers and slaughterhouses for their losses (*New York Times*, November 24, 1998).

The loss of confidence in the British government in the wake of the BSE bombshell should not surprise political scientists. In an analysis of survey data Curtice and Jowell (1997, 91; see also Hall 1997, 25) found that there had been a dramatic decline in confidence in Britain's leaders over the previous two decades. As Kenneth Newton (1997c, 2) wryly observed, perhaps the government that had gone furthest in defining citizens as "the sum of their shopping" forgot that citizens do not live by markets alone.

. . . AND SOCIAL ACTIVISTS

But all was not bleak in Britain: as if to make up for the breakdown of public confidence following publication of the SEAC report, citizens turned to their still-robust tradition of private association (Hall 1997). Farmers organized the mass slaughter of cattle, animal rights groups mobilized against the government, and the venerable Consumers' Association pushed for a new Food Standards Agency independent of the disgraced Ministry of Agriculture, Fisheries and Food (Jasanoff 1997, 225).[1] From Greenpeace's militant pronouncements to the learned discourses of scientific societies, from the efforts of private charities researching the disease to the formation of survivors' support groups, British civil society leapt into action to fill the gap produced by the decline of confidence in government.[2] People looked to other institutions—their butchers, supermarkets, restaurants, and media—for information and advice to restore their security (Jasanoff 1997, 223). Eventually, a "Great Beef" campaign was formed to lobby the EU to lift the ban and help recover Continental markets (*New York Times*, November 24, 1998). Britons' recourse to association should also have been predictable to close observers of the island's politics. Although trends vary among types of organization, writes Peter Hall (1997, 3), "average membership has grown among all the other types of organizations . . . at a rate that generally exceeds pop-

---

[1] Jasanoff's sources for this are Davies and Todd (1996) and *Health Which?* (1996).

[2] Greenpeace, for example, published a pamphlet called "From BSE to Genetically Modified Organisms" (July 1997); the Consumer's Association published a call for an Independent Food Agency (*Consumer Policy Review*, May/June 1996, 82–86); a number of private charities formed a Spongiform Encephalopathy Research Campaign (www.airtime.co.uk/bse); and the daughter of a CJD victim formed a Creutzfeldt-Jakob Disease Support Network. My thanks to Sheila Jasanoff for making these materials available to me.

ulation growth." If the BSE epidemic revealed a loss of confidence in government, it also demonstrated that social trust among citizens quietly lives on in Britain (Hall 1997). No decline of social capital here!

Not so quiet were the responses of British farmers and other groups frightened by the malady and angered at the government cover-up. Research by Evelyn Bush and Pete Simi reveals that a wave of farmers', producers', consumers', and animal rights activists' demonstrations followed in the wake of the government's announcement. For example:

- In the North Devon village of Bradworthy about 1,000 people participated in a protest march aimed at the ban on British beef.
- In Scotland beef exporters gave away 10,000 worth of prime Scottish steak to protest inadequate government assistance.
- In London animal welfare campaigners associated with the "Compassion in World Farming" group vowed to lobby sites where thousands of unwanted dairy calves were to be slaughtered.[3]

As confidence in government declined, both the social trust associated with a robust civil society and the contentious politics that Crozier, Huntington, and Watanuki feared rose in tandem. Distrust in government, social trust, and social activism: as Britain emerged from the Mad Cow episode, these three features were interlaced in a complicated pattern that was certainly contentious but looked nothing like the "anomic democracy" that the authors of *The Crisis of Democracy* worried about. On the contrary, minus the deference of traditional British political culture, it looked like a vigorous civil society crisscrossed with social networks of critical citizens.

Bennett attributes a similar phenomenon in the United States to new forms of "lifestyle politics" resulting from changes in the economy (1998, 749 ff.). Bennett found that as group membership in the United States has declined, volunteerism has increased—hardly a sign of the collapse of civil society. In this essay I make a broader argument: that activism has always taken both membership and nonmembership, contentious and noncontentious forms, and that in today's advanced industrial democracies, it is the latter that carries much of the burden of social capital. I speculate that this can be seen in the intersection between contentious and institutional politics, in activism within civil society, and in the development of ties of what I call "working trust" among activists and decision-makers. None of these relations are likely to generate "confidence in government," at least not in the generic form usually measured

---

[3] These data are culled from Reuters on-line news dispatches as part of a project on the Europeanization of Social Movements that is supported by National Science Foundation Grant SBR 961. My thanks go to Bush and Simi for allowing me to quote their unpublished paper (1999).

by survey research. But it may well generate more responsive government through a process of what E. P. Thompson once called "collective bargaining by riot" (1971). But first let us turn to social activism.

THE STUDY OF SOCIAL MOVEMENTS SINCE THE 1960s

I do not know what the authors of the Trilateral Commission Report would have made of the Mad Cow episode. But even as Crozier, Huntington, and Watanuki worried about the fate of the advanced industrial democracies, scholars of social movements had become more sanguine about the relationship between uncivil politics and democratic government. Instead of anomic behavior, they began to write of collective action (Tilly 1978); rather than how social movement organizations attack authority, they studied how they mobilize conventional resources (Zald and McCarthy 1987); instead of worrying about anti-politics, they came to regard contentious politics as a normal part of the system (Knoke 1990; McAdam, Tarrow, and Tilly 1997). Some connected social struggle with reform (Piven and Cloward 1977), and others with the consolidation of democracy (Tarrow 1989). As David S. Meyer (1998, 4–5) has recently written, activists of the 1960s and after "were more likely than their less active colleagues to be politically oriented, socially engaged, and psychologically well adapted. Policy analysts discovered that social unrest led to concessions from government, and that protest strategies were actually rational efforts by those poorly positioned to make claims on government through conventional means."

There were three main differences between this community of scholars and the mainstream political scientists who were worrying about citizens' attitudes toward authority. First, they proceeded from a conflictual rather than a consensual model of society (Tilly 1978, ch. 2). Second, this drew their attention to social mechanisms and interactions rather than to individual attitudes and dispositions. Third, rather than the survey research methods relentlessly employed by mainstream political scientists, they used case materials and historical events methods. Although this reduced the representativeness of their studies, it gave them a better purchase on the interactions of actors, their opponents, and governments (Tilly 1978; Rucht, Koopmans, and Neidhardt 1998).

This more sanguine attitude toward social activism was reinforced by the restabilization of Western politics after the 1960s. Except for savage episodes of terrorism in Italy and Germany (della Porta 1995b), the running sores of IRA and ETA violence, and the revival of "ugly" movements in the early 1990s, the increase in contentious politics has coincided with stabilizing party politics and strong support for democracy (Norris 1999). Far from spiraling into a vortex of violence, the forms of contention were by and large conventional and becoming more so. Either social movements had changed their tactics, or our understanding of them needed to be considerably broadened.

SOCIAL MOVEMENTS AND CONTENTIOUS POLITICS

Almost without realizing it, students of contentious politics were beginning to abandon established assumptions inherited from Max Weber and Robert Michels about social movements. They began to question whether activism was distinct from institutional life, whether activists mobilize their followers only to confront institutions, and whether Michels and his followers were correct in arguing that they enter these institutions at the cost of displacing their goals and becoming interest groups. Although some scholars (Burstein 1998) went so far as to deny the distinction between social movements and other types of political organizations, a growing tendency was to regard movements as a specific organizational type within a broader universe of contentious politics. That is the view advanced here. Social movements are a particular—but far from the only—form of contentious politics. They might be defined as public, collective, episodic interactions among makers of claims when (1) at least some of the interaction adopts noninstitutional forms, (2) at least one government is a claimant, an object of claims, or a party to the claims, and (3) the claims would, if realized, affect the interests of at least one of the claimants.[4]

In developed democratic states activism ranges from frontal attacks on national states, to making claims on their boundaries, to participation within their institutions. This intersection across institutional boundaries was already evident in the contentious politics of the early United States, the first mass democracy. Although America is often considered an atypical democracy, a broader perspective reveals that it was merely precocious in the interlarding of contentious with routine political processes (Tarrow 1998b). Consider the anti-slavery movement: while a minority agitated from outside the polity, its mainstream worked through accepted means on the tolerated boundaries of institutions, in journalism, and on the lecture circuit while anti-slavery congressional representatives negotiated within institutions (Weingast 1998). Operationalizing anti-slavery activism as the extreme minority abolitionist movement would make it impossible to explain how contention around the issue of slavery could have given rise to a national political and military cataclysm.

This example suggests that we locate activism within intersecting zones

---

[4] For the development of this definition and the "political process model" it implies, see McAdam, Tarrow, and Tilly (1997); Tarrow (1998a, 4); and Tilly (1995).

of public behavior vis-à-vis political authority. In both democratic and undemocratic regimes, authorities *prescribe* a certain number of political practices, such as payment of taxes and military service. They also *tolerate* a range of practices outside the prescribed zone, such as allowing leaders of established churches to take positions on current political issues. And within the limits of their capacity, they *forbid* a large array of possible ways of making claims, such as assassination or religious ecstasy. Activism overlaps to some degree with all three. In principle, it can coincide with prescribed means, such as when challengers disrupt public ceremonies; with tolerated means, such as when legal public meetings entertain seditious demands; or with forbidden means, such as when challengers of the established order attack public officials (Tilly 1998, 20).

If these assumptions are correct, then as democracies stabilize and differentiate, political contention will both increase and become more routine, more familiar, and to some extent more institutionalized. There is nothing new in this: by the time the first Reform Act was passed, much of British contention had migrated from direct attacks on opponents at the grassroots to peaceful public meetings that targeted Parliament (Tilly 1995, ch. 5). By the late nineteenth century American reform movements were operating comfortably inside as well as outside of institutions (Clemens 1997). Democracy is a form of polity characterized by broad and equal citizenship, binding consultation, and protection from governmental agents. In such a context activism is inevitable, vigorous, and bound to both intersect with and transgress institutional politics. These intersections of activism with the zones of prescription, toleration, and transgression do not mean that social movements have disappeared—or need ever disappear—from advanced industrial democracies. On the contrary, the more abundant the political opportunities, the more shifting political alignments, the more influential allies available, and the more restrictions on governmental repression, the more fertile the ground for movements to form around new claims and identities. This is especially so in periods in which new social actors are appearing, power-holders are slow to recognize their claims as legitimate, opportunities open up, and resources are widely dispersed. In such polities the goals of new movements are easily diffused, activists find niches to probe within institutions, and coalitions can form between them and members of the polity (Tilly 1995; Tarrow 1998a). But the movement of activists into institutions is neither inevitable, irreversible, nor mutually exclusive with extra-institutional activism.

Consider the recent revival of "social movement unionism" in the United States after a long period of decline in unionization and militancy (Johnston 1998). *Pace* Michels, it is not a one-way shift of activists from movements to institutions that is the most important characteristic of contemporary social movements, but their capacity to straddle institutional and noninstitutional repertoires, move back and forth between contentious and institutional politics, and engage powerholders in both cooperative and conflictual ways.

We need to dissect these interactions more precisely:

First, what has happened to the social movements that grew out of the 1960s? Did they disappear, move permanently into institutions, or give rise to other forms of contentious politics?

Second, what has been happening to more mainstream political organizations? Have they remained impervious to the movement of activism into institutions, or have they had to compete with them for political space?

Third, how do social activists behave once they experience the lures of institutional politics: do they become *un*contentious activists, or do they combine institutional and noninstitutional political means?

Fourth, how has social activism been distilled within the institutions of civil society?

THE DIFFUSION OF SOCIAL MOVEMENT FORMS

What happened to the movement organizations of the 1960s? The memoirs of "sixties" activists tell only part of the story. Some activists dispersed into private life and were never heard from again. Others—particularly in Italy and Germany—took the route of armed struggle, like the Italian and Russian anarchists of the late nineteenth century. Still others entered the talking professions, where they produced a rich memoir literature that crystallized an image of the sixties as regretted, mistaken, and dead. But many activists who had been socialized in movement organizations did not end up in private life, organized terrorism, or academia. As the politics of the Western world moved to the right, they shifted into alternative institutions, public service associations, other social movements, and political parties.

In Hanspeter Kriesi's conception, the classical social movement organizations (SMOs) of the 1960s combined two factors: the *direct participation* of their constituents in collective action, and a predominant orientation that *makes claims on authorities*. But these factors characterize only one type of movement-oriented organization; Kriesi identifies three others in terms of whether or not constituents participate directly in collective action, and whether or not they aim their activities primarily at authorities or society. As illustrated by Figure 12.1, this produces a four-cell typology of movement-related organizations.

Kriesi's typology helps us to examine different types of movement-related organizations without relegating any of them to an institutional

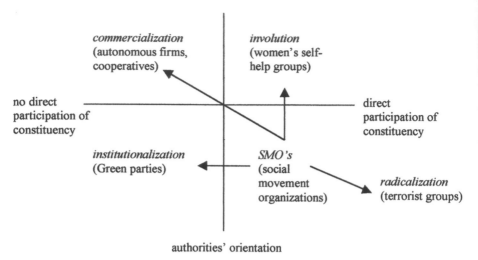

Figure 12.1. Typology of Transformations of Goal Orientations and Action Repertoires of Social Movement Organizations with Illustrative Forms
Source: Adapted from Kriesi 1996, 157.

scrap heap. For example, the many women's self-help groups that emerged from the feminist movement of the 1960s are not oriented primarily toward making claims on authorities, but they do involve the direct participation of constituents and build consensus around common goals (Taylor and Van Willigen 1996). Conversely, the European Green parties and American public-interest groups that evolved out of the same movement family no longer involve large numbers of participants in direct action, but they are oriented toward making claims on public authorities, and they share many of the goals of the movements that preceded them. Finally, while the so-called autonomous sector that developed in West Germany and Switzerland after the 1960s involved neither direct constituency participation nor an orientation toward authorities, it does provide services that helped to preserve "free spaces" outside the logic of the market.

Kriesi's perspective suggests the variety of ways in which movement militants can exit insurgent organizations without losing the potential for participating in contentious politics from time to time. By joining self-help groups, working for service organizations, and supporting parties and interest groups linked to their original movement homes, activists stay in contact with old comrades, remain available for mobilization during times of stress or opportunity, and keep the flame of activism alive for another day.

Kriesi's typology also suggests how small, weak, and impermanent movement organizations have the potential to produce explosions of protest activity with impressive support. If militants in movement organizations maintain informal links with activists in the other three types of organizations that Kriesi identifies, they can draw on them to mount collective action when political opportunities or threats arise. After the high points of contention pass, these activists remain part of critical communities connected to centers of innovation and potential insurgency (Rochon 1998).

Consider the typical set-piece demonstrations that have punctuated the politics of Western democracies since the 1960s. If they depended on classical movement organizations alone, they would be able to marshal only a fraction of the people who actually pour into the streets. By mobilizing normally nonactivist sympathizers through the intermediaries of public-interest groups, self-help organizations, and political parties, performances like Earth Day, million-people marches, and gay pride demonstrations expand the movement public's presence on the public stage. The mobilization of temporary coalitions for episodic political performances has taken the place of the steady, stolid organizing that was the stock-in-trade of the classical movement organizations of Michels's time (Gerhards and Rucht 1992). Social activism is not dead; it has evolved into a wider variety of forms—intermittent and regular, contentious and institutional.

The "Movementization" of Parties and Interest Groups

Something else has also been going on in the Trilateral democracies since the 1960s. John Aldrich has shown how American parties have been transformed from mass-centered parties-in-the-electorate to candidate-centered service organizations (1995). These changes produced a weakening of the bonds between party adherents and the party itself and a loss of a partisan sense of belonging at the grassroots. By the same token, however, movement activists began to penetrate the nominating processes of the parties with the "amateur Democrat" phenomenon of the 1950s (Wilson 1962), a trend that was reinforced and crystallized by the post-1968 reforms in the Democratic Party. With the rebirth of militant fundamentalist Christianity in the 1980s, the Republican Party, too, grew permeable to movement activism (Hertzke 1993). Although American parties continue to be candidate- and election-based organizations, activists who are more interested in achieving their ideological goals than in getting candidates elected learned to use the post-1960s rules for choosing convention delegates to advance these goals. "New" Democrats were more interested in a candidate's position on divisive issues like the Vietnam War than on distributive ones like patronage. Similarly, if somewhat more slowly, the Republican Party became prey to the ideological agenda of the Christian Coalition and other right-wing groups (Usher 1998).

European parties were slower to experience activist penetration, in part because they possessed more centralized mass organizations that filtered new adherents, and in part because they had robust mechanisms for developing their own party-based activists. But when traditional, territorially based party subcultures began to break down in the 1970s, they followed trends similar to those of American parties. During the early 1980s, for example, the British Labour Party became host to a large number of peace activists who defined themselves more in terms of their own key issues than party loyalty (Maguire 1995). Even in countries like Italy, with its strong traditions of party militancy, the mass parties were transformed from within by veterans of the social movements of the 1960s (Lange, Irvin, and Tarrow 1989).

The lowering of boundaries between conventional and unconventional politics has also affected interest-group politics. Even as local civic associations were declining in some countries, public-interest groups were multiplying (Diani 1997; Minkoff 1998). Many of these groups grew out of critical communities that had formed after the 1960s cycle of protest and learned to employ the same technological developments that mainstream electoral organizations were developing (e.g., computerized mailing lists, electronic communication with supporters, television). An emerging pattern combined passive forms of grassroots activism that are mobilized through impersonal means (e.g., check writing, petition signing) with carefully staged public performances that recall the mass militancy of the past (e.g., Earth Day, the Gay and Lesbian March on Washington), regular lobbying, and publicity activities by paid professionals.

The penetration of parties and interest groups by social activists helps explain another phenomenon of contemporary activism. As Meyer (1998, 25–26) writes, "It is not simply those outside mainstream politics . . . who use movement forms. Increasingly, even well-established groups with institutional means of political access use the social movement form to reach new constituencies and advance their claims." French or American farmers who overturn wagonloads of produce on the national border to dramatize their opposition to Spanish wine or Canadian wheat imports, British matrons in mackintoshes stopping the export of calves to Continental slaughterhouses, Italian milk producers who block the road to Milan's airport with their tractors to protest the European Union's limits on subsidies, elected officials who turn up at demonstrations and even commit civil disobedience—these and many other actors show how far the performances of activist repertoires have been diffused among well-established groups with institutional access and social resources at their command.

THE WIDENING REPERTOIRE OF CONTENTION

Not only the nature and forms, but also the rate of grassroots activism seems to have increased over the past 30 years. Comparing activism in 12 European countries as measured by the Political Action Study and the World Values Surveys, Peter Gundelach (1995, 422) reports the findings reproduced in Table 12.1: with the sole exception of Spain, the proportion of the public that reported engaging in at least two grassroots activities increased in every country between 1981 and 1990. France and Italy were at the top of the list, with 31 and 27 percent, respectively, but Switzerland was bracketed between its two neighbors with 28 percent. If pacific Switzerland resembles its uncivil Latin neighbors in its rate of activism, something new must be brewing in the Trilateral democracies.

The practice of activism has also diffused sociologically. At the end of the 1960s students and workers led most public demonstrations. By the 1990s, however, participation in unconventional political activity had increased among virtually every major subgroup of the population. The most significant increases were reported among the self-employed, citizens between 30 and 49 years of age, and especially women—the major

TABLE 12.1
Trends in Grassroots Activities in 12 Countries, 1974–90

	1974	1981	1990
Denmark	—	15	25
Iceland	—	14	24
Norway	—	19	21
Switzerland	—	16	28
Belgium	—	10	21
Britain	6	12	20
Germany	9	13	20
Ireland	—	11	16
Netherlands	7	11	23
France	—	24	31
Italy	8	18	27
Spain	—	14	11

Source: Gundelach (1995, 422). Data from the Political Action Study (1974) and European Values Study (1981, 1990).

new entrant in the public politics of contention (Dalton 1996, ch. 4; Gundelach 1995, 425).[5] Judging from survey results, Western Europe and the United States have become virtual "movement societies" in which contentious political activity has become a routine way of opposing competing groups, asserting collective identities, and influencing powerholders (Meyer and Tarrow 1998). On the whole, however, the repertoire of contentious political action has moderated over the last 30 years, privileging more conventional forms (e.g., petitions, strikes, public marches) over the uncivil ones that exploded at the end of the 1960s (Crozat 1998; Dalton 1996). Indeed, the only country in the West to have experienced a systematic increase in the more uncivil forms of protest since the 1960s is one whose politics were unnaturally pacific before then—the Federal Republic of Germany (Rucht 1998).

In the absence of more systematic data we can only speculate regarding the interaction between institutional and noninstitutional politics in this growth of activism on the basis of what can be gleaned from case studies and general impressions. We often see the following:

- Sequences of collective action that begin outside the arena of institutional politics and are absorbed by powerholders as they selectively respond to challengers by co-opting their more moderate leaders and preempting their more negotiable demands. The picture drawn by Russell Dalton (1994) of the European environmental movement in the 1980s fits this pattern fairly well.
- Sequences that begin within conventional politics but escape that arena as new actors take advantage of the opportunities created by policy debates and new political alignments to challenge powerholders. The regional mobilization growing out of use of the European Union's Regional Committee seems to follow this pattern, though in an extremely institutionalized way (Marks and McAdam 1996).
- Sequences that begin outside of conventional politics and remain there for an entire cycle of contention, such as the German cycle of skinhead violence against immigrants and the anti-skinhead response in the early 1990s.
- Sequences that combine institutional and noninstitutional contention from the beginning through the interplay among mainstream political actors, protesters, and intermediaries. Such a pattern could be observed in the formation of the Student Nonviolent Coordinating Committee from the more moderate Southern Christian Leadership Conference after the Montgomery Bus Boycott in the American South (Meyer 1998, 10).

---

[5] Katzenstein (1998, ch. 1) leaves the impression that American women protest less than they did in the 1960s and 1970s, shifting to activism within institutions. Although she marshals plenty of evidence for the latter claim, survey evidence collected by Dalton (1996) and others suggests that women are also increasingly active in the politics of protest.

Taken together, these trends suggest a range of interactions of activists within contentious and institutional politics that corresponds poorly to the classical division between parties and interest groups on the one hand and social movements on the other. They have created a movement society in which the boundaries of tolerated contention have expanded, established actors share a border region of contentious actions with new and aggressive challengers, and some disruptive tactics have been so fully accepted that they have lost much of their political clout (Meyer and Tarrow 1997).

CONTENTION WITHIN CIVIL SOCIETY

Social activism has never been directed at politics alone: social movements have always aimed at the transformation of self and community as well as at policy and social change. What seems to be unusual about the period since *The Crisis of Democracy* was published is that activism within civil society has grown out of activism in the public arena. Once social movements and political groups put issues on the public agenda, activists turn their attention from politics to community, corporation, and career. Here are two striking kinds of examples drawn from recent research.

Neighborhood Organizations, Politics, and the Police

In many ways the most fertile expansion of social activism since the 1960s has been in neighborhood and community activism. As city and metropolitan area governments have become increasingly bureaucratized and distant from citizens, a broad spectrum of activist groups has developed at the grassroots of Western societies. Focusing on issues ranging from festivals, parks, playgrounds, and waste dumps to drugs, safety, transportation, and urban planning, such groups combine socializing with friends and neighbors and self-help activities with attempts to influence municipal agendas and support candidates in local elections. A particular arena for female activism, community action groups attract parents concerned with school programs or after-school activities, retired people worried about neighborhood security or looking for a social outlet, commuters seeking better transportation facilities, residents of lower-class neighborhoods concerned with solid waste dumps in their communities, and many others.

Community activists seldom begin with politics in the conventional sense. Often meeting in schools or churches, they may focus on educational or religious issues and frequently intersect with church-based activism. Consider the congregationally linked community activists studied by Heidi Swarts in St. Louis and San Jose: if asked whether they participate in politics or social movements, most such activists would reply in the negative. Yet they attend city council sessions, question and lobby candidates for office, and organize community activities designed to increase support for their programs and develop more robust neighborhood identities—which is very similar to what social movement activists do.[6] Swarts's congregation-based activists involved themselves in institutional politics on the basis of their community concerns; other activists appear to describe the opposite trajectory. Studying three decades of Puerto Rican activism in New York, Cathy Schneider (1977) sees a shift from the nationalist movements of the 1960s to the housing movements of the 1980s to the AIDS activism of the 1990s. When Peterson and Greenstone (1977) found urban activists establishing storefront community organizations in the 1960s, they saw in it the hand of Great Society programs. No such helping hands were offered by the Reagan and Bush administrations, but New York's black and Hispanic activists became just as deeply engaged in civil society.

There is a broader way to frame the relationship between community activism and public institutions. Local communities are ecological units that are not always associated with high degrees of internal solidarity and social organization. Robert Sampson's research on the urban ghetto, for example, "has documented dense network structures that nonetheless are ineffective at the collective or political level." He underscores the "capacity of local community organizations to obtain extra-local resources . . . that help sustain neighborhood social stability and local controls. . . . The embeddedness of local communities in an interdependent system . . . points to the salience of extra-local (vertical) ties and the possibility of spatial processes of diffusion and elite influence" (Sampson 1998, 3–4).[7] Community groups become political to overcome their social-network deficits.

The community policing movement studied by Tracey Meares and Dan Kahan in Chicago is an interesting example of low-solidarity communities interacting creatively with institutions. While police usually react to community policing efforts with suspicion when they first appear, as these activities prove itself useful in spotting crime and incorporating social norms into police practice, working ties can develop between police and community associations attempting to protect their neighborhoods from drugs and other maladies. These ties are particularly effective when police cooperate with community-based religious associations. Po-

[6] I am grateful to Heidi Swarts for allowing me to cite her unpublished dissertation. See her unpublished paper "Communities, the State, and Public Policy" (1998).

[7] I am grateful to Rob Sampson for allowing me to quote his unpublished paper, and for the conversations that have led to this insight.

lice practices that reinforce social norms help to legitimate communities as well as fight crime more effectively. "Institutional integration between the police and key community organizations," write Meares and Kahan (1998), "can give a new meaning to the term 'law enforcement.'"

Feminism within Institutions

In many ways the most spectacular success of the 1960s cycle of social movement was the American women's movement. But why? Unlike some of the more dramatic movements of the 1960s, from the beginning it combined radical feminists, professional lawyers, and sedate women's groups around major themes like the Equal Rights Amendment (Mansbridge 1986). Given its heterogeneity, it is no surprise that its members' tactics ranged from consciousness-raising to "in-your-face" activism to public interest group activities to maneuvering in the party system and Congress (Mueller 1987; Costain 1992). Feminist discourse and women's activism were appearing within social organizations and institutions too. One unexpected result was ordinary citizens' growing use of the symbols—or at least the buzzwords—of feminism. In a recent study Jane Mansbridge (1993) found that the lower-class women she interviewed frequently used the term *male chauvinism*. These women were almost certainly unaware of the complex cultural and political connotations of the term, but it legitimated, justified, and dignified inchoate feelings they had about their male partners that might otherwise have remained unfocused.

More articulated and self-conscious was the appearance of feminist discourse within one of the most conservative institutions of American life: the Catholic Church. In her study of American nuns Mary F. Katzenstein (1998, ch. 5) reports the adoption and transformation of feminist discourse in the Church. Although her intent is to show that disruptive behavior can include discourse, Katzenstein (1998, 114–15) also finds it combining with "in-your-face" demonstrations of insurgency such as during the visit of Pope John Paul II to the United States in 1979. Katzenstein (1998, chs. 3–4) also reports on the growth of feminist activism in an even more conservative institution of American life: the armed forces. Often rejecting the term *feminism,* women officers combine traditional interest-group activism with insistent pressure for promotion and greater rights in all branches of the services. The infamous Tailhook Affair and the investigation that followed demonstrated that military women were able to use the media in a restrained but powerful way to increase public consciousness of the deep currents of sexism that persist at the highest levels of the services (Katzenstein 1998, 171).

TRUST AND THE DECLINE OF CONFIDENCE IN GOVERNMENT

In communities, corporations, churches, and the military, ordinary citizens are engaging in a broad array of activist performances—contentious and institutional, intermittent and continual. Some commentators might argue that these activities do not substitute for the traditional forms of social capital that are declining in America or elsewhere, and others might argue that it does not compensate for the loss of confidence in government—or worse, that they contribute to it. Certainly, activists who spend much of their time interacting contentiously with power-holders are unlikely to hold utopian expectations about their opposite numbers in government. What can this expansion in the character of social activism tell us about trust and confidence in government? Let us return to the Mad Cow episode for some clues.

First, when we compare the British public's reaction to the BSE scandal to the traditional image of the British public—class-conscious, deferential, trusting the judgment of its betters—we are clearly dealing with a more distrustful citizenry than observers found in the past (Curtice and Jowell 1997, 91). When once-deferential Britons begin to react like irascible Italians and frothing Frenchmen, political distrust has indeed diffused broadly in the advanced industrial democracies.

Second, the events surrounding that affair suggest that distrust of governmental performance is not a mechanical reflex of individual attitudes, but the result of complex and situational intersections among state and social actors. It was in the interactions among thin-lipped bureaucrats, taciturn scientists, outraged farmers, an outspoken press, and critical citizens that the episode came to be defined as a case of governmental untrustworthiness.

Third, Crozier, Huntington, and Watanuki opposed civil society and anomic democracy to one another. But in the outcry following the British government's bombshell announcement, civic association—the classic expression of civil society—and uncivil politics—the presumed expression of anomic democracy—joined hands against governmental untrustworthiness. Farmers and producers, environmentalists and consumer groups, opposition politicians and newspapers mixed conventional forms of participation with social activism in response to untrustworthy government.

What does this suggest about activism and contentious politics in the advanced industrial democracies today? This chapter has argued that routine and contentious forms of behavior have intersected more and more closely since the 1960s. This not only makes it difficult to locate the anomic democracy that seemed such a danger to Crozier, Huntington, and Watanabe in 1975, it also raises more fundamental questions about the location of the production of social capital in today's advanced industrial democracies. It may be found *precisely* in the fields of social activism that have expanded since the 1960s and that so worried the authors of *The Crisis of Democracy.*

The New Activism and Declining Confidence in Government

If social activism is having serious negative impacts on political trust, we might expect to find solid evidence of the decline of confidence in government in the social movement literature. More is the wonder, then, that a rapid survey of that literature turned up a mixed picture. Scholars of Japan, where trust in government is generally quite low, do find grassroots activism to be virtually synonymous with a lack of confidence in leaders and institutions.[8] Confidence in government has also been slipping in the United States since the 1960s.[9] Although it does not bear directly on activism, sympathy for protest activities in World Values Surveys shows a modest relationship between institutional confidence and protest potential (Norris 1999, ch. 13).[10] There is no clear cross-national evidence of a systematic correlation between social activism and a lack of confidence in government, however.

For one thing, confidence may simply represent opposition to the party that is currently in power. Working with American data, Jack Citrin (1974) found that trust in government was closely correlated with whether the respondent's preferred political party was in power or in the opposition. Citrin (1974, 976) concluded that the trust in government measure "fails to discriminate between the politically alienated and those who mistrust political leaders or politicians without repudiating regime values or institutions." Would it surprise anyone, for example, to find that those Americans who most distrusted government in the wake of the Monica Lewinsky scandal were conservative Republicans? Moreover, the cross-national correlation between political confidence and activism is weak. Examining citizens' confidence in institutions and their level of grassroots activism in the 12 nations included in the European Values Survey, Peter Gundelach (1995, 437) found only "a slight tendency for grass-roots activists to have less confidence in the institutions of government" (with correlations never exceeding $-.010$), and no important decline in activists' confidence between 1981 and 1990, when overall levels

---

[8] Of the almost 3,000 local citizens' movements formed in the early 1970s, Susan Pharr and Joseph Badaracco (1986) report that most proceeded from alienation from the ruling Liberal Democratic Party and its priorities.

[9] Paul Sniderman (1981) was so convinced of movements' alienation from government that he called his study of Bay Area activists *A Question of Loyalty.*

[10] In contrast, Norris (1999, 262–63) concludes in her review of protest potential that there is no relationship between protest potential and support for the political regime.

of confidence were declining. "Evidently," concludes Gundelach (1995, 438), "grass-roots activity is not a particularly accurate reflection of people's confidence in government."

The indeterminacy of these findings may reflect differences between Japan and the United States on the one hand and European democracies on the other: American and Japanese activists may simply be reflecting voters' high *overall* levels of distrust in their governments. The mixed findings may also reflect the relatively flat and inadequate nature of the survey questions on which much of the research is based.[11] But the most reasonable hypothesis is that they reflect the fact that activism is no longer limited to anti-system social movements located outside of and working against institutions (Knoke 1990, 58). To the extent that activism bridges conventional and unconventional forms of action, has come to involve broader sectors of the population, and includes contention around issues ranging from school safety to nuclear disarmament, there is little reason to suppose that activists as a subpopulation will be significantly less trusting in government than other citizens.

Working Trust

The diffusion of social activism throughout civil society and routine politics raises a hypothesis similar to the one formulated by Hall (1997) in his examination of social capital in Britain: involvement in protest can turn "discontent into constructive, if wary political engagement," extending social capital into new areas just as it is declining in old ones. If this is so, then the new activism may be creating networks of working relations between citizens and their governments even as those same citizens express their dismay to survey researchers about the performance of the latter. Just as industrial conflict previously gave rise to the practice of collective bargaining, regular, detailed, and routinized opportunities for conflict bring many social activists into working relations with public officials, planning boards, parties, and interest groups.

Consider the local congregational-based activists that Heidi Swarts found in San Jose and St. Louis, the police-community cooperation stud-

---

[11] It is worth observing that the data on which these findings are based are approximate in the extreme. In addition to including some highly uncommon forms of protest activities (e.g., the occupation of buildings and factories), they exclude more common forms like the sit-in—the most spectacularly successful addition to the repertoire of contention. Furthermore, the measures do not ask respondents to specify when and how often they engaged in such activities. Thus, a citizen who participated in a protest march in the 1960s may score high on the summary measure of grassroots activism in 1990 although he or she has been entirely passive since then.

ied by Meares and Kahan in Chicago, or the Puerto Rican AIDS activism Cathy Schneider has described in New York City. If interviewed by survey researchers, these activists would probably express little confidence in government, but they often find themselves engaged in working relations with their antagonists. Although activists may distrust government in the abstract—and individual officials in the flesh—in the post-1960s world of differentiated social activism, their ability to straddle the line between contentious and institutional politics can produce working trust between activists and decision-makers. Having exhaustively measured the magnitude of putative distrust by ever more sensitive survey techniques, the next step is to examine the relationships of antagonistic cooperation that stretch across the barricades of contentious politics.

UNENDURING COMMITMENTS AND UNTRUSTING CITIZENS

Contemporary contention allows ordinary citizens to draw on technical and relational skills that, in the past, were largely restricted to elites, political parties, and full-time public officials. It brings activists further into the realms of tolerated and prescribed politics and makes possible relations of working trust with public officials. It has produced hybrid forms of behavior that cross the boundaries of the polity and link grass-roots activists to public interest groups, parties, and public officials. On the one hand, these new forms of activism are unlikely to sustain high levels of confidence in government, and they may discourage public trust by demonstrating the inadequacy of governmental performance. On the other hand, they do not create enduring negative subcultures. Their variform and shifting organizations, their tendency to produce rapid and rapidly liquidated coalitions, and their focus on short- and medium-term issues rather than fully fledged ideologies do not produce enduring membership commitments or deeply held loyalties outside the polity. The grassroots activist who moves from cause to cause and coalition to coalition forms few enduring commitments and gains little confidence in elites or institutions, but neither does he or she become encapsulated in tight-knit subcultures that reject the fundamentals of democracy and produce a backlash against it among ordinary citizens. As Citrin (1974, 998) concluded in the wake of the Watergate scandal, "It is worth recalling John Stuart Mill's belief that a democratic political culture is characterized by a vigilant skepticism (or realistic cynicism) rather than an unquestioning faith in the motives and abilities of political authorities." Less trust *about* government and more activism *interacting* with government: these may be the ingredients of a less comfortable but more robust democracy.

ACKNOWLEDGMENTS

I wish to thank Mary Brinton, Pam Burke, Sam Huntington, Peter Katzenstein, Doug McAdam, David Meyer, Susan Pharr, Jonas Pontusson, Robert Putnam, Heidi Swarts, Charles Tilly, and Heather Williams for comments on an earlier version of this chapter. The article by Sheila Jasanoff (1997) referred to herein was the origin of the lead story; my thanks for her inspiration.

THIRTEEN

Political Mistrust and Party Dealignment in Japan

Hideo Ōtake

MANY ADVANCED industrial democracies are witnessing a decline of parties, political dealignment, and falling voter turnout and confidence in government. Japan is no exception. Despite a polarized structure resulting from its Cold War origins, the Japanese party system seemed exceptionally stable in terms of voter allegiance until 1993. A closer look, however, reveals that the foundations of its stability had gradually eroded since the 1970s, if not earlier, with increasing alienation among new middle-class voters (that is, urban, college-educated, relatively young, white-collar workers and their wives). The abrupt end of the reign of the conservative Liberal Democratic Party (LDP) in 1993 revealed the crisis that had been building for decades behind the facade of stability.

The LDP succeeded in institutionalizing a supportive pattern of voting behavior, and its one-party predominance, the so-called 1955 System, lasted for 38 years. In 1993, however, two groups of Diet members seceded from the LDP to initiate a "realignment of political circles" (*seikai saihen*) that has proceeded through the dissolution of existing parties and the creation of new ones. Unlike party realignment from below in other countries, including the United States, Japan's was not induced by such drastic changes as an economic crisis, the emergence of racial conflict, or defeat in war (Burnham 1970; Carmines and Stimson 1989).

Instead, a series of scandals, especially since the mid-1970s, set a process of *de*-alignment in motion by generating widespread distrust of politicians and the established parties. When new parties appeared on the scene, they flourished initially but quickly lost support once they became assimilated to the establishment. Voters' antipathy toward existing parties intensified with a new round of corruption scandals beginning in 1988. Exploiting these opportunities, some politicians attempted during the 1990s to engineer party realignment from above by introducing a neo-conservative policy package designed to alter the lines of cleavage in the party system. In creating new parties, they struggled to capture voters' anti-establishment, anti-party feelings, but it proved difficult to organize voters' transitory discontent into a stable base of electoral support, mobilize voters' support along a different issue axis, and institutionalize a new party system. Up to this point (winter 1998), the result of voter failure to understand and rally to these efforts to capitalize on their discontent has been a further decline in political confidence. Voter turnout has continued to fall since 1993. Even the surge in voter turnout and the surprise victory of the new Democratic Party in the July 1998 Upper House election seems to have been another example of extreme volatility in voter allegiance rather than the beginning of a process that could lead to stable party support.

No institutions are more basic to democracies than parties, and their failure to function effectively is a key to explaining low levels of confidence in government. In terms of the model offered in the introduction to this volume, Japan has experienced low and declining levels of confidence in government because of a long-standing and ongoing shortfall in fidelity, a disjuncture between the interests of large segments of the electorate and the interests championed by their representatives. This chapter examines party dealignment in Japan, focusing on the failure of a series of attempts by new parties to capture and institutionalize the allegiance of the new middle class. Before analyzing these attempts at party realignment from above, however, I discuss the structure of party conflict that established the dominance of the LDP for almost four decades but failed to link citizens to the state in a meaningful way. To some extent the problem is structural: the Cold War and U.S.-Japan relations coming out of the Occupation era configured a party system that has been deeply polarized around issues that became increasingly anachronistic over time. Ultimately, however, the responsibility for low confidence in government in Japan lies at the door of both party leaders, who have failed as political entrepreneurs, and ordinary citizens, who have made their leaders' tasks almost impossible.

DEFENSE AS THE DOMINANT ISSUE IN THE ONE-PARTY DOMINANT SYSTEM

Ideologies are usually conceptualized along a unidimensional left-right scale. Political parties attempt to attract voters by identifying themselves along this scale (Inglehart and Klingemann 1976). Reflecting the distinctive historical and social backgrounds of each country, the specific issues that define the left-right axis differ significantly across nations, ranging from the political regime itself to economic policy, religion, and foreign policy. Within a single country a variety of political issues may resist being shoe-horned onto a unidimensional scale (Duverger 1951), but the political system typically rotates around a single ideological axis defined by the issues that are deemed most important. The advantage of interpreting polities in this manner is that it simplifies party identification and voting decisions by significantly reducing the cost of gathering information on and evaluating political parties. For this reason parties often present a deliberately simplified image of themselves in hopes of stabilizing voter support.

Japan's basic ideological axis arose in the 1950s as a direct legacy of the Occupation (1945–52) and the Cold War. As unanimously confirmed by numerous surveys, the main line of cleavage between conservatives and progressives from the early 1950s to the 1980s ran through the issues of the status of the emperor, labor's right to strike, constitutional reform, and, especially, defense.[1] Party support was structured by acceptance of or opposition to the U.S.-Japan Security Treaty and the Self-Defense Forces, and voters generally identified political parties along a unidimensional scale that ranged from the LDP on the right to the Democratic Socialist Party, the Clean Government Party (CGP), the Japan Socialist Party (JSP), and the Japan Communist Party. Despite the emergence of various issues that fall outside this traditional cleavage (e.g., environmental protection), studies reveal that the majority of voters still identify their political ideologies along the same axis (Kabashima and Takenaka 1996, ch. 5).

Unlike many other countries, including the United States, economic policy has not been a significant issue of contention in Japan. According to a survey conducted in 1967, for example, Japanese voters were divided over whether they favored tax cuts or the expansion of welfare, but their attitudes on welfare policy had no correlation with their positions on defense and the emperor (Kabashima and Takenaka 1996, 271–77). The platforms of progressive and conservative parties alike have given high priority to the expansion of welfare benefits. This is also true of government intervention and other issues of managing the economy. Although Japanese voters have shown a high sensitivity to inflation, they have never been forced to choose explicitly between inflation and unemployment.

Underlying this progressive-conservative political cleavage was a social cleavage over values. Young, well-educated, urban, white-collar workers who exhibited a strong hostility to prewar Japanese political culture advocated pacifism. The elderly, less educated, and self-employed (including farmers) were more likely to support rearmament. Labeled "cultural" or "value politics" by Jōji Watanuki (1967), both conservatives and progressives sought to capitalize on this social cleavage to mobilize voters.

Bearing witness to the strong hold that the defense cleavage has had

---

[1] In the past Japanese labor unions, especially those in the mainstream of the labor movement, often went on strike over political issues, particularly such divisive issues as revision of the U.S.-Japan Security Treaty. The focal point of controversy over revision of the constitution has always been Article 9, which renounces war and prohibits Japan's full-fledged rearmament.

over party competition in Japan, new political parties invariably adapted to this ideological axis. Although the CGP distanced itself from the conflict over defense policy until the mid-1960s, it adopted a centrist stance on the issue once it began to make inroads in the Diet. Similarly, the New Liberal Club (NLC), which was formed in 1976 by young conservatives who abandoned the LDP, first championed the issue of political corruption, which cut across the preexisting cleavage over defense issues. When the NLC sought to shed its image as a single-issue party and draw up a more comprehensive policy platform, however, it reverted to the traditional left-right axis and portrayed itself as a middle-of-the-road conservative party. Formed around the same time as the NLC, the Social Democratic League (SDL) initially came out in favor of decentralization and citizen participation. It held the promise of becoming the party of citizens' movements and of creating a completely new pattern of political competition. Once social democrats with leftist origins took control of the party, however, the SDL proclaimed itself a middle-of-the-road progressive party and was also assimilated into the preexisting structure of conflict.

It must be noted that the nature of the defense issue changed substantially from the 1960s to the 1970s. As the LDP relinquished hopes of amending the constitution during the 1960s, the link between the defense question and the political regime was significantly weakened. As more and more information about the Eastern bloc came to light during the 1970s, the arguments of socialist and neutral countries, which had commanded widespread respect during the 1950s as the defenders of peace, lost their appeal, and it became clear that socialism did not provide a ready prescription for the troubles of the Third World. As a result, socialism rapidly lost its appeal. It became disconnected from issues of the political and economic regime, and the pacifism it inspired came to be seen as nothing more than a simplistic rationale for isolationism. It was precisely its simplicity that gave pacifism its widespread appeal, however, and mobilizing this sentiment continued to pay off electorally. The CGP, NLC, and SDL understood this when they sought to highlight their centralist position by attacking the allegedly hawkish policies of the LDP.

Despite the emergence of these and other new political parties and changes in both the domestic and international environments, the progressive-conservative cleavage over defense issues somehow survived as the only yardstick with which Japanese voters evaluated political parties until the "1955 System" of one-party predominance ended in 1993.

THE POLITICS OF INTEREST VERSUS THE POLITICS OF CLEANLINESS

Meanwhile, a clientelistic pattern of distribution of material benefits to local constituencies and occupational interest groups gained importance in electoral competition. The LDP represented the interests of local constituencies, self-employed sectors (including agriculture), and specific industries (especially the construction industry). Its main competitor, the JSP, represented the interests of public servants in railroads, the postal service, telecommunications, education, and local government. The two major parties came to compete less on the basis of policies or principles than on who would win a greater share of the pie. Voters were also mobilized directly by means of business groups and neighborhood organizations during this period (Takabatake 1980). *Kigyō-gurumi* elections, in which everyone employed by a corporation campaigns and votes for a single candidate, typify this phenomenon. Labor unions have campaigned in a similar fashion. Where workplace networks became vehicles for voter mobilization, the role of ideology in voting decisions almost vanished. Various studies have confirmed this displacement of "high politics" by patronage as the primary factor in voters' decision-making (Miyake 1995, ch. 1).

Concurrent with the sharp rise of patronage in voter mobilization, intra- and interparty politics increasingly revolved around the distribution of particularistic benefits. LDP *zoku* (or "tribe") representatives act as de facto interest representatives for a variety of groups, and Socialist Diet members acted as intermediaries for labor unions seeking parochial and short-term interests as early as the late 1950s (Taguchi 1958; Matsushita 1960). The most prominent example of such rent-seeking behavior was the active lobbying by both LDP transportation *zoku* and JSP Diet members from the Japan National Railways Union for higher railroad fares and subsidies to cover the public railroads' swelling deficits. Beneath the rhetoric of class struggle and pacifism versus anti-communism, employers and labor tacitly colluded in pursuit of the same benefits.

Patronage did not constitute a new partisan cleavage but developed parasitically alongside it. The expansion of distributive politics reduced the confidence in government of groups that could not be reached through distributive channels, however. The white-collar middle class, the young, and urban housewives, who had comprised a major wing of "value politics" in the ideological conflict over defense issues, found that no party defended their occupational and residential interests. Thus, clientelism bred growing opposition to such policies and laid the groundwork for conflict between defenders of the status quo and vested interests on the one hand and groups demanding reform of the distributive apparatus (e.g., consumers or taxpayers) on the other.

At first this new pattern of conflict appeared only intermittently, particularly in response to major political scandals, but it came to have a profound effect on electoral results and short-term partisan alignments. The founding of the NLC shortly after the Lockheed Scandal and its surge in popularity in the 1976 general elections, the "Madonna Boom" enjoyed by the JSP in the 1989 Upper House elections,[2] and the Japan New Party's triumph in the general elections of 1993 can all be interpreted as consumer and taxpayer revolts. More recently the personal popularity of Naoto Kan and Yukio Hatoyama, who founded the Democratic Party in 1996, can be viewed in similar terms. All of these successes rested on support from essentially the same social groups. Many new political parties have owed their (short-lived) popularity to the hostility of the urban new middle class to vested interests. At the core of this hostility lies a marked lack of confidence in existing political parties, party politics, the bureaucracy, and the government—in short, in all political and administrative professionals.

As long as distrust is directed against clientelism, this conflict appears to echo the traditional-modern cultural cleavage that was once dominant in Japan. As the cultural question has become detached from debates over specific issues including defense, it can be argued that this cultural cleavage has intensified and become more explicit. In spite of this continuity between the traditional-modern cleavage and urban hostility toward distributive politics, the two display important differences. First, voters from the urban new middle class have become increasingly aware that the groups that they had regarded as the champions of modern values, such as the JSP and labor unions, were merely pursuing their own narrow self-interest behind the rhetoric of peace and people. Second, elite bureaucrats, who had hitherto commanded great respect and had personified partisan neutrality, now came under severe attack as defenders of vested interests, including their own privileges. In a sense this new conflict pits citizens against government, amateurs against professionals, and exists independently of the old conservative-progressive cleavage. This hostility toward existing political parties is neither progressive nor middle-of-the-road, but is rooted at a deeper level in the political culture.

Political parties have not succeeded in exploiting this new axis of con-

---

[2] Takako Doi was elected party chair after the JSP's severe defeat in the 1986 elections for the Upper and Lower Houses of the Diet. The mass media warmly welcomed her new leadership, which emphasized a new-middle-class orientation and rejected old-style socialist and trade union rhetoric, and favorably reported on the activities of civic leaders, mostly women, who supported her. Under Doi's leadership the JSP endorsed many of these civic leaders as candidates in the 1989 Upper House elections. Female civic activists campaigned enthusiastically for these candidates, and the JSP achieved a landslide victory, gaining 46 seats (22 of them won by women) against the LDP's 36 in what was called the "Madonna Boom." Doi's attempts to reform the party ultimately failed, however, because they were blocked by party leaders and labor unions, and she resigned in frustration in 1991. Her failure was due in part to her inability to find significant numbers of fresh and attractive candidates from outside the party, namely professors, journalists, writers, and lawyers. This failure, in turn, was due to the Japanese practice of "lifetime" employment and the heavy burden of campaigning financing that each candidate was expected to bear (Doi 1993).

flict and organizing it into a stable base of support. Without exception, each of the many political parties that has appeared on the scene over the past two decades has enjoyed an initial surge in popularity but then failed to sustain its momentum because of the difficulty of transforming latent hostility toward vested interests into support for a particular political party. Failing to spark a partisan realignment and remaining nothing more than an occasional disturbance to the political system, this cleavage has only served to reduce many voters' confidence in government. Let us consider some reasons why.

First, hostility toward political elites has been based from the start on widespread disillusionment with politics itself. In the "Madonna Boom" of 1989, female candidates, mostly from the JSP, attracted votes precisely because being women distinguished them from professional politicians. For similar reasons, many candidates who entered politics from other professions also won considerable support. The outsider's advantage necessarily vanishes once one is elected and remains in office, however. Thus, anti-government sentiment requires a constant supply of fresh candidates. Furthermore, voters' hostility toward politicians readily retreats into political indifference. When political parties fail to deliver instant results, disappointed voters are quick to exit the political arena.

Second, Japanese voters' hostility toward government includes an apolitical, at times irresponsible element that regards political participation as a leisure activity rather than as a serious endeavor. The emergence of the seriousness-leisure cleavage has caused a transformation in what had hitherto been the traditional-modern cleavage (Kojima 1979, 1980). Postmaterialist values in Inglehart's (1977) sense, namely, a desire for participation that challenges authority, have had only a limited vogue in Japan, taking hold only among limited groups and for limited periods of time, such as the students' movements of the late 1960s and the citizens' movements that arose over environmental and other issues in the late 1960s and early 1970s. Rather than participating in public affairs, young people and the urban new middle class have focused on their private lives. This change can be understood as bidimensional: these groups have simultaneously shifted from traditional to modern values and from a serious orientation that emphasizes public activities to a hedonistic one that emphasizes private leisure activities (Kojima 1980, 128). The rise of a hedonistic orientation among the Japanese electorate has resulted in an attitude that regards even politics as an interesting game little different from other leisure activities.

From this standpoint the 1994 election of ex-comedians Yukio Aoshima and Nokku Yokoyama as governors of Tokyo and Osaka prefectures was due not only to these candidates' success in distancing themselves from established political parties, but also to their appeal to the increasingly hedonistic orientation of urban voters. The same can be said for the popularity of Morihiro Hosokawa, who became prime minister in 1993. With his laid-back, even flip attitude, it often seemed as if he could quit politics at any moment–which is exactly what he ended up doing in 1998. Hosokawa's appeal rested on his personification of politics as a game. To attract hedonistic voters, candidates must emphasize their personal qualities rather than party programs and the organizations to which they belong, which remain serious. These voters are strongly averse to joining or being exploited by any partisan organization whatsoever, so if new political parties initially succeeded in mobilizing such voters, they found it impossible to maintain their support. This was a major reason why the NLC and the Japan New Party failed to attract party members, not to mention membership fees, despite their strenuous efforts.

Third, many Japanese voters are quite satisfied with the social and economic—if not political—status quo. Satisfaction with one's life rose from 78 percent in 1973 to 85 percent in 1978 and remained high throughout the 1980s, reaching 87 percent in 1993. Significantly, material, spiritual, personal, and social contentment rose through 1993 among the urban new middle class and young people who have provided the bulk of new parties' support. Furthermore, a large and increasing number of voters respond that they are happy to have been born in Japan; the figure reached 93 percent in 1978 and 97 percent in 1993. Only 20 percent of the electorate feels that politics reflects public opinion, however (Akiyama 1980; Kenda 1980; NHK 1998). A logical interpretation of this disjuncture would be that most Japanese voters consider politics to be remote from their daily lives. Similarly, the declining interest of young people in politics reflects in part their contentment rather than their alienation and frustration. Because these basic conditions have persisted through the 1990s despite a long recession, the possibility that Japanese will offer sustained support for any particular political group, including one that aims to introduce a more relevant ideological cleavage, seems quite slim.

Oftentimes favorable media coverage has initially compensated for the new parties' difficulties in organizing a stable base of support. As scandals and the attempts to introduce and raise the consumption tax have clearly indicated, the mass media perform a crucial role in setting the agenda, providing the crucial impetus for both the formation of new parties and their subsequent rise in popularity. The mass media's self-proclaimed role of defending the common people often leads them to view professional politicians skeptically. After the 1960 struggle over renewal of the U.S.-Japan Security Treaty, the mass media became increasingly critical of the progressive parties, which they had previously viewed sympathetically. This disenchantment made the media lenient toward new conservative parties like the NLC and Japan New Party. As these parties themselves grew in power, however, the media were attacked for being biased and backed away. In addition, the news value of the parties inevitably fell over time. Thus, in some ways, the media actually accelerated the decline in voter interest in new parties.

Given widespread voter hostility toward existing parties, the payoff for a new party of identifying itself as middle-of-the-road or of entering into a coalition is not only greatly reduced but may even be negative because such strategies prevent the fledgling group from distancing itself from established parties. Citizens' movements have long been skeptical of allying themselves with any party, particularly because the precondition for establishing such a relationship was for many years agreement on security issues. When the new NLC and the SDL opted to identify themselves as middle-of-the-road parties in the 1970s, they essentially abandoned their attempts to forge a new axis of cleavage in place of the established conservative-progressive division. Their chief motivation was their desire to displace the LDP as the ruling party and seize power as quickly as possible.

This decision by the NLC and the SDL vividly illustrates new parties' difficulty in organizing a stable base of support. Because they were unable to mobilize and stabilize voters' support for a new policy package, if they were to develop into a significant force within the Diet, their only option was to enlist previously elected politicians who had personal support bases of their own. To bring off a political realignment, their best bet was to either become the ruling party or demonstrate the potential for becoming one, thereby sparking the breakup of the major parties. They failed. As I will demonstrate below, the same scenario was played out in the 1990s. Because voters have not rallied around a new ideological axis offered to them, a series of efforts at reforms have resulted only in political dealignment and declining confidence in government.

THE EMERGENCE OF NEO-CONSERVATISM IN JAPAN

Like other new parties, the Japan New Party (JNP) and the Renewal Party, which appeared in 1992–93, both came out strongly in favor of reforming the scandal-ridden political system. What distinguished them from previous new parties was that they unhesitatingly presented themselves as conservative. Instead of trying to position themselves to the left of the ruling LDP, they offered a reinvigorated conservativism by advocating policies that cut across the old cleavage over defense policy.[3]

---

[3] In contrast, as will be detailed in note 9 below, Sakigake gradually came to espouse the traditional leftist position on foreign policy issues because of the ideological vacuum created by the achievement of a measure of political reform.

The platforms of the JNP and Renewal Party, which signified a major break with the past, can be seen as the culmination of a process that had been evolving for some time. At the level of elites, ideological conflict between social democracy and laissez-faire economics had significantly influenced Japanese politics and administration throughout the postwar era. To varying degrees most of Japan's ministries championed big government, while the powerful Ministry of Finance (MOF), backed for the most part by the top business elite (*zaikai*), favored small government and defended the principle of a balanced budget. These conflicts over big versus small government never became issues of partisan contention, however. The major political parties were united in their support for expanding welfare and greater government intervention in the economy, particularly to appease voters when scandals surfaced (Hiwatari 1995; Ōtake 1996a).

It was the emergence of neo-conservatism among Japanese political elites after the late 1970s that propelled this cleavage over economic issues to the partisan and popular levels. As in other advanced industrial democracies, there are both domestic- and foreign-policy pillars to neo-conservative thought in Japan. On the domestic side neo-conservatism expresses doubt over the social-democratic "postwar settlement," that is, the Keynesian welfare state that was established in most of the Trilateral democracies. Although there had been numerous calls for the curtailment of particularistic benefits to local and functional interests on moral grounds, neo-conservatism provided the first coherent policy prescriptions on that issue. Typical neo-conservative programs include privatization, deregulation, and retrenchment of welfare, all of which were proposed by the Second Provisional Council for Administrative Reform (Daini Rinchō) in the early 1980s. At the level of partisan competition, the emergence of neo-conservatism stimulated the rise of political parties that sought to represent the interests of the urban new middle class, specifically consumers, the salaried class, and taxpayers, all of whom had been neglected by existing political parties. This prompted those parties, too, to attempt to shift their base of support to the urban new middle class.

On foreign policy neo-conservatives argued during the latter half of 1970s for greater Japanese contributions toward defense of the West in the face of the Soviet Union's arms buildup. After the Cold War subsided, they proposed that Japan play a more activist role in the settlement of regional disputes. In this way neo-conservatives simultaneously marginalized the traditional right wing and attacked doves within the LDP and pacifists within the JSP.

The seeds of neo-conservative economic policies can be seen in the platform of the New Liberal Club. After its emergence in the general election of 1976, the NLC decided to target the urban new middle class; it advocated reforms of education, land, and tax policies. Although its economic platform was neither coherent nor completely neo-conservative in doctrine, many of the NLC's policies were adopted by neo-conservatives during the 1980s and 1990s. A prime example was the NLC's innovative proposals for agriculture, which included plans to reduce drastically the number of farm households in Japan by encouraging large-scale, fully professionalized agribusiness (Hagiwara 1976, 146). While the rest of the opposition parties urged the expansion of pension outlays and other welfare benefits, the NLC advocated small government, calling for a reduction of the budget deficit by curtailing preferential tax treatment for doctors and freezing civil servants' salaries. Conflict among its leaders over the party's platform eventually led to the breakup of the NLC, but even if it never identified itself as neo-conservative, the party can be credited with having made the first real attempt to re-set the political agenda and create a new cleavage along neo-conservative lines.

The LDP then seized the initiative. Under Prime Minister Yasuhiro Nakasone (1982–87) the party sought to reduce its traditional dependence on the less competitive small-business and agricultural sectors and reach out to the urban new middle class and blue-collar workers outside of the leftist, public-sector unions. Nakasone advocated consumers' interests by pushing for the privatization of the National Railways and the Telephone and Telegram Corporation (whose trade unions were power bases for the JSP), drastically restructuring the welfare system, particularly pensions and medical insurance, and attempting to liberalize the education system, which was extremely centralized. He also advocated deregulation elsewhere, including the distribution sector. Administrative reform became the primary vehicle for these strategies. Under Nakasone the LDP also adopted a neo-conservative foreign policy, proposing that Japan make greater contributions toward defending the West.

Nakasone's strategies struck a severe blow to the Socialists' base of support and led to a landslide LDP victory in 1986. But if these policies were significant in the short term, they never sparked a major political realignment. The immediate reason for Nakasone's failure lay in massive popular protests against his attempt to introduce a consumption tax after the election.[4] In addition, although Nakasone's policies enhanced his per-

---

[4] The emergence of tax reform as a major issue threw the debate over neo-conservative economic policies into utter confusion. As Prime Minister Nakasone stated explicitly, reform of the consumption tax was initially designed to relieve the burden on employees, who were treated unfairly under a tax system that was skewed in favor of farmers and the self-employed. In other words, lawmakers sought to promote the interests of the new middle class and urban housewives. The consumption tax issue ran into unexpectedly staunch resistance from the very groups it was intended to benefit, however. One reason was MOF's

sonal popularity, they did not translate into greater long-term support for the LDP for several reasons (Kawato 1988).

First, modeled after American neo-conservatism, Nakasone's policies were too difficult to understand to exert a significant impact on the Japanese public (see Carmines and Stimson 1982). In the security arena, for example, the existing cleavage was not only relatively easy for voters to comprehend, but 40 years of conflict over the issue had led to widespread recognition of the relevant questions. Because the issue of whether or not Japan should assume a more activist role in international politics did not arise in the context of a major crisis, it could not radically alter the existing conservative-progressive cleavage, at least in the short term.

Similarly, neo-conservative economic ideas did not resonate well with voters, at least initially. Administrative reform in Japan meant not the reform of the governmental apparatus itself, but policies ranging from deregulation, which was expected to curb private-sector cartels, to the reform of welfare policies, particularly medical care and pensions. Whether the electorate understood this is unclear, however. For example, when voters were surveyed in 1983 as to whether they agreed with the statements "Small government is desirable, even if it accompanies a decline in the quality of government services" and "Pensions and medical care for the elderly should be expanded," the largest proportion of voters responded, "Don't know." The pattern of responses was almost the same among supporters of conservative and progressive parties (Miyake 1995; Kabashima and Takenaka 1996, 255–56). Even more surprising, many voters responded affirmatively to *both* questions, raising doubts about their understanding of these issues. One can argue that Japanese voters believed that liberalization was necessary not because of the appeal of neo-conservativism, but because they distrusted bureaucrats. Economic neo-conservatism alone was insufficient to motivate far-reaching reforms.

Second, the LDP's efforts to push neo-conservative ideas, especially in the economic area, were half-hearted. Even Nakasone was unprepared to abandon farmers and small shopowners, who constituted the LDP's traditional base of support. Other LDP Diet members were even less enthusiastic about such a shift, so Nakasone held back from his attempts to expand support among the urban new middle class.

---

failure to conceal its long-term ambition for expanding the overall tax base, but a more important reason was the widespread skepticism of the urban salaried class and housewives toward the government. For this reason, the consumption tax issue, like public outrage against political scandals, has merely served as a vehicle for voters to articulate their general lack of confidence in government and professional politicians. As a result, political scandals and the cleavage between political amateurs and professionals became the primary factor determining party support and the background to political reform during the 1990s.

For economic neo-conservatism to influence voting behavior, voters must give priority to their interests as consumers and taxpayers. On the whole, however, Japan's socio-economic culture and institutions are not conducive to neo-conservative reforms. In particular, because "lifetime" employment has been an entrenched practice and unemployment insurance provides inadequate benefits, voters have an aversion to layoffs and bankruptcies. They tend to support policies that promote the interests of producers over those of consumers and taxpayers. In addition, the fact that administrative reforms were instituted during a period in which the Japanese economy was outperforming those of other advanced industrial economies reduced the urgency of introducing reforms of the agricultural and distribution sectors drastic enough to increase unemployment and bankruptcy. Economic reforms had emerged on the political agenda during the early 1980s in reaction to a fiscal crisis; with administrative reform seeming to succeed to some extent and the bubble economy (1987–90) improving the government's fiscal balance, the perceived need for reform subsided.

NEO-CONSERVATIVE ATTEMPTS TO MOBILIZE NEW CLEAVAGES IN THE 1990s

Beginning in 1988, successive money scandals among politicians returned the interest group politics versus clean politics cleavage to center stage. This cleavage became the primary factor for determining party support until the passage of political reforms in 1994. It was not until then, after a ten-year hiatus, that the debate over neo-conservatism reemerged. It was within this context that the Renewal Party and the JNP, led by Ichirō Ozawa and Morihiro Hosokawa respectively, were formed.

Ozawa and the Renewal Party

From the late 1980s Ichirō Ozawa moved through a series of key posts within the LDP including secretary general, the party's chief electoral strategist. Among other things, Ozawa assumed responsibility for managing trade frictions with the United States and preparing Japan's response to the Gulf War. These experiences shaped his proposals for a fundamental recasting of the political system in the 1990s.

As his plans to form a new party took shape, the centerpiece of Ozawa's strategy was to use reform of the electoral system to replace the LDP's one-party dominance with a two-party system comprised of the LDP and a new, neo-conservative party. He sought to replace Japan's multimember electoral districts with single-seat districts for three reasons. First, they would weaken the JSP. Second, single-seat districts were thought to encourage electoral competition on the basis of policy differences, enabling voters to choose between reform and the status quo. Third, Ozawa thought that the introduction of British-style party politics to Japan would insulate party leaders from backbenchers, who were the primary conduit for directing pork-barrel benefits to parochial and functional interests, and strengthen political leaders' hand in the policy-making process.[5] Ozawa aimed to reinforce this shift in electoral politics by means of a major reapportionment of Diet seats that would reduce the weight of agricultural districts. By abolishing the system of parochial and functional representation that had developed behind the existing conservative-progressive cleavage, Ozawa hoped to replace that cleavage with the neo-conservative issue of small versus big government.

With the eruption of successive political funding scandals, Ozawa's proposals to introduce policy-oriented, party-centered political competition by means of electoral reform came to win widespread support from the mass media, intellectuals, big business leaders, and private-sector union leaders.[6] When Hosokawa's JNP achieved a great electoral success (the history of that party will be examined below) and the Socialists fared poorly in 1993, political realignment seemed to be unfolding in accordance with Ozawa's blueprint. As for the LDP, if it had not returned to power in coalition with the JSP and New Party Sakigake in 1994, it is unlikely the party would have recovered; the party probably would have experienced a second breakup.[7]

In the meantime the New Frontier Party (NFP), which Ozawa pieced together in 1995 out of the Renewal Party, the JNP, the CGP, and the Democratic Socialist Party, failed to convert the support previously enjoyed by these parties, which was motivated primarily by hopes for political reform, into support for a neo-conservative agenda. Although Ozawa

---

[5] Until 1994 representatives to the Lower House of the Diet were elected from multi-member districts with three to five seats. Each citizen had a single, nontransferable vote. The new system consists of two types of electoral districts, with each citizen casting two votes. There are now 300 small, single-member districts, and 11 regional districts in which parties compete for a total of 200 seats awarded on the basis of proportional representation.

[6] Although Ozawa and leftist intellectuals agreed on the need to introduce a two-party system to Japan, most of these intellectuals envisioned a two-party system in which the LDP would alternate in power with the JSP, not a neo-conservative party, as Ozawa hoped. Intellectuals had long hoped that a coalition of the JSP, CGP, and Democratic Socialists would replace the LDP, and the landslide JSP victory in 1989 revived intellectuals' hopes of putting the JSP in power. The JSP suffered a severe setback in the general elections of 1993, however.

[7] Many Sakigake Diet members have admitted to this author that the LDP-JSP coalition they played a major role in forging constituted a fatal error in strategy. They, as well as most JSP Diet members, overestimated the power of Ozawa and underestimated that of the LDP.

was successful in stimulating a reshuffling of Diet members among political parties, he accomplished little realignment on the level of the electorate, and the LDP's return to power in 1994 was accompanied by the return of traditional pork-barrel politics. Why did Ozawa's strategy fail? The essence of the problem lay in an electoral strategy that alienated the middle-class voters he was trying to reach. To win seats the NFP had no choice but to turn to established organizations: the campaign organizations (*kōenkai*) of individual Diet members, the Sōka Gakkai (a powerful Buddhist sect that had supported the CGP), and private-sector labor unions (the power base of the Democratic Socialists). Many Diet members who had belonged to the Renewal Party relied on *kōenkai* and local interest groups, and a significant proportion of them represented rural districts. Because they had joined the Renewal Party as a result of personal and factional ties with Ozawa (Ōtake 1996b, 289) rather than because they sympathized with his policies or represented urban or suburban constituencies, many of them could not afford to run on a neo-conservative economic platform. Thus, the NFP failed to project a fresh image among voters, who viewed it as nothing more than a coalition of existing political parties (which it was). Another reason for the failure of the NFP to win popular support for its neo-conservatism was Ozawa's unwillingness to present his policy platform directly to the electorate with the kind of grassroots campaigning that Nakasone had done so effectively. His ultimate goal has been to institutionalize a centralized political party that would insulate party leaders from the pressures of particularistic interest; he has shown little interest in trying to capture voters' imagination.

The Hosokawa and Hata cabinets (1993–94) behind which Ozawa stood did advance the neo-conservative agenda to some degree with partial liberalization of the Japanese rice market. Toward the end of the Hosokawa administration the cabinet also announced its intention to launch another round of administrative reform, including reform of ineffective semipublic corporations (*tokushu hōjin*) and a push for Japan to become a permanent member of the UN Security Council. There is no evidence that Japanese voters were particularly impressed with these policy initiatives, however, and an ambitious proposal for tax reform failed to win support. The majority of Japanese voters remained skeptical of the need to promote consumers' and taxpayers' interests at the expense of producers' interests, and politicians lacked both the will and ability to change the prevailing attitude.

Hosokawa and the Japan New Party

Morihiro Hosokawa formed the JNP around the same time that Ozawa formed the Renewal Party. What is important to note about the JNP was that there was a major gap between voters' expectations and the reforms Hosokawa hoped to accomplish.

Following the party's founding in May 1992, Hosokawa quickly became the darling of the mass media and came to enjoy nationwide popularity. In March 1993 the JNP's popularity rating rose to nearly 10 percent, placing it third behind the LDP and the Socialists. Despite severe difficulties in recruiting candidates,[8] the JNP won 36 seats in its first bid in the Lower House elections of 1993 (including 17 first-place winners). The JNP performed particularly well in urban districts. In these respects the JNP's early history closely resembled that of the New Liberal Club. The JNP derived its support from voters' distrust of existing parties and political professionals. In addition, with his urban lifestyle and carefree attitude, Hosokawa was adept at projecting an amateurish image.

Drafted with the help of neo-conservative intellectuals who had been part of Nakasone's brain trust, the JNP's policy platform included reform of collusive relationships between the central ministries and industries by means of decentralization, the promotion of consumer interests by means of deregulation, and the opening of Japanese markets to foreign competition. Particularly significant was Hosokawa's advocacy of liberalization of Japan's rice market, which had hitherto been a taboo subject. Hosokawa was also explicitly neo-conservative in his foreign and defense policies: he espoused the creation of a permanent UN military force, Japan's participation in that force, and greater Japanese participation in peace-keeping operations. Nevertheless, the JNP lost support within six months of Hosokawa's rise to prime minister, and he was forced to join forces with Ozawa, the CGP, and the Democratic Socialists. The party's neo-conservative policies simply did not appeal to voters. Furthermore, the party's efforts at realignment were short-circuited when personal scandal prompted Hosokawa to resign in 1994.

The failures of the NLC, Ozawa, and Hosokawa are illustrative of the difficulty of overturning a historically rooted political cleavage. It is no easy task to make the average voter understand that a party is offering a new cleavage. To interpret its platform accurately, the voter must know a great deal about both the issues in question and the ability of the party to accomplish its policies (Miyake 1985, 204). It might have been easier for voters to comprehend their policies had the new parties chosen to iden-

---

[8] The JNP encountered the same difficulty as the NLC and Doi's JSP in that it could not recruit an adequate supply of attractive, politically talented candidates. Like the NLC, it ended up with candidates recruited from the usual pool of aspiring politicians, many of whom had failed to win the endorsement of the LDP or had lost in previous elections. This proved to be fatal to the JNP when Hosokawa was forced to retire from the premiership. No other Diet members could replace him as the JNP's leader and retain voter support for the party.

tify themselves along the existing conservative-progressive cleavage over defense policy, but both the JNP and the Renewal Party sought to introduce the completely different issue axes of small versus big government and Japan's making an active versus passive contribution to international politics. Although national elites, who saw Japan's position from an international perspective, considered administrative and economic reforms to be crucial issues for the country's future, they were not necessarily regarded as urgent issues by the population at large.

According to Carmines and Stimson (1989), the recent political realignment in the United States has not only unfolded along an issue that is relatively easy for voters to comprehend, namely race, but it has also involved only existing political parties. For a new party to spark a major political realignment along a completely novel issue axis, as the JNP and Renewal Party attempted to do, is far more difficult. Given the JNP's and the Renewal Party's need to enlist the support of the Japanese urban new middle class, which is known for the fickleness of its political sympathies, these parties' efforts were almost doomed from the start. It is unclear what percentage of voters ever recognized that the Renewal Party, the JNP, and the NFP stood for neo-conservatism (Kabashima 1998, 173–77), and even if they had, it is unclear what percentage of them would have supported the parties on the basis of their ideological positions. The same can be said of New Party Sakigake, which described itself as a "third pole" or "liberal."[9]

---

[9] Although the hostility of the party founder Masayoshi Takemura and his followers toward Ozawa was a strong motivation for founding the New Party Sakigake, it is doubtful whether they seriously sought to propose an original policy program. They championed the single issue of political reform, and following the passage of electoral reform, the New Party Sakigake found itself without a raison d'être. This is ironic given that the party had called for elections that would revolve around political parties and their platforms.

The New Party Sakigake was thus reduced to identifying itself along the existing conservative-progressive cleavage and advocating backward-looking policies such as a Diet resolution that would explicitly renounce Japan's past aggression and wartime crimes and opposition to its assuming a permanent seat on the UN Security Council. Together with the JSP, Sakigake attacked Ozawa's proposals for a larger Japanese role in international affairs as a prelude to its becoming a military superpower. It treated neo-conservatism like traditional, nationalistic conservatism and tried to rouse opposition to Ozawa and his allies. This strategy was effective because the old conservative-progressive cleavage still wielded substantial symbolic power over politicians and party activists, if not the electorate in general. In addition, this strategy was conducive to Sakigake's alliance with the JSP (which had also been put on the defensive) and to its participation in a coalition government with the JSP and the LDP (which, under Yōhei Kōno's leadership, at least temporarily presented itself as a dovish party) against Ozawa's NFP. In terms of its goal of distinguishing the Sakigake's platform from that of other parties, its participation in the new coalition backfired, however. There were few policy areas left in which Sakigake could distinguish itself from the JSP and the LDP.

The New Party Sakigake had another opportunity to present a bold policy initiative with

CONCLUSION

In the first decades of the postwar era Japan had a highly polarized political system like that of France and Italy, and the chief issues put before voters were legacies of prewar fascism, World War II, and the Cold War security arrangements that grew out of the Occupation. Although a new middle class was gradually alienated from the left as it increasingly focused on the interests of organized workers, these middle-class voters failed to shift their allegiance to a succession of new parties that began to emerge in the mid-1970s. Thus, political failure in Japan as reflected in party dealignment ultimately rests on the failure of voters to reward political entrepreneurs who have sought to realign party competition around new policy axes. The result has been continuing low levels of confidence in government that have dropped still lower since 1993.

Political leaders obviously bear a share of responsibility for this failure.

---

the founding of the Democratic Party in 1996. Most Sakigake members joined, and they recruited many JSP representatives as well. They tried to establish themselves as a third pole distinct from the LDP and NFP, implicitly refusing to situate themselves in the center of the old conservative-progressive spectrum, but former Sakigake Diet members' attempt to infuse content into the "liberalism" they espoused ended in failure once again. Rather than presenting a specific policy program, the newly formed Democratic Party seemed to emphasize form over substance. Members were more concerned with criticizing their former leaders, particularly Takemura and the JSP's Murayama, and with giving the new party a youthful image. They also sought, once again, to project the image of amateurs through the new party's two leaders, Yukio Hatoyama and Naoto Kan. Kan personified anti-bureaucratic sentiment in Japan thanks to his handling of the AIDS question. Then a member of Sakigake, he joined the first Hashimoto coalition government as Minister of Health and Welfare. By dint of strenuous effort, he revealed ministry officials' responsibility for allowing doctors to continue using unheated blood products contaminated by the HIV virus to treat hemophiliacs even after research in the United States revealed the danger, and for deliberately withholding documents that revealed that (non-) decision when patients and their families demanded an investigation. Thanks to his solving this scandalous crime on the part of his own ministry, Kan suddenly became a national hero.

The Democrats owed their unexpected gains in the 1998 Upper House election to their anti-professional image and voters' dissatisfaction with the Hashimoto cabinet's mismanagement of the economy. Rather than offering a clear-cut policy package, the Democratic Party presented itself as the "citizens'" party, just as Jimmy Carter and Ronald Reagan had presented themselves as candidates of the "common people" against the Washington Establishment. As one of the founders of the Social Democratic League in 1976, Kan had particularly strong ties with citizens' movements and advocated decentralization and direct participation. It should be noted that the NLC also used the word *citizen* often. Hatoyama, as well as Kan, frequently used that word when they jointly founded the Democratic Party in 1996. It remains to be seen whether this party will avoid the fatal path of its predecessors by consolidating its position on a new axis of policy conflict, or if it will succeed in attracting voters without any coherent policy package by simply presenting itself as a more capable and accountable alternative to LDP rule.

They have been reluctant to abandon the patronage politics that middle-class voters reject, and they have lacked finesse and courage in presenting neo-conservative alternatives. Economic prescriptions like deregulation, liberalization, and the restructuring of welfare have been unfamiliar and difficult to comprehend for average, or even conscientious, Japanese voters, and political entrepreneurs have failed to get these policies across. Believing that only catch-all parties could win broad-based support and look responsible enough to govern, the new parties' leaders rarely took their neo-conservative agenda directly to the people. In addition, many of the new parties held back from presenting their programs in a clear-cut way for fear of alienating powerful political groups like farmers whose interests conflict with those of the new middle class.

But voters also deserve much of the blame. First, middle-class voters were for the most part too satisfied with their lives to be seriously interested in politics except during short periods dominated by large-scale scandals. Second, voters have not tried very hard to understand novel, "hard" issues even when new parties put those issues before them, as did the JNP. Finally, these middle-class voters' anti-establishment attitudes, their disdain for serious issues, and their preference for political amateurs have made it possible for new political parties to win initial support, but not to sustain it.

Thus, the new parties all failed to gain and stabilize electoral support on the basis of novel policy packages. The traditional left-right axis has remained, clouding policy conflicts and driving many citizens away from politics, particularly young people and the educated urban middle class. This appears to have resulted in the reemergence and entrenchment of the very mechanism of voter mobilization that reformers have attempted to uproot, namely the distribution of patronage to farmers, construction companies, and other occupational and regional groups. One-party dominance by the LDP has been revived and looks likely to continue for the foreseeable future. The nearly 50 percent of the Japanese electorate that supports no party and stays away from the polls poses a threat to stable LDP dominance, however. The party's severe defeat in the Upper House election of 1998, in which "nonvoters" suddenly went to the polls and, without agreeing on a clear alternative, cast their ballots against the LDP, seems to confirm this diagnosis.

In an era of deep recession it is, of course, possible that Japanese will become less satisfied with their lives and that dealigned voters will get more interested in politics. New political entrepreneurs, including the present leadership of the young Democratic Party, may overcome the obstacles described above and become more courageous and skillful at consolidating protest votes into support for their parties and putting across a new political agenda. It is perplexing and ironic that a dim economic future might be indispensable for the healthy development of democracy in Japan.[10]

[10] The experience of most other nations indicates that poor economic performance reduces confidence in government and, by implication, political parties (Nye et al. 1997). Thus, a more serious crisis in the Japanese economy might lead to further drops in confidence and voter turnout.

Ralf Dahrendorf

IT APPEARS that democracy is always in crisis. Twenty-five years before the present volume, in 1975, the Trilateral Commission published a report on its Kyoto Conference entitled *The Crisis of Democracy*. (In the appendix to that volume I raised a few sympathetic but skeptical questions about that crisis.) Thirty-five years before that, Harold Laski described the democratic crisis vividly in his *Reflections on the Revolution of Our Time*. In fact, the topic is of classical parentage. Tocqueville's ambivalence toward what he called democracy was coupled with the hope that it would not last. And Aristotle, of course, the father of all such theories, regarded democracy as intrinsically unstable and therefore preferred a polity that mixes democratic and oligarchic elements. So what is new today?

The contributors to the present volume provide numerous answers to this question. I want to offer five comments—no more than footnotes—to stimulate further debate. First, democracy was probably at its best when democratization itself was at issue. Where democracy still must be fought for, this is still the case.

This statement might appear to use language loosely. If by democracy we understand the institutional arrangement that regulates underlying sociopolitical conflicts peacefully and permits the removal of governments without violence, this is in principle applicable at all times. But democratic institutions are most effective when the underlying conflicts concern the extension of basic civil and political rights and the social conditions that lend substance to these rights. The demand for citizenship rights and the defense of privilege lead two parties to clash in the political arena and to accelerate—or retard—change. Once citizenship rights have become general, conflicts become more diffuse, and democracy works less well. Representative government is no longer as compelling a proposition as it once was. Instead, a search for new institutional forms to express conflicts of interest has begun.

Second, political democracy is historically, and perhaps institutionally, linked to the nation-state. Thus, democracy itself is at risk to the extent that the nation-state loses significance.

At the end of the twentieth century the nation-state is under double pressure. New demands for decentralization tend to create allegedly more homogeneous regional entities. Although this may be an understandable reaction to the remoteness of government, it also involves new dangers. Not all nation-states were ethnically or culturally heterogenous, but the great democracies were; democracy provided a framework for making heterogeneity fruitful for all. Homogeneous nations not only attract authoritarian leaders but also tend to become less tolerant within and more aggressive without. Thus, defenders of democracy do well to remain cautious of regionalism.

The more evident risk, however, is posed by internationalization. For the moment, at least, any issue that is removed from the nation-state to an international level is by the same token removed from democratic accountability. Attempts to democratize international decision-making (e.g., the Parliamentary Assembly of NATO) have failed. Even in the case of the supranational institutions of the European Union, democratic accountability remains rudimentary. Thus, in the face of increasing internationalization, one of our most urgent tasks is to devise institutions that apply democratic principles to wider political domains. These institutions probably will not copy those of nation-states; they are more likely to involve auditing and legal controls than elected bodies.

Third, aside from the effect of internationalization, national governments in even traditional democracies tend to try and bypass parliament. There is what might be called a creeping authoritarianism about.

This is a curious development that has to do with the complexities of government, the need for expertise, and the as yet undefined role of media in the democratic process. Ostensibly nonpolitical institutions are more acceptable to many citizens than explicitly political, especially party-political, ones. There is consequently much support for independent central banks and for increasing the decision-making role of the judiciary. At the same time there is little resistance to the creation of ever more "quangos," or organizations that look nongovernmental while in fact serving governmental functions. And governments like to introduce "skeleton laws" that reserve many powers to ministers rather than parliament.

The deliberative function of parliaments is much reduced, and they are often replaced by less obviously democratic mechanisms. Opinion polls everywhere play a major role in government decision-making; some governments trust focus groups more than parliaments. Then there is the influence of the media, not so much on public opinion as on governments' perception of public opinion. Because they devalue the traditional institutions of democracy, all these trends need to be deplored or reversed, but no new mechanisms have been found to control ostensibly independent bodies, rein in quangos, and channel vague expressions of public opinion.

Fourth, public apathy, the apparent unreadiness of many citizens to exercise their rights, poses a new and puzzling threat to democracy.

Democracy as defined here can also be described as a process of trial and error. Political projects are implemented for a time. They can be discontinued if they are found wanting or when their energies are spent. Defenders of some alternative project are voted into office. By allowing trial and error (it is hoped), the progress of human life chances is made possible if not certain.

But this process works only if people are prepared to try and to acknowledge their errors; it presupposes active citizens. On the basis of the long battle for democracy, democratic theorists have often assumed that people are naturally active. When basic civil rights were at stake and privilege was ruthlessly defended, it did not take much to mobilize either side. (This was true in Europe and North America, at least. China is a different case, and the debate over democracy in Hong Kong highlights the difficulty of mobilizing people who are ready to get on with their private affairs.) Nowadays many citizens are tired of what they regard as the democratic game. They shun participation and thereby strengthen the powers that be. Inactivity at the bottom represents the flip side of creeping authoritarianism at the top, and it strengthens that trend.

Fifth, a certain erosion of civil society has robbed democracy of its social base. Rebuilding civil society may therefore be the first step of democratic reform.

Several trends have combined to weaken strong, autonomous civil societies. The transformation of social conflicts into individual competition is arguably the most important one. This is in part the result of democracy's success in overcoming class-based party struggles; generalized citizenship rights are individual rights. Individual competition is also the hallmark of globalization. Such trends entail that representative democratic government based on essentially two political parties or camps no longer works. They also affect the sense of social cohesion that is often a precondition of traditional theories of democracy.

Rebuilding civil society is a difficult process, as the new democracies of the post-communist world in particular are discovering. After all, it should not be governments that produce their own counterfoil. Civil societies need not be anti-government, but they are certainly nongovernmental. They are above all separate from *central* governments. Building them may include the creation of strong local government. It also involves the growth of small businesses. A vigorous "third sector" of foundations, charities, voluntary, and volunteering bodies is important. Generally, neighborhood initiatives and associations have to be formed. Although we do not know yet what the main forces of social cohesion in tomorrow's society will be, we do know that free societies have to not only create wealth, but also maintain solidarity.

This is a considerable agenda. The Trilateral perspective adopted here has a crucial implication: there is more than one answer to the questions raised in this volume. We must not be dogmatic about either the Chicago model in economic matters or the Westminster model in political matters. An open society recognizes many different answers, and there is space for cultural variety and diverse institutional inspirations. This is why we may hope that the troubles facing contemporary democracies can be remedied—although new troubles will doubtless be discovered 25 years hence.

The Major Cross-National Opinion Surveys

Russell J. Dalton

MANY OF THE CHAPTERS in this volume present public opinion data measuring political support in one or more of the Trilateral democracies. There are several major data resources that many of the authors utilize, and I briefly describe these studies here.

In qualitative terms the most reliable and extensive data series are often derived from national election study series conducted by independent research teams in each nation (see Dalton 1999). The American National Election Studies, for example, have been conducted at each national election since 1952; extensive national series also exist for Britain, Denmark, the Netherlands, Sweden, West Germany, and several other Trilateral democracies. These surveys tend to use rigorous sampling procedures, in-person interviews, and demanding quality control measures. These studies also generally cover a long time period and include extensive measures of political support and political attitudes. In most nations the most definitive evidence of long-term changes in political support come from the national election studies series. The limitation of these surveys is that their content is generally not directly comparable across nations because the surveys are designed and executed by independent national research teams.

More recently, several large research projects have conducted coordinated, cross-national surveys in many nations. The most established is the series of Eurobarometer surveys conducted by the Commission of the European Community. The Eurobarometer series has expanded from ad hoc surveys of the six European Economic Community member states in the early 1970s to semiannual surveys of all member states of the European Union. In addition the World Values Study Group founded a cross-national data collection that has now assembled three waves of data on public values, with the most recent surveys boasting a near-global coverage. These cross-national surveys provide an extremely valuable research resource for comparative research. At the same time the quality of the sampling and survey procedures tends to be more variable in the World Values Surveys, especially for the less affluent and less democratic societies. This appendix describes these cross-national surveys in more detail. Most of these data are available for analysis from:

Inter-university Consortium for Political and Social Research
Box 1248
University of Michigan
Ann Arbor, MI 48106.

These data are also available from national archives at the University of Cologne, the University of Essex, and several other national social science archives.

THE EUROBAROMETER SURVEY SERIES

These surveys are the products of a unique program of cross-national and cross-temporal social science research. The effort began in early 1970s, when the Commission of the European Community sponsored simultaneous surveys of the publics of the European Community. These surveys measured public attitudes toward the Common Market and other European Community institutions and compared the attitudes of Europeans on social and political issues. These themes were repeated in a survey of the nine nations of the European Community countries in September 1973. In 1974 the commission launched the Eurobarometer series to provide a regular monitoring of the social and political attitudes of the publics of the member-nations: Belgium, Britain, Denmark, France, Ireland, Italy, Luxembourg, the Netherlands, and West Germany. The Eurobarometers are carried out in the spring and fall of each year. In addition to obtaining regular readings of support for European integration, the survey compares European attitudes on a variety of special issues of relevance to the Community and its policies. The Eurobarometer surveys expanded to include Greece in autumn 1980, Portugal and Spain in autumn 1985, the former German Democratic Republic in autumn 1990, Norway in autumn of 1991, Finland in spring 1993, and Sweden and Austria in autumn 1994. In the 1990s the European Union has also commissioned a series of surveys in Central and Eastern Europe, several "flash" surveys of current affairs topics, and a new survey of European social and political elites. These surveys are routinely conducted by commercial polling firms such as Gallup affiliates, which use acceptable sampling methodology and quality control. The Eurobarometers represent the largest coordinated, cross-national data collection in the Trilateral democracies and are unique in their cross-national breadth and cross-temporal length. As of January 2000 the European Union will have conducted more than 50 Eurobarometer surveys. The individual Eurobarometer surveys are available from the ICPSR and several other national archives.

THE 1981–83 WORLD VALUES SURVEY

In 1981–83 the World Values Study Group conducted a coordinated survey of the adult population in 22 societies: Australia, Belgium, Britain, Canada, Denmark, Finland, France, Hungary, Iceland, Ireland, Italy, Japan, Mexico, the Netherlands, Norway, South Africa, South Korea, the Soviet Union, Spain, Sweden, the United States, and West Germany. The survey focused on public value preferences and the correlates of these values. Among the topics covered are attitudes toward leisure, work, family life, and moral issues. The survey also includes measures of confidence in social and political institutions and participation in unconventional political activity. These data are available from the Inter-university Consortium for Political and Social Research at the University of Michigan (ICPSR Study Number 9309).

THE 1990–93 WORLD VALUES SURVEY

The World Values Study Group replicated and expanded the survey initially conducted in 1981–83. The new survey includes national surveys in 41 societies representing almost 70 percent of the world's population: Argentina, Austria, Belarus, Belgium, Brazil, Britain, Bulgaria, Canada, Chile, China, Czechoslovakia, Denmark, Estonia, Finland, France, Germany (East and West), Hungary, Iceland, India, Ireland, Italy, Japan, South Korea, Latvia, Lithuania, Mexico, the Netherlands, Nigeria, Norway, Poland, Portugal, Russia, Romania, Slovenia, South Africa, Spain, Sweden, Switzerland, Turkey, and the United States. This study is especially valuable because it includes comparative data from many newly democratizing nations in Eastern Europe and from several less-developed nations. The themes of the survey generally replicate the content of the 1981–83 World Values survey; additional questions deal with environmental quality, policy priorities, and group activity. The principal investigators note that the surveys in the Trilateral democracies are conducted by established and reputable survey firms, but many of the surveys in the newly democratizing nations are conducted without firm sampling procedures or well-established survey firms. These data are available from the Inter-university Consortium for Political and Social Research at the University of Michigan (ICPSR Study Number 6160).

THE 1995–98 WORLD VALUES SURVEY

The third wave of the World Values Survey was coordinated by Ronald Inglehart, Hans-Dieter Klingemann, and a consortium of national research teams. This wave of the survey includes data from at least 43 nations with an extremely broad international scope: Argentina, Armenia, Australia, Azerbaijan, Belarus, Brazil, Bulgaria, Chile, China, Croatia, the Dominican Republic, Estonia, Finland, Georgia, Germany, Ghana, India, Japan, Latvia, Lithuania, Mexico, Moldova, Montenegro, Nigeria, Norway, Peru, the Philippines, Poland, Romania, Russia, Serbia, Slovenia, South Africa, South Korea, Spain, Sweden, Switzerland, Taiwan, Turkey, Ukraine, the United States, Uruguay, and Venezuela. In addition to the themes of public and social values, which are replicated from the earlier surveys, the 1995–98 World Values Survey emphasizes attitudes toward democracy and environmental attitudes and includes a broader range of political attitudes. These data should be available from the Inter-university Consortium for Political and Social Research by January 2000.

Bibliography

Aarts, Kees. 1995. "Intermediate Organizations and Interest Representation." In *Citizens and the State*, ed. Hans-Dieter Klingemann and Dieter Fuchs. Oxford: Oxford University Press.

Abe, Hitoshi, Muneyuki Shindo, and Sadafumi Kawato. 1994. *The Government and Politics of Japan.* Trans. James W. White. Tokyo: University of Tokyo Press.

Adams, Michael, and Mary Jane Lennon. 1992. "Canadians, Too, Fault Their Political Institutions and Leaders." *Public Perspective* 3:6–21.

The Adjustment of National Employment and Social Policy to Economic Internationalization: Adjustment Data Set. 1988. Cologne: Max Planck Institute for the Study of Societies.

Akiyama, Toyoko. 1980. "Seikatsu no manzokukan [Satisfaction with Life]." In *Daini Nihonjin no ishiki* [Consciousness of the Japanese, 2nd ed.], ed. Nihon Hōsōkyōkai Seronchōsa Kenkyūjo. Tokyo: Shiseidō.

Aldrich, John. 1995. *Why Parties? The Origin and Transformation of Political Parties in America.* Chicago: University of Chicago Press.

Alesina, Alberto, Reza Baqir, and William Easterly. 1997a. "Public Goods and Ethnic Divisions." *National Bureau of Economic Research Working Paper* no. 6009, May.

Alesina, Alberto, Reza Baqir, and William Easterly. 1997b. "Redistributive Public Employment." Harvard University. Typescript.

Alesina, Alberto, Roberto Perotti, and José Tavares. 1998. "The Political Economy of Fiscal Adjustments." *Brookings Papers on Economic Activity* 1:197–248.

Alesina, Alberto, and Dani Rodrik. 1994. "Distributive Politics and Economic Growth." *Quarterly Journal of Economics* 109(2):465–90.

Alesina, Alberto, and Howard Rosenthal. 1995. *Partisan Politics, Divided Government and the Economy.* New York: Cambridge University Press.

Alesina, Alberto, Nouriel Roubini, and Gerald Cohen. 1997. *Political Cycles and the Macroeconomy.* Cambridge, Mass.: MIT Press.

Alesina, Alberto, Enrico Spolaore, and Romain Wacziarg. 1997. "Economic Integration and Political Disintegration." *National Bureau of Economic Research Working Paper* no. 6163, September.

Alesina, Alberto, and Romain Wacziarg. 1998. "Is Europe Going Too Far?" Carnegie Rochester Conference Series on Public Policy.

Allinson, Gary D., and Yasunori Sone, eds. 1993. *Political Dynamics in Contemporary Japan.* Ithaca: Cornell University Press.

Allport, Gordon W. 1961. *Pattern and Growth in Personality.* New York: Holt, Rinehart and Winston.

Almond, Gabriel A., and Sidney Verba. 1963. *The Civic Culture: Political Attitudes and Democracy in Five Nations.* Princeton: Princeton University Press.

Almond, Gabriel A., and Sidney Verba, eds. 1980. *The Civic Culture Revisited*. Boston: Little Brown.

Andeweg, Rudy. 1982. *Dutch Voters Adrift*. Leiden: University of Leiden.

Ansolabehere, Stephen, and Shanto Iyengar. 1995. *Going Negative: How Attack Ads Shrink and Polarize the Electorate*. New York: Free Press.

Ardener, Shirley. 1964. "The Comparative Study of Rotating Credit Institutes." *Journal of the Royal Anthropological Association of Great Britain and Ireland* 94:201–29.

Aron, Raymond. 1954. *The Century of Total War*. Garden City, N.Y.: Doubleday.

Arrow, Kenneth J. [1951] 1963. *Social Choice and Individual Values*. Reprint. New Haven: Yale University Press.

Asahi Shimbun. 1998. *Japanese Almanac*. Tokyo: Asahi Shimbun.

Asahi Shimbun. 1999. *Japanese Almanac*. Tokyo: Asahi Shimbun.

Bairoch, Paul. 1997. "Globalization Myths and Realities: One Century of External Trade and Foreign Investment." In *States against Markets: The Limits of Globalization*, ed. Robert Boyer and Daniel Drache. London: Routledge.

Baker, Kendall, Russell Dalton, and Kai Hildebrandt. 1981. *Germany Transformed: Political Culture and the New Politics*. Cambridge, Mass.: Harvard University Press.

Barber, Bernard. 1983. *The Logic and Limits of Trust*. New Brunswick, N.J.: Rutgers University Press.

Barnes, Samuel H., Max Kaase, and Klaus R. Allerbeck. 1979. *Political Action: Mass Participation in Five Western Democracies*. Beverly Hills: Sage.

Barr, Stephen. 1998. "Gore's Team Turns to Making Reinvention Deliver." *Washington Post*, March 3:A15.

Barro, Robert. 1990. "Government Spending in a Simple Model of Endogenous Growth." *Journal of Political Economy* 98(5):103–25.

Beck, J. P., and M. W. Maher. 1986. "A Comparison of Bribery and Bidding in Thin Markets." *Economic Letters* 20:1–5.

Becker, Gary S. [1964] 1975. *Human Capital: A Theoretical and Empirical Analysis, with Special Reference to Education*. Reprint. New York: Columbia University Press.

Becquart-Leclercq, Jeanne. 1989. "Paradoxes of Political Corruption: A French View." In *Political Corruption: A Handbook*, ed. Arnold J. Heidenheimer, Michael Johnston, and V. T. LeVine. New Brunswick, N.J.: Transaction.

Bellah, Robert N., Richard Madsen, William M. Sullivan, Ann Swidler, and Steven M. Tipton. 1985. *Habits of the Heart: Individualism and Commitment in American Life*. Berkeley: University of California Press.

Bennett, Stephen Earl, and Linda L. M. Bennett. 1993. "Out of Sight, Out of Mind: Americans' Knowledge of Party Control of the House of Representatives, 1960–1984." *Political Research Quarterly* 46:67–80.

Bennett, W. Lance. 1998. "The UnCivic Culture: Communication, Identity, and the Rise of Lifestyle Politics." *PS: Political Science and Politics* 31:741–62.

Berger, Suzanne, and Ronald Dore, eds. 1996. *National Diversity and Global Capitalism*. Ithaca: Cornell University Press.

Berman, Sheri. 1997. "Civil Society and Political Institutionalization." *American Behavioral Scientist* 40:562–74.

Bianco, William T. 1994. *Trust: Representatives and Constituents*. Ann Arbor: University of Michigan Press.

Biorcio, Roberto, and Renato Mannheimer. 1995. "The Relationship between Citizens and Political Parties." In *Citizens and the State*, ed. Hans-Dieter Klingemann and Dieter Fuchs. Oxford: Oxford University Press.

Black, Duncan. 1956. *The Theory of Committees and Elections*. Cambridge: Cambridge University Press.

Blendon, Robert, John M. Benson, Richard Morin, Drew E. Altman, Mollyann Brodie, Mario Brossard, and Matt James. 1997. "Changing Attitudes in America." In *Why Americans Mistrust Government*, ed. Joseph Nye Jr., Philip Zelikow, and David King. Cambridge, Mass.: Harvard University Press.

Bobbio, Norberto. 1980. "La democrazia e il potere invisibile" [Democracy and the Invisible Power]. *Rivista Italiana Scienza Politica* 10:181–203.

Boix, Arles, and Daniel N. Posner. 1996. *Making Social Capital Work: A Review of Robert Putnam's "Making Democracy Work."* The Center for International Affairs. Harvard University. Working Paper no. 96–4.

Borg, Sami, and Risto Sänkiaho. 1995. *The Finnish Voter*. Helsinki: Finnish Political Science Association.

Brehm, John, and Wendy Rahn. 1997. "Individual-Level Evidence for the Causes and Consequences of Social Capital." *American Journal of Political Science* 41(3):999–1023.

Brennan, Geoffrey. 1989. "Politics with Romance: Toward a Theory of Democratic Socialism." In *The Good Polity: Normative Analysis of the State*, ed. Alan Hamlin and Philip Pettit. Oxford: Basil Blackwell.

Broder, David S. 1998. "Trust in Government Edges Up." *Washington Post*, March 10: A15.

Bryant, Jennings, and Dolf Zillmann. 1994. *Media Effects*. Hillsdale, N.J.: Lawrence Erlbaum.

Buchanan, James M., and Gordon Tullock. 1962. *The Calculus of Consent: Logical Foundations of Constitutional Democracy*. Ann Arbor: University of Michigan Press.

Burnham, Walter D. 1970. *Critical Elections and the Mainsprings of American Politics*. New York: W. W. Norton.

Burstein, Paul. 1998. "Interest Organizations, Political Parties, and the Study of Democratic Politics." In *Social Movements and American Political Institutions*, ed. Anne Costain and Andrew McFarland. Boulder: Rowman and Littlefield.

Buruma, Ian. 1994. *The Wages of Guilt: Memories of War in Germany and Japan*. New York: Farrar, Straus, and Giroux.

Bush, Evelyn, and Pete Simi. 1999. "Harvesting Contention: European Integration, Supranational Institutions, and Farmers' Protests." Cornell University and University of Nevada at Las Vegas. Typescript.

Bushnell, John. 1990. *Moscow Graffiti: Language and Subculture*. Boston: Unwin Hyman.

Campbell, Angus, Philip Converse, Warren E. Miller, and Donald E. Stokes. 1960. *The American Voter*. New York: Wiley.

Carmines, Edward G., and James A. Stimson. 1982. "Racial Issues and the Structure of Mass Belief Systems." *Journal of Politics* 44:2–20.

Carmines, Edward G., and James A. Stimson. 1989. *Issue Evolution: Race and the Transformation of American Politics*. Princeton: Princeton University Press.

Cartier-Bresson, Jean. 1997. "Les grilles de lecture" [Frames for Reading]. In *Pratiques et controle de la corruption* [The Practices and Control of Corruption], ed. Jean Cartier-Bresson. Paris: Montchrestien.

Cattell, Ramond B. 1965. *The Scientific Analysis of Personality*. Baltimore: Penguin.

Cazzola, Franco. 1988. *Della corruzione* [On Corruption]. Bologna: Il Mulino.

Cazzola, Franco. 1993. "Storia e anatomia della corruzione in Italia" [The History and Anatomy of Corruption in Italy]. *Il Progetto* 13:50–64.

Chevallier, G., and D. Loshak. 1982. *Introduzione alla scienza dell'amministrazione* [An Introduction to Administrative Science]. Rimini: Maggioli.

Citrin, Jack. 1974. "Comment: The Political Relevance of Trust in Government." *American Political Science Review* 68:973–88.

Clarke, Harold D. 1992. *Citizens and Community: Political Support in a Representative Democracy*. Cambridge: Cambridge University Press.

Clarke Harold D., Jane Jenson, Lawrence LeDuc, Jon H. Pammett. 1995. *Absent Mandate: Canadian Electoral Politics in an Era of Restructuring*. Toronto: Gage.

Clemens, Elisabeth S. 1997. *The People's Lobby: Organizational Innovation and the Rise of Interest Group Politics in the Untited States, 1890–1925*. Chicago: University of Chicago Press.

Coase, Ronald H. 1960. "The Problem of Social Cost." *Journal of Law and Economics* 3:1–44.

Coleman, James S. 1990. *Foundations of Social Theory*. Cambridge, Mass.: Belknap Press.

Cooke, Jacob E., ed. 1961. *The Federalist*. Cleveland: Meridian Books.

Costain, Anne. 1992. *Inviting Women's Rebellion: A Political Process Interpretation of the Women's Movement*. Baltimore: Johns Hopkins University Press.

Court of Appeal of Catania. Sentence of Court in Judicial Proceeding n. 5463. 10 July 1991.

Court of Florence. Sentence of Court against Falugi +4. 28 February 1986 (excerpts in *Questione Giustizia* 1987 n.2.:337–55).

Court of Savona. Sentence of Court n. 145/85. 8 August 1985.

Craig, Stephen C. 1993. *The Malevolent Leaders: Popular Discontent in America*. Boulder: Westview.

Crosette, Barbara. 1997. "On Foreign Affairs, U.S. Public Is Nontraditional." *New York Times*, December 28: section 1, p. 10.

Crozat, Matthew. 1998. "Are the Times A-Changin'? Assessing the Acceptance of Protest in Western Democracies." In *The Social Movement Society: Contentious Politics for a New Century*, ed. David S. Meyer and Sidney Tarrow. Boulder: Rowman and Littlefield.

Crozier, Michel. 1975. "Western Europe." In *The Crisis of Democracy: Report on the Governability of Democracies to the Trilateral Commission*, ed. Michel Crozier, Samuel P. Huntington, and Jōji Watanuki. New York: New York University Press.

Crozier, Michel, Samuel P. Huntington, and Jōji Watanuki. 1975. *The Crisis of Democracy: Report on the Governability of Democracies to the Trilateral Commission*. New York: New York University Press.

Curtice, John, and Roger Jowell. 1997. "Trust in the Political System." In *British Social Attitudes—The 14th Report*, ed. Roger Jowell, John Curtice, Alison Park, Lindsay Brook, Katarina Thomson, and Caroline Bryson. Brookfield, Vt.: Dartmouth University Press.

Curtis, James E., Edward G. Grabb, and Douglas E. Baer. 1992. "Voluntary Association Membership in Fifteen Countries: A Comparative Analysis." *American Sociological Review* 57:139–52.

Cusack, Thomas R. 1997a. *On the Road to Weimar? The Political Economy of Popular Satisfaction with Government and Regime Performance in Germany*. Berlin, WZB Discussion Paper FS I, 97–303.

Cusack, Thomas. 1997b. *Social Capital, Institutional Structures, and Democratic Performance: A Comparative Study of German Local Governments*. Berlin, WZB Discussion Paper FS III, 97–201.

Dahl, Robert A. 1989. *Democracy and Its Critics*. New Haven: Yale University Press.

Dahlgren, Peter. 1995. *Television and the Public Sphere*. London: Sage.

Dahrendorf, Ralf. 1975. "Excerpts from Remarks on the Ungovernability Study." In *The Crisis of Democracy: Report on the Governability of Democracies to the Trilateral Commission*, ed. Michel Crozier, Samuel P. Huntington, and Jōji Watanuki. New York: New York University Press.

Dalton, Russell J. 1994. *The Green Rainbow: Environmental Groups in Western Europe*. New Haven: Yale University Press.

Dalton, Russell J. 1996. *Citizen Politics: Public Opinion and Political Parties in Advanced Industrial Democracies*. 2d ed. Chatham, N.J.: Chatham House.

Dalton, Russell J. 1997. "Citizens and Democracy: Political Support in Advanced Industrial Democracies." Presented at the John F. Kennedy School of Government Workshop on Confidence in Democratic Institutions: America in Comparative Perspective, Washington, D.C.

Dalton, Russell J. 1998. "Parties without Partisans: The Decline of Party Identifications among Democratic Publics." Research paper for the "Unthinkable Democracy" Project, Center for the Study of Democracy, University of California, Irvine.

Dalton, Russell J. 1999. "Political Support in Advanced Industrial Countries." In *Critical Citizens: Global Support for Democratic Government*, ed. Pippa Norris. Oxford: Oxford University Press.

Dalton, Russell J., and Manfred Kuechler, eds. 1990. *Challenging the Political Order*. New York: Oxford University Press.

Dalton, Russell J., Scott C. Falnagan, and Paul Becke. 1984. *Electoral Change in Advanced Industrial Democracies*. Princeton: Princeton University Press.

Davies, S., and S. Todd. 1996. "The Need for an Independent Food Agency." *Consumer Policy Review* 6:82–86.

della Porta, Donatella. 1992. *Lo scambio occulto* [Hidden Exchanges]. Bologna: Il Mulino.

della Porta, Donatella. 1993. "Milan: Immoral Capital." In *Italian Politics*, ed. Steven Hellman and Gianfranco Pasquino. London: Pinter.

della Porta, Donatella. 1995a. "Political Parties and Corruption." *Modern Italy* 1:97–114.

della Porta, Donatella. 1995b. *Social Movements, Political Violence, and the State: A Comparative Analysis of Italy and Germany*. Cambridge: Cambridge University Press.

della Porta, Donatella. 1996a. "Actors in Corruption: Business Politicians in Italy." *International Social Science Journal* 149:349–64.

della Porta, Donatella. 1996b. "The Vicious Circles of Corruption in Italy." In *Democracy and Corruption in Europe*, ed. Donatella della Porta and Yves Mény. London: Pinter.

della Porta, Donatella, and Yves Mény. 1996. "Democracy and Corruption: Towards A Comparative Analysis." In *Democracy and Corruption in Europe*, ed. Donatella della Porta and Yves Mény. London: Pinter.

della Porta, Donatella, and Yves Mény. 1997. *Democracy and Corruption in Europe*. London: Pinter.

della Porta, Donatella, and Alessandro Pizzorno. 1996. "The Business Politicians: Reflections from a Study on Political Corruption." *Journal of Law and Society* 23:73–94.

della Porta, Donatella, and Alberto Vannucci. 1994. *Corruzione politica e amministrazione pubblica. Risorse, meccanismi, attori* [Political Corruption and Public Administration: Resources, Mechanisms, and Actors]. Bologna: Il Mulino.

della Porta, Donatella, and Alberto Vannucci. 1995. "Politics, the Mafia, and the Market for Corrupt Exchange." In *Italian Politics: Ending the First Republic*, ed. Carol Mershon and Gianfranco Pasquino. Boulder: Westview.

della Porta, Donatella, and Alberto Vannucci. 1996. "Controlling Political Corruption in Italy: What Did Not Work and Why." *Res Publica* 38:353–70.

della Porta, Donatella, and Alberto Vannucci. 1997a. "The 'Perverse Effects' of Corruption." *Political Studies* 45:516–38.

della Porta, Donatella, and Alberto Vannucci. 1997b. "The Resources of Corruption: Some Reflections from the Italian Case." *Crime, Law and Social Change* 27: 231–54.

della Porta, Donatella, and Alberto Vannucci. 1998. *Corrupt Exchanges*. New York: Aldine de Gruyter.

Delli Carpini, Michael X., and Scott Keeter. 1996. *What Americans Know about Politics and Why It Matters*. New Haven: Yale University Press.

Dewey, John. [1935] 1987. "Liberalism and Social Action." In *The Later Works of Dewey, 1925–1953*. Vol. 11. Reprint. Carbondale: Southern Illinois University Press.

Diani, Mario. 1997. "Leaders or Brokers: On Power and Control in Social Movement Networks." Presented at the European Sociological Association Conference, University of Essex.

Dionne, E. J., Jr. 1991. *Why Americans Hate Politics.* New York: Simon and Schuster.

Dobell, Peter, and Byron Berry. 1992. "Anger at the System: Political Discontent in Canada." *Parliamentary Government* 39:5–9.

Dogan, Mattei. 1994. "The Pendulum between Theory and Substance: Testing the Concepts of Legitimacy and Trust." In *Comparing Nations,* ed. Mattei Dogan and Ali Kazancigil. Oxford: Blackwell.

Doi, Takako. 1993. *Seiippai* [As Eagerly as Possible: Memoirs]. Tokyo: Asahi Shimbunsha.

Dolan, Kathleen, Bruce McKeown, and James M. Carlson. 1988. "Popular Conceptions of Political Corruption: Implications for the Empirical Study of Political Ethics." *Corruption and Reform* 3:3–24.

Doring, Herbert. 1992. "Higher Education and Confidence in Institutions." *West European Politics* 15:126–46.

Downs, Anthony. 1957. *An Economic Theory of Democracy.* New York: Harper and Row.

Dryzek, John S. 1990. *Discursive Democracy: Politics, Policy, and Political Science.* Cambridge: Cambridge University Press.

Dunn, John. 1984. "The Concept of 'Trust' in the Politics of John Locke." In *Philosophy in History,* ed. Richard Rorty, J. B. Schneewind, and Quentin Skinner. Cambridge: Cambridge University Press.

Duverger, Maurice. 1954. *Political Parties.* Trans. Barbara and Robert North. New York: Wiley.

Easton, David. 1965. *A Systems Analysis of Political Life.* New York: Wiley.

Easton, David. 1975. "A Re-assessment of the Concept of Political Support." *British Journal of Political Science* 5:435–57.

The Economist. 1998. "He Believes in Government, So Why Doesn't America." January 24:19–21.

Edwards, Bob, and Michael W. Foley. 1997. "Social Capital and the Political Economy of Our Discontent." *American Behavioral Scientist* 40:669–78.

Elias, Norbert. 1987. "Wandlungen der Wir-Ich-Balance" [Changes in the Balance of We and I]. In *Die Gesellschaft der Individuen* [The Society of Individuals], ed. Norbert Elias. Frankfurt: Suhrkamp.

Elster, Jon. 1986. "The Market and the Forum: Three Varieties of Political Theory." In *Foundations of Social Choice Theory,* ed. Jon Elster and Aanund Hylland. Cambridge: Cambridge University Press.

Erikson, Eric H. 1950. *Childhood and Society.* New York: W. W. Norton.

Esler, Gavin. 1997. *The United States of Anger: The People and the American Dream.* London: Michael Joseph.

Estrich, Susan. 1998. *Getting Away with Murder: How Politics Is Destroying the Criminal Justice System.* Cambridge, Mass.: Harvard University Press.

Etzioni, Amitai, and Thomas A. Diprete. 1979. "The Decline in Confidence in America: The Prime Factor, a Research Note." *Journal of Applied Behavioral Science* 15:520–26.

Fair, Ray C. 1978. "The Effect of Economic Events on Votes for President." *Review of Economics and Statistics* 6(2):159–73.

Fallows, James. 1994. *Looking at the Sun: The Rise of the New East Asian Economic and Political System*. New York: Pantheon Books.

Fallows, James. 1996. *Breaking the News: How the Media Undermine American Democracy*. New York: Pantheon Books.

Federazione Italiana Pubblici Esercenti. 1992. *Malati di tangente* [Sick of Bribes]. Typescript.

Fiorina, Morris P. 1992. *Divided Government*. New York: Macmillan.

Flanagan, Scott C. 1991. "Media Influences and Voting Behavior." In *The Japanese Voter*, ed. Scott C. Flanagan, Shinsaku Kōhei, Ichirō Miyake, Bradley M. Richardson, and Jōji Watanuki. New Haven: Yale University Press.

Flanagan, Scott C. 1996. "Media Exposure and the Quality of Political Participation in Japan." In *Media and Politics in Japan*, ed. Susan J. Pharr and Ellis S. Krauss. Honolulu: University Press of Hawaii.

Flanagan, Scott C., Shinsaku Kōhei, Ichirō Miyake, Bradley M. Richardson, and Jōji Watanuki. 1991. *The Japanese Voter*. New Haven: Yale University Press.

Flexner, Abraham. 1910. *Medical Education in the United States and Canada: A Report to the Carnegie Foundation for the Advancement of Teaching with an Introduction by Henry Pritchett*. Bulletin Number 4. New York: Carnegie Foundation for the Advancement of Teaching.

Foley, Michael, and Bob Edwards. 1997. "Escape from Politics? Social Theory and the Social Capital Debate." *American Behavioral Scientist* 40:550–61.

Freeman, Laurie Anne. 1995. "Ties That Bind: Press, State and Society in Contemporary Japan." Ph.D. diss. University of California at Berkeley.

Fuchs, Dieter, Giovanna Guidorossi, and Palle Svensson. 1995. "Support for the Democratic System." In *Citizens and the State*, ed. Hans-Dieter Klingemann and Dieter Fuchs. Vol. 1 of *Beliefs in Government*, ed. Kenneth Newton. Oxford: Oxford University Press.

Fuchs, Dieter, and Hans-Dieter Klingemann. 1995. "Citizens and the State: A Relationship Transformed." In *Citizens and the State*, ed. Hans-Dieter Klingemann and Dieter Fuchs. Vol. 1 of *Beliefs in Government*, ed. Kenneth Newton. Oxford: Oxford University Press.

Fukuyama, Francis. 1992. *The End of History and the Last Man*. New York: Maxwell Macmillan.

Fukuyama, Francis. 1995. *Trust: The Social Virtues and the Creation of Prosperity*. New York: Free Press.

Gabriel, Oscar W. 1995. "Political Efficacy and Trust." In *The Impact of Values*, ed. Jan van Deth and Elinor Scarbrough. Oxford: Oxford University Press.

Gallup Organization. 1997. *Gallup Political and Economic Index*. Report 441, 30.

Galston, William A., and Peter Levine. 1997. "America's Condition: A Glance at the Evidence." *Brookings Review* 15(4):23–26.

Gamson, William A. 1968. *Power and Discontent*. Homewood, Ill.: Dorsey.

Garment, Suzanne. 1991. *Scandal: The Crisis of Mistrust in American Politics*. New York: Times Books.

Garrett, Geoffrey. 1998. "Global Markets and National Politics: Collision Course or Virtuous Circle?" *International Organization* 52, no. 4.

Garrett, Geoffrey. 1998. *Partisan Politics in the Global Economy*. New York: Cambridge University Press.

Geertz, Clifford. 1962. "The Rotating Credit Associations: A 'Middle Rung' in Development." *Economic Development and Cultural Change* 10:241–63.

Gelman, Andrew, and Gary King. 1993. "Why Are American Presidential Election Campaign Polls So Variable When Votes Are So Predictable?" *British Journal of Political Science* 23:409–51.

Gerbner, George, Larry Gross, Michael Morgan, and Nancy Signorielli. 1994. "Growing Up with Television: The Cultivation Perspective." In *Media Effects*, ed. Jennings Bryant and Dolf Zillmann. Hillsdale, N.J.: Lawrence Erlbaum.

Gerhards, Jürgen, and Dieter Rucht. 1992. "Mesomobilization: Organizing and Framing in Two Protest Campaigns in West Germany." *American Journal of Sociology* 98:555–96.

Giddens, Anthony. 1990. *Consequences of Modernity*. Stanford: Stanford University Press.

Giglioli, P. P. 1996. "Degrading in Public: Some Aspects of the Italian Political Corruption Trials." In *The Art of Persuasion*, ed. L. Cheles and L. Sponza. Manchester: Manchester University Press.

Greeley, Andrew. 1997. "Coleman Revisted: Religious Structures as a Source of Social Capital." *American Behavioral Scientist* 40:587–94.

Greven, Michael. 1998. "Der Zweck heiligt die Mittel in der Demokratie nicht" [The End Cannot Justify the Means in Democracy]. In *Opposition als Triebkraft der Demokratie: Bilanz und Perspektiven der zweiten Republik. Jürgen Seifert zum 70. Geburtstag* [Opposition as a Driving Force in Democracy: Survey and Perspectives of the Second Republic. To Jürgen Seifert on His 70th birthday], ed. Michael Buckmiller and Joachim Perels. Hannover: Offizin-Verlag.

Gundelach, Peter. 1995. "Grass-Roots Activity." In *The Impact of Values*, ed. Jan W. Van Deth and Elinor Scarbrough. Vol. IV of *Beliefs in Government*, ed. Kenneth Newton. Oxford: Oxford University Press.

Habermas, Jürgen. 1962. *Strukturwandel der Öffentlichkeit: Untersuchungen zu einer Kategorie der bürgerlichen Gesellschaft* [Structural Transformation of the Public Sphere: An Inquiry into a Category of Bourgeois Society]. Neuwied: H. Luchterhand.

Habermas, Jürgen. 1996. *Between Facts and Norms: Contributions to a Discourse Theory of Law and Democracy*. Trans. William Rehg. Cambridge, Mass.: MIT Press.

Hachten, William A. 1998. *The Troubles of Journalism: A Critical Look at What's Right and Wrong with the Press*. Mahwah, N.J.: Lawrence Erlbaum.

Hagiwara, Michihiko. 1976. *Kōno shintō no subete* [All about Kōno's New Party]. Tokyo: Jibunsha.

Hall, Peter A. 1997. "Social Capital in Britain." Presented at the Bertelsmann Stiftung Workshop on Social Capital, Berlin.

Hallenstvedt, Abraham. 1974. "Formal Voluntary Associations in Norway." In *Voluntary Action Research*, ed. D. H. Smith. Lexington, Mass.: Lexington Books.

Hamilton, Richard F., and James D. Wright. 1986. *The State of the Masses.* New York: Aldine.

Harden, Blaine. 1997. "Meeting for Martinis in Manhattan? See You at the Bowling Alley." *Washington Post,* December 18: A3.

Hardin, Russell. 1991. "Trusting Persons, Trusting Institutions." In *The Strategy of Choice,* ed. Richard J. Zeckhauser. Cambridge, Mass.: MIT Press.

Hardin, Russell. [1992] 1993. "The Street-Level Epistemology of Trust." Reprint. *Politics and Society* 21:505–29.

Hardin, Russell. 1996. "Trustworthiness." *Ethics* 107:26–42

Hardin, Russell. 1998a. "Trust in Government." In *Trust and Governance,* ed. Valerie Braithwaite and Margaret Levi. New York: Russell Sage Foundation.

Hardin, Russell. 1998b. "Institutional Commitment: Values or Incentives?" In *Economics, Values, and Organization,* ed. Avner Ben Ner and Louis Putterman. Cambridge: Cambridge University Press.

Hardin, Russell. 1999a. "Do We Want Trust in Government?" In *Democracy and Trust,* ed. Mark Warren. New York: Cambridge University Press.

Hardin, Russell. 1999b. "Social Capital." In *Competition and Cooperation: Conversations with Nobelists about Economics and Political Science,* ed. James Alt and Margaret Levi. New York: Russell Sage Foundation.

Hardin, Russell. 1999c. *Liberalism, Constitutionalism, and Democracy.* Oxford: Oxford University Press.

Hardin, Russell. 1999d. "Democracy and Collective Bads." In *Democracy's Edges,* ed. Ian Shapiro and Casiano Hacker-Cordon. Cambridge: Cambridge University Press.

Hardin, Russell. Forthcoming. "Democratic Epistemology and Accountability." *Social Policy and Philosophy* 17(1).

Hart, Roderick. 1994. *Seducing America.* Oxford: Oxford University Press.

Hartz, Louis. [1955] 1991. *The Liberal Tradition in America: An Interpretation of American Political Thought since the Revolution.* Reprint. New York: Harcourt Brace.

Hastings, Elizabeth, and Phillip Hastings, eds. 1994. *Index to International Public Opinion.* Westport, Conn.: Greenwood.

Hastings, Sally Ann. 1995. *Neighborhood and Nation in Tokyo, 1905–1937.* Pittsburgh: University of Pittsburgh Press.

Hayama, Tsutomu. 1994. "Pachinko: The Lonely Casino." In *The Electric Geisha: Exploring Japan's Popular Culture,* ed. Atsushi Ueda. Tokyo: Kodansha.

Health Which? 1996. "BSE: What Have We Learned?" June: 89–91.

Heimer, Carol. 1990. "Comment: On Russell Hardin's 'The Social Evolution of Cooperation.'" In *The Limits of Rationality,* ed. Karen Cook and Margaret Levi. Chicago: University of Chicago Press.

Hertzke, Allen D. 1993. *Echoes of Discontent.* Washington, D.C.: CQ Press.

Hicks, Alexander M., and Duane H. Swank. 1992. "Politics, Institutions, and Welfare Spending in Industrialized Democracies, 1960–1982." *American Political Science Review* 86:658–74.

Hirst, Paul, and Grahame Thompson. 1995. "Globalization and the Future of the Welfare State." *Economy and Society* 24:408–42.

Hiwatari, Nobuhiro. 1995. "Gojūgonen taisei no 'shūen' to sengo kokka" [The "End" of the 1955 System and the Postwar State]. *Leviathan* 16:121–44.

Hofstadter, Richard. 1967. *The Paranoid Style in American Politics and Other Essays.* New York: Vintage Books.

Holmberg, Sören. 1997. "Down and Down We Go: Political Trust in Sweden." In *Critical Citizens: Global Support for Democratic Government,* ed. Pippa Norris. Oxford: Oxford University Press.

Holtz-Bacha, C. 1990. "Videomalaise Revisited: Media Exposure and Political Alienation in West Germany." *European Journal of Communication* 5:78–85.

Huntington, Samuel P. 1968. *Political Order in Changing Society.* New Haven: Yale University Press.

Huntington, Samuel P. 1974. "Postindustrial Politics: How Benign Will It Be?" *Comparative Politics* 6:147–77.

Huntington, Samuel P. 1975a. "The United States." In *The Crisis of Democracy: Report on the Governability of Democracies to the Trilateral Commission,* ed. Michel Crozier, Samuel P. Huntington, and Jōji Watanuki. New York: New York University Press.

Huntington, Samuel P. 1975b. "The Democratic Distemper." *Public Interest* 41:9–38.

Huntington, Samuel P. 1981. *American Politics: The Promise of Disharmony.* Cambridge, Mass.: Belknap Press.

Huntington, Samuel P. 1982. "American Ideals versus American Institutions." *Political Science Quarterly* 97(1):1–38.

Huntington, Samuel P. 1991. *The Third Wave: Democratization in the Late Twentieth Century.* Norman: University of Oklahoma Press.

Imig, Doug, and Sidney Tarrow, eds. Forthcoming. *Contentious Europeans: Popular Politics in an Emerging Europe.*

Inglehart, Ronald. 1977. *The Silent Revolution: Changing Values and Political Styles among Western Publics.* Princeton: Princeton University Press.

Inglehart, Ronald. 1990. *Culture Shift in Advanced Industrial Societies.* Princeton: Princeton University Press.

Inglehart, Ronald. 1996. "Changing Values in Japan and the United States, 1981–1995." Presentation for Dentsu Institute for Human Studies, Tokyo.

Inglehart, Ronald. 1997a. *Modernization and Postmodernization: Cultural, Economic, and Poltical Change in 43 Societies.* Princeton: Princeton University Press.

Inglehart, Ronald. 1997b. "Postmodernization Brings Declining Respect for Authority but Rising Support for Democracy." Presented at the John F. Kennedy School of Government Workshop on Confidence in Democratic Institutions: America in Comparative Perspective, Washington, D.C.

Inglehart, Ronald. 1997c. "Postmaterialist Values and the Erosion of Institutional Authority." In *Why People Don't Trust Government,* ed. Joseph S. Nye Jr., Philip D. Zelikow, and David C. King. Cambridge, Mass.: Harvard University Press.

Inglehart, Ronald. 1999. "Postmodernization, Authority and Democracy." In

Critical Citizens: Global Support for Democratic Government, ed. Pippa Norris. Oxford: Oxford University Press.

Inglehart, Ronald, and Paul Abramson. 1994. "Economic Security and Value Change." *American Political Science Review* 88:336–54.

Inglehart, Ronald, and Hans D. Klingemann. 1976. "Party Identification, Ideological Preference and the Left-Right Dimension among Western Publics." In *Party Identification and Beyond,* ed. Ian Budges, Ivor Crewe, and Dennis Farlie. New York: Wiley.

Ingram, Helen, and Steven Smith, eds. 1993. *Public Policy for Democracy.* Washington, D.C.: Brookings Institution Press.

Inoguchi, Takashi. 1980. "Economic Conditions and Mass Support in Japan, 1960–1976." In *Models of Political Economy,* ed. Paul Whiteley. London: Sage.

Inoguchi, Takashi. 1997. "The Decline of Social Capital and Political Culture as a Condition of Democracy: The Japan Paradox." University of Tokyo. Typescript.

Iyengar, Shanto, and Donald Kinder. 1987. *News That Matters.* Chicago: University of Chicago Press.

Jamieson, Kathleen. 1992. *Dirty Politics.* Oxford: Oxford University Press.

Jasanoff, Sheila. 1997. "Civilization and Madness: The Great BSE Scare of 1996." *Public Understanding of Science* 6:221–32.

Jennings, M. Kent, and Jan van Deth. 1989. *Continuities in Political Action.* Berlin: de Gruyter.

Johnson, Chalmers. 1986. "Structural Corruption and the Advent of Machine Politics in Japan." *Journal of Japanese Studies* 12(1):1–28.

Johnston, Paul. 1998. "Social Movement Unionism: Labor as Citizenship Movement." Presented at the conference "The Revival of the American Labor Movement," School of Labor and Industrial Relations, Cornell University.

Jowell, Roger, and Richard Topf. 1988. "Trust in the Establishment." In *British Social Attitudes: The 5th Report,* ed. R. Jowell, S. Witherspoon, and L. Brook. Brookfield: Gower.

Just, Marion. 1998. "Candidate Strategies and the Media Campaign." In *The Election of 1996,* ed. Gerald M. Pomper. Chatham, N.J.: Chatham House.

Kaase, Max. 1997. "Trust and Participation in Contemporary Democracies." Wissenschaftszentrum Berlin. Typescript.

Kaase, Max, and Kenneth Newton, eds. 1995. *Beliefs in Government.* Vol. 5 of *Beliefs in Government,* ed. Kenneth Newton. Oxford: Oxford University Press.

Kabashima, Ikuo. 1987. "Kiken no kenkyū [Research on Rights]." Zasshi Senkyo.

Kabashima, Ikuo. 1998. *Seiken kōtai to yūkensha no taido henyō* [Changes in Administration and Changes of Attitude in the Electorate]. Tokyo: Bokutakusha.

Kabashima, Ikuo, and Yoshihiko Takenaka. 1996. *Gendai Nihonjin no ideorogi* [Ideology of Contemporary Japanese]. Tokyo: Tōkyō Daigaku Shuppankai.

Kagan, Robert A. 1991. "Adversarial Legalism and American Government." *Journal of Policy Analysis and Management* 10:369–406.

Kagan, Robert A., and Lee Axelrad. 1997. "Adversarial Legalism: An International Perspective." In *Comparative Disadvantages: Social Regulations and the*

Global Economy, ed. Pietro S. Nivola. Washington, D.C.: Brookings Institution Press.

Kaiser, Karl. 1971. "Transnational Relations as a Threat to the Democratic Process." In *Transnational Relations and World Politics*, ed. Robert O. Keohane and Joseph S. Nye Jr. Cambridge, Mass.: Harvard University Press.

Katz, Richard S., and Peter Mair. 1992. "The Membership of Political Parties in European Democracies, 1960–1990." *European Journal of Political Research* 26:329–45.

Katzenstein, Mary Fainsod. 1998. *Faithful and Fearless: Moving Feminist Protest Inside the Church and Military*. Princeton: Princeton University Press.

Katzenstein, Peter J. 1984. *Corporatism and Change: Austria, Switzerland, and the Politics of Industry*. Ithaca: Cornell University Press.

Katzenstein, Peter J. 1985. *Small States in World Markets: Industrial Policy in Europe*. Ithaca: Cornell University Press.

Katzenstein, Peter J. 1996. *Cultural Norms and National Security: Police and Military in Postwar Japan*. Ithaca: Cornell University Press.

Katzenstein, Peter J., ed. 1997. *Tamed Power: Germany in Europe*. Ithaca: Cornell University Press.

Katzenstein, Peter J., and Takashi Shiraishi, eds. 1997. *Network Power: Japan and Asia*. Ithaca: Cornell University Press.

Kawato, Sadashi. 1988. "Shūsan dōjisu senkyo to Nakasone ninki" [The Simultaneous Lower and Upper House Elections and Nakasone's Popularity]." *Hokudai Hōgaku Ronshū* [Hokkaido University Law Review] 39(2):180–238.

Kenda, Sosuke. 1980. "Nanajū-nendai ni okeru seinenzō no henbō" [Transformation of the Young during the 1970s]. In *Daini Nihonjin no ishiki* [The Consciousness of Japanese, 2nd ed.], ed. Nihon Hōsōkyōkai Seronchōsa Kenkyūjo. Tokyo: Shiseidō.

Kielmansegg, Peter, ed. 1976. *Legitimationsprobleme politischer Systeme* [Legitimation Problems of Political Systems]. Special issue of *Politische Vierteljahresschrift* [Political Quarterly], vol 7.

Kilz, Hans Werner, and Joachim Preuss. 1983. *Flick: Die gekaufte Republik* [Flick: The Purchased Republic]. Hamburg: Rowolt.

Kinder, Donald R. 1981. "Presidents, Prosperity, and Public Opinion." *Public Opinion Quarterly* 45:1–21.

Kinder, Donald R., and D. R. Kiewiet. 1979. "Economic Discontent and Political Behavior." *American Journal of Political Science* 23:495–527.

Kinder, Donald R., and D. R. Kiewiet. 1981. "Sociotropic Politics." *British Journal of Political Science* 11:129–61.

King, Anthony. 1986. "Sex, Money and Power." In *Politics in Britain and the United States: Comparative Perspectives*, ed. Richard Hodder-Williams and James Ceaser. Durham: Duke University Press.

King, David C. 1997. "The Polarization of American Parties and Mistrust of Government." In *Why People Don't Trust Government*, ed. Joseph S. Nye Jr., Philip D. Zelikow, and David C. King. Cambridge, Mass.: Harvard University Press.

Kirchgässner, Gebhard. 1992. "Towards a Theory of Low-Cost Decisions." *European Journal of Political Economy* 8:305–20.

Kitschelt, Herbert. 1989. *The Logics of Party Formation.* Ithaca: Cornell University Press.

Klingemann, Hans-Dieter. 1999. "Mapping Political Support in the 1990s: A Global Analysis." In *Critical Citizens: Global Support for Democratic Government,* ed. Pippa Norris. Oxford: Oxford University Press.

Klingemann, Hans-Dieter, and Dieter Fuchs, eds. 1995. *Citizens and the States.* Vol. 1 of *Beliefs in Government,* ed. Kenneth Newton. Oxford: Oxford University Press.

Klite, Paul, Robert M. Bardwell, and Jason Salzman. 1997. "Local TV News: Getting Away with Murder." *Harvard International Journal of Press and Politics* 2(2):102–12.

Knoke, David. 1990. *Political Networks: The Structural Perspective.* New York: Cambridge University Press.

Kohut, Andrew, and Robert Toth. 1997. "The Fault Line in Foreign Affairs: What the Public Doesn't Know—And What the Elites Don't Seem to Hear." *Washington Post,* December 28: C1, C5.

Kohut, Andrew, and Robert C. Toth. 1998. "The Central Conundrum: How Can People Like What They Distrust?" *Harvard International Journal of Press and Politics.* 3(1):110–17.

Kojima, Kazuto. 1979. "Ishiki henka no hōkō to tokushitsu" [The Direction and Nature of Change in Consciousness]. In *Gendai Nihonjin no ishiki kōzō* [The Structure of Contemporary Japanese Consciousness], ed. Nihon Hōsōkyōkai. Tokyo: Nihon Hōsōkyōkai Seronchōsa Kenkyūjo.

Kojima, Kazuto. 1980. "Gendai seinen no seijiteki mukanshin no keisei [The Formation of Political Apathy among Contemporary Youth]." In *Daini Nihonjin no ishiki* [The Consciousness of Japanese, 2nd ed.], ed. Nihon Hōsōkyōkai Seronchōsa Kenkyūjo. Tokyo: Shiseidō.

Kramer, Gerald H. 1971. "Short Term Fluctuations in U.S. Voting Behavior, 1896–1964." *American Political Science Review* 65(1):131–43.

Kriesi, Hanspeter. 1996. "The Organizational Structure of New Social Movements in a Political Context." In *Comparative Perspectives on Social Movements: Political Opportunities, Mobilizing Structures, and Cultural Framings,* ed. Doug McAdam, John McCarthy, and Mayer N. Zald. New York: Cambridge University Press.

Krauss, Ellis S., and Bradford L. Simock. 1980. "Citizens' Movements: The Growth and Impact of Environmental Protests in Japan." In *Political Opposition and Local Politics in Japan,* ed. Kurt Steiner, Ellis S. Krauss, and Scott C. Flanagan. Princeton: Princeton University Press.

Krugman, Paul. 1995. "Growing World Trade: Causes and Consequences." *Brookings Papers on Economic Activity* 1:327–77.

Kull, Steven, I. M. Destler, and Clay Ramsay. 1997. *The Foreign Policy Gap: How Policymakers Misread the Public.* Center for International and Security Studies, Program on International Policy Attitudes, University of Maryland.

Ladd, Everett C. 1996. "The Data Just Don't Show Erosion of America's 'Social Capital.'" *Public Perspective* (June/July):1–22.

Ladd, Everett C. 1998. *Silent Revolution: The Reinvention of Civic America.* New York: Free Press.

Ladd, Everett C., and Karlyn H. Bowman. 1998. *What's Wrong: A Survey of American Satisfaction and Complaint.* Washington, D.C.: AEI Press.

Lane, Robert E. 1965. "The Politics of Consensus in an Age of Affluence." *American Political Science Review* 59:874–95.

Lange, Peter, Cynthia Irvin, and Sidney Tarrow. 1989. "Phases of Mobilization: Social Movements and the Italian Communist Party since the 1960s." *British Journal of Political Science* 22:15–42.

Langer, John. 1998. *Tabloid Television.* London: Routledge.

Lawrence, Robert Z. 1997. "Is It Really the Economy, Stupid?" In *Why People Don't Trust Government,* ed. Joseph S. Nye Jr., Philip D. Zelikow, and David C. King. Cambridge, Mass.: Harvard University Press.

Lax, David A., and James K. Sebenius. 1986. *The Manager as Negotiator: Bargaining for Cooperation and for Competitive Gain.* New York: Free Press.

LeDuc, Lawrence. 1995. "Citizens' Revenge: The Canadian Voter and the 1993 Federal Election." In *Politics: Canada.* 8th ed., ed. Paul Fox and Graham White. Toronto: McGraw-Hill Ryerson.

Leff, N. 1964. "Economic Development through Bureaucratic Corruption." *American Behavioural Scientist* 8:8–14.

LeRoy, Michael K. 1995. "Participation, Size, and Democracy: Bridging the Gap between Citizens and the Swedish State." *Comparative Politics* 27:300–301.

Levi, Margaret. 1996. "Social and Unsocial Capital: A Review Essay of Robert Putnam's *Making Democracy Work." Politics and Society* 24:45–55.

Levi, Margaret. 1997. *Consent, Dissent and Patriotism.* New York: Cambridge University Press.

Lewis-Beck, Michael. 1988. *Economics and Elections: The Major Western Democracies.* Ann Arbor: University of Michigan Press.

Lichter, Robert, and Ted Smith. 1996. "Why Elections Are Bad News: Media and Candidate Discourse in the 1996 Presidential Primaries." *Harvard International Journal of Press and Politics* 1(4):15–35.

Lien, D. D. 1986. "A Note on Competitive Bribery Games." *Economic Letters* 22:337–431.

Lijphart, Arend. 1984. *Democracies: Patterns of Majoritarian and Consensus Government in Twenty-one Countries.* New Haven: Yale University Press.

Lijphart, Arend. 1991. "Majority Rule in Theory and Practice. The Tenacity of a Flawed Paradigm." *International Social Science Journal* 129:483–93.

Lind, E. Allan, and Tom R. Tyler. 1988. *The Social Psychology of Procedural Justice.* New York: Plenum.

Lindner, Clausjohann. 1990. *Kritik der Theorie der partizipatorischen Demokratie* [The Theory of Participatory Democracy: A Critique]. Opladen: Westdeutscher Verlag.

Lipset, Seymour Martin. 1977. "Why No Socialism in the United States." In *Sources of Contemporary Radicalism,* ed. Serwyn Bialer and Sophis Sluzar. Boulder: Westview.

Lipset, Seymour Martin. 1994. "American Democracy in Comparative Perspective." In *A New Moment in the Americas*, ed. Robert S. Leiken. New Brunswick, N.J.: Transaction.

Lipset, Seymour Martin, and William Schneider. 1983. *The Confidence Gap*. Baltimore: Johns Hopkins University Press.

Listhaug, Ola. 1995. "The Dynamics of Trust in Politicians." In *Citizens and the State*, ed. Hans-Dieter Klingemann and Dieter Fuchs. Vol. 1 of *Beliefs in Government*, ed. Kenneth Newton. Oxford: Oxford University Press.

Listhaug, Ola, and Matti Wiberg. 1995. "Confidence in Political and Private Institutions." In *Citizens and the State*, ed. Hans-Dieter Klingemann and Dieter Fuchs. Vol. 1 of *Beliefs in Government*, ed. Kenneth Newton. Oxford: Oxford University Press.

Lodge, Milton, Marco Steenburgen, and Shawn Blau. 1995. "The Responsive Voter: Campaign Information and the Dynamics of Candidate Evaluation." *American Political Science Review* 89:309–26.

Lowi, Theodore J. 1969. *The End of Liberalism: Ideology, Policy, and the Crisis of Public Authority*. New York: W. W. Norton.

Luhmann, Niklas. 1980. "Trust: A Mechanism for the Reduction of Social Complexity." In *Trust and Power*, ed. Niklas Luhmann. New York: Wiley.

Luhmann, Niklas. 1988. "Familiarity, Confidence, Trust: Problems and Perspectives." In *Trust: Making and Breaking of Cooperative Relations*, ed. Diego Gambetta. Oxford: Basil Blackwell.

Lull, James, and Stephen Hinerman, eds. 1997. *Media Scandals*. Cambridge: Polity.

Lupia, Arthur, and Matthew D. McCubbins. 1997. *The Democratic Dilemma*. Cambridge: Cambridge University Press.

Luthardt, Wolfgang. 1994. *Direkte Demokratie: Ein Vergleich in Westeuropa* [Direct Democracy: A Comparison in Western Europe]. Baden-Baden: Nomos.

MacDougall, Terry. 1988. "The Lockheed Scandal and the High Costs of Politics in Japan." In *The Politics of Scandal: Power and Process in Liberal Democracies*, ed. Andrei S. Markovits and Mark Silverstein. London: Holmes and Meier.

Madison, James, Alexander Hamilton, and John Jay. 1961. *The Federalist Papers*. Ed. Clinton Rossiter. New York: New American Library.

Maguire, Diarmuid. 1995. "Opposition Movements and Opposition Parties: Equal Partners or Dependent Relations in the Struggle for Power and Reform?" In *The Politics of Social Protest: Comparative Perspectives on States and Social Movements*, ed. J. Craig Jenkins and Bert Klandermans. Minneapolis: University of Minnesota Press.

Maier, Charles S. 1994. "The Moral Crisis of Democracy." *Foreign Affairs* 78(4):48–64.

Manin, Bernard. 1987. "On Legitimacy and Political Deliberation." *Political Theory* 15:338–68.

Mansbridge, Jane. 1986. *Why We Lost the ERA*. Chicago: University of Chicago Press.

Mansbridge, Jane. 1993. "Feminist Identity: Micronegotiation in the Lives of

African-American and White Working Class Women." Presented at Cornell University.

Markovits, Andrei S., and Mark Silverstein, eds. 1988. *The Politics of Scandal: Power and Process in Liberal Democracies.* London: Holmes and Meier.

Marks, Gary, and Doug McAdam. 1996. "Social Movements and the Changing Structure of Political Opportunity in the European Community." *West European Politics* 19:249–78.

Massing, Michael. 1998. "The Blue Revolution." *New York Review of Books,* November 19: 32–36.

Matsushita, Keiichi. 1960. "Rōdōkumiai no Nihongata seiji katsudō" [Political Activities of Labor Unions, Japanese Style]. In *Nihon no atsuryoku dantai* [Pressure Groups in Japan], ed. Nihon Seijigakkai. Tokyo: Iwanami Shoten.

McAdam, Doug, Sidney Tarrow, and Charles Tilly. 1997. "Towards an Integrated Perspective on Social Movements and Revolution." In *Ideals, Interests, and Institutions: Advancing Theory in Comparative Politics,* ed. Marc Irving Lichbach and Alan Zuckerman. Cambridge: Cambridge University Press.

McAllister, Ian. 1999. "The Economic Performance of Governments." In *Critical Citizens: Global Support for Democratic Government,* ed. Pippa Norris. Oxford: Oxford University Press.

McCarthy, John D., and Mark Wolfson. 1992. "Consensus Movements, Conflict Movements and the Cooperation of Civic and State Infrastructures." In *Frontiers of Social Movement Theory,* ed. Aldon Morris and Carol McClurg Mueller. New Haven: Yale University Press.

McKean, Margaret A. 1981. *Environmental Protest and Citizen Politics in Japan.* Berkeley: University of California Press.

Meares, Tracy L., and Dan M. Kahan. 1999. "Law and (Norms of) Order in the Inner City." *Law and Society Review* 32(4):805–38.

Meehl, P. E. 1977. "The Selfish Voter Paradox and the Thrown-Away Vote Argument." *American Political Science Review* 71:11–30.

Mehnert, John Siegfried. 1997. *Die Gewerkschaftsbande* [The Union Gang]. Hamburg: Rotbuch.

Meltzer, Alan, and Scott Richard. 1981. "A Rational Theory of the Size of Government." *Journal of Political Economy* 89:914–27.

Mény, Yves. 1992. *La corruption de la république* [Corruption of the Republic]. Paris: Fayard.

Mény, Yves. 1997. "France: The End of the Republican Ethic." In *Democracy and Corruption in Europe,* ed. Donatella della Porta and Yves Mény, London: Pinter.

Merton, Robert K. 1957. *Social Theory and Social Structure.* New York: Free Press.

Meyer, David S. 1990. *A Winter of Discontent: The Nuclear Freeze and American Politics.* New York: Praeger.

Meyer, David S. 1998. "Social Movements: Creating Communities of Change." In *Feminist Approaches to Social Movements, Communities and Power,* ed. Mary Ann Tetrault and Robin L. Teske. Columbia: University of South Carolina Press.

Meyer, David S., and Sidney Tarrow, eds. 1998. *The Social Movement Society: Contentious Politics for a New Century.* Boulder: Rowman and Littlefield.

Mill, John Stuart. 1977. "De Tocqueville on Democracy in America, II." In *Essays on Politics and Society.* Ed. J. M. Robson. Vol 18 of *Collected Works of John Stuart Mill.* Toronto: University of Toronto Press.

Miller, Arthur H. 1974. "Political Issues and Trust in Government 1964–1970." *American Political Science Review* 68:951–72.

Miller, Arthur H., Edie Goldenberg, and Erbring Lutz. 1979. "Set Type Politics: Impact of Newspapers on Public Confidence." *American Political Science Review* 73:67–84.

Miller, Arthur H., and Ola Listhaug. 1997. "Failed Government Performance and Growing Political Distrust." Presented at the John F. Kennedy School of Government Workshop on Confidence in Democratic Institutions: America in Comparative Perspective, Washington, D.C.

Miller, Gary. 1992. *Managerial Dilemmas: The Political Economy of Hierarchy.* Cambridge: Cambridge University Press.

Miller, Gary. 1998. "Why Is Trust Necessary in Organizations? The Moral Hazard of Profit-Maximization." Washington University. Typescript.

Minkoff, Debra C. 1998. "Producing Social Capital: National Social Movements and Civil Society." *American Behavioral Scientist* 40:606–19.

Mischler, William, and Richard Rose. 1997. "Trust, Distrust, and Skepticism: Popular Evaluations of Civil and Political Institutions in Post-Communist Societies." *Journal of Politics* 59(2):418–51.

Miyake, Ichirō. 1985. *Seitō shiji no bunseki* [An Analysis of Party Support]. Tokyo: Sōbunsha.

Miyake, Ichirō. 1995. *Nihon no seiji to senkyo* [Japanese Politics and Elections]. Tokyo: Tōkyō Daigaku Shuppankai.

Mogiliansky, A. 1994. "Corruption in Procurement: The Economics of Regulatory Blackmail." Research paper in economics. Department of Economics. University of Stockholm.

Montgomery, John. 1957. *Forced to Be Free: The Artificial Revolution in Germany and Japan.* Chicago: University of Chicago Press.

Moravcsik, Andrew. 1993. "Preferences and Power in the European Community: A Liberal Intergovernmentalist Approach." *Journal of Common Market Studies* 31:473–524.

Moravcsik, Andrew. 1994. "Why the European Community Strengthens the State: Domestic Politics and International Cooperation." Center for European Studies, Harvard University Working Paper 52.

Morlino, Leonardo. 1996. "Crisis of Parties and Change of Party System in Italy." *Party Politics* 2:5–30.

Morlino, Leonardo. 1998. *Democracy between Consolidation and Crises: Parties, Groups, and Citizens in Southern Europe.* Oxford: Oxford University Press.

Morlino, Leonardo, and Marco Tarchi. 1996. "The Dissatisfied Society: The Roots of Political Change in Italy." *European Journal of Political Research* 30:41–63.

Mortimore, Roger. 1995. "Public Perceptions of Sleaze in Britain." Special Issue on "Sleaze: Politics, Private Interests and Public Reaction," ed. Alan Doig. *Parliamentary Affairs* 48(4):579–90.

Mueller, Carol McClurg. 1987. "Collective Consciousness, Identity Transformation, and the Rise of Women in Public Office in the United States." In *The Women's Movements of the United States and Western Europe: Consciousness, Political Opportunity and Public Policy*, ed. Mary F. Katzenstein and Carol McClurg Mueller. Philadelphia: Temple University Press.

Mueller, John. 1999. *Democracy, Capitalism, and Ralph's Pretty Good Grocery*. Princeton: Princeton University Press.

Muramatsu, Michio, Mitsutoshi Itō, and Yutaka Tsujinaka. 1986. *Sengo Nihon no atsuryoku dantai* [Pressure Groups in Postwar Japan]. Tokyo: Tōyō Keizai Shinpōsha.

Nannestad, Peter, and Martin Paldam. 1994. "The VP-Function: A Survey of the Literature on Vote and Popularity Functions after 25 Years." *Public Choice* 79:213–45.

Nettl, J. P. 1968. "The State as a Conceptual Variable." *World Politics* 20: 559–92.

Newhouse, Joseph. 1997. "Europe's Rising Regionalism." *Foreign Affairs* January/February:67–84.

Newton, Kenneth. 1997a. "Social and Political Trust." Presented at the John F. Kennedy School of Government Workshop on Confidence in Democratic Institutions: America in Comparative Perspective, Washington, D.C.

Newton, Kenneth. 1997b. "Politics and the News Media: Mobilization or Videomalaise?" In *British Social Attitudes: The 14th Report, 1997/8*. Vol. 14, ed. Roger Jowell, John Curtice, Alison Park, Lindsay Brook, Katarina Thomson, and Caroline Bryson. Aldershot: Ashgate.

Newton, Kenneth. 1997c. "Social Capital and Democracy." *American Behavioral Scientist* 40(5):575–86.

Newton, Kenneth. 1998. "Trust in People and Confidence in Institutions: Trends and Patterns in the Trilateral Countries." Presented at the conference on Public Trust and Governance in the Trilateral Democracies, Bellagio, Italy.

Newton, Kenneth. 1999. "Social and Political Trust." In *Critical Citizens: Global Support for Democratic Government*, ed. Pippa Norris. Oxford: Oxford University Press.

NHK, Hōsōbunka Kenkyūjo. 1998. *Gendai Nihonjin no ishiki kōzō* [The Structure of Contemporary Japanese Conciousness]. 5th ed. Tokyo: Nihon Hōsōkyōkai.

NHK. 1995. *A Bilingual Guide to the Japanese Economy*. Tokyo: NHK Overseas Broadcasting Department Economic Project and Daiwa Institute of Research.

Niedermayer, Oskar, and Richard Sinnott, eds. 1995. *Public Opinion and Internationalized Governance*. Vol. 2 of *Beliefs in Government*, ed. Kenneth Newton. Oxford: Oxford University Press.

Niemi, Richard G., John Mueller, and Thomas W. Smith. 1989. *Trends in Public Opinion*. New York: Greenwood.

Noack, Paul. 1985. *Korruption: Die andere seite der Macht* [Corruption: The Other Side of Power]. Munich: Kindler.

Noelle-Neumann, Elisabeth, and Renate Koecher. 1993. *Allensbacher Jahrbuch für Demoskopie*. Allensbach, Germany: Allensbach Institute.

Norris, Pippa. 1997a. "Designing Democracies: Institutional Arrangements and System Support." Presented at the John F. Kennedy School of Government Workshop on Confidence in Democratic Institutions: America in Comparative Perspective, Washington, D.C.

Norris, Pippa. 1997b. *Electoral Change since 1945*. Oxford: Blackwell.

Norris, Pippa. 1998. "The Battle for the Campaign Agenda." In *New Labour Triumphs: Britain at the Polls*, ed. Anthony King. Chatham, N.J.: Chatham House.

Norris, Pippa, ed. 1999. *Critical Citizens: Global Support for Democratic Government*. Oxford: Oxford University Press.

Norris, Pippa, John Curtice, David Sanders, Margaret Scammell, and Holli Semetko. 1999. *On Message: Communicating the Campaign*. London: Sage.

Nye, Joseph S., Jr. 1967. "Corruption and Political Development. A Cost-Benefit Analysis." *American Political Science Review* 61:417–27.

Nye, Joseph S., Jr. 1997a. "Introduction: The Decline of Confidence in Government." In *Why People Don't Trust Government*, ed. Joseph S. Nye Jr., Philip D. Zelikow, and David C. King. Cambridge, Mass.: Harvard University Press.

Nye, Joseph S., Jr. 1997b. "In Government We Don't Trust." *Foreign Policy* 108:99–111.

Nye, Joseph S., Jr., and Zelikow, Philip. 1997. "Conclusion: Reflections, Conjectures, and Puzzles." In *Why People Don't Trust Government*, ed. Joseph S. Nye Jr., Philip D. Zelikow, and David C. King. Cambridge, Mass.: Harvard University Press.

Nye, Joseph S., Jr., Philip D. Zelikow, and David C. King, eds. 1997. *Why People Don't Trust Government*. Cambridge, Mass.: Harvard University Press.

Oates, Wallace E., ed. 1977. *The Political Economy of Fiscal Federalism*. Lexington, Mass.: Heath.

Offe, Claus. 1985. "New Social Movements: Challenging the Boundaries of Institutional Politics." *Social Research* 52:817–68.

Offe, Claus. 1997. "The Decline of Social Capital: German Country Report." Humboldt University. Typescript.

Offe, Claus. 1998. "How Can We Trust Our Fellow Citizens?" Social Science Department, Humboldt University. Typescript.

Olson, Mancur. 1982. *The Rise and Decline of Nations: Economic Growth, Stagnation and Social Rigidities*. New Haven: Yale University Press.

Orren, Gary. 1997. "Fall from Grace: The Public's Loss of Faith in Government." In *Why People Don't Trust Government*, ed. Joseph S. Nye Jr., Philip D. Zelikow, and David C. King. Cambridge, Mass.: Harvard University Press.

Ostrom, Elinor. 1990. *Governing the Commons: The Evolution of Institutions for Collective Action*. New York: Cambridge University Press.

Ōtake, Hideo. 1996a. *Sengo Nihon no ideorogi tairitsu* [Ideological Conflicts in Postwar Japan]. Tokyo: San'ichi Shobō.

Ōtake, Hideo. 1996b. "Forces for Political Reform: The Liberal Democratic

Party's Young Reformers and Ozawa Ichiro."*Journal of Japanese Studies* 22(2): 269–94.

Ozawa, Ichirō. 1993. *Blueprint for a New Japan: The Rethinking of a Nation.* Trans. Eric Gower. Tokyo: Kodansha International.

Page, Benjamin I., and Robert Y. Shapiro. 1992. *The Rational Public: Fifty Years of Trends in Americans' Policy Preferences.* Chicago: University of Chicago Press.

Paldam, Martin. 1991. "How Robust Is the Vote Function? A Study of Seventeen Nations over Four Decades." In *Economics and Politics: The Calculus of Support,* ed. Helmut Norpoth, Michael Lewis-Beck, and Jean-Dominique Lafay. Ann Arbor: University of Michigan Press.

Parsons, Talcott. [1937] 1968. *The Structure of Social Action.* Reprint. New York: Free Press.

Pasquino, Gianfranco. 1997. *Corso di scienza politica* [Political Science: A Handbook]. Bologna: Il Mulino.

Patterson, Thomas E. 1993. *Out of Order.* New York: Alfred Knopf.

Pempel, T. J. 1990. *Uncommon Democracies: The One-Party-Dominant Regimes.* Ithaca: Cornell University Press.

Peters, John G., and Susan Welch. 1980. "The Effects of Charges of Corruption on Voting Behavior." *American Political Science Review* 74(3):697–710.

Peterson, Paul E., and J. David Greenstone. 1977. "Racial Change and Citizen Participation: The Mobilization of Low-Income Communities through Community Action." In *A Decade of Federal Antipoverty Programs,* ed. Institute for Research on Poverty. Madison: University of Wisconsin Press.

Pew Research Center for the People and the Press. 1997. *America's Place in the World II.* Washington, D.C.: Pew Research Center for the People and the Press Report.

Pew Research Center for the People and the Press. 1998. *Deconstructing Distrust: How Americans View Government.* Washington, D.C.: Pew Research Center for the People and the Press Report.

Pharr, Susan J. 1990. *Losing Face: Status Politics in Japan.* Berkeley: University of California Press.

Pharr, Susan J. 1996. "Media and Politics in Japan: Historical and Contemporary Perspectives." In *Media and Politics in Japan,* ed. Susan J. Pharr and Ellis S. Krauss. Honolulu: University Press of Hawaii.

Pharr, Susan J. 1997a. "Japanese Videocracy." *Harvard International Journal of Press and Politics* 2(1):130–38.

Pharr, Susan J. 1997b. "Public Trust and Democracy in Japan." In *Why People Don't Trust Government,* ed. Joseph S. Nye Jr., Philip D. Zelikow, and David C. King. Cambridge, Mass.: Harvard University Press.

Pharr, Susan J. 1998. "'Moralism' and the Gender Gap: Judgments of Political Ethics in Japan." *Political Psychology* 19(1):211–36.

Pharr, Susan J., and Joseph Badaracco. 1986. "Coping with Crisis: Environmental Regulation in Japan and the U.S." In *America versus Japan: The Business-Government Connection,* ed. Thomas McCraw. Cambridge, Mass.: Harvard Business School.

Pharr, Susan J., and Ellis S. Krauss. 1996. *Media and Politics in Japan.* Honolulu: University Press of Hawaii.

Pierson, Paul. 1997. "Path Dependence, Increasing Returns, and the Study of Politics." Center for European Studies Program for the Study of Germany and Europe, Harvard University. Working Paper Series no. 7.7. Cambridge, Mass.

Piven, Frances Fox, and Richard Cloward. 1977. *Poor People's Movements: Why They Succeed, How They Fail.* New York: Vintage Books.

Pizzorno, Alessandro. 1992. "La corruzione nel sistema politico" [Corruption in the Political System]. In *Lo scambio occulto* [Hidden Exchanges], ed. Donatella della Porta. Bologna: Il Mulino.

Poguntke, Thomas. Forthcoming. "Explorations into a Minefield: Anti-Party Sentiment." *European Journal of Political Research.*

Polanyi, Karl. 1957. *The Great Transformation: The Political and Economic Origins of Our Time.* Boston: Beacon.

Poole, Keith T., and Howard Rosenthal. 1984. "The Polarization of American Politics." *Journal of Politics* 46:1061–79.

Portney, Kent E., and Jeffrey M. Berry. 1997. "Mobilizing Minority Communities: Social Capital and Participation in Urban Neighborhoods." *American Behavioral Scientist* 40:632–44.

Postman, Neil. 1985. *Amusing Ourselves to Death.* London: Methuen.

Poterba, James. 1997. "Demographic Structure and the Political Economy of Public Education." *Journal of Policy Analysis and Management* 16(1):48–66.

Powell, G. Bingham, and Guy D. Whitten. 1993. "A Cross-National Analysis of Economic Voting: Taking Account of the Political Context." *American Journal of Political Science* 37(2):391–414.

Putnam, Robert D. 1988. "Diplomacy and Domestic Politics: The Logic of Two-Level Games." *International Organization* 42:429–60.

Putnam, Robert D. 1993a. *La tradizione civica nelle regioni italiane* [The Civic Tradition in the Italian Regions]. Milano: Rizzoli.

Putnam, Robert D. 1993b. "The Prosperous Community: Social Capital and Public Life." *American Prospect* 21:35–42.

Putnam, Robert D. 1995a. "Bowling Alone: America's Declining Social Capital." *Journal of Democracy* 6:65–78.

Putnam, Robert D. 1995b. "Tuning In, Tuning Out: The Strange Disappearance of Social Capital in America." *PS: Politics and Political Science* 28(4):664–83.

Putnam, Robert D. 1996. "The Strange Disappearance of Civic America." *The American Prospect* 24:34–48.

Putnam, Robert D. 2000. *Bowling Alone: The Collapse and Revival of American Community.* New York: Simon and Schuster.

Putnam, Robert D. Forthcoming. *The Dynamics of Social Capital.* Princeton: Princeton University Press.

Putnam, Robert D., with Robert Leonardi and Raffaella Y. Nanetti. 1993. *Making Democracy Work: Civic Traditions in Modern Italy.* Princeton: Princeton University Press.

Putnam, Robert D., and Steven Yonish. 1998. "New Evidence on Trends in

American Social Capital and Civic Engagement: Are We Really 'Bowling Alone'?" Harvard University. Typescript.

Ramseyer, J. Mark, and Frances Rosenbluth. 1993. *Japan's Political Marketplace*. Cambridge, Mass.: Harvard University Press.

Reed, Steven R. 1994. "Democracy and the Personal Vote: A Cautionary Tale from Japan." *Electoral Studies* 13(1):17–28.

Reed, Steven R. 1996. "Political Corruption in Japan." *International Social Science Journal* 149:395–405.

Richardson, Bradley M. 1974. *The Political Culture of Japan*. Berkeley: University of California Press.

Richardson, Bradley M. 1991. "Japanese Voting Behavior in Comparative Perspective." In *The Japanese Voter*, ed. Scott C. Flanagan, Shinsaku Kōhei, Ichirō Miyake, Bradley M. Richardson, and Jōji Watanuki. New Haven: Yale University Press.

Richardson, Bradley M. 1997. *Japanese Democracy: Power, Coordination, and Performance*. New Haven: Yale University Press.

Riker, William H. 1982. *Liberalism against Populism. A Confrontation between the Theory of Democracy and the Theory of Social Choice*. San Francisco: W. H. Freeman.

Robinson, Michael. 1976. "Public Affairs Television and the Growth of Political Malaise: The Case of 'The Selling of the Pentagon.'" *American Political Science Review* 70:409–32.

Rochon, Thomas R. 1988. *Mobilizing for Peace: The Antinuclear Movements in Western Europe*. Princeton: Princeton University Press.

Rochon, Thomas R. 1998. *Culture Moves: Ideas, Activism and Changing Values*. Princeton: Princeton University Press.

Rodrik, Dani. 1997. *Has Globalization Gone Too Far?* Washington, D.C.: Institute for International Economics.

Rose, Richard. 1994. "Postcommunism and the Problem of Trust." *Journal of Democracy* 6:18–30.

Rose, Richard, ed. 1980. *Challenge to Governance*. Beverly Hills: Sage.

Rose, Richard, William Mischler, and Christian Haerpfer. 1998. "Social Capital in Civic and Stressful Societies." *Studies in International Comparative Development* 32:85–111.

Rosenberg, Morris. 1956. "Misanthropy and Political Ideology." *American Sociological Review* 12:690–95.

Rosenberg, Morris. 1957. "Misanthropy and Attitudes toward International Affairs." *Journal of Conflict Resolution* 1:340–45.

Rosencrance, Richard. 1986. *The Rise of the Trading State: Commerce and Conquest in the Modern World*. New York: Basic Books.

Rostagno, Massimo, and Francesca Utili. 1998. "The Italian Social Protection System—The Poverty of Welfare." IMF Working Paper no. 98/74.

Roth, Guenther. 1963. *The Social Democrats in Imperial Germany: A Study on Working-Class Isolation and National Integration*. Totowa, N.J.: Bedminster.

Rothstein, Bo. 1998. "Social Capital in the Social Democratic State: The Swedish

Model and Civil Society." Presented at the Eleventh International Conference of Europeanists, Baltimore.

Rucht, Dieter, Ruud Koopmans, and Friedhelm Neidhardt. 1998. *Acts of Dissent: The Study of Protest in Contemporary Democracies.* Berlin: Sigma.

Ruggie, John Gerard. 1982. "International Regimes, Transactions, and Change: Embedded Liberalism in the Postwar Economic Order." *International Organization* 36:379–415.

Sabato, Larry. 1991. *Feeding Frenzy: How Attack Journalism Has Transformed American Politics.* New York: Free Press.

Sabetti, Filippo. 1996. "Path Dependency and Civic Culture: Some Lessons from Italy about Interpreting Social Experiment." *Politics and Society* 24(1):19–44.

Sampson, Robert J. 1998. "Neighborhood Activism and Collective Efficacy in Chicago: A Comparative Network Approach." Center for Advanced Study in the Behavioral Sciences, Stanford. Typescript.

Sandel, Michael J. 1996. *Democracy's Discontent: America in Search of a Public Philosophy.* Cambridge, Mass.: Belknap Press.

Sartori, Giovanni. 1965. *Democratic Theory.* New York: Praeger.

Scarrow, Susan. 1997. "Wither the Grassroots? Mass Party Membership at Century's End." Research paper series of the Center for German and European Studies, University of California, Berkeley.

Scharpf, Fritz W. 1970. *Demokratietheorie zwischen Utopie und Anpassung* [Democratic Theory between Utopia and Adjustment]. Konstanz: Universitätsverlag.

Scharpf, Fritz W. 1988. "The Joint-Decision Trap: Lessons from German Federalism and European Integration." *Public Administration* 66:239–87.

Scharpf, Fritz W. 1996. "Negative and Positive Integration in the Political Economy of European Welfare States." In *Governance in the European Union,* ed. Gary Marks, Fritz W. Scharpf, Philippe C. Schmitter, and Wolfgang Streeck. London: Sage.

Scharpf, Fritz W. 1997a. *Games Real Actors Play: Actor-Centered Institutionalism in Policy Research.* Boulder: Westview.

Scharpf, Fritz W. 1997b. "Introduction: The Problem-Solving Capacity of Multi-Level Governance." *Journal of European Public Policy* 4:520–38.

Scharpf, Fritz W. 1999. *Governing in Europe: Democratic and Efficient?* Oxford: Oxford University Press.

Schattschneider, Elmer Eric. 1960. *The Semi-Sovereign People.* New York: Holt, Rinehart, and Winston.

Schmalz-Bruns, Rainer. 1995. *Reflexive Demokratie: Die demokratische Transformation moderner Politik* [Reflexive Democracy: The Democratic Transformation of Modern Politics]. Baden-Baden: Nomos.

Schmidt, Susanne K. 1998. "Commission Activism: Subsuming Telecommunications and Electricity under European Competition Law." *Journal of European Public Policy* 5:169–84.

Schmidt, Vivien A. 1990. *Democratizing France: The Political and Administrative History of Decentralization.* Cambridge: Cambridge University Press.

Schmidt, Vivien A. 1997. "Discourse and (Dis-)Integration in Europe: The Cases of France, Great Britain, and Germany." *Daedalus* 126:229–41.

Schmidt, Vivien A. 1998. "Democracy and Discourse in an Integrating Europe and a Globalizing World." Center for German and European Studies, University of California at Berkeley. Working Paper.

Schneider, Cathy. 1997. "Framing Puerto Rican Identity: Political Opportunity Structures and Neighborhood Organizing in New York City." *Mobilization* 2:227–45.

Schneider, Friedrich, and Bruno S. Frey. 1988. "Models of Macroeconomic Policy." In *Political Business Cycles*, ed. Thomas D. Willett. Durham: Duke University Press.

Schudson, Michael. 1995. *The Power of News*. Cambridge, Mass.: Harvard University Press.

Schudson, Michael. 1996. "What if Civic Life Didn't Die?" *American Prospect* 25:17–20.

Schumpeter, Joseph A. 1952. *Capitalism, Socialism, and Democracy*. 4th ed. London: Allen and Unwin.

Schwartz, Michael, and Shuva Paul. 1992. "Resource Mobilization versus the Mobilization of People: Why Consensus Movements Cannot Be Instruments of Social Change." In *Frontiers of Social Movement Theory*, ed. Carol McClurg Mueller. New Haven: Yale University Press.

Scott, James C. 1986. *Weapons of the Weak: Everyday Forms of Peasant Resistance*. New Haven: Yale University Press.

Seibel, Wolfgang. 1997. "Corruption in the Federal Republic of Germany: Before and in the Wake of Reunification." In *Democracy and Corruption in Europe*, ed. Donatella della Porta and Yves Mény. London: Pinter.

Seligman, Adam B. 1997. *The Problem of Trust*. Princeton: Princeton University Press.

Semetko, Holli. 1996. "Political Balance on Television: Campaigns in the United States, Britain and Germany." *Harvard International Journal of Press and Politics* 1(1):51–71.

Sherman, L. W. 1980. "Three Models of Organizational Corruption in Agencies of Social Control." *Social Problems* 27:478–91.

Skocpol, Theda. 1996. "Unravelling from Above." *American Prospect* 25:20–25.

Smith, Robert J. 1985. *Japanese Society: Tradition, Self, and the Social Order*. Cambridge: Cambridge University Press.

Sniderman, Paul. 1981. *A Question of Loyalty*. Berkeley: University of California Press.

Somogyi, G. 1992. "L'economia della corruzione" [The Economy of Corruption]. *Mondoperaio* 11:76–80.

Stanley, Harold W., and Richard G. Niemi. 1994. *Vital Statistics on American Politics*. 4th ed. Washington, D.C.: CQ Press.

State Auditors Department Reports to the Parliament, 1987–92.

Stolle, Dietlind, and Thomas R. Rochon. 1996. "Are All Associations Alike? Member Diversity, Associational Type and the Creation of Social Capital." Presented at the Europeanist Conference, Chicago.

Sutherland, E. H., and D. R. Cressey. 1974. *Criminology*. 9th edition. Chicago: Lippincott.

Svallfors, Stefan. 1995. "The End of Class Politics? Structural Cleavages and Attitudes to Swedish Welfare Policies." *Acta Sociologica* 38:53–74.

Swarts, Heidi J. 1998. "Communities, the State and Public Policy: Agenda Setting by Community Organizations in U.S. Cities." Presented to the Mellon/ CASBS Conference on Contentious Politics, Center for Advanced Study in the Behavioral Sciences, Stanford, Calif.

Sztompka, Piotr. 1996. "Trust and Emerging Democracy." *International Sociology* 11(1):37–62.

Taguchi, Fukuji. 1958. "Nihon shakaitō ron [An Analysis of the Japan Socialist Party]." *Chūō Kōron* 73(9):124–43.

Takabatake, Toshimitsu. 1980. *Gendai Nihon no seitō to senkyo* [Parties and Elections in Contemporary Japan]. Tokyo: San'ichi Shobō.

Talmon, Jacob L. 1955. *The Origins of Totalitarian Democracy*. London: Secker and Warburg.

Tarrow, Sidney. 1989. *Democracy and Disorder: Protest and Politics in Italy, 1965–1975*. Oxford: Oxford University Press.

Tarrow, Sidney. 1996. "Making Social Science Work across Space and Time: A Critical Reflection on Robert Putnam's *Making Democracy Work*." *American Political Science Review* 90:389–97.

Tarrow, Sidney. 1998a. *Power in Movement: Social Movements and Contentious Politics*. New York: Cambridge University Press.

Tarrow, Sidney. 1998b. "'The Very Excess of Democracy': State Building and Contentious Politics in America," In *Social Movements and American Political Institutions*, ed. Anne Costain and Andrew McFarland. Boulder: Rowman and Littlefield.

Taylor, Verta, and Marieke Van Willigen. 1996. "Women's Self-Help and the Reconstitution of Gender: The Post-Partum Support and Breast Cancer Movements." *Mobilization* 2:123–43.

Thompson, E. P. 1971. "The Political Economy of the English Crowd in the Eighteenth Century." *Past and Present* 50:76–136.

Thurow, Lester. 1993. *Head to Head: The Coming Economic Battle among Japan, Europe, and America*. New York: Warner Books.

Tilly, Charles. 1978. *From Mobilization to Revolution*. Reading, Mass.: Addison-Wesley.

Tilly, Charles. 1995. *Popular Contention in Great Britain, 1758–1834*. Cambridge, Mass.: Harvard University Press.

Tilly, Charles. 1998. "Armed Forces, Regimes, Contention, and Democratization in Europe since 1650." University of California, Irvine, Center for the Study of Democracy Research Monograph Series no. 19.

Topf, Richard. 1995. "Beyond Electoral Participation." In *Citizens and the State*, ed. Hans-Dieter Klingemann and Dieter Fuchs. Vol. 1 of *Beliefs in Government*, ed. Kenneth Newton. Oxford: Oxford University Press.

Tsebelis, George. 1995. "Decision Making in Political Systems: Comparison of Presidentialism, Parliamentarism, Multicameralism, and Multipartism." *British Journal of Political Science* 25:289–325.

Tsujinaka, Yutaka. 1986. *Rieki shūdan* [Interest Groups in Japan]. Tokyo: Tōkyō Daigaku Shuppankai.

Tsujinaka, Yutaka. 1996. "Interest Group Structure and Regime Change in Japan." Maryland/Tsukuba Papers on U.S.-Japan Relations 12–13.

Tyler, Tom R. 1990. *Why People Obey the Law: Procedural Justice, Legitimacy, and Compliance.* New Haven: Yale University Press.

Ulram, Peter. 1994. "Political Culture and Party System in the Kreisky Era." In *The Kreisky Era in Austria*, ed. Günther Bischof and Anton Pelinka. New Brunswick, N.J.: Transaction.

Usher, Douglas. 1998. "Party Institutions and Issue Activists Strength: The Impact of Rules on Republican National Convention Delegations, 1976–1996." Cornell University, Department of Government. Typescript.

Uslaner, Eric M. 1993. *The Decline of Comity in Congress.* Ann Arbor: University of Michigan Press.

Uslaner, Eric M. 1995. "Faith, Hope, and Charity: Social Capital, Trust, and Collective Action." University of Maryland. Typescript.

Valelly, Richard M. 1996. "Couch-Potato Democracy?" *American Prospect* 25: 25–29.

van Deth, Jan, and Elinor Scarbrough. 1995. *The Impact of Values.* Oxford: Oxford University Press.

van Wolferen, Karel. 1989. *The Enigma of Japanese Power.* New York: Alfred Knopf.

Vanucci, Alberto. 1997. *Il mercato della corruzione* [The Corruption Market]. Milano: Società Aperta.

Verba, Sidney, Kay Schlozman, and Henry Brady. 1995. *Voice and Equality: Civic Volunteerism in American Politics.* Cambridge, Mass.: Harvard University Press.

Visser, Jelle, and Anton Hemerijck. 1997. *A Dutch Miracle: Job Growth, Welfare Reform and Corporatism in the Netherlands.* Amsterdam: Amsterdam University.

Vogel, David. 1978. "Why Businessmen Distrust Their State: The Political Consciousness of American Corporate Executives." *British Journal of Political Science* 8:45–74.

Vogel, Ezra F. and George C. Lodge, eds. 1987. *Ideology and National Competitiveness.* Boston: Harvard Business School.

Watanuki, Jōji. 1967. "Patterns of Politics in Present-Day Japan." In *Party Systems and Voter Alignments: Cross-National Perspectives*, ed. Seymor M. Lipset and Stein Rokkan. New York: Free Press.

Watanuki, Jōji. 1977. *Politics in Postwar Japanese Society.* Tokyo: University of Tokyo Press.

Wattenberg, Ben. 1985. *The Good News Is the Bad News Is Wrong.* New York: Simon and Schuster.

Wattenberg, Martin. 1996. *The Decline of American Political Parties.* Cambridge, Mass.: Harvard University Press.

Weiler, Joseph H. H. 1982. "The Community System: The Dual Character of Supranationalism." *Yearbook of European Law* 1:267–306.

Weiler, Joseph H. H. 1996. "European Neo-Constitutionalism: In Search of Foundations for the European Constitutional Order." *Political Studies* 44:517–33.

Weingast, Barry R. 1998. "Political Stability and Civil War: Institutions, Commitment and American Democracy." In *Analytic Narratives*, ed. Robert H. Bates, Avner Greif, Margaret Levi, Jean-Laurent Rosenthal, and Barry R. Weingast. Princeton: Princeton University Press.

Weir, Margaret, Anna Shola Orloff, and Theda Skocpol. 1988. "Understanding American Social Politics." In *The Politics of Social Policy in the United States*, ed. Margaret Weir, Anna Shola Orloff, and Theda Skocpol. Princeton: Princeton University Press.

Weisberg, Herbert. 1981. "A Multidimensional Conceptualization of Party Identification." *Political Behavior* 2:33–60.

Weymouth, Tony, and Bernard Lamizet. 1996. *Markets and Myths: Forces for Change in the European Media*. London: Longman.

Williams, Bernard. 1988. "Formal Structures and Social Reality." In *Trust: Making and Breaking Cooperative Relations*, ed. Diego Gambetta. Oxford: Blackwell.

Wilson, James Q. 1962. *The Amateur Democrat: Club Politics in Three Cities*. Chicago: University of Chicago Press.

Wilson, William Julius. 1996. *When Work Disappears: The World of the New Urban Poor*. New York: Alfred Knopf.

Wolfe, Alan. 1997. "Is Civil Society Obsolete? Revisiting Predictions of the Decline of Civil Society." *Brookings Review* 15(4):9–12.

Wood, Richard L. 1997. "Social Capital and Political Culture: God Meets Politics in the Inner City." *American Behavioral Scientist* 40:595–605.

Wright, James D. 1976. *The Dissent of the Governed*. New York: Academic.

Wuthnow, Robert. 1997a. "The Role of Trust in Civic Renewal." National Commission on Civic Renewal, Working Paper no. 1.

Wuthnow, Robert. 1997b. "The Changing Character of Social Capital in the United States." Princeton University. Typescript.

Yamamoto, Shinichirō. 1995. *Akarui senkyo suishin no tebiki* [Clean Election League Guide]. Tokyo: Tōkyō Gyōsei.

Younnis, James, Jeffrey A. McLellan, and Miranda Yates. 1997. "What We Know about Engendering Civic Identities." *American Behavioral Scientist* 40(5): 620–31.

Zajonc, Robert B. 1980. "Feeling and Thinking: Preferences Need No Inferences." *American Psychologist* 35:151–75.

Zald, Mayer, and John D. McCarthy. 1987. *Social Movements in an Organizational Society*. New Brunswick, N.J.: Transaction.

Zürn, Michael. 1998. *Regieren Jenseits des Nationalstaates: Globalisierung und Denationalisierung als Chance* [Governing beyond the Nation-State: Globalization and Denationalization as Chance]. Frankfurt: Suhrkamp.

Contributors

ALBERTO ALESINA is a professor of economics and government at Harvard University. A Research Fellow of the National Bureau of Economic Research in Cambridge and of the Centre for Economic Policy Research in London, his research focuses on the politics of monetary and fiscal policy, economic growth, and formal modeling of elections.

RALF DAHRENDORF is former executive director of Bankgesellschaft Berlin (UK) plc. A sociologist by training, he has written extensively on problems of the advanced industrial societies. His own role in helping make the European Community a reality establishes him as a leading commentator on trends and developments in the Trilateral countries.

RUSSELL J. DALTON is a professor of political science and director of the Research Program on Democratization at the University of California at Irvine's Center for the Study of Democracy. He has written extensively on the political beliefs of contemporary publics and the linkage between these beliefs and ongoing changes in citizen behavior, partisan politics, and policy outcomes.

DONATELLA DELLA PORTA is a professor of political science at the University of Florence. She has investigated social movements, political violence, and the problem of corruption in a number of countries including Italy, France, Germany, Spain, and the United States. She is currently involved in comparative research on transformations in environmental activism.

RUSSELL HARDIN is a political philosopher and chair of the Department of Politics at New York University. His work centers on intellectual problems associated with theories of rational choice, collective action, ethnic conflict, and social trust; the morality behind law; and moral and political philosophy.

SAMUEL P. HUNTINGTON is a University Professor in the Department of Government at Harvard University. A coauthor of the original 1975 Trilateral Commission report, he has contributed a wealth of work on democracy and its problems and tensions at all stages of political development.

PETER J. KATZENSTEIN is a political scientist at Cornell University. His work focuses on both international and comparative political analysis, and he has intensively researched the issue of transnational effects on domestic politics.

ANTHONY KING is a professor of government at the University of Essex. He conducts research on domestic politics in Britain and Europe, and in his role as journalist and broadcaster he commissions and analyzes the Gallup Poll for the *Daily Telegraph* and is a frequent commentator on politics for the BBC.

KENNETH NEWTON is a professor of government and executive director of the European Consortium for Political Research at the University of Essex. He has written extensively on political beliefs and attitudes of mass publics and the roles of social capital and the media, particularly in European democracies.

PIPPA NORRIS is associate director of research and a lecturer at the Shorenstein Center on the Press, Politics, and Public Policy in the Kennedy School of Government at Harvard University and is an associate of the Center for Research on Elections and Social Trends in London. A political scientist, she focuses on comparative political behavior in the context of elections, parties, gender politics, and political communication.

HIDEO ŌTAKE is a professor in the Faculty of Law at Kyoto University. His work has compared state-society relations in Japan with Germany and elsewhere in Europe, and he currently heads a major project comparing political change in Japan and France.

SUSAN J. PHARR is a political scientist at Harvard University. She conducts research on political behavior, the social basis for democracy, and social change. Her current work deals with political ethics and public trust focusing on Japan in comparison with Italy and the United States.

ROBERT D. PUTNAM is a political scientist in the Department of Government and the Kennedy School of Government at Harvard University. At the Kennedy School he is the principal investigator of The Saguaro Seminar: Civic Engagement in America and is currently engaged in an investigation of civic engagement and social trust in America.

FRITZ W. SCHARPF is the Director of the Max Planck Institute for the Study of Societies in Cologne. A political scientist with broad interests in political theory and political economy, he has done extensive research on the relation between economic globalization and democratic legitimacy.

SIDNEY TARROW is a political scientist at Cornell University. The author of *Power in Movement*, he is currently working on the Europeanization of collective action in the European Union and on a joint book with Doug McAdam and Charles Tilly, *Dynamics of Contention*.

ROMAIN WACZIARG is an economist and an assistant professor in the Graduate School of Business at Stanford University. He specializes in international economics and econometrics.

Index

accountability of government, 94–95
activism: benefits to citizens of, 289; changing forms of social, 277–79; contentious politics and social, 275–77; corruption and, 213, 216; declining public confidence and new, 287–88; democracy strengthened by political, 146; grassroots, 281–83, 287–88; growth of feminist, 285; health of U.S. voluntary, 123; Japanese voluntary and nonvoluntary, 186–87; in local neighborhoods, 283–85; media and British/U.S. political, 245; new pattern of U.S. political, 268; social capital built through, 181–88, 203–4; social movements since 1960s, 274–75; social trust, institutional confidence and voluntary, 63–64; social trust, television and voluntary, 235–37; Sweden voluntary, 139; television viewing and political, 240–43; within political parties, 279–81; working trust and, 273, 287–89. *See also* interest groups
adversarial legalism, 83–84
AIDS activism, 284, 289
Aldrich, John, 279
Alesina, Alberto, 24, 157, 162, 164, 168, 180, 189
Almond, Gabriel, 85
"amateur Democrat" phenomenon (U.S.), 279
American National Election Studies, 13, 18, 86–87, 88, 315
American presidential approval ratings (1953–99), 90
American presidents, 87, 89–91
anomie relationships, 205
Ansolabehere, Stephen, 96, 233
anti-communism: end of Cold War impact on, 131; political institution confidence and, 130
anti-slavery movement (U.S.), 275
Aoshima, Yukio, 297
apathy indicators, 58
Aristotle, 311
armed forces. *See* military
Aron, Raymond, 134

Arrow, Kenneth, 46
Asahi Corruption Report Database (1948–96), 194, 195
Asahi Shimbun (Japanese newspaper), 194
Asahi Shimbun surveys (1978 and 1996), 174
associations: Japanese, 185; percentage of TV users as members of, 238; social capital and, 203–4. *See also* activism
Austria, 18, 51, 120
automotive safety equipment, 46–47
Axelrad, Lee, 84
axis of conflict (Japan), 293–94, 296–97, 299, 306–7

bad social capital: corruption favored by, 223–24; created by corruption, 225; good vs., 203; vicious circle creating, 227. *See also* social capital
banking crisis (U.S. and Japan), 37
Baqir, Reza, 162, 164
BATNA (best alternative to the negotiated agreement), 117
BBC, 244
Beck, Paul, 201
Becker, Gary, 39
beliefs in government: attitude, behavior differences and, 213, 216; Eurobarometer measurement of, 206. *See also* public confidence; trust
Bellah, Robert, 131
Bennett, Linda L. M., 93
Bennett, Stephen Earl, 93
Bennett, W. Lance, 270, 273
Berlin Wall, 4
BES (British Election Study of 1997), 231, 243
Black, Duncan, 151
Blair, Tony, 44, 49, 75
"blessed communities," 203, 205
Bobbio, Norberto, 224
Boix, Arles, 204
"bowling alone" metaphor, 121
Brandt, Willy, 252
bribery corruption costs, 219–21. *See also* corruption

strength and public dissatisfaction in, 180; legacy of W.W. II in, 130; media reported corruption in, 194–99; mercantilist economic management in, 43, 50–51; neo-conservatism of, 299–310; pattern of public distrust in, 174–76; *Pax Americana* remake of, 131; political confidence trends in, 124–25; political satisfaction and misconduct in, 189–99, 197–99, 200–201; political satisfaction and political party strength in, 189; political satisfaction and social capital in, 186–87; politics of interest vs. cleanliness in, 294–99; progressive-conservative cleavage in, 293–94, 296–97, 299, 306–7; public disillusionment in, 12–13; public distrust and economic policy performance in, 177–81; recession (1992) of, 4; revenue and spending as GDP percentage, 159; self-identified middle class in, 178; voter preferences in, 303. *See also* LDP (Liberal Democratic Party) [Japan]; one-party dominant system (Japan)

Japan Community Party, 293
Japan National Railways Union, 295
Japan New Party (JNP), 296, 298, 299, 300, 304, 305–7
Japanese civil servants, 82
Japanese Elections and Democracy Survey study (1996), 193
Japanese Occupation (1945–52), 293
Japanese social traveling activities, 184
Jasanoff, Sheila, 271, 290
JEDS (Japan Election and Democracy Study) of 1996, 185, 201
Jefferson, Thomas, 86
JNP (Japan New Party), 296, 298, 299, 300, 304, 305–7
Jobs, Steve, 40, 44
Johnson, Lyndon, 47, 90
Jospin, Lionel, 75
Jowell, Roger, 272
JSP (Japan Socialist Party) [Japan], 293, 295–96, 304
jūmin (Japanese residential membership), 185

Kaase, Max, 63, 126, 127, 128, 132, 133, 146, 148
Kagan, Robert, 83, 84
Kahan, Dan, 284, 285, 289

Kan, Naoto, 296
Katzenstein, Mary F., 148, 285
Katzenstein, Peter J., 24, 25, 98, 170, 290
Kennedy, John F., 86, 90
kigyō-gurumi elections (Japan), 295
King, Anthony, 96, 139, 147, 191, 201
Kitschelt, Herbert, 264
Klaas, Polly, 45
Klingemann, Hans-Dieter, 53, 56, 126, 148, 317
Kneeshaw, Jack, 98
Knights of the Holy Sepulchre (Italy), 224
Knights of Malta (Italy), 224
Kohl, Helmut, 5, 48, 167
Kosovo media coverage, 233
Krauss, Ellis, 201
Kriesi, Hanspeter, 277, 278–79

laissez faire movement, 43
Laski, Harold, 311
Lawrence, Robert, 178
LDP (Liberal Democratic Party) [Japan]: attacked by other parties, 294; claims credit for prosperity, 47; neo-conservative foreign policy by, 301, 302; 1955 System of Japan and, 291, 294; politics of interest vs. cleanliness and, 294–99; predominance during Cold War of, 133, 175; scandals and defeat of, 12, 13, 193, 291–92; voter disaffection and, 176, 179–80, 192, 309. *See also* Japan; one-party dominant system (Japan)
leadership. *See* political leadership
legitimacy. *See* democratic legitimacy
Levi, Margaret, 204
Levine, Peter, 123
Lewinsky, Monica, 91n.9, 233, 287
Lewis-Beck, Michael, 157, 179
lifestyle politics, 273
Lincoln, Abraham, 86, 87, 102, 103
Lind, E. Allan, 200
Listhaug, Ola, 53, 137, 138, 139, 258
Lockheed scandal of 1976 (Japan), 195, 295
London Times, 271
Lowi, Theodore, 130
Lutz, Erbring, 233

Maastricht Treaty, 111, 228
McAdam, Doug, 290
McAllister, Ian, 127